Normative Health Economics

Normative Health Economics

A New Pragmatic Approach to Cost Benefit Analysis, Mathematical Models and Applications

Sardar M.N. Islam and Christine Suet Yee Mak

palgrave
macmillan

First published 2006 by
PALGRAVE MACMILLAN
Houndmills, Basingstoke, Hampshire RG21 6XS and
175 Fifth Avenue, New York, N.Y. 10010
Companies and representatives throughout the world

PALGRAVE MACMILLAN is the global academic imprint of the Palgrave Macmillan division of St. Martin's Press, LLC and of Palgrave Macmillan Ltd. Macmillan® is a registered trademark in the United States, United Kingdom and other countries. Palgrave is a registered trademark in the European Union and other countries.

ISBN 13: 978–1–4039–8749–5   hardback
ISBN 10: 1–4039–8749–1   hardback

This book is printed on paper suitable for recycling and made from fully managed and sustained forest sources.

A catalogue record for this book is available from the British Library.

Library of Congress Cataloging-in-Publication Data

Islam, Sardar M.N., 1950–
    Normative health economics : a new pragmatic approach to cost benefit analysis, mathematical models and applications / by Sardar M.N. Islam and Christine Suet Yee Mak.
      p. cm.
    Includes bibliographical references and index.
    ISBN 1–4039–8749–1 (cloth)
      1. Medical economics–Australia. 2. Medical care, Cost of–Australia. 3. Mathematical optimization. I. Mak, Christine Suet Yee. II. Title.

RA410.55.A8.I85 2006
338.4′336210994–dc22   2006048585

10   9   8   7   6   5   4   3   2   1
15 14 13 12 11 10 09 08 07 06

Printed and bound in Great Britain by
Antony Rowe Ltd, Chippenham and Eastbourne

Contents

List of Tables and Figure

Tables

Figure

List of Appendices

Preface

In this book, a new approach to normative health economics, called new[3] cost benefit analysis and based on new[3] welfare economics, is developed. The integration of economics and moral philosophy, which provides a new approach to valuation and analysis of economic activities, is increasing within the literature in welfare economics. It is argued in this book that valuation and analysis in health economics and health programs (normative health economics) should be based on this approach in welfare economics. An appropriate integration of moral philosophy in welfare economics which is useful operationally, is yet to be done. The objectives of this book are to modify the existing economic theory in welfare economics for health analysis by integrating the issues and principles of moral philosophy and develop some operational mathematical models in order to show how the proposed welfare economics framework (called new[3] welfare economics) integrating moral philosophy in the area of health economics can be applied to health economics and policy evaluation (see Chapter 3).

On the application side, this book operationalises social choice theory and welfare economics by applying different elements of new[3] welfare economics such as possibility of social choice, measurability of utility and interpersonal comparison. Scientific (or clinical) information, expert opinions, as well as social value judgement are used to estimate and analyse the social costs and social benefits (called new[3] cost benefit analysis) of the listing decisions or social choice of the Pharmaceutical Benefits Scheme (PBS) in Australia *as an illustrative but realistic case study*. In this approach, the social choice theory, individual choices (preferences, costs and benefits) are added or considered, along with scientific information, expert opinions and social value judgments (derived from constitution and public policy statements) in making social choices. An operational social welfare function can define a desirable social state.

The book demonstrates the possibility for adopting the principles of new[3] welfare economics, and operations research techniques such as dynamic optimisation to operationalise normative social choice theory in the new integrated approach. The new modified framework including both deterministic and stochastic sets of operational models is used for analysis and health sectoral planning. In applying the elements of new[3] cost benefit analysis to the Australian PBS, only those which are realistic for present health sector and public policy conditions of Australia, have been implemented based on the integration of ethics and economics, computer programs using GAMS system and EXCEL software are used to solve these models. The policy implications of the new[3] cost benefit analysis of the PBS in Australia are discussed in detail (Chapter 7).

The elements of new[3] welfare economics and new[3] cost benefit analysis which are relevant in the Australian PBS setting have been adopted in this study. Following the discussion of the present application of the new[3] cost benefit analysis in Section 3.6.2, economics and ethics have been considered in estimating costs and benefits of listing medications on the PBS in Australia. The present application assumes the measurability of social welfare and other extra-welfaristic components of costs and benefits of listing a medication on the PBS on the basis of social value judgment and public policy objectives. In this PBS application, social welfare is represented by the social benefits of a medication which consists of improvement in productivity, avoidance of hospitalisation and other costs, and improvement in the quality and expectancy of life. In the present application in this study, costs and benefits have been estimated by using scientific information, expert opinions and social preferences. As consideration for equity are addressed in the PBS setting by other health and social support schemes, equity consideration have not been incorporated in the present new[3] cost benefit analysis.

This book shows that application of the new set of valuation principles developed in this book with existing methods in health economics techniques provides an accurate health sector policy evaluation (normative health economics) framework and makes such an evaluation operational, useful and effective. It demonstrates the advantages of the proposed new extended framework of valuation. This book also shows that applications of social choice theory and new[3] welfare economics resulted in new[3] cost benefit analysis provide a more operational and appropriate framework in assessing and analysing costs and benefits of health programs compared to the traditional cost benefit analysis method. Since the new method is more operational and flexible to incorporate ethics, extra-welfaristic elements and social preferences.

The authors thank Dr. Ruchi Gupta, Margarita Kumnick and Kashif Rashid for editorial assistance.

Sardar M.N. Islam & Christine Suet Yee Mak
Decision Sciences and Modelling Program
Victoria University,
Australia

Foreword

The development of a normative approach to health economics and public health by integrating economics and moral philosophy in computerised mathematical models is being studied by Sardar M.N. Islam and Christine Mak in this book, titled *Normative Health Economics*.

A new approach to valuation and analysis of economic activities is provided by integrating economics and moral philosophy, and is well presented in this book. Such a new approach is enriching the present literature in health economics analysis. This book argues that valuation and analysis in health economics, public health, and health programs should be based on the recent advances such as the integration of economics and moral philosophy.

However, an appropriate integration of moral philosophy in the area of health economics has not yet been done. The integration of the issues and principles of moral philosophy and the development of some operational mathematical models to demonstrate how the proposed framework for integration of moral philosophy in the area of health economics can be applied to health economics and policy evaluation are accomplished in this book, with the primary objective to modify the existing economic theory of health analysis.

The applicability of this book is that it operationalises the social choice theory and new[3] welfare economics by combining the human capital approach, the preference approach, scientific (or clinical) information, expert opinions as well as social value judgement, in order to estimate the social costs and social benefits of listing decisions of the Pharmaceutical Benefits Scheme in Australia.

The advantages for adopting the principles of welfare economics, and operations research techniques such as dynamic optimisation and integer programming to operationalise the new integrated approach are revealed and argued in this book. A modified framework including operational models are also developed in this book for the analysis and planning in the health economics sector. Computer programs GAMS and EXCEL are subsequently used in this book to solve these models. In achieving its objective, this book discusses in detail the policy implications of the new[3] cost benefit analysis of the Pharmaceutical Benefits Scheme in Australia.

This book demonstrates that an application of the new set of valuation principles with existing methods in health economics techniques provides an accurate health sector policy evaluation framework and makes such an evaluation useful and effective. It demonstrates the advantages of the extended framework of valuation, which is capable of addressing a wide range of economic, ethical, socio-philosophical and policy issues. This book also shows that applications of social choice theory and welfare economics provide an easier and more operational framework in assessing costs and benefits of health programs.

The existing research on the normative aspects of health economics and public health is relatively scarce. Therefore, this book makes a significant contribution to enrich the literature in this area. I believe that researchers, academics, practitioners, policy makers and students of health economics, public health, economics, and development policy and management will benefit from this book.

Victoria University is proud to be associated with the publication of this book by a commercial publisher.

Professor Elizabeth Harman
Vice Chancellor
Victoria University
Australia

July 2005

1
Introduction

1.1 Introduction

Health economics is largely a sub-discipline of normative economics and applied welfare economics. Health economics provides, among other things, methods and principles for evaluation of different health programs from an economic and social welfare perspective for ranking programs, as well as guides health policy and resource allocation that maximise social welfare. Health economics, especially economic evaluation of health programs, is therefore substantially based on the principles of normative economics or welfare economics, a discipline concerned with finding a normative framework to make social choices regarding the socially desirable state of the economy.

Hurley (2000, p. 61) argued that the near exclusive focus on efficiency concerns over distributional equity was the result of two 'fundamental' theorems of welfare economics. The first theorem states that the allocation of resources generated by a perfectly competitive market process is Pareto optimal, achieving technical, cost-effective and allocative efficiency. The second theorem states that a Pareto optimal allocation can be achieved through a perfectly competitive economy. Under the assumption that utility is ordinally measurable and inter-personally non-comparable, the second theorem provides economists with a rationale to separate efficiency from distributional concerns. Some economists analyse only questions of efficiency and leave questions of distributional equity regarding resource allocation to the political process. In the absence of a perfectly competitive market, Reinhardt (1992) argued that economists ignore the distributional concerns by focusing only on efficiency issues.

With its foundation in welfare economics, cost benefit analysis under the normative social choice theory (Sen 1999b), which has been termed as 'social choice theory in practice' (Stiglitz 2000) or 'operational social choice theory' (Clarke and Islam 2004), has started to address the issues of efficiency, distributive equity, and other extra-welfaristic issues of resource allocation (Drummond et al. 1997; Hurley 2000; Stiglitz 2000; Carter 2001; Clarke and Islam 2004) by integrating economics and moral philosophy or ethics (Hausman and McPherson 1996). Two useful principles of operational, practical normative social choice theory are the measurability and interpersonal comparison of welfare, based on subjective and objective information (see Section 3.4.1). These have paved the way for wider applications of cost benefit analysis to public policy issues including those in health sector. These developments have also influenced the nature of health economics and have provided solid foundations for health economics and economic evaluation of health programs as normative economics (Hurley 2000).

In most OECD countries, the healthcare system is financed by public money either through direct government funding or through tax expenditures such as tax exemption of healthcare benefits (OECD 1998). Economic evaluation is used as an aid in policy-making in the health sector and decision-making of resource allocation in health programs such as the Pharmaceutical Benefits Scheme (PBS) in Australia. Results of economic evaluation are used in the processing of applications of PBS listings of medications (formulary decision), and in establishing the amount of government subsidy (reimbursement decision). In 1993, Australia became the first jurisdiction in the world to make economic evaluation mandatory in the submission process of applying for reimbursement or government subsidy of pharmaceuticals (see Henry 1992; Johannesson and Henry 1992; Aristides and Mitchell 1994; Kemp and Wlodarczyk 1994). The Canadian province of Ontario followed the Australian lead in requesting economic evaluation and data on the listing decision of the Ontario provincial formulary (see Detsky 1993; Ontario Ministry of Health 1994). However, the present state of development in the theory and applications of cost benefit analysis has several weaknesses (discussed further in Sections 1.4 and 2.6). This requires further study to improve the method and application of cost benefit analysis. There is a need for integrating recent developments in welfare economics and social choice theory with cost benefit analysis to improve its normative economic foundations.

1.2   Economic evaluation methods in normative economics

There are four main methodologies commonly used in the economic evaluation of social, economic and health projects, policies and programs, namely cost benefit analysis, cost effectiveness analysis, cost utility analysis and cost minimisation analysis. Cost effectiveness analysis, cost utility analysis and cost minimisation analysis generally consider the monetary estimates of costs of projects, thus addressing the issues of technical and cost-effectiveness efficiency only. Cost benefit analysis is the only methodology that measures both benefits and costs (net social welfare) of projects in monetary terms, thus addressing the issues optimal allocation of resources (allocative efficiency). The differences between the four methodologies will be discussed in details in Section 2.2.2.

Jules Dupuit (1844) is referred to as the 'intellectual' father of the cost benefit analysis technique. In his article 'On the Measure of the Utility of Public Works', Dupuit wrote about the concept of consumer surplus. Dupuit recognised that benefits from public works went beyond the direct revenues generated from the projects (Kneese and Schulze 1985; Johannesson 2000). Cost benefit analysis was empirically operationalised in the 1930s to evaluate water resources investment by US federal water agencies such as the United States Bureau of Reclamation and the United States Corps of Engineers. The objective of the analysis was to evaluate the costs and benefits from investing in water development projects.

The application of cost benefit analysis in normative health economics for economic evaluation of health programs began with the work of Burton Weisbrod of the University of Wisconsin on measles vaccination in 1961. In 1967, Dorothy Rice of US Social Security Administration estimated the economic costs of illness as the resources consumed in treatment plus the foregone economic production. Early work in economic evaluation of health programs generally adopted this approach to define health-related benefits as the estimated reduction or avoidance of future treatment costs plus increased production due to improved health status (Rice 1967). This approach is based on *human capital theory* (Becker 1964), and is generally known as the *human capital approach* (Johannesson 2000) or the *cost of illness approach* (Jack 1999). The human capital approach measures the value of life and the benefits of health in terms of the economic contribution made by an individual to society.

Jack (1999) argued that low value was placed on the health or life of individuals that are not in the labour force, such as the elderly, the unemployed, the homemakers, and so on. Analyses based on market production would tend to inappropriately bias project analysis towards interventions that improved the health of working-age individuals. The issues regarding quality of life, improvement of health status, as well as increase in personal utility are largely ignored (Jack 1999, p. 240).

Thomas Schelling argued that the theoretical foundation of the human capital approach came from the concept of willingness-to-pay (WTP) (see Kaldor 1939; Hicks 1941). There are two types of preference-based approaches used to measure WTP concerning health changes, namely the *revealed preference approach* and the *expressed preference approach*.

Under the *revealed preference approach*, WTP can be inferred from actual decisions that involve tradeoffs between money and health, time trade-off and person trade-off, etc. Most of the work on revealed preference was done in studies of labour markets with a wage premium being offered to workers for riskier jobs (Abel-Smith 1985; Viscusi et al. 1987, 2003). Under the *expressed preference approach*, WTP is assessed by a survey or the *contingent valuation* method where respondents are given hypothetical choices involving health. The *contingent valuation* method was first used to assess WTP in mobile coronary care units that reduced the risk of death after heart attack (Acton 1973). Cost benefit analysis, based on these preference approaches, is adopted in evaluation of projects and programs, especially in the health sector such as PBS in Australia.

1.3 Pharmaceutical Benefits Scheme in Australia

The Australian PBS is a prominent example of health projects or programs. It is a Commonwealth-funded health program through which pharmaceuticals are provided with government subsidy to the Australian society. Given its significance and controversial nature in the Australian health sector, a study dealing with the applications of evaluation methods in the context of PBS is an interesting academic exercise with practical importance. Economic evaluation of a medication is mandatory in its application to be listed on the PBS of Australia. The healthcare expenditure escalates with an ageing population and the advance in technology (Mooney and Scotton 1999). This is especially the case of pharmaceutical expenditures as poly-pharmacy is prevalent in the elderly population. Economic evaluation is important in comparing the costs and consequences of listing different medications on the PBS, to assist decision-making in resource allocation, and to maximise the health and welfare of Australian society. As it will be shown that it is the societal perspective of a new cost benefit analysis developed in this research being most relevant in assisting the selection of medications which offer maximum social benefits to be included in the PBS. This study is therefore, important in influencing Australian health policy in terms of government subsidy for pharmaceuticals.

1.4 Limitations of existing literature – cost benefit analysis in health economics

1.4.1 Cost benefit analysis

In spite of the persuasiveness of the use of cost benefit analysis, there are several limitations in the existing literature in applying cost benefit analysis to health economics and other areas in economics and social sciences. Present applications of cost benefit analysis in health economics focus predominantly on financial and economic analysis rather than *real* social and welfare economic analysis based on principles of ethics, social and extra-welfaristic considerations. The rationale for economic evaluation stemmed from the economic concepts of resource scarcity, choices among alternative programs and opportunity costs (Donaldson et al. 2002). In the presence of resource scarcity, Williams (1983) considered economic evaluation as a way of *'ensuring that the value of what is gained from an activity outweighs the value of what has to be sacrificed'*. Economic evaluation goes beyond simply the identification, measurement and comparison of consequences and costs to incorporate the valuation of these effects or impacts (Donaldson et al. 2002).

A *true* social cost benefit analysis of health programs is yet to be developed and most of the existing literature consists generally of cost comparisons that use methods such as cost effectiveness analysis rather than quantifying benefits and costs in monetary and ethics-based social welfare terms (Drummond et al. 1997; Brent 2003). There is also inadequate discussion about issues and topics such as the social discount rate, shadow pricing and the social valuation of costs and benefits of a health project (Jack 1999; Johannesson 2000).

Rigorous specifications of health sector planning based on cost benefit analysis of programs and policies are still not well developed. Furthermore, certain useful mathematical methods of capital budgeting and project appraisal have not yet been applied in health sector planning and project evaluation (Brent 2003, Pearce and Nash 1981).

There are other limitations in existing work where ethics and moral philosophy are not well integrated into the economic evaluation of health programs (Hurley 2000; Carter 2001). In the current setting of the Australian PBS, financial and economic analysis rather than real social cost benefit analysis is used, and thus issues of welfare economics are ignored in the process. Essentially, the economic evaluation in health program deals with issues of technical and cost-effectiveness efficiency. The allocative efficiency and distributional equity is largely ignored from the evaluation and ultimately the decision-making process.

Furthermore, Johannesson (2000) argued that there was an emphasis in the literature on the use of WTP to reveal the preferences of households and thus the benefits of health programs. There are limitations in this preference-based method (Mitchell and Carson 1989). WTP is inevitably a function of ability to pay. Respondent's valuation is influenced by a range of reasons such as self-interest, interviewers or sponsors, statistical problems due to sample design, execution of the study, etc. In addition, the respondent's valuation can also be skewed by starting point bias or range bias, relation bias, importance bias, or position bias. From the time the contingent study is carried out to the time of decision-making, preferences may change and lead to inference bias. There are also indications that the hypothetical WTP exceeds real WTP (Duffield and Patterson 1991).

In addition to the above issues, there are other limitations of cost benefit analysis which makes the technique less satisfactory as a decision-making method. For example, as preference methods of cost benefit analysis has several limitations, especially in providing reliable estimates of benefits of projects. The preference-based method should be used in conjunction with other methods such as expert opinions, scientific information, social preferences and value judgements in order to estimate health benefits without bias. In Islam (2001), the paradigm of new[3] welfare economics is developed where the applications of these methods have been proposed to make social decisions and choices (see also Clarke and Islam 2004; Craven and Islam 2005).

In new[3] welfare economics, making social choices and decisions is feasible since quantifiability, measurability, and comparability of social benefits or welfare are assumed in this paradigm on the basis of the possibility perspective (Sen 1999b) in social choice theory (discussed further in Chapter 3). This paradigm also provides a framework for incorporating ethics and non-economic elements in economic analysis (therefore also in cost benefit analysis) relatively conveniently and appropriately. This approach has not yet been applied to economic evaluation of projects for making decisions or social choices in general and in the health sector. It is possible to develop a kind of cost benefit analysis (which we can name new[3] cost benefit analysis) on the basis of the principles of new[3] welfare economics. In new[3] cost benefit analysis, social choice can be operationalised for practical application and social value judgements, expert opinion, and scientific information need to be applied to the social decision making process (as discussed in Chapter 3). This paradigm can enable the development of a full social cost benefit analysis with plausible estimates of social costs and benefits of health programs.

1.4.2 Cost benefit analysis in the setting of PBS in Australia

Cost benefit analysis has extensively been adapted in the PBS context. However, there are several limitations in the literature in applying cost benefit analysis in the PBS listing process in Australia. The Pharmaceutical Benefits Advisory Committee (PBAC) guidelines state that economic evaluation should be societal in perspective, but indirect social benefits are not included in the evaluation. Cost effectiveness analysis, rather than cost benefit analysis, is the pre-ferred methodology under the PBAC guidelines. Reinhardt (1992) argued that the analysis focused only on efficiency issues and ignored the concerns of distributional equity, and therefore, has ignored the ethical dimensions of social choices and decision-making. There is also no distinction between social cost benefit analysis and financial cost benefit analysis. Use of intermediate effectiveness measures narrows the scope of comparison in an econ-omic evaluation and makes the results of cost effectiveness analysis difficult to interpret. The theoretical welfare economic foundation of the application of cost benefit analysis to PBS listing is also not yet developed.

1.5 Aims of the research

1.5.1 Main aims

The above state of developments in the literature justifies undertak-ing further research in this area of cost benefit analysis as a topic in applied welfare economics or normative economics. The first specific aim of this research is to *develop a new social choice based cost benefit analysis framework*. As stated in the previous section, the human capital approach of cost benefit analysis remains the most commonly used methodology in the economic evaluation of health programs. No consideration is given to the issues of valuing health improvements in terms of other extra-welfaristic, ethical and social benefits (Birch and Donaldson 1987; Donaldson et al. 2002). The omission of these social welfare changes reduces the cost benefit analysis to mere cost analyses or cost comparisons and thus elimi-nates its many essential elements of normative economics.

In order to overcome this limitation, the objective of this research is to develop a new cost benefit analysis approach with an appropri-ate basis of normative economics, where the emphasis is on the preference-based and human capital-based valuation methods. The intent is to measure the social benefits in terms of WTP as well as other measures (external, indirect, intangible benefits) based on expert opinion, scientific information and social preferences. Concerning the field of health economics, most of the valuation methods in the healthcare literature are in the experimental stage. This research attempts to further develop the valuation methods in assessing the full net benefits of health programs. This task involves application of the practical social choice methods explored in Stiglitz (2000) who estimates the net social benefit or welfare of a program. In applying this social choice method, it is necessary to adopt some assumptions of welfare economics to make social choice theory practical. In the present work, the assumptions adopted in welfare economics (Islam 2001; Clarke and Islam 2004; Craven and Islam 2005) are applied. This approach is called new[3] cost benefit analysis since it is based on the elements of new[3] welfare economics (Islam 2001; Clarke and Islam 2004; Craven and Islam 2005).

The second specific aim of this research is *to apply improved models in the PBS in Australia*. The cost benefit analysis model under the new social choice approach in the new[3] welfare economics paradigm discussed in Chapter 3 will then be applied to the economic evaluation for listing of six medications in the PBS. They are, namely Atorvastatin and Clopidogrel for cardiovascular diseases, Pioglitazone for type 2 diabetes, Letrozole for breast cancer, Tiotropium for chronic obstructive pulmonary disease, as well as Fluticasone/Salmeterol for asthma. The above medical conditions account for about 70% of the total burden of diseases in Australia and are identified by Australian Health Ministers for priority action under the National Health Priority Areas (NHPA) initiatives (see further discussion in Section 5.1). This research attempts to evaluate the full social benefits of inclusion of these six medications on the PBS, and to compare the results of the new[3] cost benefit analysis with those from the economic evaluation in the PBAC submission for the six medications.

1.5.2 Other aims of this research

In addition to the specific aims discussed in Section 1.5.1, the other important aim of this research is *to review the current application of cost benefit analysis in health programs*. One of the objectives of this study is to undertake a critical literature review in order to argue that although the dominating practice in health economics is to adopt a cost effectiveness analysis, the appropriate method to be used is cost benefit analysis (preferably the new[3] cost benefit analysis developed in this study). In the past few decades, cost benefit analysis has been receiving limited acceptance from healthcare professionals. This is mainly because the human capital approach of cost benefit analysis is widely viewed as inequitable and the social benefits of health programs are difficult to estimate and largely ignored in the mainstream approach which is focused on financial cost benefit analysis (Drummond et al. 1997; Carter and Harris 1999; Johannesson 2000).

Furthermore, this research aims *to apply the recent advances of cost benefit analysis to health program evaluation*. With the recent advances of valuation methodologies in environmental economics, there is a renewed interest in the application of cost benefit analysis in a healthcare setting. This research attempts to develop a comprehensive approach of social cost benefit analysis for health programs by extending the current literature on the applications of cost benefit analysis in health economics and incorporating the recent developments in cost benefit analysis and its application. The developed social cost benefit analysis methodology will then be applied in the PBS setting to demonstrate its validity and its suitability, by applying it in the economic evaluation of Atorvastatin, Clopidogrel, Pioglitazone, Letrozole, Tiotropium and Fluticasone/Salmeterol for the hypothetical PBAC submission seeking PBS listing.

1.6   Research methodology, approach and strategy

1.6.1   Research approach

Research can be classified into four different types according to the purpose of the study, namely, exploratory, descriptive, analytical and predictive (Hussey and Hussey 1997; Sekaran 1992; Zikmund 1994). The research approach used in this study involves a combination of four approaches to research and is in conformity within the properties of scientific research such as objectivity, rigour and generalisation ability. The applications of these approaches in this research are discussed below.

Exploratory research is conducted when there is limited existing knowledge of the phenomena or research problem, or there are few or no previous studies done on the issue. Exploratory studies are performed to allow better comprehension of the phenomena or research problem. Exploratory research aims at identifying patterns, ideas or hypothesis, rather than testing hypothesis. Through data collection based on observation and experience, empirical evidence of the phenomenon or research problem is gathered. The empirical evidence may reveal certain patterns regarding the phenomenon or research problem, theories are then developed and hypotheses are formulated. Thus, exploratory research concentrates on gathering evidence, and guiding future studies rather than on providing specific answers to problems. Exploratory research may take the form of case studies, observation and historical analysis. The present research involves an exploratory component since very limited work has been done on incorporating social choice in evaluating health programs.

A *descriptive* study is conducted to ascertain and describe the different characteristics of a phenomenon or research issue that is of interest. It is used to obtain specific information and describe the relevant aspects of the research issue from an individual, societal, organisational, industry, or other perspective. Descriptive research aims at answering questions of *who*, *what*, *when*, and *where*. Statistical techniques are used to analyse the quantitative data collected. This research involves a descriptive component of the PBS in Australia, as well as similar schemes in other countries.

Analytical research continues from descriptive research and goes beyond the mere description of the characteristics of the research issue. Through analysis of the information collected, analytical research aims at understanding the research issue, identifying and measuring any causal relationships among the different variables, and answering the question *how*. This study involves an analytical component by analysing the cost and benefit estimates of the PBS in Australia.

Predictive research goes one step further than analytical research. Based on the empirical evidence gathered, the theories developed and the hypotheses formulated and tested, predictive research aims at forecasting the likelihood of a phenomenon, and generalising from the analysis by predicting certain phenomenon to happen. This research involves a predictive component in the form of health sector planning for proactive allocation of resources in health programs. This research aims at applying normative social choice theory of welfare economics in the form of cost benefit analysis in health economics, using the PBS as an illustrative example. There is little existing literature on normative social choice welfare economics in the healthcare area. Therefore, this research ultimately aims at extending the application of social cost benefit analysis from the PBS to health sector planning.

The nature of a research largely depends on the level of existing knowledge regarding the phenomenon or research issue. The rigour of research design increases progressively from the exploratory stage, to the descriptive stage, to the analytical stage, and lastly to the predictive stage. Accordingly, this study adopts a combination of these approaches to make a scientific study in the area of social cost benefit analysis in general, and to apply in particular in the economic evaluation in health programs in Australia.

1.6.2   Methodologies of economic evaluation

As noted earlier, there are four main methodologies in the economic evaluation of health programs, namely cost benefit analysis, cost effectiveness analysis, cost utility analysis and cost minimisation analysis (see Bootman et al. 1996).

Since a comprehensive analysis of costs and benefits showing the net social welfare of projects or policies is possible in cost benefit analysis, it is a preferred method of economic evaluation. Cost benefit analysis is a form of economic evaluation in which monetary values are determined for both the inputs and the outcomes of the intervention, thus offering a single measurement unit for different outcomes, and allowing comparison between multiple outcomes. There are two types of cost benefit analysis, namely financial cost benefit analysis and social cost benefit analysis. These will further be discussed in Chapter 2.

Although cost benefit analysis is the preferred method for economic evaluation, it is not generally adopted in analyses in the health sector largely due to the difficulties in valuation of health benefits. The PBAC does not specify the type of methodologies to be used in formal economic evaluation; but it prefers cost effectiveness analysis to other analyses. Although the PBAC does not prohibit the use of cost benefit analysis, it does not encourage cost benefit analysis in its submission guidelines for the pharmaceutical industry (Commonwealth Department of Health and Ageing 2002 p. 66). Consequently, many submissions take the form of cost effectiveness analysis.

A social cost benefit analysis (discussed below and in Chapter 3) based on the principles of new[3] welfare economics can be adopted to evaluate the PBS in Australia. This new cost benefit analysis model, under the normative social choice approach using a combination of human capital, revealed preference and expressed preference approaches (contingent valuation) along with expert opinion, and social value judgements. The new[3] cost benefit analysis is suitable for social cost benefit analysis of health programs. This cost benefit analysis model under the normative social choice approach will then be applied in economic evaluation studies of submissions for listing a number of medications in the PBS in order to examine whether such listings would be socially beneficial to Australia.

1.6.3 Operations research methods

Operations research (OR) methods (Craven and Islam 2005) have been applied to healthcare since the 1960s. The application of OR models in healthcare broadly covers six areas, namely scheduling, allocation, forecasting demand, supplies/materials planning, medical decision-making, and quality and efficiency (Gass and Harris 2001). While there has been major growth of their application in healthcare, OR methods (such as linear, non-linear, parametric and stochastic programming) have not been widely applied in the economic evaluation of health programs. The allocation and forecasting demand perspectives of OR are the most relevant in the economic evaluation of health programs such as the PBS. OR provides an excellent set of tools of decision-making in pharmacoeconomics. Decisions to select or to reject the PBS listing of new medications are made before long-term trials or database studies can be conducted. Information available is mainly from clinical trials. OR models utilises this information to predict expected costs and benefits of long-term treatment use within a given population, and provide valuable additional information for decision makers (Richter 2004).

Operational models for social cost benefit analysis, especially for sectoral analysis, are not well developed. It is argued that cost benefit analysis of health programs should be based on the normative social choice approach of welfare economics, and operations research techniques such as dynamic optimisation and stochastic programming should be used to operationalise this approach (Islam and Mak 2002).

In this research, OR models and capital budgeting techniques will be applied to evaluate the costs and benefits of listing the six medications chosen on PBS in Australia for developing PBS sector planning.

1.6.4   Data sources

As all the submissions of pharmaceutical companies to PBAC are confidential commercial documents, such data is not available to the general public. Secondary data obtained from published sources along with expert opinion (including the views of the present authors) and social value judgements and policy preferences in Australia will be adapted to undertake the present research on economic evaluation of health programs. As majority of the PBAC proceedings and decision-making process are all classified as confidential commercial documents, the authors can only conduct the study using the published PBAC submission guidelines (as available from the website of PBAC) and the secondary data that are readily available to the public.

About 70% of the total burden of diseases in Australia has been attributed to cardiovascular diseases, diabetes mellitus, cancers, injuries, mental problems, as well as asthma (AIHW 2002). Most medications treating the above conditions are available through the PBS to the Australian public. In order to examine whether the PBS listing decision is socially beneficial to Australia, six medications are selected for cost benefit analysis under the PBAC submission guidelines, for cost benefit analysis under the financial analysis framework, as well as for the new[3] cost benefit analysis under the social choice theory of welfare economics. The medications selected are Atorvastatin and Clopidogrel for cardiovascular diseases, Pioglitazone for type 2 diabetes mellitus, Letrozole for breast cancer, Fluticasone/Salmeterol for asthma, as well as Tiotropium for chronic obstructive pulmonary diseases. These medications are selected because the medical conditions they treated contributed significantly to the total burden of diseases in Australia.

In order to undertake a new[3] cost benefit analysis of the PBS listing of Atorvastatin, Clopidogrel, Pioglitazone, Letrozole, Fluticasone/Salmeterol and Tiotropium, the data requirements include the following.

1. Costs of listing medications on PBS including the acquisition cost, distribution cost and cost of adverse effects of the drugs plus the operating cost of the PBS.
2. Benefits of listing Atorvastatin, Clopidogrel, Pioglitazone, Letrozole and Fluticasone/Salmeterol and Tiotropium on the PBS.

3. Discount rate and other parameters in capital budgeting models.

The following three sources are used in this study to obtain the above data.

1. Scientific information such as the data quoted in annual report of PBAC and Australian Bureau of Statistics (ABS), and Australian Institute of Health and Welfare (AIHW); information of Atorvastatin, Clopidogrel, Pioglitazone, Letrozole and Fluticasone/Salmeterol and Tiotropium from clinical and pharmacoeconomic journals, information from manufacturer of medications.
2. Expert opinions.
3. Social value judgement and preferences.

1.6.5 Computer programs

Two computer programs, EXCEL and GAMS, are used in this study. Using EXCEL, the costs and benefits of Atorvastatin, Clopidogrel, Pioglitazone, Letrozole and Fluticasone/Salmeterol and Tiotropium are estimated. These figures are then used to calculate cost benefit ratios and net present values when undertaking the cost benefit analysis of the six medications. A set of figures of costs, benefits, cost-benefit ratios and net present values is calculated using EXCEL under PBAC submission criteria, the financial cost benefit analysis approach, as well as the new[3] cost benefit analysis approach.

To demonstrate the application of this new social choice approach in new[3] cost benefit analysis, a set of operations models of cost benefit analysis and health sector planning, both deterministic and stochastic, are developed. A computer program based on the General Algebraic Modelling System (GAMS) is used to solve these models (Brooke et al. 1992).

1.7 Contributions of this research

This research makes a conceptual and methodological contribution to the literature of health economics by developing the new[3] cost benefit analysis framework which is based on recent developments in welfare economics and social choice theory and is appropriate for normative decision-making, and social choices in economics and health economics.

The contributions of this research may further be elaborated as the following.

1. Operationalisation of the normative social choice approach based on new[3] welfare economics in health economics.
2. Argument for the need for and the possibility of incorporating issues such as ethics, moral philosophy and welfare economics into health economics, especially in form of new[3] cost benefit analysis.
3. Application of the new[3] cost benefit analysis under the new social choice approach to the PBS.
4. Development of an appropriate framework to evaluate PBS issues and policies, and to suggest any improvement.
5. Demonstration that within the proposed framework of new[3] cost benefit analysis can be effectively applied in health economics.
6. Application of new[3] cost benefit analysis in a holistic approach to the PBS setting to go beyond a single program consideration and towards health sector planning.
7. Application of OR methods in economic evaluation of health programs.
8. Comprehensive incorporation of issues such as quality of life, utility, and so on; thus extending the scopes of cost benefit analysis to welfare economics.
9. Bring uncertainty into the discussion of the PBS.

1.8   Outline of the book

The book is divided into nine chapters as discussed below

Chapter 1 is the introduction, outlining the objectives and aims of this research, methodology and approach adopted.

Chapter 2 discusses the present state of the art and its limitations in the economic evaluation of the health programs.

Chapter 3 discusses the new[3] cost benefit analysis under the new framework of normative social choice theory of new[3] welfare economics based on the social welfare function.

Chapter 4 describes the issues in the PBS in Australia and in other countries, present economic evaluation practices in the PBS and an appropriate framework for cost benefit analysis of the PBS.

Chapter 5 discusses the principles adopted in estimating the costs and benefits of medications examined by applying new[3] cost benefit analysis and report their details..

Chapter 6 analyses the social cost and benefit estimates of the selected medications in the PBS setting in Australia by applying new[3] cost benefit analysis for making social choices for listing medications on PBS.

Chapter 7 discusses other issues of cost benefit analysis such as uncertainty, the social discount rate, sustainability, public objectives, health sector planning, policy implications, and optimisation models of the PBS.

Chapter 8 is the concluding chapter; it summaries the arguments presented and outlines possible areas for future research.

Appendices consist of formulae and data tables referred to and discussed in the research.

This research operationalises normative social choice theory in the area of cost benefit analysis based on the new[3] welfare economics framework. It is argued here that a new[3] cost benefit analysis is the preferred methodology in the economic evaluation of health programs (and all economic and social programs) as it addresses the issues of allocative efficiency, ethics and extra-welfaristic elements of welfare, in addition to technical efficiency and cost-effectiveness efficiency.

2
Economic Evaluation of Health Programs: The Case for Cost Benefit Analysis

2.1 Introduction

Arrow's (1963) seminal work on 'Uncertainty and the economics of medical care' laid the foundation of welfare economics analysis of health programs. An important area of health economics is the application of cost benefit analysis and its associated methodologies in project planning and economic evaluation of health policies and health programs. Economic evaluation in the area of reimbursement of pharmaceuticals attracts most attention. Cost benefit analysis estimates net social welfare changes as a result of a program or a policy, with social welfare being measured in terms of net benefits of the program. A body of literature exists in this area following Arrow's (1963) seminal work (Drummond et al. 1997; Williams 1997; Carter and Harris 1999; Jack 1999; Johannesson 2000; Carter 2001; Islam 2001; Brent 2003). However, there are significant limitations in the current literature. In order to improve its effectiveness and usefulness, economic evaluation of health programs requires adjustment based on normative social choice theory.

As stated in Chapter 1, this book develops an improved and comprehensive cost-benefit methodology under normative social choice theory within the framework of welfare economics. The proposed methodology is useful in evaluating health programs in general such as the reimbursement scheme of pharmaceuticals. The Pharmaceutical Benefits Scheme (PBS) in Australia is used as an illustrative example in this research. In pursuit of these tasks, the objectives of this chapter are the following:

a. to provide a discussion of evaluation methods in health economics;
b. to argue the relevance of cost benefit analysis for health programs evaluation;
c. to discuss the basic methods of cost benefit analysis;
d. to discuss the corresponding issues in the application of cost benefit analysis for the evaluation of health programs; and
e. to highlight the limitations of existing methods of cost benefit analysis in order to provide justifications for developing improved methods for cost benefit analysis suitable for all branches of economics including health economics.

This chapter is structured as follows. Section 2.2 discusses the different methodologies of economic evaluation. Section 2.3 argues the case for cost benefit analysis as being the preferred methodology among the four alternatives. Section 2.4 discusses the financial approach of cost benefit analysis and its inadequacies to address the social issues of health programs. Section 2.5 discusses the social approach of cost benefit analysis. Section 2.6 reviews the contemporary issues in the application of social cost benefit analysis to the economic evaluation of health programs. Section 2.7 discusses the limitations of the existing evaluation methods and Section 2.8 is the conclusion.

2.2   Methodologies of economic evaluation

Economic evaluation in normative economics starts from the fundamental assumption of resource scarcity. Due to existence of finite resources, it is important for us to undertake evaluations and to make choices. The use of resources in one program is at the expense of other alternative programs. By using a resource for a selected program, one is forgoing the opportunity of using that resource elsewhere, and an *opportunity cost* is incurred. Economic evaluation is an analytical tool used to assess the social desirability of a health program relative to other alternatives, with emphasis on social efficiency (Carter and Harris 1999). 'If no other alternative is considered, the health program is being *described* but not *evaluated*' (Brent

2003 p. 4). As alternative options exist, one needs to make choices. Economic evaluation is conducted to assist the decision-making processes.

Marginal costs and marginal benefits are the change in total costs and benefits of producing one additional unit of output. If marginal benefits are greater than or equal to marginal costs, the output of a health program is guaranteed at an optimal level. Without budget constraints, a program can be expanded or contracted until marginal benefits equal marginal costs. With budget constraints, programs should operate at a level whereby the ratio of marginal benefits to marginal costs is the same for all (Mooney 1993).

2.2.1 Components of an economic evaluation

Production in a healthcare system is a two-step process. Health programs transform inputs (such as labour and capital) into outputs in the form of health intervention. Inputs are resources consumed by health programs. Examples of resources consumed as input include prescription drugs, laboratory tests, hospital stays, and so on (Bootman et al. 1996). The aggregate input is called a *cost* and is measured by valuing labour and capital using market prices in monetary units (Brent 2003).

Ultimate outputs of healthcare system are health interventions that cure, prevent or alleviate disease and thus improve health status. These outputs are called *effects*, and are expressed in natural units (such as unit changes in blood pressure). These effects can be measured in relation to utilities (estimates of the satisfaction of the effects), and the output unit is called Quality Adjusted Life-year (QALY). The outputs can also be expressed in monetary units and the effects are called *benefits* (Brent 2003).

Benefits and costs of health programs can be classified into three categories: direct, indirect and intangible (Drummond et al. 1997; Johannesson 2000). *Direct* benefits and costs are those related to the healthcare industry. *Indirect* refers to inputs and outputs occurring or taking place outside of the healthcare industry. *Intangible* refers to pain and suffering caused or alleviated by healthcare interventions.

2.2.2 Methodologies of economic evaluation

There are four types of economic evaluation incorporating these different components of inputs and outputs, namely cost benefit

Table 2.1   Measurement of costs and consequences of economic evaluation

Methodology	Cost measurement unit	Outcome/Output unit
Cost benefit	Dollars	Dollars
Cost effectiveness	Dollars	Natural units (e.g. life-years gained, mmol/L blood glucose lowered, mmHg blood pressure lowered)
Cost minimisation	Dollars	Assume to be equivalent in comparative groups
Cost utility	Dollars	Quality adjusted life-year or other utilities

Source: Bootman et al. 1996.

analysis (CBA), cost effectiveness analysis (CEA), cost utility analysis (CUA) and cost minimisation analysis (CMA).

Cost benefit analysis

Cost benefit analysis is a means of comparing the beneficial and adverse consequences of a health program in order to determine whether the expected outcomes of the health program are in public interest. Cost benefit analysis requires that both the inputs and outputs of a health program to be measured in comparable monetary units. The benefits of an output are evaluated by quantifying it into monetary terms. Benefit estimation of an intervention that transforms an input into an output involves assigning a *pricing* (P) to an *effect* of intervention (E). There are various approaches to valuate benefits of health programs, namely human capital or cost of illness, revealed preferences and expressed preferences approaches. These approaches are discussed in Section 3.8.2. In order to rank different health programs, a cost benefit ratio is calculated by dividing the benefits of a program by its costs. A health program is selected if its cost benefit ratio is higher than that of other alternatives.

Benefit (B) = Effect (E) × Pricing (P):

$$\frac{P_1 E_1}{C_1} > \frac{P_2 E_2}{C_2} \tag{2.1}$$

Cost effectiveness analysis

Cost effectiveness analysis is an analytical tool used in a decision-making process by identifying a preferred choice among possible alternatives. Cost effectiveness analysis is generally a series of analytical and mathematical procedures that aid in selecting a course of action from various approaches (Bootman et al. 1996). Cost effectiveness analysis avoids the difficulties involved in valuing costs and benefits in monetary terms. Although the valuation of outcomes in cost effectiveness analysis uses measurement in natural units such as life-years gained which are not constrained by the level of income, this does not mean that such measures are unaffected by the distribution of income (Donaldson et al. 2002).

Cost effectiveness (C/E) ratio is used to measure the worthiness of a health program in cost effectiveness analysis and is calculated as the amount of cost per unit of effect. A fixed budget constraint is the basic requirement in a cost effectiveness analysis model. Different health programs are ranked in ascending order of their C/E ratio, and approved until the budget is exhausted. However, the fixed budget usually considers only healthcare expenditures, but not the non-healthcare costs or social costs. Indirect costs are paid by patients, and do not constitute part of the costs (or fixed budget constraints) borne by the agency making such decisions. Ignoring the social costs is consistent with maximising the effect for a *given agency budget*, it does not contribute to the selection of the most socially worthwhile health programs.

The predominance of cost effectiveness analysis over cost benefit analysis in the economic evaluation of health programs arises from the concern about the validity of evaluation methods, especially those related to the hypothetical nature of the willingness-to-pay (WTP) questions and the dependence of the responses on the distribution of incomes, wealth or 'ability to pay' (Donaldson et al. 2002). Kenkel (1997) argued that this concern about the validity of measurement was not confined only to methods for monetary valuation. Non-monetary methods of valuation used in cost effectiveness analysis, such as time trade off and standard gamble, are also based on hypothetical settings (Pauly 1995).

The outcome measurement in natural units of health effects is a fundamental problem of cost effectiveness analysis. In order to compare different programs by cost effectiveness analysis, outcomes of these programs must be measured in the same units of effectiveness. In order to apply cost effectiveness analysis, health programs must share a common objective such as lowering blood pressure by a specified amount. Cost effectiveness analysis cannot compare programs that achieve different kinds of effects, such as antihypertensive lowering blood pressure versus an hypoglycaemic lowering blood glucose level. Cost effectiveness analysis can determine whether one medication can achieve a given clinical effect with fewer resources than alternative medications, but it cannot ascertain that use of such medication is socially worthwhile. This uni-dimensional nature of outcome measurement greatly reduces the range of problems that can be addressed by cost effectiveness analysis. Cost effectiveness analysis is a useful tool only where there is a single unambiguous objective for a health intervention (Carter and Harris 1999).

For cost effectiveness analysis, we set $P_1 = P_2 = P$:

$$\frac{E_1}{C_1} > \frac{E_2}{C_2} \qquad (2.2)$$

Cost utility analysis

Cost effectiveness analysis fails to capture all the relevant dimensions of benefits and treats all life-years as having equal value, regardless of the quality of life. Cost utility analysis is an economic tool in which output of health programs is measured in terms of quantity and quality of life. QALY is the tradeoff between the quantity of life and the improved quality of life. QALY is calculated by multiplying quality weights or preference of health states with time duration spent in those health states. There are a number of approaches to determine preferences attached to health states, namely contingent valuation, conjoint analysis and health state valuation techniques (Green et al. 2000).

Cost utility analysis can be regarded as a form of cost effectiveness analysis that can analyse multiple forms of output, or alternatively as a form of cost benefit analysis, where QALYs are the criteria of value (rather than dollars) and where rankings can be made for setting priorities within a fixed health sector budget (Carter and

Harris 1999). However, cost utility analysis cannot decide which program is socially desirable as it works on a similar set of decision rules as cost effectiveness analysis. Unlike cost benefit analysis that considers all benefits and effects of a health program, cost utility analysis focuses mainly on survival and quality of life effects at the expense of imposing restrictions on the form of utility function (Brent 2003). Cost utility analysis is thus appropriate for a clinical decision setting rather than in a social decision-making context.

For cost utility analysis, we set E = Quality Adjusted Life-Year (QALY):

$$\frac{QALY_1}{C_1} > \frac{QALY_2}{C_2} \tag{2.3}$$

Cost minimisation analysis

When two or more programs are assumed to be equivalent in terms of a given output, costs associated with each program are examined and compared and programs with lower costs should be selected (Bootman et al. 1996). In a cost minimisation analysis, consequences do not form part of the evaluation. As output or benefits of the two programs are assumed equivalent, the analysis focuses only on input or cost.

A typical example of cost minimisation analysis with regards to pharmaceuticals is the evaluation of two generically equivalent drugs in which the outcomes have been proven equal, but acquisition and administration costs of the two drugs may be significantly different. For example, the unit cost of a metronidazole 500mg infusion bag is higher than that of metronidazole 500mg in a glass vial. However, the latter requires an infusion set to administer the medication. The total cost of the medication in a glass vial plus the infusion set is higher than the unit cost of the medication in an infusion bag. It is in deciding the optimal mix of inputs that the principle of cost minimisation analysis becomes important.

For cost minimisation analysis, we set $P_1E_1 = P_2E_2 = PE$:

$$\frac{1}{C_1} > \frac{1}{C_2} \tag{2.4}$$

Comparison between CBA, CEA, CUA and CMA

There is a fundamental philosophical difference between cost effectiveness analysis, cost utility analysis and cost benefit analysis (Drummond 1997). Cost effectiveness analysis and cost utility analysis assist decision makers in deciding the values of competing programs, are often referred as the decision maker's approach to economic evaluation (Johannesson 2000). Cost benefit analysis has its origin in welfare economics. Under cost benefit analysis, it is the value of individuals rather than those of the program being examined.

However, Brent (2003) considered cost benefit analysis as the primary evaluation technique, and cost effectiveness analysis, cost utility analysis and cost minimisation analysis as special cases of cost benefit analysis. Cost effectiveness analysis is a special case of cost benefit analysis when we set *pricing* of two *effects* to be equal. Cost utility analysis is a special case of cost benefit analysis when we express *effect* in terms of QALY and set *pricing* of two QALYs to be equal. Cost minimisation analysis is a special case of cost benefit analysis when we set both effects and *pricings* to be equal.

2.3   The case for cost benefit analysis

2.3.1   Capital budgeting

Cost benefit analysis is developed on the basis of capital budgeting technique. Capital budgeting is an operations research technique designed to select an optimal portfolio of investment among a set of alternative investment proposals. An optimal portfolio of investments is defined as a set of investments that makes the greatest possible contribution to the goals of an organisation, given its constraints such as limited supplies of capital or other resources (Gass and Harris 2001).

Social cost benefit analysis is an exercise of capital budgeting under capital rationing. Capital rationing is a constraint in which the amount of capital available for investment is limited. The techniques of social cost benefit analysis are essentially similar to those of financial cost benefit analysis. However, the issues considered by the analyst when performing a social cost benefit analysis are different from those considered by management of a private firm or fund managers of the finance sector. All the policy recommendations from a social cost benefit analysis can only be interpreted in terms of the chosen *social objective function* (Dinwiddy and Teal 1996). In addition to the financial benefits such as a decrease in health expenditure and increase in economic production, a social cost benefit analysis should also consider the social benefits such as the improvement of health status, improved quality of life, an increase in life expectancy, a decrease in mortality and morbidity, etc. As discussed in Section 2.2, cost benefit analysis is the only methodology that can determine the social worthiness of health programs and address the issues of allocative efficiency. A health program is selected on the basis that it maximises health and utilities of patients, as measured by the social welfare function (see discussion of social welfare function in Section 3.6.1).

2.3.2 The need of extending existing cost benefit analysis

The early attempts of cost benefit analysis to valuate benefits of health programs solely under the human capital approach led to the perception that cost benefit analysis was not a useful evaluation technique in the health sector (Abel-Smith 1985) and normative health economics. However, with the development of a contingent valuation technique in environmental economics, there is an increasing interest of applying cost benefit analysis in the health sector (Tolley 1994; Johannesson 2000).

As discussed in Section 1.4.1, there are several limitations in the existing literature in the area of cost benefit analysis application within the healthcare sector. An appropriate and comprehensive discussion of costs and benefits of health programs such as the PBS in Australia has not been undertaken. The focus is more on financial analysis rather than economic and welfare analysis. The full set of comprehensive cost benefit analysis techniques under social choice approach is not applied in the economic evaluation of health programs.

Although cost benefit analysis is a technique of social choice theory (Sen 1999b) and welfare economics (Broadway and Bruce 1984), cost benefit analysis of health programs (such as PBS listing decisions in this case) has not been developed within the framework of the recent developments in welfare economics (Hausman and McPherson 1996; Broome 1999), unlike the case in environmental economics. Also, ethics is not incorporated in the economic evaluation of health programs. There is little discussion about issues such as the social discount rate, shadow pricing and social valuation of costs and benefits of a health program, sustainability and intergenerational equity. Finally, mathematical methods (such as optimisation, general integer programming and Stochastic programming) of project planning are yet to be applied in sectoral planning of health.

This book argues that cost benefit analysis of health programs should be based on the recent advances in normative social choice theory of welfare economics. By applying the full set of cost benefit analysis techniques, a project plan is provided to health sector project evaluation, and thus improving the usefulness and effectiveness of such an evaluation. However, if the cost benefit analysis techniques are only partially applied, all the relevant economic principles may not be fully considered. Moreover, ethics and moral philosophy should be incorporated in the economic evaluation of health programs. The extent of the adoption and implementation of the suggested extended cost benefit analysis framework depends on the analyst's value judgement and the underlying public perspective.

Social cost benefit analysis helps to ascertain estimates of the net social benefits or welfare of listing a medication in the PBS and is a better methodology than cost effectiveness analysis in addressing allocative efficiency. In this book, *social cost benefit analysis* is performed on six medications, namely Atorvastatin, Clopidogrel, Pioglitazone, Letrozole, Fluticasone/Salmeterol and Tiotropium. The results of the social cost benefit analysis are then compared with results from the financial cost benefit analysis and from the type of criteria listed under The Pharmaceutical Benefits Advisory Committee (PBAC) submission guidelines.

Several methods of normative economics for economic evaluation of health programs are discussed in Section 2.2. From these methodologies, we have chosen cost benefit analysis because of its broader scope and its ability to address the issues of allocative efficiency in order to establish the social worthiness of a health program. Cost benefit analysis is an amalgam of classical and neoclassical utilitarianism ideas (Kneese and Schulze 1985) and helps to incorporate ethics into the economic evaluation of the PBS in Australia. The neoclassical perspective of cost benefit analysis assumes maximisation of individual utilities rather than utility of the whole, however, its classical perspective in the quantitative application contrasts the neoclassical tradition of assuming both measurable and comparable utility (Kneese and Schulze 1985).

2.4 Cost benefit analysis: Financial analysis

Financial cost benefit analysis is commonly used in evaluating financial investment. When a private sector firm considers an investment decision, management will examine a range of issues such as financial profitability of the project, cash flow analysis of costs and revenues, internal rate of return at which the project breaks even, as well as the risks associated with the project. Management also considers other alternatives in order to select the project that maximises the return of investment for the firm as well as its shareholders. After evaluating and selecting the proposed investment project, management will then consider the financing decision (Peirson et al. 1995; Dinwiddy and Teal 1996).

The same principles of cost benefit analysis can be applied in the project selection process of health programs. When medications are listed on PBS, costs are incurred and benefits are generated to the government and the public (or patients). To apply principles of financial cost benefit analysis in the PBS setting, costs and benefits of these medications are identified and valuated into monetary terms in the year they occur, and are discounted to net present values using the chosen discount rate. A low discount rate favours programs with benefits in the distant future, while a high discount rate favours those with benefits in the near future.

2.4.1 Discounted cash flow analysis

Discounted cash flow (DCF) analysis refers to the process of discounting a series of cash flows due in future periods to their present values when analysing and evaluating a program or a project (Peirson et al. 1995; Campell and Brown 2003). Two most frequently employed DCF methods are the net present value (NPV) and the internal rate of return (IRR) methods.

NPV is the difference between the present value of the net cash generated by a project and the initial cash outlay.

$$NPV = \frac{C_1}{(1+k)} + \frac{C_2}{(1+k)^2} + \ldots + \frac{C_n}{(1+k)^n} - C_0 \qquad (2.5)$$

$$NPV = \sum_{t=1}^{n} \frac{C_n}{(1+k)^n} - C_0$$

where: C_0 = the initial cash outlay on the project;
C_t = net cash flow generated by the project at time t;
n = the life of the project; and
k = required rate of return.

The study on direct cost savings from the prevention of myocardial infarction and stroke from cessation of smoking by Lightwood and Glantz (1997) is an example of using net present value in estimating benefit of health program (see Table 2.2).

The IRR is the rate of return that equates the present value of the net cash flows generated by a health program with its initial cash outlay. The internal rate of return is the best index to use when there is a capital constraint. IRR is the discount rate when the net present value equals zero. It is the highest rate of interest that one can afford without losing money on the project. Weisbrod (1971) was the first to calculate the internal rate of return of a medical research program on poliomyelitis, estimate at 11–12%.

$$C_0 = \frac{C_1}{(1+r)} + \frac{C_2}{(1+r)^2} + \ldots + \frac{C_n}{(1+r)^n}$$

$$C_0 = \sum_{t=1}^{n} \frac{C_1}{(1+k)}$$

$$\sum_{t=1}^{n} \frac{C_1}{(1+k)} - C_0 = 0$$

where: C_0 = the initial cash outlay on the project;
C_t = net cash flow generated by the project at time t;
n = the life of the project; and
r = the internal rate of return.

Table 2.2 **Results of study on cost savings from cessation of smoking ($)**

	Year 1	Year 2	Year 3	Year 4	Year 5	Year 6	Year 7
Undiscounted	47	155	299	462	634	811	990
Discount Factor	1.000	0.976	0.952	0.929	0.906	0.884	0.862
Discounted at 2.5%	47	151	284	429	575	717	853

Source: Lightwood and Glantz 1997.

2.4.2 Time discounting

The time value of money implies that a sum of money in the present is worth more than the same amount in the future. The real worth of $100 is more now than that in a year time. The $100 can be invested or be banked to accumulate interest. If the rate is 5%, there is an additional $5 as interest at the end of the year. That is a total of $105 at the end of the year if one takes the $100 now. Alternatively, the present value (at the beginning of the year) of $105 receivable at the end of the year with an annual rate of interest of 5% is $100. This comparison of the present value and the future value of a health program is done by discounting the future value by a factor (e.g. market rate of interest) and calculating the present value of the future stream.

Discounting is particularly important for health programs because the costs are immediate, but some benefits or health effects are in the future. Hurley et al. (1996) demonstrated the role of discounting in calculating the lifetime cost of HIV in Australia. The lifetime costs are dependent on whether the discounting is done on the first day of phase 1 or first day of each of the four phases.

2.4.3 Net present value, cost benefit ratio and decision rules

The present value (*PV*) can be calculated as:

$$PV = FV/(1 + r)^n \tag{2.6}$$

Where: *FV* = future values
r = discount rate/rate of interest
n = number of years

In this case, the future value is \$105.00, the discount rate is 5% and the number of years is one. The present value is calculated as:

$$PV = FV/(1 + r)^n$$
$$= 105/(1 + 0.05)^1$$
$$= 100$$

A general statement of the net present value formula is as follows:

$$PV = \frac{FV_1}{(1+r)^0} + \frac{FV_2}{(1+r)^1} + \cdots + \frac{FV_n}{(1+r)^n} \qquad (2.7)$$

The net discounted present value of a project is calculated as:

$$NPV = \frac{B_0 - C_0}{(1+r)^0} + \frac{B_1 - C_1}{(1+r)^1} + \cdots + \frac{B_n - C_n}{(1+r)^n} \qquad (2.8)$$
$$= \sum_{t=0}^{n} \frac{B^t - C^t}{(1+r)^t}$$

If the NPV is positive, the health program generates benefits more than its costs. If the NPV equals zero, benefits of the health program equal its costs. If the NPV is negative, the costs of the health program are more than its benefits.

The cost benefit (C-B) ratio reveals the dollars gained on each dollar of cost.

$$\text{C-B ratio} = \frac{\displaystyle\sum_{t=0}^{N} \frac{B_t}{(1+r)^t}}{\displaystyle\sum_{t=0}^{n} \frac{C_t}{(1+r)^t}} \qquad (2.9)$$

If the C-B ratio is greater than one, the health program is of value. If the C-B ratio is equal to one, the benefit equals the cost. If the C-B ratio is less than one, the health program is not beneficial.

Decision rules

In selecting a medication to be listed on the PBS, several criteria can be considered:

a. If NPV is positive (> zero), the medication should be listed;
b. If the C-B ratio is greater than one, the medication should be listed; and
c. Reject the PBS listing of the medication if conditions (a) or/and (b) do not hold true.

2.4.4 Example

On the basis of the human capital or cost of illness approach, health benefits are estimated as an increase in economic production and reduction/avoidance of future treatment costs. In a hypothetical example, drug A is a hypolipidaemic agent which lowers blood cholesterol level and is to be considered for listing on the PBS. The NPV and C-B ratio of drug A are calculated using a discount rate of 5%. The details of the calculations are shown in Appendix 2.2. For drug A, the NPV over a period of five-year is 132.76 and the C-B ratio is 1.37. Since the NPV is positive and the C-B ratio is greater than one, drug A should be included in PBS listing.

2.5 Social cost benefit analysis for health programs

2.5.1 Social cost benefit analysis

The appraisal of a public sector program, such as the PBS, requires a social cost benefit analysis of the project, rather than just a financial cost benefit analysis (Campbell and Brown 2003). Medications should be selected to be included in the PBS listing on the basis of maximising net social benefits in addition to net financial benefits. In PBS setting, social cost benefit analysis attempts to convert all social benefits and costs to a single monetary measurement unit, the dollar. There are several reasons for which this distinction between financial and social cost benefit analysis is made, such as the presence of the externalities, market distortions, trade restrictions, and capital market restrictions, etc.

2.5.2   Cost benefit analysis: Assumptions and steps

Cost benefit methodology is based on certain assumptions. Firstly, it is possible to separate one program from another. Secondly, there is a possibility of choice between programs. Thirdly, it is possible to estimate the outcomes associated with each program. In addition, it is possible to value the outcomes and to estimate the cost of providing each program; as well as to weigh benefits and costs of the program. Finally, a program should be rejected if its costs exceed its benefits (Culyer and Maynard 1997).

In conducting a cost benefit analysis, alternative ways of achieving the desired objectives are considered. In order to choose among these alternatives, a cost benefit analysis requires a precise definition of the variables and objectives; criteria for judging results; quantification of the results of each alternative; formal exposition of alternatives; and examination of the effects of assumptions and uncertainties.

A cost benefit analysis in a health program such as PBS involves several steps (Conyers and Hills 1984). The first step is to define the program of the PBS. The second step is to identify all the relevant consequences of a particular policy decision, which is the policy decision to accept or reject listing of a medication on the PBS in this case. The third step is to evaluate all the consequences in the same monetary unit, so as to derive values for the costs and benefits accrued to the society as a result of PBS listing decision of a medication. The fourth step is to discount the costs and benefits of the PBS to their net present values in order to allow comparison between different medications listing (multiple outcomes), in the form of an overall cost benefit ratio. The results are compared in order to determine the feasibility of listing these medications on the PBS. Medications with cost benefit ratio greater than one are selected for PBS listing and those with cost benefit ratio less than one are rejected from PBS listing. The final step is to present the results of analysis in an appropriate format.

2.6   Social cost benefit analysis and health program evaluation: Recent issues

As discussed in Section 2.2, cost benefit analysis is the preferred methodology for economic evaluation of health programs because the issues of allocative efficiency and social worthiness are addressed. However, the majority of the existing literature focuses on cost effectiveness analysis, with a small percentage on cost benefit analysis. Among the published studies of cost benefit analysis, outcome measures are often not quantified into monetary terms (see for examples in Zarnke et al. 1997). Some crucial areas of controversy and limitations in cost benefit analysis in health economics include valuation of benefits and costs; quality of life measurements; and incorporation of ethics and equity.

2.6.1 Valuation of benefits and costs

The main difficulty in applying social cost benefit analysis in the evaluation of the health programs is monetary quantification of social costs and benefits estimates. Cost benefit analysis is a method for social choice and decision-making. A proper integration of cost benefit analysis with recent developments in social choice theory is necessary to produce a useful evaluation method. There is a need to develop an approach in applying cost benefit analysis to health program evaluation that overcomes the difficulties mentioned above.

There is a lack of consensus in the existing literature of what constitutes an acceptable method in evaluating social costs and social benefits of health programs. Methodological developments tend to focus on the benefits side of the equation, with vigorous debates on the outcomes to be included, how they are to be measured, valued and aggregated, and the nature of the social welfare function (Hurley 2000 p. 98). Many studies focus only on narrow socioeconomic benefits and ignore wider issues such as extra-welfaristic factors (equity, freedom, and so on). Methods integrating economic, social, welfaristic as well as extra-welfaristic issues are yet to be developed.

A typical economic evaluation of a health program divides costs into three categories, namely direct (the health expenditure), indirect (forgone earnings) and intangibles (pain and suffering associated with the conditions and treatment). Benefits can be interpreted as negative costs, and can be divided into direct (savings in health expenditure), indirect (restored earnings) and intangible (alleviation of pain and suffering). When applying social cost benefit analysis, direct and indirect benefits can be measured under the human capital approach and intangibles can be estimated by valuation methods.

Rice (1967) of the US Social Security Administration estimated the economic costs of illness as the sum of resources consumed in treatment and forgone economic production, which are the direct economic cost of the illness (Jack 1999). In early economic evaluations, health-related benefits are defined as estimated reductions or avoidance of future treatment cost plus increased economic production due to health improvement. This is generally known as the *human capital approach* (Johannesson 2000) or the *cost of illness approach* (Jack 1999).

The possible valuation methods for measuring intangible costs are shown below in Figure 2.1. The non-demand curve approaches are well defined and rely on existing markets to determine the valuation. Under the demand curve approaches, the revealed preference method also relies on existing markets and hence valuation can be imputed by reference to markets. The contingent valuation

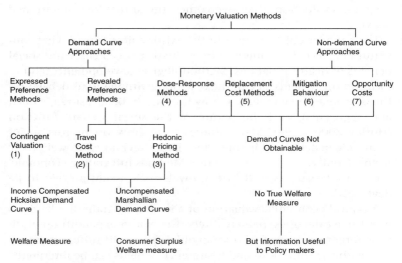

Figure 2.1   A typology of valuation approaches

Sources: Islam and Gigas 1996 (1) Cummings et al. 1896. (2) Turner et al. 1993 (3) Streeting 1990. (4) Turner et al. 1993. (5) Dixon et al. 1986. (6) Perkins 1994. (7) Krutilla et al. 1985.

approach, which is an expressed preference method, does not rely on market information to achieve a valuation. By combining the human capital approach and valuation methods, all costs and benefits can be estimated and included in the social cost benefit analysis so that a full evaluation of the health program is made possible.

Conjoint analysis is a technique used to establish the relative importance of attributes in the provision of a good or service. By including different cost attributes in a conjoint analysis study, estimates of WTP for changes in the levels of attributes of importance can be derived using regression techniques (McIntosh et al. 1999).

The human capital approach estimates the costs of the PBS based on resources consumption. Benefits are estimated in terms of decreased consumption of healthcare resources, and an increase in economic production (using market wage rates) due to the improved status of individuals. The value of life and the benefits of health are measured in terms of economic contribution an individual makes to the society (see further discussion in Chapter 3). Consequently, low value is placed on the health and/or life of individuals that are not in labour force, such as the elderly, the unemployed, the homemakers, etc.

Thomas Schelling (1968) argued that the theoretical foundation of the human capital approach came from the concept of WTP (see also Kaldor 1934 and Hicks 1941). The value of a livelihood measured by the human capital approach is distinguished from the value of a statistical life measured by individual WTP for decrease in probability of death. WTP is a relevant measure of economic benefit for health programs that 'saved lives' and should reflect the probabilistic nature of outcome of health programs.

Abelson (2003) argued that WTP is 'an *ex-ante* measure of the amount an individual is willing to pay to prevent an impaired health state'. This is in contrast to the 'traditional cost of illness approach to valuing health benefits as the *ex-post* sum of identifiable costs, such as loss of output and medical expenses'. Abelson further argued that the ex-post measure 'does not account for pain and suffering and cannot account for changes in lifestyles' and the '*ex-ante* measure of WTP is the appropriate value of health for most policy purposes'. There are two types of approaches used to measure WTP related to health changes, namely the revealed preference approach and the expressed preference.

Under the revealed preference approach, WTP can be inferred from actual decisions that involve a trade-off between money and health. Most work on revealed preference was done in a study of the labour market with a wage premium being offered to workers for more risky jobs (Viscusi et al. 1987, 2003). Under the expressed preference approach, WTP is assessed by a survey or the *contingent valuation* method where respondents are given hypothetical choices involving health. The contingent valuation method was first used to assess WTP in mobile coronary care units that reduced the risk of death after heart attack (Acton 1973).

Under the human capital or cost of illness approach, there are difficulties in valuating benefits due to imperfections in the labour market. Jack (1999) argued that the value of new production arising from the effects of health program on individuals' health and productivity was not necessarily restricted to market production only, but in the form of domestic economic activities as well. There is difficulty in determining a price on non-marketed resources (shadow pricing). Analyses based on market production tend to bias towards interventions that improve health of working-age individuals, and less value is placed on the health of elderly, homemakers, and the unemployed who largely do not contribute to increased economic production even with improved health status. The wage rate may not reflect the true value of economic production because of other inequities such as gender or race.

Many benefits of health programs are in the form of improvement in health status, time and health of homemakers. Such costs and benefits do not have market prices; and are difficult to be estimated and included in a project appraisal exercise. The analyst may have to supply alternative prices when market prices do not exist. Such prices are referred as shadow prices (Dinwiddy and Teal 1996; Little and Mirrlees 1974). The weakness of the human capital approach has led to the development of other valuation methods such as those based on measuring WTP and health-related quality of life. 'A defining element in the historical development of outcome measures is the fact that the primary "output" of many health care interventions is life-years, and in particular, life-years of varying quality' (Hurley 2000 p. 98).

The contingent valuation method involves individuals undertaking surveys to determine the monetary value they place on a health program. When conducting a contingent valuation study, health effects associated with an intervention is described to respondents who determine the amount they are willing to pay for that intervention. There is an emphasis in the literature on the use of WTP to reveal the preferences of households and thus the benefits of health programs. As discussed in Section 1.4.1, there are also limitations to this method in PBS setting. Measurement of WTP can be subject to strategic bias, interviewer bias, sponsor bias, starting point bias, range bias, relation bias, importance bias, position bias, inference bias, etc. Statistical problems due to sample design and execution of the study also lead to bias in the respondent's valuation. Hypothetical WTP may exceed real WTP (Johannesson 2000).

All the approaches mentioned above have limitations in different perspectives. A combination of the human capital or cost of illness approach and preference-based approaches should be used in the social cost benefit analysis of the PBS, where the human capital or cost of illness approach is used to measure the tangible inputs and outputs; and the preference-based approach is used to measure the intangible effects.

2.6.2   Quality of life measurements

The constitution of the World Health Organisation (1948) defines health as more than freedom from disease and includes complete physical, mental, and social well-being. Health services providers and researchers consider the impact of disease and its treatments on patients' lives, in addition to the traditional measures of laboratory results and clinical opinions. When evaluating a health program, stakeholders (such as government or fund holders, policy makers, as well as patients) require information as how the program improves and promotes health. Information about the social functioning and mental well-being is equally important in the decision of a project appraisal of a health program. The study of health related quality of life (HRQOL) is particularly relevant in this respect.

Quality of life refers to an evaluation of all the different aspects of people's lives including work, leisure, daily living, etc. HRQOL encompasses those aspects of our lives that are significantly influenced by our health, or our activities to maintain or to improve health. With the advance in technology, medical treatments aim at improving both the quantity of life (through death-averting treatments), as well as the quality of life (through treatment of many chronic conditions such as arthritis and diabetes).

With scarcity of resources, economic evaluation is conducted to test the social worthiness and merits of a health program in order to justify the resource allocation. Both costs and benefits of the competing alternatives are examined in order to determine the financial, economic and social viability of a health program. People's preferences regarding the benefits of a health program play an important role in the decision-making process. Health outcomes are interpreted in terms of improved quantity and quality of life. In addition to describe the benefits of the health program, it becomes increasingly necessary to give an indication of the value attached to such benefits in terms of HRQOL (Green et al. 2000).

There are a number of approaches to determine the values attached to HRQOL, namely contingent valuation, conjoint analysis and health state valuation or health state utilities approach. Contingent valuation (CV) study places a monetary value to health change, and is the main source of WTP values derived from a stated preference survey. Conjoint analysis is used to establish the relative importance of attributes in the provision of a good or service. By including different amount of money as cost attributes in a conjoint analysis study, estimates of WTP for changes in the level of attributes are derived by regression techniques (McIntosh et al. 1999).

Health state valuation or health state utilities approach elicits preferences for different health states on a scale from one (full health) to zero (dead). Techniques used to elicit preferences of health states include category rating scale, magnitude estimation, standard gamble, time trade-off and personal trade-off technique (Green et al. 2000). Health state valuation helps to determine quality weights (preferences) in the calculation of QALYs. QALY is intended to be a general health measure that captures the effects of a healthcare intervention on both the quantity of life (mortality) and quality of life (morbidity), so that it can serve as an outcome measure for a range of health programs and/or health interventions (Hurley 2000). There are different methods to estimate the weights of QALY such as psychometric principles and using utility theory. HRQOL is the QALY constructed by the utility weights. The weights are preference-based, but QALY is a utility score. HRQOL can be interpreted as a preference-based measure of subjective health or as a utility itself depending on the assumptions made regarding the nature of individual utility function. HRQOL measures are used as both extra-welfarist measures of health and as utility measures within the welfarist framework.

The value of a QALY is referred to as value of a life-year (VOLY) derived indirectly from the estimated statistical value of life (VOSL). VOLY is assumed to be a constant sum over the remaining life span and has a discounted value equal to the estimated VOSL. The average value of QALY is used as a measure of benefits in the cost benefit analysis of health programs (Abelson 2003).

Preference-based approaches place monetary values on outcomes of health programs on the basis of individual maximum WTP for a health gain. Developments in measuring WTP in environmental economics revived interest in applying cost benefit analysis in the economic evaluation of health programs (Tolley 1994; Johannesson 2000). WTP can be assessed directly by a survey using the expressed preference approach or contingent valuation method; or be determined, using the revealed preference approach, from actual decisions made by individuals that involved trade-offs between health and money (Viscusi 2003). WTP is a measure of the welfare, economic and social benefits of a program.

2.6.3 Incorporation of ethics and equity

During the process of assessing the efficiency and effectiveness of health programs, there are certain assumptions and procedures of economic evaluations that have equity implications. These include the methodology of measuring and valuing outcomes, aggregating outcomes (benefits or utility), as well as the associated maximising decision criterion.

The equity principle is embodied in the outcome measurement technique of health programs. WTP links health effect to a person's economic resources, as compared to QALY which is supposed to be independent of an individual's economic resources. QALY is developed to be a non-monetary measure in order to avoid monetary valuation, and to incorporate the equity assumptions of the analysts (Hurley 2000). Although QALY is not directly constrained by the income level of an individual, this does mean that QALY is unaffected by the distribution of income (Donaldson et al. 2002).

The techniques of estimating utility weights of QALYs are from the egalitarian perspective. The difference in utility across different health states and age groups are set equal, resulting in a simple unweighted aggregation of QALY. In reality, analysts empirically estimate utilities. Consequently, utilities are not consistently scaled, and making it difficult to incorporate distributional equity principles into aggregation procedures (Bleichrodt 1997; Hurley 2000).

Methodologies of aggregating utilities, either over time or across individuals, both contain distributional equity principles. If benefits or health outcomes are aggregated over time, issues of intergeneration equity and discount rate (of costs and benefits) should be considered. There are two philosophical bases for selecting discounting rate. The first argument is that market interest rate is chosen as discount rate to represent the opportunity cost of fund used in the health programs instead of other alternative options. Based on individual sovereignty, the second argument sets the discount rate as the social rate of time preference of individuals at the time the health programs are implemented.

Benefits or health outcomes can also be aggregated across individuals. However, the anonymity principle of the simple unweighted aggregation of QALYs under the egalitarian approach may impede distributional equity. The focus of the maximisation criterion of cost benefit analysis is on total outcome rather than the distribution of outcome. Distributional equity demands recognition of the moral claims of different individuals to healthcare due to their different characteristics. Differential weights should be attached to health benefits of individuals according to their identifiable characteristics such as family status, age, initial health states, etc.

Results of economic evaluations should support allocation decisions based on both efficiency and equity criteria, providing information for making allocations to achieve a relatively equal distribution of health. In addition to the effectiveness and efficiency of interventions, achieving an equal distribution of health relies also on the initial levels of health of individuals.

2.7 Limitations and problems of the existing methods

Economic evaluation of health program should consider the economic efficiency, allocative efficiency and distributional equity of the program. As discussed in Chapter 1 and previous sections of Chapter 2, cost benefit analysis is the preferred methodology as it deals with issues of allocative efficiency and social desirability of the programs that the other methodologies fail to address.

There are several problems with the existing practices of cost benefit analysis. Firstly, there are theoretical difficulties. The neo-classical welfare economics framework of cost benefit analysis assumes utility maximisation, individual (consumer) sovereignty, consequentialism and welfarism (Hurley 2000). However, standard demand theory assumes utility functions are ordinal. Interpersonal comparisons of utility are impossible. This weakens the argument of utility maximisation, as it is no longer possible to maximise the sum of utilities aggregated across individuals (Kneese and Schulze 1985). There is also the likelihood of preference failure due to information asymmetry, poor knowledge (especially in the area of health), rational thinking, or impact of context. All these cast doubts on the concept of utility maximisation.

The concept of consumer sovereignty is also questionable as individuals may not have the professional knowledge to judge which medication will be suitable for their conditions. Society may override individual preference in the notion of merit good argument (see further discussion in Section 3.4.1). Consequentialism holds that a program or policy is only judged in terms of the results or consequent, not the process. Thus, the issues associated with the process may be ignored due to the over-emphasis of the outcomes. Also, focus on efficiency of the outcome may be at the expense of the equity of the outcome (Carter 2001).

As discussed in Section 2.6.1, there is a lack of consensus in definition and evaluation of social costs and social benefits. This is clearly evident in the *2002 Guidelines for the Pharmaceutical Industry on Preparation of Submissions to the Pharmaceutical Benefits Advisory Committee including major submissions involving economic analyses*, which is an important reference document for the illustrative example in this study, that is the Australian PBS. In the PBAC submission guidelines, costs generally include direct medical expenses and health services consumption, valuation of outcomes is not recommended, and inclusion of indirect costs and benefits are not recommended. As a matter of fact, cost benefit analysis methodology is not recommended (see also www.health.gov.au/internet/wcms/publishing.nsf/content/health-pbs-general-pubs-guidelines-content.htm).

Another problem is choosing a proper discounting rate for the costs and benefits accrued from the health programs, as well as addressing the issues of intergenerational equity. To the issues of selectivity, there are practical problems to identify all the relevant consequences of a particular health program or policy. The monetary valuation of costs and benefits, and intangibles is also problematic. The most complex issue of cost benefit analysis is distributional equity. Simple aggregation of costs and benefits may ignore individual circumstances and their specific needs. The application of differential weights to costs and benefits according to individual demographics and needs is an attempt to address the issue of distributional equity.

Cost benefit analysis can be used to substitute political process because of its image of scientific objectivity basis for decision, thus undermining the effect of public participation. This is a general problem of extending economic analyses to serve as a basis for practical decision-making in a political economic context.

In order to address the above problems, there are some major areas to be considered for a social cost benefit analysis:

1) identification and inclusion of indirect, external and intangible costs and benefits;
2) social valuation of benefits and costs;
3) shadow pricing of benefits and costs;
4) the use of a social discount rate;
5) incorporation of public policy objectives:
6) incorporation of ethics and moral philosophy; and
7) incorporation of issues such as sustainability and intergenerational equity.

While the first two areas are relatively well developed in health economic evaluation practices, the rest are not as evident from literature in this area (Carter and Harris 1999; Johannesson 2000; Brent 2003) and require further developments in health economics. The cost benefit methodology has been developed under the framework of normative welfare economics (Hurley 2000). However, cost benefit analysis is a social choice and decision method (Islam

2001a), and should be developed within the foundations of normative social choice theory. The application of social choice theory foundations of cost benefit analysis is not well articulated in the existing literature. The improved social cost benefit analysis framework is developed from a foundation of social choice theory, and can then be applied to test the social worthiness of programs and policies. However, a major limitation in cost benefit analysis in health economics is it is a social choice and decision-making method; existing cost benefit methods are not founded in social choice theory.

It is discussed above that one of the contemporary areas of controversies in the application of cost benefit analysis is the incorporation of ethics. This requires the consideration of social value judgements and preferences to provide the ethical perspective to be incorporated in cost benefit analysis. In order to incorporate ethics and moral philosophy into the cost benefit analysis framework, a number of issues need to be addressed (Kneese and Schulze 1985):

1) establish shadow prices for public goods or services that have no market prices;
2) establish normative values of individual preferences;
3) address the distributional issues including moral hazard (tendency for insurance coverage to induce behavioural responses that raised expected losses that are insured); and
4) address the issues of intergenerational equity.

The resolution of these issues can only be achieved through social value judgements and preferences since these are normative issues. As social choice theory is a framework for normative decision-making (Sen 1999b), cost benefit analysis based on this theory is a suitable framework for incorporating the above issues in the economic evaluation of programs and policies.

2.8 Conclusion

As discussed in this chapter, there are different methodologies for the economic evaluation of health programs. Social cost benefit analysis is the preferred methodology as it addresses the issues of allocative efficiency and social worthiness of the program. However, there are still some limitations and difficulties in applying social cost benefit analysis in the economic evaluation in a health setting. Therefore, an extended cost benefit analysis is needed, based explicitly on social choice theory. This new technique is named as the new[3] social cost benefit analysis and will be discussed in Chapter 3.

3
New³ Cost Benefit Analysis

3.1 Introduction

As discussed in previous chapters, there are limitations in the existing methods of cost benefit analysis. For economic evaluation of health programs to be useful and meaningful, certain adjustments are needed. Omission of extra-welfaristic elements in social costs and social benefits, inappropriate measures of benefits, difficulties in measuring benefits and a lack of proper integration of cost benefit analysis methods of health programs with the underlying evaluation processes which make it difficult to understand how the cost benefit analysis is being used for social choices, narrow the scope of analysis. An evaluation method needs to be developed on the basis of the right and relevant principles of welfare economics and social choice theory (by explicating social preferences), so that it can test the economic and social efficiency of health programs, containing the benefits and costs which are measured adequately and appropriately. Extra-welfaristic considerations (such as equity, freedom, and so on) in ethics, incorporated in the integrated operational framework and methods of cost benefit analysis, can then be applied in the evaluation.

To overcome the limitations in cost benefit analysis and to develop an appropriate evaluation method, the paradigm of new³ welfare economics developed in Islam (2001) where the preference methods are used in conjunction with expert opinions, scientific information, social preferences and value judgements to evaluate benefits and costs can be adopted. As cost benefit analysis is a discipline in applied welfare economics, any particular form of cost benefit analysis is based on the principles and theories of a corresponding school of thought in welfare economics. A cost benefit analysis of health programs developed under the new[3] welfare economics paradigm can be named as new[3] cost benefit analysis. The objective of this chapter is to specify and discuss the elements of new[3] cost benefit analysis applicable to health economics and all other branches of economics.

This chapter is structured as follows. Section 3.2 discusses the foundation of welfare economics and Section 3.3 looks at the applied welfare economics framework. Section 3.4 is about the history of modern welfare economics. Section 3.5 considers the social choice theory, while Section 3.6 discusses the elements of the new[3] cost benefit analysis. Costs and benefits in the new approach are identified in Section 3.7 and their valuation is examined in Section 3.8. Section 3.9 deals with the social discount rate. Section 3.10 considers the welfare weights of the new[3] cost benefit analysis. Section 3.11 is about sustainability, weighting and intergenerational equity. Section 3.12 looks at public policy objectives. Section 3.13 discusses the new[3] cost benefit analysis of health programs. Examples of new[3] cost benefit analysis are presented in Section 3.14. Section 3.15 discusses the advantages of the proposed framework. Section 3.16 is the conclusion.

3.2   Welfare economics foundations and limitations

As stated above, welfare economics theory provides the conceptual foundation for methodology of cost benefit analysis. Hurley (2000, p. 97) puts it in the following way:

> ... welfare economics theory provides the intellectual pretext for the practice of assessing programs and services by measuring the costs and benefits in monetary units, calculating the net benefits (benefits less costs), and ranking the allocative efficiency of those programs and services on the basis of net benefit.

The basic objective of welfare economics (see Clarke and Islam 2004) is to evaluate the alternate states of an economy, and to determine the impact of economic, social, environmental, or political interventions on the welfare of individuals and that of society at large. In a healthcare setting, welfare economics is about ranking, resource allocation of health programs and policies. Welfare economic analysis ranks different health programs in terms of net changes in social welfare or health benefits, and aids in program selection in order to achieve an optimal social outcome. Ranking a policy requires a positive analysis that describes the effects of the policy on resource allocation and the ethical criteria of what constitutes a *better* resource allocation (Hurley 2000).

Although cost benefit analysis is a sub-discipline in welfare economics and the principles of cost benefit analysis are derived from welfare economics, there are some weaknesses in the present state of welfare economics foundation of cost benefit analysis. In the mainstream welfare economics, especially in new welfare economics, measurability and interpersonal comparison of welfare are ruled out. In cost benefit analysis under this situation, social welfare is measured by aggregation of consumer surplus caused by price changes to be induced by the proposed program or policy. Non-price change measures of social welfare such as increase in life expectancy, happiness, and so on are not captured by the measures of consumer surpluses. Extra-welfaristic elements of social welfare such as liberty, freedom, ethics, etc are not incorporated into consumer surplus measures of social welfare in cost benefit analysis. Therefore, the mainstream welfare economics cannot provide a comprehensive foundation for cost benefit analysis, especially social cost benefit analysis. Therefore, there is a need for a paradigm in welfare economics which can provide an appropriate foundation for (social) cost benefit analysis. A review of the different schools of welfare economics (classical, new and new² welfare economics) is provided below to highlight the above limitations of the present welfare economics foundation of cost benefit analysis and to look for another paradigm (new³ cost benefit analysis) which can overcome the above limitations.

Moreover, there is a lack of consensus in defining welfare, as well as in defining a methodology for measuring welfare (Clarke and Islam 2004). Despite advance of mathematical modeling and calculation, determination of optimal social states rests on value judgements of individuals, analysts, policy makers, and society at large. Economics is a subject about making the *best* use of scarce resources. However, the definition of *best* must have a reference point in order to be meaningful. The presumption underlying neoclassical economics is the more goods and services the better. The best allocation of resources is maximising the flows of goods and services in any time period for given resource constraints. To decide on the *best* use of resources implies value judgement of individuals (Pearce and Nash 1981). Welfare economics is a discipline of economics and is no exception. Welfare economics deals with the logical implication of value judgements of the society and emphasises policy recommendation (Samuelson 1947; Maler 1985; Salvaris 1998; Altman 1996; Osberg and Sharpe 1998). Value judgements reflect the philosophical paradigm of an individual, and thus vary from market capitalism to communism to utilitarianism (Broadway and Bruce 1984; Johansson 1991).

A value judgement can be neither verified nor falsified in the way that an empirical statement can be. Economics is not only about optimal allocation of scarce resources, and this implies some value judgement about the desirability of economic activities. The meaning of economics is 'value-laden'. There is no such thing as a 'value-free' welfare economics (Pearce and Nash 1981; Hurley 2000).

3.3   Applied welfare economics framework

Welfare economics is about ranking the different social states. The principle of welfare economics is to maximise social welfares and to determine the optimal social states for people. Welfare economic analysis defines social welfare and its criterion, identifies factors prohibiting achievement of optimal levels of social welfare, and sets out policies to maximise social welfare (Oser and Brue 1988; Islam 1998; Clarke and Islam 2004). For applying welfare economics, it is necessary to choose a set of concepts and methods related to each application in evaluating the alternative state of the economy. Application of cost benefit analysis requires estimation of net social welfare (social benefits minus social costs of a health program) and choosing appropriate concepts and methods among other issues in applied welfare economics. Several of these conceptual and methodological issues in applied welfare economics (Lahiri and Moore 1991; Ravallion 1994; Johnson 1996; Islam 2001; Arrow et al. 2003; Clarke and Islam 2004) have been addressed and defined by different schools of thought in welfare economics.

A summary of alternative concepts and methods in applied welfare economics is discussed as follows. There are different concepts of welfare: well-being, benefit, or preference satisfaction. Welfarists adopt utility as benefit measures and extra-welfarists opt for health outcome. There are different approaches for specifying an aggregate social welfare function such as the possibility and the impossibility theorems. There is an extensive range of numeraire for performance and welfare such as utility, consumption, gross domestic product, capabilities, entitlement, wealth, capital stock, clean environment, level of human development or a combination of extra-welfaristic factors such as rights, freedom, opportunity, equity, and so on. There are also a number of different measurement units such as monetary units or physical units, market prices, shadow prices, and contingent valuation. Measurement can be at the aggregative (macro) level or disaggregative (micro) level. Models for measurement and analysis include gross domestic product or other performance indices, economy-wide macroeconomic models, econometric estimates of demand functions, constrained optimisations, and macro or microeconomic growth models.

It appears from the above analyses that there is a need to choose a set of concepts and methods in applying welfare economics. Different sets of concepts and methods belong to different schools of welfare economics. It is essential to understand different school of thought in welfare economics in order to understand the different sets of concepts and methods of application. Therefore, a brief survey of different schools of thought in welfare economics is provided below.

3.4 History of modern welfare economics

The foundations of welfare economics date back to Adam Smith's *Wealth of Nations* (1776). Under the utilitarian approach, welfare improvement of a society depends on increasing the utility level of individuals, but utility is not a sole function of income level. Jeremy Bentham (1789) aggregated the personal interests of individuals in the form of their respective utilities by using utilitarian calculus in order to obtain social judgement. The result was about the total utility of the community irrespective of distributional issues, diminishing the ethical and political importance of the informational base

(Sen 1999b). John Stuart Mill's *Utilitarianism* (1863) linked utilitarianism with economics. Until the 1890s, welfare economics assumed that marginal utility could be measured on a cardinal scale; and consumers sought to maximise utility in the way that firms sought to maximise profits (Ackerman 1997). Social welfare of individuals could be measured and compared in order to derive an economic decision.

In the early 1900s, Marshall (1890) and Pigou (1912, 1920) questioned the approach of cardinally measuring and comparing social welfare. Their new approach distinguished between material and non-material aspects of utility, and economics could only determine the material aspects of utility. Under Pigou's (1920) assumption of an 'unverified probability' that there was a positive relationship between material aspects and social welfare, it was possible to determine total welfare by measuring only the material aspects of utility. From the egalitarian viewpoint of Pigou, all individuals experience roughly the same relationship between utility and income and share similar needs. Thus the average utility for large groups could be meaningfully compared and it is possible to make welfare judgements on this basis (Kneese and Schulze 1985, Clarke and Islam 2004). In periods of extreme poverty or when externalities threatened the efficiency of competition, a government might choose to adopt a normative social choice perspective and intervene by redistributing income or resources in order to increase social welfare provided there was no interference with economic growth (Ackerman 1997, Clarke and Islam 2004).

Jevons (1871), Fisher (1906) and Pareto (1906) questioned the measurability of utility. The shift from cardinal measures to ordinal measures of utility led to a reduced emphasis on policy intervention to increase social welfare through resource redistribution. Without interpersonal comparison of utility, the informational base for making social choice decision is substantially reduced. From 1940 onwards, this approach quickly became established as the *new welfare economics*, using 'Pareto comparison' as the only basic criterion of measuring social improvement without addressing the distributional issues. Bergson (1938) and Samuelson (1947) explored further criterion for making social welfare judgements. Arrow (1950, 1951) formulated the 'social welfare function' by relating social preferences to the set of individual preferences and his *impossibility theorem* (1951) stated that it is impossible to measure utility cardinally in a practical sense (Quirk and Saposnik 1968; Ng 1979; Sen 1985, 1999b; Gaspert 1997).

3.4.1 New and new² welfare economics assumptions

There are two important assumptions in new welfare economics which base *Pareto criteria* on either *originality of ranking* or on *rationality* (for details see Arrow, Sen and Szumura 2003; and also Clarke and Islam 2004).

Different social states (of space, time, or information content) can be compared and ranked according to the *Pareto criteria*. Using this concept, unambiguous normative judgements can be made. If the social state change from $(c^1, \ldots, c^n)$ to $(c^{1'}, \ldots, c^{n'})$ and nobody is made worse off and at least one person is made better off, welfare has increased. According to this *Pareto 'unanimity' principle*, a policy is judged socially beneficial if and only if it increases the welfare of at least one individual and leaves no single individual with reduced welfare. However, a health program incurs social costs as well as creates social benefits for individuals of a society. The uneven distribution of social costs and social benefits creates winners and losers. When opportunity costs of resource allocation are considered, it is impossible to have a policy that benefits someone and does not harm the others. The gain of an individual is always at the expense of the loss of the others. In the 1930s, it was recognised that this *Pareto 'unanimity' principle* was not practical in real-life applications (Pearce and Nash 1981).

The *Kaldor-Hicks compensation* approach was developed as a solution to the *Pareto 'unanimity' principle* (Kaldor 1934; Hicks 1941). Pareto *compensation* exists if winners of a policy change can secure sufficient benefit to compensate losers for their loss. If losers are compensated to the extent they neither gain nor lose, they will be indifferent to the policy. If winners still have net benefits after compensating the losers, they will still prefer the policy. With an actual Pareto improvement, the program leads to at least one individual being better off and none worse off. With a potential Pareto improvement, the program creates gainers and losers in terms of welfare or social benefits; winners themselves remain better off after they compensate losers.

However, the compensation case can work in reverse. It is possible to change from $(c^1, \ldots, c^n)$ to $(c^{1'}, \ldots, c^{n'})$, and from $(c^{1'}, \ldots, c^{n'})$ back to (c^1, ... , c^n), and still satisfy the Kaldor-Hicks criteria. Winners compensate losers to move to a new social state and find that relative prices change in the transition; losers might be able to compensate winners to return to the original social state. This problematic situation is known as the *Scitovsky reversal* (Quiggin 1996).

The *Pareto compensation* case generates criticism because it is a hypothetical situation and does not require actual transfer of money from winners to losers. Losers are meant to be 'better off' when they actually still lose (Sen 1979a, 1979b; Pearce and Nash 1981; Hausman and McPherson 1996; Altman 1996). Another problem is that a *Pareto compensation* case is efficiency-oriented but equitably neutral; it does not address distributive justice.

The second assumption of modern welfare economics is *rationality* in which individuals' decisions result in optimal social outcomes. Under the *collective rationality* argument, it is legitimate to aggregate individual preferences in such a way that the difference between those in favour and those against defines the concept of *net social benefit*. There are problems in the simple summation of individual preferences to form an expression of net social benefit based on the concept of rationality (see Pearce and Nash 1981; Hurley 2000; Arrow, Sen and Suzumura 2003; Anand and Sen 2000).

Under the Pareto principle, social benefit is assumed the aggregation of benefits of individual members of a society. However, it is not always possible and practical to use simple aggregation of individual preferences in order to find an optimal level of social welfare. As discussed in Section 2.6.3, the anonymity principle of the simple unweighted aggregation of Quality Adjusted Life-years (QALYs) under the egalitarian approach may impede distributional equity. The aggregate of individual preferences revealed within market place does not necessarily reflect an optimal outcome of social welfare. Individuals may act irrationally, place self interest ahead of those of the society, or simply fail to judge the scenario. The value system of consumer sovereignty holds when consumers can easily understand the nature, costs, risks and benefits of the products or services they are going to purchase. In the health sector, individuals generally do not possess adequate professional knowledge, or have little access to the appropriate technical information in order to make decisions in their best interests (Carter and Harris 1999).

Individual preferences do not safeguard optimal social outcomes. In an ideal situation, individuals make choices with full knowledge of different health programs available, as well as the consequence of such programs with certainty. Individuals are assumed to be rational thinkers and have the technical or professional knowledge to understand the clinical and social consequences of the health programs. When making choices, individuals consider altruism and non-welfarism (Sen 1995). As discussed above, the reality can be very different from ideal situations (Basu 1980; Varoufakis 1998; Altman 1996; Paavola and Bromley 2002).

The concept of consumer sovereignty and willingness-to-pay (WTP) is debatable in the field of health economics (Kneese and Schulze 1985; Carter and Harris 1999; Hurley 2000). Health is perceived as a 'merit good' that decision makers representing social values could override in the case of certain individual preferences on health. Consumption of a merit good is regarded as socially desirable irrespective of consumers' preference. Governments are prepared to suspend consumers' sovereignty by subsidising the provision of such goods and services (Bannock et al. 1998).

Altruism and caring are matters of preference, but equity and social justice are not. Equity is the source of value for making equitable judgements and is extrinsic to preferences (Wagstaff and van Doorslaer 2000 p. 1807). Despite the assumption of full knowledge about different alternatives and their consequences, individual preferences do not necessarily enhance utility and welfare, or lead to equitable or optimal welfare outcomes (Stoleru 1975; Sen 1977; Broome 1999; Ehrlich et al. 1999). Individuals may prefer to take hypolipidaemic agents and antihypertensive agents rather than to decrease dietary intake of fat and salt (sodium). Individuals may prefer to use bronchodilator and corticosteroid inhalers for relieving symptoms of their comprised airways rather than to quit smoking.

Individuals may also make decisions as individuals within the market place as well as citizens within a society (Sen 1995; Clayton and Radcliffe 1996; O'Neill 2001). As citizens, individuals consider value judgements such as equity, freedom or altruism in addition to their own utilities. Social choice decisions made under this framework are more likely to lead to socially optimal outcomes (Sen 1995). This is very much the case in the healthcare area. Individuals are more likely to hold an egalitarian view in healthcare that the well-being of a society is measured by the well-being of the worst off person in that society (Kneese and Schulze 1985), and access to health is every citizen's right like access to the ballot box or to courts of justice (Williams 1993, p. 291). Individuals are unlikely to object to inclusion of medications on the Pharmaceutical Benefits Scheme (PBS) for conditions such as cardiovascular diseases, diabetes, cancer, etc., even though they do not suffer from such medical conditions themselves. On the contrary, individuals are more likely to be outraged if medications for common chronic medical conditions are not subsidised under the PBS.

The above limitations of new welfare economics have motivated the development of a welfare economics which is realistic, practical and useful. Two such developments in the literature are new^2 welfare economics (Reiter 1986) and normative social choice theory. New^2 welfare economics has the advantage that it is relatively operational and overcomes some limitations of new welfare economics such as the measurement of utility, the summation of aggregate benefits, and the implication of potential Pareto improvement on welfare. However, it retains some of the difficulties of new welfare economics. The second line of development, i.e. normative social choice theory, is relatively more promising and discussed further below.

3.5   Normative social choice theory: Theory and practice

The problems of new welfare economics such as the weakness of the Pareto criteria, ordinality, non-comparability, anonymity and rationality assumptions can be addressed by performing a more realistic and appropriate welfare economic analysis based on normative social choice theory (Sen 1999b; Islam 2001; Arrow, Sen and Suzumura 2003; Clarke and Islam 2004). Normative Social Choice Theory is a recent development in social choice theory. Therefore, we first provide below a discussion of social choice theory.

3.5.1   A social choice theory

The difficulties in judging and ranking different social welfare states have been a problem for researchers as early as Borda (1781) and de Condorcet (1785). Bergson (1938) and Samuelson (1947) defined social welfare as a function of utility levels of households in society. The Bergson-Samuelson social welfare function is defined under the assumption of cardinal measurability and interpersonal comparability of utility. Arrow (1951) formulated social welfare function by relating social preferences to the set of individual preferences.

Standard demand theory assumes that utility functions are ordinal and utility levels cannot be compared between households. According to Arrow (1963), it is impossible to have a democratic social welfare function simultaneously satisfying the conditions of *non-negative association, independence of irrelevant activities, non-imposition, non-dictatorship*, as well as the *free triple* condition. However, it is possible to ease these restrictions in order to allow a democratic ordering of social states. Arrow's 'reasonable' conditions were restrictive and essentially ruled out the Kaldor-Hicks compensation assumption that gains of winners could be weighed against losses of losers.

For a constructive social choice theory, Sen (1970a, 1970b) argued that interpersonal comparisons can be 'fully axiomatised and exactly incorporated in social choice procedures' and even partial comparability allows consistency in making social welfare judgements, satisfying Arrow's conditions, as well as being sensitive to distributional issues (Sen 1999b). Measurability and interpersonal comparison of welfare based on subjective and objective information is approximate but acceptable under the normative social choice theory, as distinguished from other approaches of welfare economics. All ethical systems require interpersonal comparisons of well-being (Hausman and McPherson 1996). Theoretical results demonstrate the existence of logically consistent, non-dictatorial social welfare functions in the 1980s (Slesnick 1998).

Benefits of health programs such as the PBS range from number of lives saved, increase in life expectancy, the improvements in the quality of life, reduction in risk of illness and death, decrease in morbidity and injury, etc. This broader concept of 'benefit' makes measurement difficult in an economic appraisal exercise. In addition to benefits of PBS, other social objectives such as equity and fairness should also be considered. Extra-welfarists argue that health, not utility, is the most relevant outcome when conducting normative analysis in the health sector (Culyer 1989, 1990). In this book, health gain as benefits of medication therapy is measured in terms of decreased consumption of health services, increased economic productivity, improved life expectancy, and decreased consumption of complementary medicines due to improved health status. Patients' preference for health gain is measured by WTP for the medications in the absence of government subsidies.

Economists try to analyse social choice using consumer choice framework. When considering individual or consumer choice, the opportunity set is defined by individual budget constraints. When considering social choices, the opportunity set is defined by utility possibilities schedule. An economy is Pareto-efficient when it operates along the utilities schedule which describes the trade-off between utilities of individuals. Individual preference is defined by individual indifference curve while social preference is defined by social indifference curve. Social indifference curve describes how society might make trade-off between utility levels of different individuals. Programs are selected on the basis that they increase social welfare and put society on the highest social indifference curve. The preferred point is the one tangent between the social indifference curve and the utility possibilities schedule (Stiglitz 2000).

According to Sen (1999a), choices made by society are not dictational under a different set of assumptions (the possibility perspective of social choice). When there is a difference in opinions or with no general agreement, methods need to be found to bring together different opinions in decisions that concern everyone, linking individual values with collective choices. Social choice theory allows the normative significance of economic and non-economic events to be evaluated in a formal framework (Boadway and Bruce 1994). With operationalisation of social choice theory, it is possible to address a range of questions. These include society's choices, individual preferences, community value and preferences, value judgements on economic equity and efficiency, intergenerational equity, the relationship between individual preferences and community preferences, social justice, poverty, measurement and market perspectives versus social perspectives. (Arrow and Scitovsky 1969; Sen 1982; Boadway and Bruce 1984; Kneese and Schulze 1985; Bonner 1986; Altman 1996; Wagstaff and van Doorslaer 2000). This line of thought has been defined as normative social choice theory and is discussed below.

3.5.2   Recent developments of welfare economics and health economics

In addition to the traditional approach of welfare economics, there are other alternative approaches for comparing different social (welfare) states in the context of health economics, namely Sen's approach of 'capability' and 'functionings', extra-welfarism, communitarianism and empirical ethics (see Hall et al. 2005).

Sen's capability approach

Sen defined utilitarianism as a combination of welfarism, sumranking and consequentialism. Sen argued that the utilitarian approach of traditional welfare economics (Edgeworth 1881, Marshall 1890, Pigou 1920) neglected the distributional issues and concentrated single-mindedly only on the maximisation of utility sumtotal. Under Sen's alternative framework, the well-beings of individuals depend on their *functionings* (what they achieve) and *capabilities* (the opportunities that open to individuals), as well as their efficiency of transforming relevant input into well-beings. The social preferences of individuals are influenced by their view of a social good based on their concept of a good society (Hall et al. 2005).

Sen considered health equity as a multi-dimensional concept. Sen argued that health was an important condition of human life and a significant constituent of human capabilities, and equity in achievement and distribution of health is essential in terms of social justice. 'An injustice is the lack of opportunity that some may have to achieve good health because of inadequate social arrangement (Sen 2002 p. 660). Sen further argued that health equity was more than just an issue of distribution of health care, but was influenced by other factors ranging from genetical propensities, individual incomes, living standards, to the epidemiological environment and work conditions. Fairness in social processes, social procedures, and resource allocation, reduction in health inequality, as well as social arrangements linking health with other features of states of affairs are all relevant to concerns of social justice and health equity. Sen considered health equity as a broad and inclusive discipline and argued against arbitrary narrowing of the domain and rejected the approach of pursuing a single maximand such as health gain (Sen 2002).

Extra-welfarism

Extra-welfarism brings non-utility information to supplement utility information in the process of judging social welfare and decision-making in resource allocations in principle (Culyer 1989), but tends to focus on the maximisation of health gain in application. In addition to health, other relevant individual characteristics such as consumer choice, privacy, timeliness of services, etc, are also important factors in defining social welfare and individual well-being. The extra-welfarists selected and measured relevant characteristics, applied weights to characteristics which are then used in the measurement of social welfare. Culyer (1991) argued that both *individual characteristics* and *extra-welfarist characteristics* should be used in evaluating alternatives, without clear specification of these two sets of characteristics are to be used in social welfare function. The economist is supposed to play the role of consultant or decision maker, who is the source of information on the objectives of economic evaluation. Value judgements of the decision maker are incorporated into the maximand of the analysis (Culyer 1991). Individual preferences are obtained through survey with the average value is used as QALY weight, excluding any consideration of heterogeneity. The exclusive emphasis on health and the lack of consideration of other characteristics (e.g. education, literacy, living standards, etc.) limits the generalisability of extra welfarism (Hall et al. 2005).

Communitarianism

From the Avineri and de Shalit communitarian perspective, individuals cannot be understood outside the context of community. Healthcare is a community good. Healthcare system is a community institution. Using a communitarian perspective as an alternative basis for healthcare resource allocation, greater emphasis is given to equity in resource allocation (Mooney 1996). Communitarians argue that there are two sources of utility, namely normal utility and participation utility. Participation utility is derived from the membership of the community and is not captured by the consequentialism of the traditional welfarist approach.

Communitarians assess welfare at both the personal level and the community level. The personal level is concerned with individual health and the community level is concerned with the social choices an individual has to make. Avineri and de Shalit argued that rational individuals do not choose freely, but rather in their social, cultural and historical context. Communitarianism places community at the centre of the analysis and value system (Mooney 2001). It is the task of the community to decide what constitutes the communitarian claims, irrespective of individual perception and utility. Communitarian claims override individual preferences. It is the duty of the community to allocate claims and to assess the relative strength of different claims (Mooney 1998). The community appoints healthcare decision maker, policy makers or bureaucrats as its informed social agents to evaluate and make decision about different types and forms of healthcare. Rules and values are derived from the community. Citizens are supposed to be educated and informed in setting up such values as well as to monitor decision makers in their application of such rules. However, it is unclear about the practical procedures of setting up communitarian claims, and or citizen rules and values.

Empirical ethics

Empirical study of population values and ethical analysis of the results leads to formulation of a set of principles which are used to guide resource allocation under the empirical ethics approach (Richardson 2002).

Utility or well-being is not specifically defined at the individual level, but social choice rather than individual choice is the main concern of empirical ethics. Social welfare is maximised with resources are allocated according to ethically justified population values (Richardson and McKie 2005). Under the empirical ethics approach, preference information is derived from community through careful and considered population survey. But the validity of the methodology and the process remains an issue. There is no specific direction about the consideration and weighting of information from alternative sources.

However, Olsen and Richardson et al. (2003) argued that decision makers should not always accept majority view as that might express ethically unacceptable preferences and the community may not agree on different ethical issues. Empirical ethics argues that policy makers and ethicists will then be informed about the extent of disagreement and the strength of preferences of the population and arrive at their decision. Policy makers and ethicists are then given a powerful role in judging the ethical acceptability of majority views, adjudicating between conflicting values as well as modifying population preferences.

3.5.3 Normative social choice theory

Normative social choice refers to the ranking of alternative social states on the basis of choices, preferences and value judgements of individuals in order to determine the optimal social state. It incorporates issues (various social concerns such as happiness) that are inadequately addressed using the individual preference satisfaction technique within the market place.

Although there has been significant progress in normative social choice theory in order to make welfare economics a practical discipline for social decision-making, further development of normative social choice theory is still necessary. An important area of development is the full operationalisation of this theory, which enables practical application of welfare economics in ranking alternative social states, making social choices, measuring and comparing social welfare, specifying socially optimal programs, preparing economic and social planning, evaluating costs and benefits of alternative policies, and economic organisation (Clarke and Islam 2004). Such an effort to make social choice and welfare economics is discussed in the next section.

3.6 New[3] cost benefit analysis: An extended approach

3.6.1 New[3] welfare economics and new[3] cost benefit analysis

To further advance developments in and especially to operationalise normative social choice theory, Islam (2001a) has developed the new[3] welfare economics (see also Clarke and Islam 2004; Craven and Islam 2005). In new[3] welfare economics, Islam (2001a) has developed a new paradigm of welfare economics which provides a suitable normative framework for social choice and decision-making (including cost benefit analysis of projects, policies and programs) that facilitates the selection of public programs, plans and policies. The main elements of new[3] welfare economics are the possibility for social choices, the measurability of social welfare, interpersonal comparability, and the necessity for extra-welfaristic and ethical elements in social welfare analyses, operationalisation of welfare economics and social choices theory and democratic decision-making (Islam 2001a).

Under new³ welfare economics, it is assumed that welfare can be measured and a social choice can be made on the basis of expert opinions, scientific information and social value judgement. In this approach to social choice, individual choices (preferences, costs and benefits) are aggregated along with expert opinions, scientific information and social value judgements (derived from explicating the preferences of the society). There are a lot of arguments in favour and against the elements of welfare economics (Boadway and Bruce 1984, Johannesson 2000). The arguments in favour of these elements have been accepted in new³ welfare economics since acceptance of these elements make welfare economics operational and socially useful in making social choices and public policies.

The principles of new³ welfare economics include:

1) measurability and interpersonal comparison of welfare based on subjective and objective information, which is approximate but acceptable;
2) possibility of social choice based on a social welfare function;
3) incorporation of welfaristic and extra-welfaristic elements of welfare in a social welfare analysis; and
4) incorporation of market non-existence and imperfections, information asymmetry, incomplete contracts, unequal exchange and other social and institutional factors that can transform a social choice problem into a constrained social optimisation problem, making the resultant optimum lower than the full potential social welfare.

In new³ welfare economics, social choices can be estimated using expert opinions, government formulated public policy, or specific interviews of individuals on social welfare outcomes (Clarke and Islam 2004). Using one, or a combination of the above, it is possible to determine the social choice perspective on various social welfare issues.

With its allocative, regulatory, and distributive roles, the state or government should enforce these social choice preferences, as well as the moral and political will of the people (Musgrave 1959; Stoleru 1975). This is achieved by quantification of individual preferences and weighting of such preferences through some form of consensus. For certain issues (such as sustainability), it is difficult to reach a consensus. The state or the analyst must interpret and act on these preferences in order to achieve an optimal social outcome (Ehrlich et al. 1999; Pezzey 2001, 2002). New[3] welfare economics extends this consensus from a household to society. In addition to issues of social welfare based on individual preference, new[3] welfare economics also studies requirements for achieving an optimal social outcome.

The extended cost benefit analysis developed in this study is based on the principles of new[3] welfare economics. Therefore, we name the extended cost benefit analysis developed in this study as the *new[3] cost benefit analysis*. The *new[3] cost benefit analysis* adopts the following principles for measurement of social welfare and economic performance. The concept of well-being and welfare is defined through the utilitarian preference satisfaction as well as extra-welfaristic elements, with a view that the propensities of consumption, demand functions and information which reflects not only the preference satisfaction but also the extent of fulfilment of capabilities. The aggregate social welfare function and index to measure the net benefits of projects are specified through the possibility theorem perspective. The numeraire of welfare and performance include consumption and expenditures, is affected by income and other socio-economic factors envisaged in recent theories of social welfare such as Sen's capabilities approach (1985a). Units of measurement are market prices of goods and services adjusted by expert opinions. Methods of measurement for cost benefit analysis are net present values and cost benefit ratios.

Later in this chapter, discussion is provided on how the *various aspects of new[3] cost benefit analysis can be specified to develop and apply a unified approach of the new[3] cost benefit analysis*.

A complete ranking of all social states is referred to as a social welfare function (Johannesson 2000). Bergson (1938) and Samuelson (1947) defined social welfare as a function of the utility levels of the households. The social welfare function holds under the assumption of measurability and comparability of utility levels. Arrow's Impossibility Theorem argued that no social welfare function exists that consistently ranks social states because the measurement of utility is ordinal and interpersonal comparison is not possible.

Under the normative social choice theory as prepositional in new[3] welfare economics, measurability and interpersonal comparison of welfare is approximate but acceptable. By incorporating the above elements of social choice and new[3] welfare economics, a social welfare function can be developed. It provides a social and economic evaluation and value judgement framework incorporating costs and benefits of health programs in general and the PBS in particular. The social welfare function is expressed as follows:

$$SWF_t = W_t (NB_t\{P_t\}) \tag{3.1}$$

where: W_t = welfare measured by applying social choice theory based on moral philosophy;

t = times;

$NB_t = \dfrac{[(B_t\{P_t\}) - (C_t\{P_t\})]}{(1 + r)^t}$ = net benefits of a health program;

B_t = benefits of a health program;

C_t = costs of a health program;

r = discount rate; and

P_t = the health program.

This welfare function provides a normative economic framework that incorporates guidelines for social choices in considering and estimating social benefits and costs, social time preference, incorporating extra-welfaristic judgements in cost benefit analysis, efficient and intertemporal valuation of inputs and outputs, and so on; as required in the new[3] cost benefit analysis. This social choice framework for health programs is applied in the rest of this book (see Chapters 5, 6 and 7). It should be noted that in existing literature the specification and application of social welfare function are based primarily on economic considerations without explicit and comprehensive consideration of moral philosophy and social value judgement issues derived from operational social choice methods as specified in new[3] cost benefit analysis.

Several methods can be adopted to incorporate identifying, analysing and quantifying social value judgements and preferences and public policy objectives into a social welfare function and thus into cost benefit analysis (Fox, Sengupta and Thorbecke 1973; Islam 2001a). These methods include interviewing and analysing actual (or imaginary) policy makers, analysing social preferences from surveys, opinion polls or social documents, as well as polls or referendum.

These methods can be adopted to incorporate social value judgements and preferences (and public policies) in new[3] cost benefit analysis.

In the following sections of this chapter, a discussion is provided on how the various aspects of the new[3] cost benefit analysis can be specified on the basis of the above principles of welfare economics, to develop and to apply a unified approach of the new[3] cost benefit analysis in economics and public policy formulation, with a special emphasis on the health sector.

3.6.2 The elements of the new[3] cost benefit analysis

The normative social choice approach to cost benefit analysis based on the principles of new[3] welfare economics requires that both economic and ethical factors be considered when undertaking the cost benefit analysis exercise – in estimating costs and benefits, determining the social discount rate, and valuation of resources. This new[3] cost benefit analysis approach assumes measurability of social welfare and net benefits, non-economic costs and benefits on the basis of social value judgements, preferences, and public policy objectives; and aims to estimate the costs and benefits of a health program by using a combination of *scientific information, expert opinions and social preferences*. In uncertain and risky situations, the new[3] cost benefit analysis also adopts the standard approach of numerical specification, estimation and management of uncertainty (Brent 2003) as discussed in Chapters 5, 6, and 7. In this approach, a social choice is made on the basis of individual and social preferences reflected in a social welfare function consisting of the net benefits of a project.

3.7 Identification of costs and benefits in new[3] cost benefit analysis

A project or a health program such as the PBS generates costs and benefits directly as well as indirectly; some of these are internal or tangible whilst others are external or intangible. Resource consequence from inputs into health programs are classified as *direct costs*, as these resources are consumed directly in the activities of health programs. *Indirect costs* are resource consumption that do not arise due to an activity or a disease; and usually depict changes in production and amount of leisure time, or other indirect effects generated by the health program.

Conyers and Hills (1984) define tangibles as those effects that can be converted into or be measured in monetary terms, such as acquisition cost of drugs, costs of dispensing, costs of freight, savings or avoidance of future medical costs, etc. Intangibles can be of either be effects that may be qualified but not measured in monetary terms (e.g. improved quality of life of patients); or those that can neither be measured nor be quantified (such as the improved sense of well-being of patients). Quantification of intangible effects is an important but difficult task in project appraisal; estimation of such effects is normally required in practical appraisal work. In the new³ cost benefit analysis, a comprehensive set of economic and social costs and benefits in direct and indirect, tangible and intangible, internal and external forms should be included on the basis of scientific information, expert opinion, social value judgement and preferences.

3.8   Valuation in new³ cost benefit analysis

Numerical estimation of the costs and benefits of health programs is a difficult task. Under the new³ cost benefit analysis, these costs and benefits can be estimated by utilising scientific information, expert opinion and social judgements and preferences if necessary. This makes the task of estimation relatively easy since social judgements and expert opinions can be used in the cases where data from other sources are not available.

3.8.1   Estimation of costs

The first step in cost estimation is to estimate the quantity of inputs consumed by a health program. The next step is to estimate the unit cost of each input. The final step is to calculate the total cost by multiplying the unit costs with quantities of inputs. Johannesson (2000) identified three types of costs for health programs, namely *program costs*, *morbidity costs* and *mortality costs*. In the PBS setting, program costs include the acquisition and distribution costs of drugs, administrative costs, monitoring costs, as well as costs of adverse effects arising from drugs. Morbidity costs and mortality costs are generally not included in a Pharmaceutical Benefits Advisory Committee (PBAC) submission. Johannesson further divided each type of cost into three components – *health inputs, market production* and *leisure of individuals.*

3.8.2   Valuation of benefits of health programs

There are controversies regarding how to estimate social benefits of a health program. As benefits of health programs are not sold at market prices, they cannot be calculated in monetary terms by simple multiplying quantities sold with the unit market price. Hence the traditional consumer surplus method based on compensation or equivalent variations cannot be applied to health programs. There are other different approaches to measure benefits of health program in monetary terms, namely the *human capital* or *cost-of-illness* approach, the *revealed preferences* approach, and the *expressed preferences* approach. In the new[3] cost benefit analysis, a combination of these approaches supplemented by expert opinion and social preferences about values of different health programs can be adopted in the valuation of the benefits of health programs.

As discussed in Section 2.6, under the human capital or cost of illness approach, costs of health programs are estimated as the sum of resources consumed in treatment and forgone economic production. Health-related benefits of health programs are defined as the estimated reductions or avoidance of future treatment cost plus increased economic production due to improved health (Jack 1999; Johannesson 2000). In the PBS setting, the human capital approach estimates costs of the PBS on the basis of resources consumed and benefits in terms of decreased consumption of healthcare resources, and an increase in economic production (using market wage rate) as a result of the improved health status of individuals.

Under the human capital approach, there are difficulties in the valuation of benefits:

1) imperfections in the labour market;
2) the wage rate may not reflect the true value of economic production because of other inequities such as gender or race;
3) difficulty in determining a price on non-marketed resources (shadow pricing); and
4) analyses based on market production tend to inappropriately bias programs towards interventions that improved the health of working-age men and women; and

5) less value is placed on the health of the elderly, homemakers, and the unemployed who largely do not contribute to increased economic production even with improved health status.

The limitations of the human capital or cost of illness approach leads to other developments such as the valuation method based on the measurement of WTP. Many benefits of health programs are in the form of improvement in health status, time and health of homemakers. Under the revealed preference approach, the values attached to health-related quality of life are determined by techniques such as contingent valuation, conjoint analysis, and health states valuation. Some costs and benefits may not have market prices, and are difficult to be estimated and included in a project appraisal exercise. The analyst need to use alternative prices called *shadow prices*, when market prices do not exist (Little and Mirrlees 1974; Dinwiddy and Teal 1996; Campbell and Brown 2003).

The approaches mentioned above have their own share of limitations. A combination of the human capital or cost of illness approach and preference-based approaches should be used in new³ cost benefit analysis. The human capital or cost of illness approach is used to measure the tangible inputs and outputs and the preference-based approach is used to measure the intangible effects. Therefore, in the new³ cost benefit analysis, costs and benefits need to be identified, conceptualised and measured by a combination of these methods supplemented by scientific information, expert opinions and social value judgements and preferences.

Under the human capital or cost of illness approach, benefits of health programs are defined as the cost savings or cost avoidance from future treatment cost plus increase in economic productivity due to improved health. Abelson (2003) argued that these health benefits measures are the *ex-post* sum of identifiable costs such as loss of output and medical expenses, and do not account for pain and suffering, or changes in life-styles. Schelling (1968) argued that this definition of benefits measure the value of a livelihood. Under the new³ cost benefit analysis, the benefit estimates include the components of increase in economic productivity, cost avoidance of hospitalisation, as well as cost saving decreased health services consumption in form of consultation with general and/or specialist medical practitioners.

Under the preference-based approaches, WTP is used to measure benefits of health programs. The WTP estimates of health changes are obtained by either *revealed preference* as observed in *actual choices* and *expressed preference* as observed in hypothetical choices in surveys (Johannesson 2000). Schelling (1968) argued that WTP measure the statistical value of life rather than just the value of a livelihood. Under the new[3] cost benefit analysis, WTP is estimated by the amount patients pay for their medications in the absence of government subsidy. In other words, WTP is the amount what patients pay for their medications as privates scripts rather than as PBS scripts.

In addition to increase in productivity, cost savings and/or avoidance of medical treatment, WTP of individuals for their medication, the quality of life measurement (as discussed in Section 2.6.2) is also incorporated in the benefits estimates in the form of QALYs under the new[3] cost benefit analysis approach. The outcomes of health programs are interpreted in terms of improved quantity and quality of life. Technique such as health state valuation is used to estimate the *quality weight* or *preferences* in the calculation of QALY. The principles of numerical estimates of costs and benefits under the new[3] cost benefit analysis will be further discussed in details in Chapters 5 and 6.

Ethics deals with fairness. Following the literature in this area, we argue that in the new[3] cost benefit analysis, fairness is ensured by attaching distributional weights to incidents or benefits occurring to the relatively disadvantaged section of the community. Higher weight is given to the benefits for those who are relatively poor in the society. However, in the Australian context, this is not done in the illustrative example of the PBS in Australia because equity and fairness is ensured through the social security system in Australia (see further discussion in Section 4.8). Individuals eligible for commonwealth income support programs are issued with Pension cards, Health Care cards, or Commonwealth Seniors Health Card, thus allowing them access to PBS under concessional category of patient co-payment. In 2005, they pay $4.60 instead of $28.60 for a basic PBS item. These include retired people, families of low income or sole parents with dependent children, young people who attend tertiary education or are on newstart program, the unemployed, and so on. The safety net scheme is established to provide further assistance to those who suffer from chronic medical conditions and require constant supply of medications. These will be further discussed in Chapter 4.

3.8.3 Shadow pricing of inputs and outputs

In the new³ cost benefit analysis, it is argued that in an economy where market prices of inputs and outputs do not exist or are imperfect, shadow prices can be used. In a non-perfectly competitive market with distortions, market prices do not reflect the true social values of costs and benefits. The usual practice is to use shadow prices for valuation of inputs and outputs of a development project.

As market imperfections and the non-existence of market prices of costs and benefits of health programs are common, health programs should be undertaken by using shadow pricing in the relevant situations. Shadow prices are the opportunity costs of benefits foregone for using resources in alternative ways. Determination of shadow prices is the most difficult and controversial task in a project appraisal exercise.

The OECD's (Little and Mirlees 1974) approach to shadow pricing is based on the classification of goods and services as traded goods and non-tradable goods. Traded goods are valued at their broader (imports or exports) prices. In the case of non-tradable goods, a conversion factor can be used. A conversion factor is the ratio between the world price, in terms of foreign exchange, and the domestic price of a good. There are several other non-tradable goods or services (e.g. labour) that require special treatment for shadow pricing. Formulae that can be adopted to estimate shadow prices, especially in developing countries, are given in Appendix 3.1. Shadowing pricing of inputs and outputs is a more important factor in conducting cost benefit analysis in developing countries. It plays a less important role in health program in developed countries such as PBS in Australia, and is not applied in this research.

3.9 Social discount rate in new³ cost benefit analysis

In a financial analysis of a health program, the market risk-free interest rate (e.g. government bond rate) is used as the discount rate.

Some argue that costs and benefits of the PBS should be discounted at different rates. In terms of improvement of health status or health gain, future benefits are as important as those in the present and should not be discounted at all. The discount rate for costs is different from that for benefits and some economists suggest that more than one discount rate is needed for health programs with a long time horizon, as the inter-temporal preferences may change over generations (Aylward and Porras 1998). One operational approach is to set the discount rate equal to the social opportunity cost of funds. With the changes in technology and the availability of new drugs, it is reasonable to analyse the costs and benefits of the PBS listing over a period of five years. A single discount rate is used for such a short time horizon in this research.

3.10   Welfare weights in new[3] cost benefit analysis

The net present value of health programs such as the PBS should be adjusted by a factor that shows the relative importance of sustainability, equity, and others, as compared to economic growth. The method of using weighting enables the analyst to perform a project appraisal on the basis of social objectives rather than just on net present value.

Addressing the issues of intergenerational equity in new[3] cost benefit analysis, the welfare weights were those discussed by Littles and Mirrlees (1974) and operationalised by Squires and van der Tak (1975) with the distribution parameters being the ratio of the *marginal utility* of *target income groups* to the *marginal utility* of the *average income group*. The relative weights, in term of the differential effects of income on social welfare, can be derived as:

$$d_{ij} = (Y_j / Y_i)^{\eta} \tag{3.2}$$

where: Y = income of persons i and j; and
η = elasticity parameter.

In estimation of social welfare and benefits, social discount rate, shadow prices as well as incorporation of the public policy objectives in economic evaluation of projects, such welfare weights or distributional weights can be used. Application of welfare weights is discussed below and in Chapter 7.

3.11   Sustainability, weighting and intergenerational equity

When conducting an economic evaluation of health programs and policies, the effects of interventions are aggregated across affected individuals. If equal weights are allocated to each individual, issues of distribution equity are ignored. Mooney (1998) argued that society welfare is more than the sum of utility across individual programs and individuals.

A system of differential aggregation weights reflecting different levels of concern among the population may better address distributional issues than a system of equal weighting. Harberger (1984) argued against differential aggregation weights because they were arbitrary. Culyer (1989) argued that a differential aggregation weighting system helped to reconcile efficiency and distributional equity concerns by allocating resources to maximise the weighted sum of the health of a society (Hurley 2000).

In addition to distributional equity among the current generation, sustainability is about managing resources to preserve intergenerational equity. Talbot (1977) argued that preserving opportunities for future generations is a common sense of intergenerational justice. The present generation should not deplete the opportunities afforded by a resource base since it does not *own* it (Kneese and Schulze 1985).

3.12   Public policy objectives

An important aspect of a new³ cost benefit analysis should incorporate the underlying government social and economic policies (see Islam 2001) including extra-welfaristic outcomes of economic programs such as liberty, freedom, and equity. (Hausman and McPherson 1996). For example, the objectives of a macroeconomic policy include increasing employment, keeping the interest rates down, keeping the inflation rate and the balance of payments level down, economic development and growth, and so on. The main objectives of health programs are health maximisation, improved health status, improved quantity and the quality of life of members of the community. A health program chosen for its highest net social benefit (including welfaristic and extra-welfaristic outcomes), on the basis of the aggregation of individual utility and health gain, will contribute most to the economic development of a country. Additionally, the macroeconomic policies of the government can be incorporated in the evaluation by giving higher weights to medications that contribute relatively higher to the existing public policy objectives.

3.13   New[3] cost benefit analysis of health programs

One of important application of welfare economic analysis in the healthcare area is economic evaluation of health programs. Project appraisal or economic evaluation has been defined as 'a process of analysing a number of plans or projects with a view to searching out their comparative advantages and disadvantages and the act of setting down the findings of such analysis in a logical framework' (Lichfield et al. 1975). With scarcity of resources, economic evaluation is performed to test the social worthiness of a health program, and to justify the resource allocation, as well as to assess the relative merits of different programs. The PBS in Australia is a typical example of such health program. For a full economic evaluation, both the costs and benefits of competing alternatives must be examined in order to determine the financial and economic viability (i.e. the social desirability) of listing a drug on the PBS.

In order to decide about the listing of a medication on PBS, an economic evaluation is conducted. Information required for such economic evaluation includes: the amount and types of resources consumed; the nature and level of effects, costs and benefits produced; the incidence of these effects; and the social, cultural and environmental effects of the PBS listing decision. Conclusions of the evaluation are made (Conyers and Hills 1984). Result of economic evaluation of the medication is then submitted to the PBAC. After considering the submission, the Committee makes its recommendation to the Minister for Health and Ageing regarding the listing of the medication.

Only direct costs are considered in the economic evaluation of a PBAC submission, but there is a need for including indirect costs in the PBS submission as well. Inclusion of indirect costs in a submission is not encouraged by the PBAC (Commonwealth Department of Health and Ageing 2002). In the PBS setting, only 'health inputs' are considered in cost estimation, market production and leisure of individuals are considered indirect costs and are not included in the cost estimation.

According to the submission guidelines of the PBAC (2002), costs and benefits are discounted at an annual rate of 5%. A new³ cost benefit analysis and evaluation of health programs should adopt a social discount rate. But in a social cost benefit analysis of the PBS, the choice of a social discount rate is relatively complicated. Formulae for estimating the social discount rate are discussed further in Chapter 7.

This application of the proposed new³ cost benefit analysis makes some important extensions to the existing methods of cost benefit analysis and the PBS by undertaking a comprehensive discussion of cost and benefit estimates of PBS in Australia.

The new³ cost benefit analysis incorporates recent issues of welfare economics (such as the social choice theory) in order to develop an appropriate framework for economic evaluation of health programs such as the PBS. By adopting a social choice approach, this new approach incorporates ethics, moral philosophy and other interdisciplinary issues (such as clinical science) into health economics by addressing technical issues such as estimation of demand functions for various outputs; shadow pricing of non-tradable goods; normative value of individual preferences; distribution of costs, benefits, risks and moral hazards; sustainability and intergenerational equity (Kneese and Schulze 1985; Hurley 2000).

The new³ cost benefit analysis provides a balanced decision-making framework based on scientific knowledge, social value judgement, social and individual benefits and costs, thus making it easier and more operational to estimate social costs and benefits of health programs, as well as to provide appropriate quantitative information for decision-making in PBS.

3.14   Examples of new³ cost benefit analysis

The numerical examples in this section show how a standard cost benefit analysis of the health program presented in Section 2.4.4 can be changed into a new³ cost benefit analysis by including some simple modifications which underline the paradigm of this analysis.

A *restrictive* human capital approach is adopted from the PBAC type of submission criteria. Indirect costs and indirect benefits are not encouraged to be included in the submission. The details of the calculation are shown in Appendix 3.2. The discount rate is set at 5% (PBAC requirement). Indirect economic benefits, social costs and social benefits are excluded. For drug A, the NPV over a period of five years is –292.76 and the C-B ratio is 0.2. Since the NPV is negative and the C-B ratio is less than one, drug A would be rejected for PBS listing.

For academic argument, the same analysis is converted into a social cost benefit analysis with a social discount rate of 0% and inclusion of social costs and benefits. The details of calculation are shown in Appendix 3.3. Under the social cost benefit analysis, drug A gives a net present value of 150 over five years and a cost benefit ratio of 1.33. Since the net present value is positive and the cost benefit ratio is greater than one, drug A should be included for listing on PBS.

As discussed in Section 3.12, public policy objectives can be incorporated into the evaluation criteria of the cost benefit analysis. The details of the calculation are shown in Appendix 3.4. Assuming that drug A is exclusively manufactured in Australia as part of the agreement between the pharmaceutical company (manufacturer of drug A) and the Australian government, leading to increase in employment for the five-year period. Improved employment is included as part of the social welfare and benefits. This gives drug A gives a net present value of 190 over five years and a cost benefit ratio of 1.42. When comparing with other drugs of the same therapeutic effects, drug A offers higher social welfare due to the effect of increased employment of the Australian community.

As discussed in Sections 3.8.2, and 3.10, welfare weights or distributional weights can be incorporated into the evaluation criteria of the cost benefit analysis. The details of the calculation are shown in Appendix 3.5. Assuming that higher distributional weights are attached to the relatively disadvantaged section of the community, an extra 50% health gain is included as social welfare or benefit of drug A. Instead of the health gain of ten counted in the previous scenario, an additional of five is counted due to the incorporation of distributional weights. This gives drug A gives a net present value of 170 over five years and a cost benefit ratio of 1.38.

Comparing the above scenarios, the PBS listing decision of drug A changes with a different discount rate as well as the definition and valuation of costs and benefits. This demonstrates the importance of the theoretical framework behind an economic evaluation, which allows the appropriate selection criteria to be established for a PBAC submission. These criteria ensure the PBS listing decision gives the maximum net social benefits.

3.15 Advantages of the proposed framework

In this chapter, we have provided a discussion of the new³ cost benefit analysis being developed and applied to the health sector. We have shown the mechanism of the integration of recent developments in welfare economics, especially from the area of economics and moral philosophy, with the standard cost benefit analysis. It has been argued in this chapter that new³ cost benefit analysis is a relatively more appropriate framework in health economics for project and policy evaluation. New³ cost benefit analysis is an improved method for evaluation (see different chapters of this book).

This new³ cost benefit analysis essentially makes the following extensions to the existing methods for cost benefit analysis:

a) it proposes a comprehensive discussion of cost and benefit estimates;
b) it incorporates recent issues of welfare economics in cost benefit analysis in order to develop an appropriate framework for health program evaluation;
c) it develops and applies a social choice approach with the following characteristics:
   • it incorporates moral philosophy into health economics;
   • it adopts the social choice approach;
   • it provides appropriate quantitative information for decision-making in health sector;
   • it incorporates interdisciplinary issues into economics such as clinical science, ethics and economics; and
   • it makes it easier and more operational to estimate the social costs and benefits of health programs;
d) it provides a balanced decision-making framework-based scientific knowledge, social value judgement, social and individual benefits and costs;

e) it highlights a complete application of cost benefit analysis with the possible and required extension to health programs for its comprehensive and complete applications; some areas of its extension are social cost benefit analysis, shadow pricing, social discount rate, uncertainty analysis, and health sector planning; and

f) it incorporates ethics by addressing technical issues such as: estimation of demand functions for various outputs; shadow pricing of non-tradable goods; normative value of individual preferences; distribution of costs and benefits as well as possible risks and moral hazards; sustainability and intergenerational equity (Kneese and Schulze 1985; Hurley 2000).

3.16 Conclusion

New[3] cost benefit analysis is an economic evaluation method based on the following assumptions and principles. Firstly, it is possible to make a democratic decision for society's individual and collective choices and consensus. Secondly, net social benefit or welfare should consist of welfaristic and extra-welfaristic elements. Thirdly, evaluation of programs and projects should be based on efficiency (economic), social and ethical (morality, justice, freedom, and equity) considerations. Fourthly, a combination of scientific information, expert opinion and social value judgements and preferences should be utilised in applying evaluation methods. A combination of market and social perspectives should be incorporated in evaluation methods. Based on the standard principles for estimation and management of uncertainty and risk, it is possible to make decisions under uncertainty

New[3] cost benefit analysis is an improved method for economic evaluation of programs and projects. Various aspects of the new[3] cost benefit analysis are well developed in the literature. However, a unified method for evaluation based on all the principles of new[3] cost benefit analysis does not exist in the current literature. It is a general method and can be applied to all areas of projects or program evaluation. In the remaining part of the book, this new approach will be applied to the evaluation of the PBS in Australia. In this regard, the next chapter presents a brief review of the issues of the PBS in Australia, and the background for the application of the new cost benefit analysis to PBS in Australia.

4
Economic Evaluation: The Case of the Australian PBS

4.1 Introduction

One of the important areas of economic evaluation of health programs is in the Pharmaceutical Benefits Scheme (PBS). As part of total healthcare spending, pharmaceutical expenditure attracts the attention of government regulators, the public or private fund holders because absolute expenditure continues to grow; pharmaceuticals are perceived more as products than as services; and there is a growing concern that new biotechnology and biogenomic products will push pharmaceutical expenditure to an unprecedented level. All countries are faced with the dilemma of an increasing demand for healthcare to be financed by finite or even diminishing resources (Bootman et al. 1996). Economic evaluation becomes an integral part of the applications of pharmaceutical companies to governments of different countries worldwide for subsidies.

From the egalitarian viewpoint, the healthcare sector should be predominantly financed by public fund according to 'ability to pay' and healthcare should be distributed according to 'need'. From the libertarian viewpoint, health care sector should be privately funded and healthcare should be rationed according to willingness-to-pay (WTP) and 'ability to pay' (Wagstaff and van Doorslaer 2000). The Australian PBS generally adopts the egalitarian viewpoint.

This chapter is structured as follows. Section 4.2 discusses the international perspective of a PBS. Section 4.3 looks at the Australian case of a PBS. Section 4.4 sets out in detail the Pharmaceutical Benefits Advisory Committee (PBAC), its submission guidelines and the economic evaluation involved in such submissions. Section 4.5 examines the Pharmaceutical Benefits Pricing Authority (PBPA) and Section 4.6 the Therapeutic Goods Administration. Section 4.7 discusses the process of Australian PBS listing. Section 4.8 discusses the social security system of Australia as well as the level of patient co-payment under PBS. Section 4.9 considers the safety net arrangement of the PBS. Section 4.10 looks at generic medicines and their pricing policy. Section 4.11 discusses different types of special patient contributions under the Australian PBS. Section 4.12 discusses freezing of the pharmacy approval number. Section 4.13 examines the impact of a free trade agreement with the United States on the PBS in Australia. Section 4.14 presents the Intergeneration Report. Section 4.15 discusses the issues of economic evaluation in a PBS setting and the need of new[3] cost benefit analysis. Section 4.16 is the conclusion.

4.2   PBS: An international perspective

As part of the healthcare expenditure of a country, a pharmaceutical benefits scheme is financed from a mixture of four sources, namely taxes, social insurance, private insurance and patients' direct contribution. While private insurance is voluntary, social insurance is compulsory. Taxes are usually assessed on taxable income and social insurance is levied on earnings. Healthcare funding comes from: general tax revenue in the United Kingdom; mainly from local income taxes in Scandinavian countries; from social insurance in France, Germany and the Netherlands; from private insurance in the US and Switzerland; and from a mixture of tax and social insurance in Italy. The role of private insurance also varies from country to country. Private insurance covers: those sections of the population without any public cover in Ireland, Switzerland and the United States; those who opted out of the public sickness funds in Germany; those who do not have comprehensive public cover in the Netherlands; those against the co-payment levied by public sector in Denmark and France; and provides double cover to those who have comprehensive public cover in Italy, Portugal, Spain and the United Kingdom (Wagstaff and van Doorslaer 2000). Pharmaceutical benefit schemes take different forms and shape in countries worldwide. A few examples are discussed in the following part of this section.

4.2.1 Greece

Government-funded pharmaceutical care provides cover for the entire Greek population. Retail pricing is based on the wholesale price plus the pharmacists' profit and value added tax (VAT). The hospital price is 13% lower than the wholesale price. Aiming for cost-containment of its pharmaceutical expenditure, the Greek government introduced a positive reimbursement list for all social security organisations in 1998. Pharmaceutical companies were forced to cut prices of products in order to be included on the list. This led to a 21% reduction of the average weighted price. However, taxes on the final price of a medicine; and taxes paid to fund third parties (such as public institutions and insurance funds) were abolished. The Greek government had to commit further funds to subsidise the scheme. In 2000, the Greek government introduced a reform on the pharmaceutical subsidy scheme such as inclusion of clinical and economic criteria in the reimbursement procedure, and introduction of a hospital formulary for medications (Kontozamanis et al. 2003).

4.2.2 Ireland

In Ireland, healthcare policy and expenditure are governed by the Department of Health and Children (DHC) and administered through ten regional health boards. Healthcare expenditure is funded through taxation (75%), private insurance (11%) and patient direct copayment (14%). In 2002, pharmaceutical expenditure accounted for ∈ 960 million or 10% of the total healthcare expenditure. The terms and conditions of supply as well as pricing of medications are negotiated between the DHC and the Irish Pharmaceutical Healthcare Association. Cost-effectiveness is a not a pre-requisite for reimbursement. Although the DHC can demand cost benefit studies for any medicines introduced after 1997; but it rarely does so. There are five main types of community drug schemes. Patients under the General Medical Services Scheme (GMS) are means tested. Patients must have one of the 15 specified chronic conditions to be eligible under the Long-Term Illness Scheme (LTI). The European Economic Area Scheme (EEA) covers visitors from other member states of the European Union. There is no patient co-payment under the GMS, LTI and EEA schemes. The Drug Payment Scheme (DP) covers patients that are not eligible for free medicines, with a monthly co-payment capped at ∈ 78 (Barry et al. 2004).

4.2.3   Denmark

The Danish healthcare system is tax-financed and operated through the 14 counties and the Copenhagen Hospital Corporation. Pharmaceutical benefits are financed by the national health insurance that is a tax funded system payment for pharmaceutical, medical and dental services. The Danish Medicine Agency is the central authority making decisions on reimbursement of a particular medication, based on the legislation passed by the Danish Parliament. The Medicine Agency receives recommendations from a standing committee composed of seven appointed members with a medical or pharmaceutical background. There are general reimbursements and four types of individual reimbursements (single reimbursement, reimbursement for the chronically ill, reimbursement for the dying and increased reimbursement).

Pharmaceutical companies apply to the Medicine Agency for reimbursement from the national health insurance. Economic evaluation of a medication is not compulsory for these medications. The exact role of economic evaluations in the deliberations of the standing committee is unclear. There are nine instances in which a general reimbursement submission is rejected. For instance, there is a risk that the drug will be used outside the approved indication ('indication creep'). If one or more of the nine instances are identified, the submission will be rejected even with a high-quality health economic evaluation. The current reimbursement scheme was introduced in March 2000. Under the Danish system, patients with higher pharmaceutical expenditure will receive a higher level of reimbursement (Pederson 2003). This is similar to the safety net arrangement of the PBS in Australia.

4.2.4   Spain

In 1999, pharmaceutical expenditure accounted for 23% of total healthcare spending in Spain. Under the Spanish system, pharmaceutical products are patentable from 8 October 1992 and their patent expires after 2017. True generic medications will have to appear in Spanish market after that. As a result, generics currently have a very low market share in Spain. In 1996, the Spanish Medicines Law was modified to include new generic substitution. The introduction of a reference system in 2000 to encourage generic substitution was aimed at slowing the rapid growth of pharmaceutical expenditure. The

Spanish government introduced a negative list of non-reimbursable active principles (atenolol, ciprofloxacin, enalapril, famotidine and omeprazole). This only shifted usage from the non-reimbursed market to the reimbursed market that includes more expensive products. During 1998–2001, cost-containment measures of the Spanish government failed to control pharmaceutical expenditure. Inclusion of cost effectiveness evidence should form the basis of the government decision on reimbursement and pricing of new drugs (Darba 2003).

4.2.5 Central European countries

The transition from a central planning to a regulated market economy led to major changes in healthcare systems in Central and Eastern European countries. The Semaskho model was a uniform model of organising health services introduced after WWII. Health services are financed entirely through the state budget, with publicly owned healthcare facilities and publicly provided services. The Semaskho model was abolished in the 1990s and replaced by the market model. The Czech Republic, Hungary, Poland, Slovakia and Slovenia have introduced co-payments and other out-of-pocket user fees for pharmaceuticals. Co-payments range from 5 to 50% of the total costs. In Croatia, patients pay for their pharmaceuticals without government subsidy.

Guidelines for health economic evaluation are developed in Hungary and Poland. The Polish guidelines recommend performing an analysis from a societal perspective. The Hungarian guidelines require analysis from the purchaser's perspective, with inclusion of additional impact analyses with respect to budget, healthcare service, equity and clinical guidelines (Nuijten et al. 2003).

4.3 The Australian PBS

Many countries have adopted some form of pharmaceutical benefits scheme, but only a few countries (such as Australia, Canada and the United Kingdom) have incorporated economic evaluation as mandatory criteria when pharmaceutical companies apply for government subsidy of medications. Australia was the first jurisdiction to adopt such mandatory approach, which makes it an example for others to discuss and examine. The Australian case of the PBS is discussed in detail in the following sections.

Pharmaceuticals have been provided to the Australian community through the PBS for over 50 years. The PBS was first implemented in 1950 to provide 139 life-saving and disease-preventing medications free to the whole community. The *Pharmaceutical Benefits Act 1947–1949* restricted benefits to items listed in the Commonwealth Pharmaceutical Formulary, which was compiled by a committee. PBS subsidies are only available from an approved pharmacy via a PBS prescription written by a registered medical practitioner. The Commonwealth government supplies PBS stationery to all registered and approved medical practitioners. In 1954, PBS was included as Part VII of the *National Health Act 1953*.

Over the last five decades, the total cost of PBS has risen from $50 million in the 1950s, to $1.5 billion in the 1990s and to $5 billion in 2004 (see Appendices 4.1 and 4.2). The exponential increase in government expenditure on the PBS triggered a number of changes to achieve cost-containment. These include patient co-payments and safety net arrangements; minimum and generic pricing policy as well as restrictions of issuing pharmacy approval numbers in order to achieve economies of scale.

In 1987, the *National Health Act 1953* was amended to expand membership of the PBAC. This was done in order to consider comparative cost-effectiveness and cost in recommending listing of new drugs, or amending the listing of currents drugs; create the Economic Subcommittee (ESC) and Drug Utilisation Subcommittee (DUSC) to assist the PBAC in performing its function; and establish the PBPA as a price negotiator.

4.4   Pharmaceutical Benefits Advisory Committee

The PBAC was established as a statutory body in 1954 under Section 101 of the *National Health Act 1953* to recommend to the Commonwealth Minister for Health and Ageing which items should be available as pharmaceutical benefits, and to advise the Minister about other matters relating to the PBS. The committee is also required by the Act to consider the effectiveness and cost of a proposed benefit relative to other therapies. Unless a new medication is recommended by the PBAC to be listed on the PBS, it does not attract any government subsidy as pharmaceutical benefits (Commonwealth Department of Health and Ageing 2002).

The PBAC considers cost effectiveness and clinical efficacy of a product relative to other products already listed for the same or similar indications. The choice of comparator (which could be a non-drug therapy) should be the therapy which most prescribers would use as alternative in practice, in order to avoid bias. If no other alternatives are listed, the committee considers the benefits that the new product will provide for patients compared with the cost of achieving those benefits.

The Economic Subcommittee was established in 1993 under section 101A of the *National Health Act 1953* to review and interpret economic analyses of medications submitted to the PBAC; and advises PBAC on these analyses as well as the technical aspects of requiring and using economic evaluations. The Drug Utilisation Subcommittee was established in 1998 under the same section of *National Health Act 1953* to collect and analyse data on drug utilisation in Australia for use by the PBAC; to make inter-country comparisons of drug utilisation statistics; and to assist in generating information relating to the rational use and prescribing of medicines.

4.4.1 PBAC submission guidelines

PBS expenditure increased dramatically in the 1980s. Cost containment rather than cost-effectiveness was the primary concern at the time. There was no systematic approach to evaluating whether the drugs listed on the PBS represented a good value for public money. The *National Health Act 1953* was amended in 1987; the Minister for Health and Ageing specified that the cost-effectiveness requirement was to achieve 'value' for taxpayers' dollar and to improve efficiency. When developing a cost-effectiveness policy in the decision-making process, the following issues needed to be addressed, namely: the efficiency criteria to be used; the perspective to be adopted in economic evaluation; the types of economic evaluation required in order to meet such efficiency criteria; and the basis on which the outcomes of new pharmaceuticals are to be valued.

The Australian authorities were the first jurisdiction to include economic criteria in the decision-making process in listing new drugs for government subsidy. The PBAC guidelines were prescriptive in how to prepare a submission containing an economic evaluation. An evidence-based approach was required to compare the incremental costs and benefits of a new medication. The hierarchy of levels of evidence was stated explicitly in the submission guidelines, starting with randomised controlled trials preferred to the lower level of expert opinion (Salkeld et al. 1999).

Submissions to PBAC include the following information:

1) details of the proposed drug and its proposed use in the PBS, its comparison with the 'main comparator';
2) data from comparative randomised trials for the main indication;
3) modelled economic evaluation for the main indication; and
4) estimated extent of use and financial implications.

Listing decisions on the PBS need to be made before long-term trials or database studies can be conducted. The potential long-term impacts of new medications cannot be determined from short-term clinical trials (Richter 2004). The PBAC also requested a preliminary trial-based economic analysis, but the industry argued that controlled trials were not predicative of 'real-world' situations (Carmine 1996). The guidelines require a preliminary economic evaluation based on evidence from comparative randomised trials, with specified outcomes to be described in terms of a natural unit of measurement with 95% confidence intervals. Companies can submit a modelled economic evaluation, which allows the extrapolation from trials to final outcomes.

4.4.2   Economic evaluation for a PBAC submission

In terms of the methodology of an economic evaluation, the PBAC prefers a cost effectiveness analysis, cost minimisation analysis and cost utility analysis. A cost benefit analysis is not the preferable methodology as stated in the PBAC submission guidelines:

> ... *In contrast to other forms of analysis, cost benefit analysis (CBA) expresses all outcomes in monetary rather than physical units. This requires a monetary valuation of these outcomes and CBA often relies heavily on calculations of indirect costs and benefits, principally changes in production capacity. Such analyses are not likely to be helpful to the PBAC in its deliberations and are not encouraged.*
> (Commonwealth Department of Health and Ageing 2002, p. 65)

As discussed previously, cost benefit analysis is the only methodology that can address issues of allocative efficiency and distributive equity. With the PBAC preferred other methodologies such as cost effectiveness analysis, cost minimisation analysis and cost utility analysis, only technical efficiency and cost-effectiveness efficiency are addressed, and allocative efficiency is ignored in the guidelines. It is debatable that the issues of social welfare and utility are addressed by cost effectiveness analysis, cost minimisation analysis and cost utility analysis. Yet, the guidelines clearly state that an economic evaluation should be conducted from a societal perspective. Pharmaceutical companies are required to justify the inclusion of indirect benefits in their economic appraisal and to present the results with and without the indirect benefits and costs included. We argue that the new[3] cost benefit analysis (as discussed in Chapter 3) is the only methodology that captures all the costs (financial or social) and considers all the benefits and changes in social welfare. New[3] cost benefit analysis is a better methodology in adopting societal perspectives in economic evaluation as compared with other methodologies.

It is stated in the PBAC guidelines, 'for many drugs the intended final outcome is the improvement in quality of life through alleviation of distress. Where the final outcome of drug therapy is a change in quality of life, a quality of life measure should be considered' (Commonwealth Department of Health and Ageing 2002, p. 74). However, the PBAC stops short of developing a set of guidelines for measuring and valuing utility weights for its submissions (Salkeld et al. 1999).

It also specifically rules out the inclusion of indirect economic outcomes (or indirect benefits). The reasons given are that production will made up on the return to work for short-term absence, employers usually have excess capacity in the labour to cover absenteeism, and production will be made up by a replacement worker otherwise unemployed in the case of long-term absence (Commonwealth Department of Health and Ageing 2002, p. 68).

In reality, not every employer has the capacity and resources to put on a casual worker in case of sick leave. This is even more so in the case of small businesses, and especially for those requiring special or professional training. Even if the employers are lucky enough to find a replacement worker, there is still a cost involved. If the employee off sick is a permanent staff, the employer has to pay his or her sick leave as well as the wages for the replacement casual staff. That is the employer is paying two lots of wages for no additional productivity (if s/he is lucky enough to secure the same productivity from the replacement worker). If the employee off sick is a causal staff, s/he is not entitled to sick leave payment and looses that day (or days of) wages. Furthermore, certain tasks or duties at workplace cannot wait until tomorrow. Retail industry is a classic example. It there are insufficient staff on the shop floor due to sick leave, impatient and unsatisfied customers leave the shop because they cannot wait or they do not want to wait. These represent lost sales at least and lost clientele if under-staff situation persists. Ultimately, the cost of lost productivity is captured by the society. This is why we include the increase in economic productivity as benefits under the social choice approach (Mak and Islam 2004b).

4.5   Pharmaceutical Benefits Pricing Authority

The PBPA is the price negotiator of the Commonwealth government. The PBPA was established in January 1988 as a non-statutory body, independent of the Commonwealth Department of Health and Ageing. It makes recommendation on prices for new items that have been recommended for PBS listing by the PBAC, and for medications that have their uses extended or changed.

The PBPA reviews prices of all PBS listed items at least on an annual basis. Items are divided into therapeutic groups with members of the same group being reviewed at the same time. For pricing reviews, the PBPA meets on a quarterly basis, in line with the PBAC meeting schedule and the quarterly editions of the Schedule of Pharmaceutical Benefits.

In the pricing review, the PBPA considers the followings:

1) PBAC comments on clinical and cost effectiveness aspects of items;
2) the prices of alternative brands of a drug;
3) information on costs provided by the supplier or estimated by the PBPA;
4) prescription volumes, economies of scale and other factors such as expiry date;
5) storage requirements, product stability and special manufacturing requirements;

6) the level of activity being undertaken by the company in Australia, including new investment, production, and research & development;
7) the price of the drug in reasonably comparable overseas countries;
8) other relevant factors presented by the applicant company; and
9) any direction as advised by the Minister.

4.6 Therapeutic Goods Administration

The Therapeutic Goods Administration (TGA) is a regulatory body within the Commonwealth Department of Health and Ageing which processes applications of new drugs to be released in the Australian market. The TGA carries out a range of assessment and monitoring activities to ensure therapeutic goods available in Australia are of an acceptable standard with the aim of ensuring that the Australian community has access, within a reasonable time, to therapeutic advances.

The TGA assesses new medications on their clinical efficacy and safety, pharmacology as well as toxicology. The Australian Drug Evaluation Committee (ADEC) is the technical body of the TGA examining the quality, safety and efficacy based on the data presented from the clinical trials conducted by the manufacturer of the medication. The TGA proceeds to register the new medication based on the advice from ADEC. ADEC is also responsible for the post-market surveillance of the safety of the medication, and is the watchdog body monitoring the incidence of adverse effects following the release of new medications. The TGA also issues alert and recall notice for medications or medical devices if the safety of such products are in doubt.

4.7 PBS listing process

The process of listing a medication on PBS is a two-step process. Firstly, the PBAC considers cost and therapeutic need of the medication in the community, its clinical effectiveness and safety when compared to the similar medications currently listed, and then decides whether to recommend the listing of such medication. After receiving the recommendations from the PBAC, the Commonwealth Minister for Health and Ageing considers whether to accept the PBS listing of the medication, the extent of government subsidy (e.g. the proposed price of the medication), or the extent of availability of the medication to the community. The PBPA provides pricing information to the Minister making the PBS listing decisions (Salkeld et al. 1999).

A new medication may be recommended for listing under one of the three circumstances. Firstly, the medication is needed for prevention or treatment of significant medical conditions and the clinical profile of the medication is not covered by existing PBS listed drugs. It must also be of acceptable cost-effectiveness. Secondly, the medication is more effective and/or less toxic than existing PBS listed drugs for the same indications and is of acceptable cost-effectiveness. Thirdly, the medication is at least as effective and safe as currently PBS listed drugs for the same indications and is of comparable cost-effectiveness.

A medication may be removed from PBS listing for a number of reasons. A more effective or equally effective but less toxic drug becomes available. There is evidence from post-market surveillance by ADEC that the effectiveness of the medication is unsatisfactory. Evidence becomes available that the toxicity or abuse potential of the drug outweighs its therapeutic value. The medication has fallen into disuse or is no longer available. Treatment with the medication is no longer deemed cost-effective relative to other therapies (Salkeld et al. 1999).

4.8 The social security system, patient co-payment and equity issues

4.8.1 The social security system in Australia

The social security system is an integral part of Australia's social justice system, funded from consolidated revenue, and directed at providing support to low income and/or disadvantaged individuals and families. Individuals have a right to claim social security payments and benefits upon sickness, retrenchment, unemployment and retirement. There is also assistance for families and people with caring responsibilities.

Family Tax Benefit Part A is a payment to assist low-income and middle-income families with the cost of raising children. It is paid to each dependent child aged under 21 and/or dependent full-time

Table 4.1   Commonwealth government income support programmes

Income for families with children	Income for retired people	Income for those of workforce age	Income for young people
• Family Tax Benefit Part A • Family Tax Benefit Part B • Child Care Benefit • Parenting Payment • Maternity Allowance • Maternity Immunisation Allowance • Jobs, Education and Training Program (JET)	• Age Pension • Wife Pension • Pension Bonus Scheme	• Newstart Allowance • Partner Allowance • Mature Age Allowance • Disability Pension • Sickness Allowance • Widow Allowance	• Youth Allowance • Austudy • Loan Supplement • Abstudy • Assistance for Isolated Children Scheme

Source: Australia's Welfare 2003 (AIHW 2003).

students aged 21 to 24. Family Tax Benefit Part A payment is subject to income and assets test. There are three rates of payment namely *maximum rate* payable below a low-income threshold; *part rate* payable for families with incomes between the low-income threshold and the base rate threshold; and the *base rate* payable for families with incomes above the base rate threshold and below the means-tested threshold. Maximum and part rates vary with the age of the child, with payments increasing for teenagers and young people. In 2005, the income threshold for the maximum rate of the Family Tax Benefits Part A is $33,361. Families with income below $33,361 annually are eligible for Health Care cards. This threshold will increase to $37,500 in July 2006.

Family Tax Benefit Part B payment provides additional assistance to single-income families with a child aged under 16 or a child aged 16–18 years studying full-time. Extra assistance is given to families with a child under the age of five. The payment is not mean-test for sole parent families. For couple families, the payment is means-tested on the income of the partner with the lower income.

Eligibility for social security payments and allowances requires three basic criteria, namely residential requirements, basic eligibility conditions, as well as assets and income tests. The social security system provides income support to people with different types of payments, benefits and allowances, which are regulated by Federal Government acts of Parliament. The *Social Security Act 1991* provides the authority for making those payments and defines the conditions for qualification for payment, amount and calculation of payment and termination of payment.

4.8.2 Patient co-payment and equity issues

Patient co-payment for the general public was first introduced in 1960. A flat rate patient contribution of $0.50 per script was imposed. The patient contribution rose steadily over the next few decades, from $0.50 in 1960 to $28.60 in 2005. Co-payment for welfare recipients (or healthcare card holders) was introduced in 1971 at $0.50, and increased to $3.30 in 2000. Co-payment for pensioners started in 1990 at $2.50 per script, and increased subsequently to $2.60 and to $4.60 in 2005 (see Appendix 4.3).

In order to ensure *equity* in the distribution of medications under the PBS, welfare recipients, pensioners, war veterans, the unemployed and low-income earners receive additional subsidy from the Australian Government. There are two levels of patient co-payments under the PBS, namely the general co-payment and the concession co-payment depending on the entitlement status of the individuals.

Holders of *Pensioner Concession Cards, Health Care Card* or *Commonwealth Seniors Health Cards* are eligible to concession co-payment under the PBS, thus ensuring access to cheaper medications with additional government subsidy. In addition, the Pharmaceutical Allowance offsets the cost of prescription medications available through PBS and is paid as part of the total pension, allowance or benefit payment to recipients of social security pension, Mature Age Allowance, Sickness Allowance, Youth, Newstart or Widow Allowance during a period of temporary illness, or Newstart, Widow, Parenting Payment, or Special Benefit and turned 60, and has been receiving income support payments continuously for at least nine months.

A Pensioner Concession Card is issued to:

1) all Social Security and Department of Veteran Affairs (DVA) pensioners, Mature Age, Mature Age Partners and Bereavement allowees, single Parenting Payment recipients; and

2) Newstart Allowance, Widow Allowance, Partner Allowance, Sickness Allowance, Special Benefit and Partnered Parenting Payment recipients aged 60 years or older and in receipt of income support for nine months or more.

A Health Care Card is issued to recipients of social security payment including:

1) Newstart Allowance, Widow Allowance, Partner Allowance, Special Benefit and some Parenting Payment recipients who are not eligible for a Pensioner Concession Card (the card may be retained for six months from employment date after loss of allowance by returning to work, if the allowees were in receipt of payments for a period of at least twelve months);
2) all maximum rate Family Tax Benefit recipients (every six months);
3) children of Child Disability Tax Benefit recipients;
4) Family Tax Benefit Part B recipients who return to work and have been in recipient of an income support payment for more than 12 months are issued a Health Care Card for six months of their payment is cancelled due to income from employment; and
5) Mobility Allowance recipient who are not eligible for a Pensioner Concession Card, and low income earners who are income tested and found to be eligible for a Health Care Card.

Commonwealth Seniors Health Card gives non-pensioners of Age Pension age or Service Pension age access to concessional prescription medicines through the PBS. It is available to Australian residents with an annual income not exceeding $50,000 for singles, $80,000 for couples, and $50,000 each for couples separated by illness. It is for these arrangements that the distributional weight is not used in the valuation of benefits in PBS setting.

4.9 Safety net arrangement

With the introduction of patient co-payment, a safety net scheme was implemented to protect patients with chronic medical conditions and their polypharmacy needs. In 1986, the safety net arrangement was implemented as a protection measure for chronically ill patients who had a large of number of prescriptions dispensed per year. Initially, patients (either as a single person or as a family unit) were entitled to pharmaceuticals free of charge after reaching an annual threshold of 25 scripts.

In 1990, the criterion of the safety net threshold was changed from 'the number of script per year' to 'the amount of individual or family expenditure per year'. A two-tier safety net was introduced for general patients. The annual safety net threshold for concessional patients remains at 52 scripts for the last few years. The safety net threshold will increase to 54 scripts in 2006 and 56 scripts in 2007.

The safety net threshold for general patients for 2005 is $874.90, and will increase by the dollar equivalent of two co-payments each year from 1 January 2006 until 1 January 2009. This will take the safety net threshold for general patients well over $1,000 over the next two years. After reaching the safety net threshold, general patients are entitled to pharmaceuticals at a reduced rate rather than free of charge.

Under the PBS, there is mandatory time interval specified between supplies of medications. If the time interval is less than that specified, the medication falls into the 'immediate supply' provision. From 2006, supply of some medications under the 'immediate supply' provision will be excluded from the PBS safety net entitlements and the patient co-payments for these medications will not count towards their safety net total. If patients are already on Safety Net, they are not eligible for a lower co-payment for any prescriptions dispensed under 'immediate supply' provision. In other words, concessional or general patients who have reached the Safety Net will have to pay the normal concessional or general co-payment when their prescriptions are dispensed under the 'immediate supply' provision. The measure is introduced to address the issues of moral hazard, or to remove the financial incentive for patients to use immediate supply arrangements to obtain supplies in excess of their needs.

4.10 Generic medications and pricing policy

The Commonwealth government has been actively promoting generic medicines, including information brochures and advertisement on television. Medical practitioners are required to endorse the prescription as 'brand substitution not permitted' if they prefer patients stay with brands they prescribed. The government argued that the cost of generic drugs to the PBS being only 3% less than formerly patent-protected drugs, and believed that Australia had not gained the same benefit from generic drugs as other countries such as the United States, the United Kingdom and New Zealand where generic drugs comprise about 50% of the market and generally cost much less than patent-protected drugs (Pharma in Focus 2005).

However, there is a lack of central policy in governing the entry of generics into the market. There are so many different generic brands of the same product, and this makes it is extremely confusing to the general public. At one stage, there were 12 brands of amoxycillin, a commonly prescribed antibiotic, on the market (Amoxil from GSK, Cilamox from Sigma, Alphamox from Alphapharm, Moxacin from CSL, Amohexal from Hexal, Bgramin and Amoxycillin-DP from Douglas, Amoxycillin-BC from Biochemie, Chem-mart amoxycillin, Terry White amoxycillin, Healthsense amoxycillin, and GenRx amoxycillin). Some of the generic brands and 'house brand' from pharmacy banner groups are not available directly from full-line pharmacy wholesaler. Patients may face a different brand of the same medication each time when their scripts are dispensed. The health outcome of brand substitution can be a therapeutic nightmare, especially in the case of ongoing medications such as antihypertensives, hypolipidaemic, oral hypoglycaemics, and especially for the elderly patients, patients of poor command of English, or patients of poor literacy.

In 2005, a 12.5% price cut is introduced to new generic and benchmark PBS prices. The government aims at cutting PBS outlays by $830 million over four years. The pharmaceutical industries believe the potential savings from this measure is much higher than the estimated $830 million. From 1 August 2005, a price reduction of at least 12.5% must be offered by the manufacturer for the first new generic brand of a PBS medication.

Prices of medications listed on PBS are linked if they work in the same way or have the same health outcomes. PBS medications are grouped under the same *Reference Pricing Group* based upon the relativities between medications as outlined in the PBPA's Therapeutic Relativity Sheets. Further information on reference pricing group refer to http://www.health.gov.au/internet/wcms/publishing.nsf/ Content/health-pbs-general-pricing-therelativity.htm. As the PBS is based on a reference pricing system, the price reduction will flow on to: all brands of that medication; all strengths and preparation forms of that medication which are administered in the same way; all other medications in the same reference pricing groups which are administered in the same way; and be applied to combination preparation on a pro-rata basis.

The flow-on effect of the generic pricing policy is confusing and lacks transparency in its mechanism. The Commonwealth government states that the price reduction will apply only to the first new brand of any PBS medication listed, not to subsequent new brands of the same medication. It also maintains that price reduction will apply once only for each medication, including for medications in a reference pricing group where the reduction has occurred as a flow-on from another medication. Atorvastatin, Fluvastatin, Pravastatin and Simvastatin are in the same reference pricing group number 26 for serum lipid reducing agents. From 1 August 2005, there are six new generic brands added to PBS listing in addition to the existing four brands of Zocor,, Lipex,, Simvar, and Zimstat,. The flow-on effect leads to price reduction for Fluvastatin, Pravastatin and Simvastatin, but Atorvastatin is specifically exempted by the Minister for Health and Ageing from recommendation of PBAC.

4.11   Special patient contributions

The government only subsidises to the level of the lowest price brand for any therapeutic products. Special patient contributions apply when there is a disagreement between the manufacturer and the commonwealth government about the price for subsidy purpose. Despite the disagreement about price, the medication continues to be listed and subsidised, but patients are required to pay an additional amount on top of the normal PBS patient co-payment. Special patient contributions can be in three forms, namely brand premium, therapeutic premium and other special patient contributions.

Brand premium arises when manufacturer of a certain brand of medication disagrees with the commonwealth government on price reduction on introduction of new generic brands. Patients are required to pay the difference if they insist on the more expensive brand. Patients can avoid brand premiums by asking the doctor or pharmacist to prescribe or dispense a less expensive brand. A substitute brand is available for each medication.

In 1997, a therapeutic group premium was introduced for high cost items such as Calcium channel antagonists, Angiotensin converting enzyme inhibitors, etc. Therapeutic group premiums apply within narrowly defined therapeutic sub-groups where medications concerned are of similar safety and health outcomes. Patients are required to pay the extra cost unless medical practitioners obtain authority from the Medicare Australia to exempt the therapeutic premium on clinical ground. There will no new therapeutic group premiums due to the 12.5% price reduction policy from 1 August 2005.

Some medications in the same reference pricing groups are not interchangeable for patients although they deliver similar health outcomes. If manufacturers of these medications have pricing disagreement with the Commonwealth government, patients will have to pay the additional cost in the form of special patient contributions. Patients are required to pay the special patient contribution unless medical practitioners obtain authority from the Medicare Australia to exempt the extra payment on clinical ground.

4.12   Freezing pharmacy approval number

The number of community pharmacies authorised to dispense pharmaceutical benefits has been reduced through amalgamation and regulating the issuing of pharmacy provider numbers (see Appendix 4.4). Since 1990, a new pharmacy approval number is only issued to an area where there is no existing pharmacy. There are strict rules regarding relocation of existing pharmacies in order to prevent overcrowding. Relocation of a community pharmacy must be applied for and approved by the Australian Community Pharmacy Authority of the Medicare Australia (formerly Health Insurance Commission). A new approval number is granted for relocation; otherwise, the pharmacy is not eligible for the PBS. This policy has been criticised by many as anti-competitive since the approval number becomes a trading commodity that fetches an unrealistic price that serves an entry barrier for pharmacists pursuing pharmacy ownership.

4.13   Free Trade Agreement with US

The Free Trade Agreement (FTA) between Australia and the United States commences in January 2005. Under the FTA, there are measures agreed by both countries to enhance the transparency and accountability of the operation of the PBS. Some academics believe that the FTA will delay the listing of generic medicines, put undue pressure on the PBAC, redefine intellectual property laws and forfeit substantial export opportunities for Australian generic drug companies (Drahos et al. 2004). The Australian government is confident that the AUSFTA will not impact on the integrity and sustainability of the PBS (Abbott 2004).

4.14   Intergeneration report

The Commonwealth government of Australia spent about 4% of GDP on healthcare expenditure in 2003. Non-demographic factors such as listing new medications are likely to generate the greatest cost pressure on the PBS. There has been a rapid growth on PBS expenditure, average 6.1% over the last 20 years. The government believes that fiscal sustainability is the key to managing its finances. In the context of the PBS, sustainability of the program stems from the general health of the population and cost-efficiency of the program. There are always new medications for which a PBS subsidy is sought after. In reviewing a PBS listing, the PBAC should consider the impact of the medication from a societal perspective. As discussed in the previous sections, the new[3] cost benefit analysis is the only methodology capable of addressing issues of allocative efficiency, distributive equity and social welfare changes.

4.15   Economic evaluation in the PBS: The need for new[3] cost benefit analysis

Australia is one of the first few countries to adopt economic evaluation as part of the pharmaceutical subsidy program. The above analysis provides a comprehensive survey of economic evaluation issues confronting the PBAC in Australia. In its submission guidelines, the PBAC prefers that cost effectiveness, cost minimisation and cost utility analyses be carried out and reported. However, a new[3] cost benefit analysis is the better alternative in selecting medications that maximise social benefits to Australian society.

As discussed in Section 3.15, the new[3] cost benefit analysis integrates the standard cost benefit analysis with recent development in welfare economics, scientific information from clinical studies, as well as ethics and moral philosophy. The new[3] cost benefit analysis is the only methodology of economic evaluation that addresses allocative efficiency, distributive equity, as well as issues of ethics and moral philosophy.

The new[3] cost benefit analysis measures costs and benefits of a program such as the PBS under the new[3] welfare economics framework. The new[3] cost benefit analysis considers social costs and social benefits, truly adopting a societal perspective by measuring the net changes of social welfare rather than just from the perspective of a single agency (e.g. the PBAC on behalf of the Australian Commonwealth government). Welfare changes are measured by using scientific information, expert opinions and social value judgement. In addition to financial costs, social costs (such as indirect costs and opportunity costs) are taken into consideration so that the true cost picture is captured in the new[3] cost benefit analysis. Benefits are measured by a combination of the human capital approach, the expressed and revealed preferences approach so that changes in welfare as a result of PBS are quantified in monetary terms. This allows economic evaluation to be done across therapeutic classes, so that a meaning comparison can be made when considering listing of medications on the PBS.

4.16 Conclusion

The PBS provides a good case for applying the new[3] cost benefit analysis. The advantages for applying the new[3] cost benefit analysis to the PBS are discussed in Section 3.15. In addition to incorporating welfare economics, ethics and clinical science, the new[3] cost benefit analysis is also easier and more operational to apply when estimating the social costs and benefits of a health program such as the PBS. Details of applying the new[3] cost benefit analysis in a PBS setting is discussed in Chapters 5 and 6.

5
Cost and Benefit Estimates

5.1 Introduction

In this chapter, we discuss the general principles and methods of estimating costs and benefits of six medications (namely Atorvastatin, Clopidogrel, Pioglitazone, Letrozole, Fluticasone/ Salmeterol and Tiotropium) while the detailed estimates of the costs and benefits and their analysis will be provided in the next chapter.

About 70% of the total burden of diseases in Australia has been attributed to cardiovascular problems, cancers, injuries, mental health problems; diabetes mellitus and asthma, as identified by Australian Health Ministers for priority action under the National Health Priority Areas (NHPA) initiatives (see Appendix 5.1). The NHPA initiative is a collaborative effort involving commonwealth, state and territory governments. The aim of the NHPA is to focus public attention and health policy on areas that simultaneously contribute significantly to the burden of disease in Australia, and show potential for improvement (AIHW 2004).

In this research, discussion is focused on the following conditions, namely cardiovascular diseases with specific references to coronary heart disease (heart attack) and stroke, type 2 diabetes mellitus, breast cancer, asthma and chronic obstructive pulmonary disease. Medications play an integral part in the management of these chronic conditions. The majority of these medications are provided under the Pharmaceutical Benefits Scheme (PBS) in Australia. Nine out of the top 15 generic medications prescribed in 2002–03 are for cardiovascular diseases (see Appendix 5.2). Medications for cardiovascular diseases, respiratory diseases, diabetes mellitus and neoplasm account for 46% of the pharmaceutical expenditure in 2000–01 (see Appendix 5.1).

5.2   General principles of numerical estimates

5.2.1   Application of new[3] cost benefit analysis

As discussed in Section 3.6.1, the new[3] cost benefit analysis is developed under the new[3] welfare economics that provides a suitable normative framework for social choice and decision-making for selecting health programs. The new[3] cost benefit analysis is applied to the PBS setting in order to select medications for government subsidy that will maximise the health and social welfare of the Australian public.

5.2.2   New[3] cost benefit analysis in the PBS setting: Essential elements

As discussed in Section 3.6.2, the new[3] cost benefit analysis approach considers economics and ethics in estimating costs and benefits of listing medications on the PBS in Australia. This new approach assumes the measurability of social welfare and other extra-welfaristic components of costs and benefits of listing a medication on the PBS on the basis of social value judgement and public policy objectives. In this PBS application, social welfare is represented by the social benefits of a medication which consists of improvement in productivity, avoidance of hospitalisation and other costs, and improvement in the quality and expectancy of life. This new approach aims at estimating costs and benefits by using scientific information, expert opinions, social preferences and social value judgements.

In Chapter 3, a general framework is given for new[3] cost benefit analysis which can be applied to any countries in any situations. However, not every component is applicable in the PBS setting in Australia. Only the components relevant to the PBS in Australia are applied in this research. These include the consideration of ethics, as well as direct and indirect benefits. The social choice approach is applied in estimating costs and benefits from scientific information, expert opinions and social value judgements. The valuation method used is a combination of the human capital approach and the preference (expressed and revealed) approach. Shadow pricing is important in developing countries but not relevant in the PBS setting as market price is more efficient in Australia. A social discount rate of zero percent is used in order to address the issues of intergenerational equity. As considerations for equity are addressed in the PBS setting by other health and social support schemes, equity have not been incorporated in the present new[3] cost benefit analysis. Current data on the avoidance of health costs and increase in economic productivity are used in determining the financial costs and benefits of listing the above six medications on the PBS under the new[3] cost benefit analysis. Scientific information, expert opinions and social value judgements are used to determine net social welfare, i.e. the values of social benefits (such as improved life expectancy, improved health status and patients' preference) and social costs.

5.2.3   General principles of numerical estimates of costs and benefits

The assumptions, concepts and methods of operationalising economics and new[3] cost benefit analysis as discussed in Chapter 3 are adapted in estimating costs and benefits of medications in the present study.

The cost stream

As discussed in Section 2.6, a healthcare program such as the PBS generates costs and benefits directly as well as indirectly. Some of these costs and benefits are internal or tangible whilst others are external or intangible. The resource consequences from the inputs into PBS health programs are classified as direct costs, as these resources are consumed directly in the activities of the health programs. These include the acquisition cost of the medications supplied, the internal administrative cost of the program via a government department, as well as the external administrative cost of the program via community and hospital pharmacies.

The acquisition cost of the medications is negotiated between the Pharmaceutical Benefits Pricing Authority (PBPA) and the manufacturer of the medications (i.e. the individual pharmaceutical company). The acquisition cost is the amount paid by community pharmacists to wholesaler or manufacturers for purchase of the medication. The external administrative cost of the PBS is the remuneration paid to pharmacies for dispensing prescriptions under the

PBS as discussed in Chapter 4. The pharmacy remuneration or pharmacy mark-up is made up of a fixed dispensing fee and percentage mark-up of the acquisition cost of the medications. The dispensing fee is negotiated between the Pharmacy Guild of Australia and the Minister of Health and Ageing as specified in the Community Pharmacy Agreement. The percentage mark-up for high cost item is usually 10%, and higher for low cost items.

For medications listed on PBS under Section 85 of *National Health Act*, the sum of the acquisition cost and external administrative costs is the 'approved price to pharmacist'. The 'approved price to pharmacist' of each PBS listed medication is published in the *Schedule of Pharmaceutical Benefits* or the Yellow Book (Department of Health and Ageing 2004b) as 'dispensed price for maximum quantity' by the Department of Health and Ageing, for circulation among approved pharmacists and medical practitioners. These prices are reviewed on a quarterly basis with new prices (if any) effective from February, May, August and November, which are traditionally the change months in the PBS calendar, but the changes in 2005 took place in April, August and December. The internal administrative cost of the program refers to the operating costs of the PBS such as wages of operating personnel, stationery and printing, computer hardware and software, research and development cost (such as the PBS online program). However, this internal program cost is generally insignificant when compared with other costs and is not considered in the economic evaluation.

All medications have potential adverse effects because none of them have absolute specificity in their actions. Adverse drug effects are the unwanted effects other than the therapeutic actions intended, as a result of medications even if they have been used correctly. As discussed in Section 4.6, the Therapeutic Goods Administration is the regulatory body that examines the safety efficacy of medications and monitors the incidence of adverse effects after the release of the medication. Treatment of these adverse effects of medications incurs a cost which forms part of the direct costs of the PBS. In 2001–02, the clinical incidence of adverse drug effects amounts to 68,008 hospital separations, or 1.1% of the diagnostic category of injury, poison and toxic effects of drugs (AIHW 2004 p. 293). The average cost per hospital separation for injury, poison and toxic effects of drugs is $2691.00 in 2001–02

(AIHW 2004 pp. 438–439), and costs of adverse drug effects is estimated to be $29.60 ($2691 × 1.1%).

Only direct costs (i.e. acquisition cost of drugs and the administrative costs of the programs) are considered in the economic evaluation of a Pharmaceutical Benefits Advisory Committee (PBAC) submission. Indirect costs are resource consumption that do not arise due to an activity or a disease; and usually depict changes in production and amount of leisure time, or other indirect effects generated by the health program. Indirect costs are not included in cost estimation under the PBAC submission guideline.

Social costs include those other than the financial costs of supplying the medications on the PBS to the general public of Australia. Opportunity costs refer to the forgone opportunities of using the funds to pay for the medications instead of other alternatives. The opportunity cost dose not represent the physical sum of money paid by the government for the subsidised medications and is not considered by the PBAC. Under the social choice approach of the new[3] cost benefit analysis, the opportunity cost of the medication is included in order to determine whether the higher premium paid for the medication will be offset by the benefits it generates (Mak and Islam 2004b).

The benefit stream: measures of social welfare

The benefits of the PBS can be estimated by increase in economic productivity; decrease or avoidance of consumption of healthcare resources; and health gain in terms of improvement of health status or quality of life. Increase in economic productivity or decrease in resource consumption fall under the *human capital approach* or the *cost of illness approach* (Johannesson 2000; Jack 1999). However, the PBAC type of criteria generally adopt a restricted human capital approach and estimates the benefits of the PBS only on the basis of the decreased consumption of healthcare resources. The issue of increase in economic productivity is excluded. The benefit is thus estimated as a decrease in resource consumption in hospital separations.

Under the preference based approach, the benefit is estimated as the willingness of the patients to pay for the medication supplied as private prescriptions in the absence of government subsidy, as well as the improvement of health status and life expectation in terms as

Quality Adjusted Life-years (QALYs) (i.e. the improvement in quantity and quality of life).

Improvement in productivity

According to the Australian Bureau of Statistics, the average weekly earning is about $690.00 in Australia in May 2002 (ABS 2005, Cat. Nos 6305.0, 6306.0). This corresponds to about $18.15 per hour for a 38-hour week, and about $145.00 for an average 8-hour working day.

The increase in economic productivity is calculated by multiplying a daily wage rate of $145.00 with the number of days off work due to hospitalisation and medical consultation. The average length of hospital stay for coronary heart disease, stroke, breast cancer, type 2 diabetes mellitus, asthma and chronic obstructive pulmonary diseases is used to calculate the productivity gain if hospitalisation is avoided for these medical conditions.

Use of medication is only justified with health improvement and better control of the medical conditions of the patients. With such health improvement, it is assumed patients should have less frequent need to visit their general and specialist medical practitioners. When their medical conditions stabilise, the number of visit to medical practitioner should decrease. According to our professional opinion and social value judgement, successful medication therapy should result in patients' medical conditions being stabilised over the period of five years (time span of the study) with only a bi-annual visit to general medical practitioner and an annual visit to specialist medical practitioner is required. The details of the estimates in decrease in number of visits to medical practitioners are listed in Table 5.1, and this translates into decrease in the number of work days lost. Based on average wage of $145.00 per day, the resulting increase in economic productivity is calculated as shown in the Table 5.1.

Avoidance of hospitalisation cost

The clinical information of the average length of stay of the four different types of hospital separation is used to calculate their corresponding average cost per patient day. The average cost per patient day for each type of hospital separation is calculated by dividing the total estimated costs by the total number of that type of hospital separation, as shown in Table 5.2.

Table 5.1   Increase in economic productivity due to less visits to medical practitioners

Year	Without health improvement		With health improvement		No. of work days lost**	Increase in economic productivity
	No. of visit/year*		No. of visit/year*			
	GP	Specialist	GP	Specialist		
0	12	4	4	2	5	$725.00
1	12	4	4	2	5	$725.00
2	6	2	2	1	2.5	$362.50
3	6	2	2	1	2.5	$362.50
4	6	2	2	1	2.5	$362.50

Notes:
* Assume each medical visit = half a work day lost.
** Less amount of work days with health improvement.

Source: Authors' estimates.

Table 5.2   Separations, same-day separations, patient-days, average length of stay and cost for the major diagnostic category, 2001–02

Major Diagnostic Category	Separations[a]	Percentage same-day separation	Patient-days	ALOS[b] (days)	ALOS[c] (days)	Estimated cost ($'000)	Average cost per day ($)
Circulatory System 05	472610	23.9	1920935	4.06	5.03	1919045	999.02
Endocrine, Nutritional, metabolic 10	70977	24.7	349629	4.93	6.21	276003	789.42
Neoplastic disorders 17	309340	90.4	500568	1.62	7.45	375994	751.13
Respiratory system 04	301634	13.7	1498513	4.97	5.60	987115	658.73

Notes:
a. Separations for acute and unspecified episodes of care only.
b. Average length of stay including same-day separation.
c. Average length of stay excluding same-day separation.

Source: *Australian Health* (AIHW 2004 pp. 438–439).

Coronary heart disease and stroke is under by the circulatory system category. Type 2 diabetes mellitus is covered under the endocrine, nutritional and metabolic category. Breast cancer is covered under neoplastic disorder category. Asthma and chronic obstructive pulmonary diseases are covered under the respiratory system category. The cost avoidance of an episode of hospital separation is calculated as the average cost per patient day multiplied by the average length of stay of that medical condition.

Decrease in visits to general and specialist medical practitioners

As discussed in the section on increase in economic productivity, the number of visits to a medical practitioner decreases provided that their medical conditions stabilise and their health improves with the use of medications prescribed. According to authors' expert opinion and social value judgement, patients are likely to visit their general medical practitioners on a quarterly or bi-annual basis rather than on a monthly basis if their medical conditions are under control.

Assuming patients attend their general medical practitioners for a level 'C' consultation, the cost savings of decreased visits to general medical practitioners are shown in Table 5.3. The fee for a level 'C' surgery consultation is $57.35 (Medicare Benefits Schedule May 2004). If the number of visits decreases from 12 monthly visits to four quarterly visits, this represents a savings of: $458.80 (8 × $57.35).

Using the same argument, the need for visiting a consultant physician or specialist medical practitioners should decrease with health improvement. According to authors' expert opinion and

Table 5.3   Cost savings of decrease in visits to general medical practitioners

| | No. of GP visit per year | | | Cost savings |
Year	Without health improvement	With health improvement	Decrease in no. of GP visit	of health services ($)*
0	12	4	8	458.80
1	12	4	8	458.80
2	6	2	4	229.40
3	6	2	4	229.40
4	6	2	4	229.40

Note: * Level C consultation fee at $57.35 per visit (Medicare Benefits Schedule May 2004).
Source: Authors' estimates.

Table 5.4   Cost savings of decrease in visits to specialist medical practitioners

| Year | No. of specialist visit per year | | Decrease in no. of specialist visit | Cost savings of health services ($)* |
	Without health improvement	With health improvement		
0	4	2	2	250.80
1	4	2	2	250.80
2	2	1	1	125.40
3	2	1	1	125.40
4	2	1	1	125.40

Note: * Level C consultation fee at $125.40 per visit (Medicare Benefits Schedule May 2004).

Source: Authors' estimates.

social value judgement, patients should visit their specialist medical practitioners on an annual or a bi-annual basis rather than on a quarterly basis if their medical conditions are stabilised with successful medication therapy.

The Medicare scheduled fee for a referral to a consultant physician is $125.40 (Medicare Benefits Schedule May 2004). The cost saving in decrease in visit to specialist medical practitioners are calculated as in Table 5.4.

Complementary medications

The benefits of improvement of health status is estimated as the decrease of health service consumption such as consultation with general and/or specialist medical practitioners, diagnostic services (such as radiological examination or pathology tests) as well as the decrease in consumption of complementary medications. Patients resort to alternative medicines to control conditions (e.g. vitamins, herbal and homeopathic remedies). According to authors' professional opinion, a monthly supply of complementary medicines is estimated to range from $20.00 to $50.00. If the medical conditions are controlled, this represents a substantial saving for the patients for not consuming complementary medicines. An annual savings of $400.00 is estimated from a decrease in usage of complementary medicines.

Increase in life expectancy

As stated in Section 5.1, the discussion of this research focuses on a number of medical conditions, namely coronary heart disease, stroke, type 2 diabetes mellitus, breast cancer, asthma and chronic obstructive pulmonary diseases. Among these medical conditions, some of them are the main causes of death in Australia.

The use of medications is aimed to improve the quantity and quality of life for patients. Benefits from improved life expectancy are estimated by the number of healthy life-years gained (or the number of healthy life-years lost if without the medications) and the average value of the Quality Adjusted Life-Years (QALY $/year).

In order to estimate the benefits as a result of increase in life expectancy, the value of a statistical life is calculated. As discussed in Section 2.6, the value of a statistical life (VOSL) is an inference made by evaluating individuals' preferences for risk avoidance or

Table 5.5   Ranking of NHPA diseases and conditions as underlying causes of death, 2002

NHPA	Underlying cause of death	Deaths		Ranks	
		Number	% of all deaths	Males	Females
Cardiovascular	Coronary heart disease	26063	19.5	1	1
	Stroke	12533	9.4	2	2
	All cardiovascular diseases	50294	37.6		
Cancer	Lung cancer	8110	6.1	3	6
	Breast cancer	2698	2.0		5
	Colorectal cancer	4649	3.5	7	8
	Prostate cancer	2852	2.1	6	
	Lymphomas	1597	1.2	18	16
	All cancers	37622	28.1		
Injury and poisoning	Suicide	2320	1.7	8	20
	Land transport accident	1826	1.4	13	
	All injury and poisoning	7820	5.8		
Diabetes	**All diabetes**	3329	2.5	9	10
Mental disorders	**All mental disorders**	3172	2.4		
Asthma	**Asthma**	397	0.3		
Arthritis	**All arthritis**	1015	0.8		

Note: See also Appendix 5.3.

Source: *Australia's Health* (AIHW 2004 p. 392).

Table 5.6   Literature review of values of a statistical life

Author (year)	Value of a life	Notes
Nordhaus (2002)	$3 million (1990)	
Murphy and Topel (1999)	$5 million	
Viscusi (2003)	$7 million (2000)	Median from labour based estimates
	$3 million (1996)	Federal Aviation Administration
	$5.5 million (1996)	Food & Drug Administration
	$6.3 million (1999)	EPA
Blomquist (2001)	$1 million to $9 million	
Hirth et al. (2000)	$460,000 to $2 million	Human capital
	$680,000 to $26 million	Willingness to pay
	$920,000 to $9 million	Willingness to accept

Source: MEDTAP International 2003.

improvement in their situations, and expressing such preferences in monetary terms (Green et al. 2000; Abelson 2003; MEDTAP 2003). The VOSL have been obtained from three main types of studies, namely estimates of willingness-to-pay for reduced risks, estimates of willingness to accept compensations for increased risks, and estimates of human capital value of lost earnings and leisure time with premature mortality.

The average value of a life-year or a QALY is calculated by dividing the VOSL by the discounted or undiscounted remaining life expectancy for the surveyed population. From the literature review, the average value of QALY ranges from $24,777 to $428,286 in US dollars. The average values of QALYs are converted to A$ using the exchange rates of A$1 = US$0.70. Benefits of improved life expectancy for the six medications are calculated using the lower estimates of A$35,395.00.

For the six medications being examined, the increase in life expectancy as measured in QALYs for individual medication is either quoted from published scientific or clinical journal, or obtained from authors' expert opinion or social value judgement if no such published figure is found.

Table 5.7   Average value of QALY under different approaches

Type of study	Average value of QALY	
Human capital	US$24777	A$35395
Willingness to pay	US$265345	A$379064
Job risk	US$428286	A$611837

Note: Assume A$1 = US$0.70.

Source: MEDTAP International 2003.

With this background of general principles provided here, the remaining part of this chapter provides a detailed discussion of the estimates of costs and benefits. For each of the chosen medical conditions, there is a brief discussion on the incidence, the mortality, the burden of the diseases, the medications used, the health services consumed, as well as the estimates of the costs and the benefits.

5.3   Cardiovascular disease

Cardiovascular diseases comprise all diseases and conditions involving the heart and the circulatory system such as coronary heart disease, stroke, peripheral vascular disease, heart failure and hyper-

Table 5.8   Deaths from cardiovascular diseases, 2000

Causes of death	Males			Females		
	Number	Rate*	Change**	Number	Rate*	Change**
All cardiovascular diseases	23774	255.7	−4.2	25967	172.9	−4.0
Coronary heart disease	14052	150.2	−4.8	12469	84.0	−4.7
Stroke	4931	53.7	−2.9	7423	48.5	−3.1
Heart failure	982	10.9	−5.3	1662	10.0	−5.3
Peripheral vascular disease	1108	11.9	−3.8	938	6.5	−1.8
Hypertensive disease	449	4.9	−2.7	753	5.0	−2.3
Rheumatic heart disease and fever	101	1.1	−3.0	164	1.3	−3.0
All causes of death	66817	712.7	−2.5	61474	450.7	−2.0

Notes:
*   Age-standardised rate per 100,000 population.
**   Annual change in the age-standardised death rate over the period 1989 to 2000.

Source: AIHW National Mortality Databases, *Australia's Health* 2002 (AIHW 2002 p. 44).

tension. Cardiovascular disease is at its most serious stage when end-organ damage is involved, such as heart (causing angina, heart attack or sudden death) and brain (leading to stroke).

5.3.1 Incidence and mortality

In the National Health Survey 2001, 19.4% of the population (or 3.7 million of Australians) reported a long-termed cardiovascular condition, with hypertension being the most common of all. Cardiovascular diseases are Australia's greatest health problem. The health and economic burden of cardiovascular disease exceeds that of any other diseases.

In 2002, cardiovascular disease was the leading cause of death, accounting for 50,294 deaths or 38% of all death (see Appendix 5.3). Death rates for cardiovascular disease increases dramatically with age, with 82% of deaths occurring among those aged 70 and over, compared with less than 5% for those aged below 55. Over the last three decades, there has been a considerable decline in cardiovascular death rates due to the reduction of prevalent risk factors (high levels of blood pressure, tobacco smoking and saturated fat intake), and medical interventions such as counseling, use of medications, emergency care, medical and surgical treatment and follow-up care.

Coronary heart disease (CHD) is the largest single cause of death, accounting for 26,063 (19%) of all deaths in Australia in 2002 (AIHW 2004). In 2000–01, it is estimated that there were 48,700 coronary events (mainly heart attacks) among people aged 40–90, with one-half of the cases being fatal. Non-fatal heart attacks were three times more common in males than females in the 35–69 age group (AIHW 2002). Each year, around 40,000 to 48,000 Australians have a stroke. Stroke is the second largest cause of death, accounted for 12,533 deaths (9% of all deaths) in Australia in 2002 (AIHW 2004). Stroke is a major cause of disability with over three-quarters of survivors needing assistance and ongoing care (AIHW 2004).

5.3.2 Health services consumed

In 2002–03, patients with cardiovascular problems represented 11% of the workload of general medical practitioners in Australia (Britt et al. 2003). Hypertension was the most common problem presented and managed by general medical practitioners, accounting for 8.9% of all problems. Lipid disorders (elevated blood levels of cholesterol, triglycerides or related substances) accounted for 3% of all problems. Several classes of anti-hypertensives and hypolipidaemic agents were among the top 15 generic medications consumed (see Appendix 5.2), reflecting the large number of cases managed by general medical practitioners.

For hypolipidaemic medications, 'statins' are the main drugs prescribed. The top two drugs most commonly prescribed are Atorvastatin and Simvastatin, followed by Pravastatin and Fluvastatin. For hypertension, there are at least six different therapeutic classes commonly prescribed, namely diuretics, beta-blockers, calcium antagonists, angiotensin converting enzymes inhibitors, angiotensin receptor antagonist as well as the partial alpha-agonist. Diltiazem, Ramipril, Irbesartan, Irbesartan with hydrochlorothiazide, and Amlodipine, make the top 15 list (see Appendix 5.2). For stroke, the medications commonly prescribed are Clopidogrel 75mg, Dipyridamole/aspirin 200/25mg (Asasantin-SR) and Aspirin 100mg.

In 2001–02, cardiovascular diseases accounted for 441,002 hospital separations (7% of all hospitalisation) in Australia. Coronary heart disease accounted for 36% and stroke for 12% of all cases. Hospitalisation for cardiovascular disease increases rapidly with age. Patients above 55 represent 21% of the total population, but 77% of hospital separations are for cardiovascular diseases. The average length of hospital stay for cardiovascular diseases was 8.1 days in 2001–02 (AIHW 2004). In 1999–00, stroke accounted for the longest hospital stay of 9.7 days and coronary heart disease accounted for 4.5 days (AIHW 2002).

5.3.3   Burden of cardiovascular diseases

In 2000–01, cardiovascular disease accounted for the largest proportion of health system costs in Australia, $5.5 billion or 11.2% of total health system costs (AIHW 2004). Cardiovascular diseases accounted for 22% of the disease burden in Australia in 1996, 33.1% of premature mortality (YLL) and 8.8% of years of equivalent 'healthy' life lost through disease, impairment and disability (YLD) (Mathers et al. 1999).

5.3.4   Cardiovascular medications: Costs

A health program such as the PBS generates costs and benefits directly and indirectly, some internal or tangible and others external or intangible. Direct costs are the resource input consumed directly in the activities of health programs.

As discussed in Section 3.8, direct costs of the PBS include the acquisition costs of medications, external programs costs such as remuneration to pharmacies to dispense and distribute medications, internal programs such as administrative costs of Medicare Australia implementing PBS, monitoring costs, as well as costs of adverse effects arising from medications.

The drugs costs and external program costs of the three cardiovascular medications selected (namely Atorvastatin, Simvastatin and Clopidogrel) are listed in Appendix 5.4. The internal program costs of the PBS include the administrative costs per script as well as the overheads of the PBS program. However, the internal program cost is insignificant when compared with other costs. The costs of adverse drug effects were estimated in Section 5.2.3.

Indirect costs are resource consumption that do not arise due to an activity or a disease; and usually depict changes in production and amount of leisure time, or other indirect effects generated by the health program. Indirect costs are not considered under the PBS submission guidelines (see Department of Health and Ageing 2002 Appendix I).

5.3.5 Cardiovascular medications: Benefits

Improvement in health status

As discussed in Section 5.2.2, coronary heart disease is the most common cause of death in Australia. Clinical studies such as the Myocardial Ischaemia Reduction with Aggressive Cholesterol Lowering (MIRACL) trial demonstrated that intensive lipid lowering significantly reduced the risks of complications of coronary heart diseases such as heart attack, deaths, and myocardial infarction. The MIRACL study was a randomised, double-blind, placebo-controlled trial conducted at 122 centres in North and South America, Europe and Australia, with a sample of 3,086 patients aged over 18 years. Patients were randomised to receive either Atorvastatin 80mg daily or a placebo 24–96 hours after hospitalisation for acute coronary syndrome for 16 weeks. The results demonstrated that intensive lipid lowering significantly reduced the risk of primary combined endpoints such as death, non-fatal acute myocardial infarction (AMI), cardiac arrest with resuscitation or recurrent symptomatic myocardial ischaemia with objective evidence requiring emergency hospitalisation.

Improvement in productivity

As discussed in Section 5.2.3, the average wage is $145.00 for an 8-hour working day. In 1999–2000, the average length of hospitalisation was 9.7 days for stroke and 4.5 days for coronary heart disease. The increase in productivity as a result of decreased amount of sick leave due to avoidance of hospitalisation is $1,406.50 (9.7 days × $145/day) in the case of stroke, and $625.50 (4.5 days × $145/day) in case of coronary heart diseases. The increase in productivity due to a decrease in visits to medical practitioners is estimated in Section 5.3.

Avoidance of hospitalisation cost

The results of the MIRACL study demonstrated that intensive lipid lowering significantly reduced the risk of primary combined endpoint as well as the risk of stroke or recurrent symptomatic myocardial ischaemia. From Table 5.2, the average cost per patient day for cardiovascular type of hospital separation is $999.02. The cost avoidance of an episode of hospital separation is $9,690.50 ($999.02 × 9.7 days) for stroke and $4,495.59 ($999.02 × 4.5 days) for coronary heart diseases.

Decrease in visits to general and specialist medical practitioners

Assuming that their cardiovascular conditions are under control, patients attend their general and specialist medical practitioners on a less regular basis. The cost savings of these reduced service consumption are calculated in Section 5.2.3.

Increase in life expectancy

Cardiovascular diseases have been the leading cause of death in Australia for the last eight decades. With the improvement in medical technology, the death rates of cardiovascular diseases have steadily declined and the life expectancy of patients has improved. Twenty-one per cent of the population is over 55 years of age. These patients account for 75% of the hospital separations for cardiovascular diseases. Once over 65 years of age, cardiovascular diseases surpass the other causes as the leading cause of death.

Assuming that the average life expectancy from birth is 80 years of age (82 for females and 76.6 for males), there are potentially 10–15 years of life lost prematurely if there is no health intervention. Cardiovascular diseases accounts for 9% of years of equivalent 'healthy' life lost through disease, impairment and disability (AIHW 2004). If cardiovascular conditions are monitored and controlled, the number of healthy life-years lost can be reduced. Using expert opinion and social value judgement, the author assumed that the number of healthy life-years lost is 1.35 years (9% × 15 years) through cardiovascular diseases in the absence of intervention.

Atorvastatin achieves a relative risk reduction of coronary events by 36% and that of non-fatal myocardial infarction by 45% (Sever et al. 2003). With the scientific information available, the author assumes that Atorvastatin achieves a relative risk reduction of 40% for coronary heart diseases. This translates into an improvement of 0.54 healthy life-years (40% × 1.35 years). As discussed in Section 5.2.3, the values of QALY range from $35,395 to $611,837. The lower estimate of $35,395 per year is used and the benefit of improved life expectancy for Atorvastatin is calculated as $19,113.30 (0.54 years × $35,395/year).

Clopidogrel achieves a relative risk reduction of primary end-points (death, myocardial infarction, stroke and re-hospitalisation) of 36.3% (Durand-Zaleski and Bertrand 2004). Using the above scientific information, the author assumes that Clopidogrel achieves an improvement of 0.5 healthy life-years (36.3% × 1.35 years) in the case of stroke. Using the lower estimate of $35,395 per year, the benefit of improved life expectancy for Clopidogrel is calculated as $17,697.50 (0.5 years × $35,395/year).

Complementary medications

As discussed in Section 5.2.3, patients may resort to alternative medicines to control conditions if their medical conditions are not properly controlled and maintained. In the case of cardiovascular conditions, complementary medications in the form of vitamins and herbal preparations (such as Polcosanol, Basikol, fish oil capsules, and Coenzymes Q10) are common alternatives. A monthly supply of such complementary medicines ranges from $20.00 to $50.00. If the cardiovascular conditions are controlled, this represents a substantial saving for patients by not consuming complementary medicines. Based on the authors' judgement, the saving is estimated to be about $400 per year.

5.4   Type 2 diabetes mellitus

Diabetes mellitus has become a worldwide epidemic. In 1995, an estimated 135 million people had diabetes and by the year 2025 the number of diabetic patients is expected to reach 300 million worldwide (Ettaro et al. 2004). Diabetes mellitus is a chronic metabolic disorder characterised by inherited and/or acquired deficiency in the production of insulin by the pancreas or by resistance of tissues to insulin. Insulin is the hormone involved in the metabolism of carbohydrates, proteins and lipids of the body. Consequently, diabetic patients are presented with an elevated blood glucose level because the body cannot produce sufficient insulin or cannot use insulin effectively to regulate the blood glucose level. In 2002, diabetes was the ninth and tenth leading cause of death in Australia among males and female (AIHW 2004). Diabetes mellitus contributes to significant illness, disability, diabetes, poor quality of life and premature mortality. Elevated blood glucose levels damage blood vessels and end organs supplied by blood vessels such as eyes, kidneys, and nerves.

In type 1 diabetes, there is a failure in production of insulin as a result of β cell destruction in the Islet of Langerhans of the pancreas. Type 1 diabetes is often diagnosed in childhood or adolescents, accounting for 5 to 10% of the cases. Most of the remaining cases are type 2 diabetes (Foster and Plosker 2002). Type 2 diabetes is the predominant form existing among middle-aged and elderly persons on account of a rapid increase in its prevalence after the age of 45. Type 2 diabetes is characterised by a reduced level of insulin or insulin resistance. Type 2 diabetes is the most common among people over 45 years of age and accounts for 85–90% of all diabetic patients. The risk factors of type 2 diabetes include obesity and ethnicity (AIHW 2002).

5.4.1   Incidence

The Australian Diabetes, Obesity and Lifestyle Study (AusDiab) was conducted in 1999 and 2000 to determine the prevalence of diabetes, obesity and other cardiovascular disease risk factors including behavioural and biomedical risk factors, such as high blood pressure and abnormal lipid profiles.

The AusDiab study estimated that about 1 million Australians aged 25 or over had diabetes, 7.6% of the population. The prevalence increased with age, from less than 1% for those aged below 45 to 10% in those aged 65–74 (AIHW 2004). Type 2 diabetes is the predominant form among middle-aged and elderly people with the rapid increase in prevalence after the age of 45. The prevalence rates of diabetes in Australia increased dramatically in the last 20 years, with obesity being a significant contributing factor. The prevalence rate was 7.6% in 2001 as compared with 3.4% in 1981 (Dunstan et al. 2002).

5.4.2   Diabetes-related complications

Poorly controlled diabetes leads to a range of macro-vascular and micro-vascular complications. Macro-vascular complications range from coronary heart diseases, to stroke and peripheral vascular diseases. Micro-vascular complications include conditions such as nephropathy, neuropathy and retinopathy. The risk of micro-vascular complications is the same in both type 1 and type 2 diabetes. Macro-vascular complications are more common among type 2 diabetes.

In addition to uncontrolled glucose levels and duration of disease, other risk factors contributing to complications include age, genetic predisposition, obesity, high blood pressure, high cholesterol and tobacco smoking. Avoidance or reduction of risk-increasing behaviours and conditions can delay the onset or slow the progression of complications associated with diabetes. Diabetes share several risk factors with cardiovascular diseases and is itself is a risk factor for cardiovascular disease.

5.4.3   Health services consumed

From Table 5.9 above, diabetic patients are more likely to suffer other cardiovascular conditions and kidney diseases as compared with non-diabetic patients. Diabetic patients are thus more likely to consult health professionals or use hospital services. This higher rate is related to treatment for blood glucose control, diabetic complications, as well as other medical conditions of the diabetic patients. According to the BEACH survey 2002–03, diabetes represented 2%

Table 5.9   **Prevalence of medical conditions with and without diabetes**

	Incidence (%), AusDiab study 1999–2000	
Condition	Diabetic patients	Patients without diabetes
Hypertension	69.3	25.8
Angina	16.9	3.8
Heart attack	11.8	2.7
Stroke	9.3	1.7
Kidney disease	6.8	1.5

Source: Australia's Health 2002 (AIHW 2002 p. 69).

of all problems managed by general medical practitioners and 2.9% of all consultations. In addition to blood glucose level control, other concomitant problems of diabetic patients include hypertension, lipid disorder and osteoarthritis.

In 2001–02, diabetes was the principal diagnosis in 53,224 hospital separations or 0.8% of all hospital separations. Diabetes was often reported as an additional diagnosis rather than the principal diagnosis, particularly in association with primary diagnoses of coronary heart disease, stroke and kidney disease. When separations for diabetes as the principal diagnosis and as an additional diagnosis are combined, the total number rises to 389,940 or 6.1% (AIHW 2004).

The impact of diabetes on the health system is further increased by the long periods that patients with diabetes spend in hospital. The average length of stay in hospital with diabetes as principal diagnosis is 10 days in 1999–00 (compared with nine days for all other diagnoses). When diabetes as an additional diagnosis is included, the average length of stay increased to 11 days.

5.4.4   Mortality and burden of diabetes

Diabetes was the underlying cause of 3,329 deaths or 2.5% of all deaths in 2002, but it was listed as an associated cause in 11,467 deaths (AIHW 2004). Diabetes is rarely listed as the sole cause of death, only in 1.7% of the cases. Diabetes is listed as the associated causes of death with coronary heart diseases (50% of the cases), stroke (22%) and renal failure (15.0%).

The chronic nature of diabetes and its devastating complications make it a very costly disease. Diabetes accounted for 3% of the disease burden in Australia in 1996. 2% of years of life are lost due to premature mortality as a result of diabetes. Diabetes and its complication were also responsible for much disability in 1996, 4% of years of 'healthy' life (YLD) lost due to poor health or disability (AIHW 2004).

As a result of the high impact of the disease, a substantial proportion of healthcare expenditure is spent on diabetes and its complications. The direct costs of diabetes and its complications in 1993–94 were estimated to be $681 million or 2.2% of total health system costs (Mathers et al. 1999; AIHW 2004). Examples of direct and indirect costs of Type 2 diabetes are listed in Appendix 5.5.

5.4.5   Type 2 diabetes medications: Costs

As discussed in Section 3.8, direct costs of type 2 diabetes medications include acquisition costs of medications, external program costs such as remuneration to pharmacy, as well internal program costs of administration of the PBS, as well as the cost of adverse drug effects. The medications commonly prescribed for type 2 diabetes include Sulphonylureas (Gliclazide, Glipizide, Gliclazide and Glimepiride), Biguanide (Metformin) and Thiazolidinediones (Pioglitazone and Rosiglitazone).

The acquisition costs and external program costs of these medications are listed in Appendix 5.6. As discussed in Section 5.2.3, the internal program cost of the PBS is insignificant. Costs of adverse drug effects are estimated in Section 5.2.3. Indirect costs are resource consumption that does not arise due to an activity or a disease. Under the PBAC submission guidelines, only direct costs are considered, but not indirect costs.

5.4.6   Type 2 diabetes medications: Benefits

Improvement in health status

Poor glycaemic control in diabetic patients is associated with chronic complications, may lead to premature death or disabilities. Research studies have shown that improved glycaemic control substantially decreases the risks of micro-vascular complications such as retinopathy and nephropathy (Stratton et al. 2000).

Correction of hyperglycaemia and improved glycaemic control helps to alleviate diabetes-related symptoms such as polyuria, polydipsia, polyphagia, bodyweight loss, fatigue, blurred vision, cognitive dysfunction and susceptibility to infection and to prevent ketoaci-dosis and hyperglycaemic nonketonic syndrome.

Improvement in productivity

As discussed in section 5.2.3, the average wage for an 8-hour day is $145.00. The average length of hospital stay for patients with dia-betes as the principal diagnosis in Australia in 2001–02 is ten days. When hospital separations for diabetes as an additional diagnosis are taken into considerations, the average length of hospital stays increases to 11 days (AIHW 2004).

Hospitalisation could be avoided with intensive control of blood glucose, blood pressure and lipid profiles of diabetic patients. Using the clinical information above, the increase in productivity as a result of decreased amount of work days lost due to avoidance of hospitalisation is $1,595.00 (11 days × $145/day) in case of diabetes mellitus. The increase in productivity due to decrease in visits to medical practitioners is estimated in Section 5.3.

Avoidance of hospitalisation cost

The results of the Diabetes Control and Complications Trails (DCCT) and the United Kingdom Prospective Diabetes Study (UKPDS) demonstrated the benefits of intensive glycaemic control, with normoglycaemia as the treatment goal in diabetic patients. Maintenance of normoglycaemia significantly reduced the risk of clinical endpoint of macro-vascular complications (such as myocar-dial infarction and stroke) and of micro-vascular complications (such as nephropathy, retinopathy and neuropathy). As seen in Table 5.2, the average cost per patient day for endocrine, nutritional and metabolic type of hospital separation is $789.42. The cost avoidance of an episode of hospital separation for type 2 diabetes is $8,683.62 ($789.42/day × 11 days).

Decrease in visits to general medical practitioners

Assuming that their diabetic conditions (such as blood glucose level, blood pressure and cholesterol levels) are under control, there is lesser need for patients to attend their general and specialist medical practitioners. The cost savings from decrease visits to general and specialist medical practitioners are calculated in Section 5.2.3.

Increase in life expectancy

Diabetes is rarely listed as the only cause of death, accounting for less than 1.5% of deaths in 2000. However, diabetes is frequently listed as the associated cause of death included with in 51% cases of coronary heart disease, 22.6% cases of kidney-related diseases, 21.4% cases of stroke and 18.6% cases of heart failure. A Pioglitazone-based strategy was estimated to reduce the cumulative incidence of severe clinical events and long-term complications by between 23 and 36%, and to increase discounted life expectancy by between 0.13 and 0.35 life-years (Coyle et al. 2002). By using the clinical information above, the benefits of increased life expectancy of Pioglitazone is $12,388.25 (0.35 years × $35,395/year).

Complementary medications

As discussed in Section 5.2.3, patients venture with complementary medicines (e.g. vitamins, herbal remedies, and others) when their diabetic conditions are not controlled. With successful medication therapy with Pioglitazone, the diabetic conditions of patients are assumed to be controlled and monitored; they are less likely to consume complementary medications for their condition. This represents a substantial saving of $400 annually for patients as estimated in Section 5.2.3.

5.5 Breast cancer

Cancer is a diverse group of diseases in which different parts of the body can be involved. Cancer cells are different from normal cells in four aspects, namely clonality, autonomy, anaplasia and metastasis. Cancer originates from a single stem cell and proliferates to form a clone of malignant cells. Growth of cancer cells is not regulated by normal biochemical and physical influences in the environment. There is a lack of normal, coordinated cell differentiation. Cancer cells develop the capacity for discontinuous growth and dissemination into other parts of the body.

5.5.1 Incidence and mortality

In 2002, cancer accounted for 37,622 deaths in Australia or 28.1% of all deaths (see Table 5.5), 21,041 males and 16,581 females giving age-standardised rates of 241 per 100,000 for males and 150 per 100,000 for females. Breast cancer was the leading cause of death, accounting for 16% of all deaths among females, followed by lung cancer (15.0%) and colon-rectal cancer (13.0%). The incidence of breast cancer has been on the rise since the early 1980s, but the death rate remains relatively stable over the period. The death rate of breast cancer is 24.9 deaths per 100,000 in 1980 and 23.0 deaths per 100,000 in 1998. Improvement in earlier detection and treatment, as well as the effects of screening programs contribute to the relative reduction of mortality (AIHW 2004).

5.5.2   Survival following cancer diagnosis

Survival after a diagnosis of cancer is a measure used in assessing the impacts of early detection methods such as screening and treatment. The five-year relative survival proportion is the ratio between what actually happened to a group of people with cancer and what would normally have occurred to them in the absence of cancer over the first five-year following a diagnosis of cancer. Relating to the diagnosis periods 1982–86 and 1992–94, five-year survival for all registrable cancers increased on average from 55.3% to 63.4% for females, and that for breast cancer increased from 72.3% to 84.4% (see Appendix 5.7).

5.5.3   Burden of breast cancer

Cancer caused 19% of the disease burden in Australia in 1996, and accounted 30% of years of life lost due to premature mortality (YLL) and 7% of years of 'healthy' life lost due to poor health or disability (YLD) (Mathers et al. 1999). Breast cancer is the leading cause of the cancer burden among females, accounting for 24% of that burden in 1996 (AIHW 2004). The life-time risk of developing breast cancer before 75 years of age is one in 11. The total health cost for female breast cancer was estimated to be $184 million in 1993–94.

5.5.4   Breast cancer medications: Costs

Aromatase is a critical enzyme in the biosynthetic pathway of local production of oestrogen in breast tissue, promoting the carcinogenic process in breast cancer. Letrozole (Femara®) is a third-generation aromatase inhibitor, competitively binding to the haem-region of the aromatase (Higa 2000). Apart from Letrozole, Tamoxifen is an anti-oestrogen that is commonly used in treating breast cancer. As discussed in Section 3.8, direct costs of breast cancer medications include acquisition cost of medications, external program costs such as pharmacy remuneration, as well as internal program costs of administration of the PBS, costs of adverse reactions and other social costs. Acquisition costs and external program costs of Letrozole and Tamoxifen are listed Appendix 5.8. The internal program costs are considered insignificant in the analysis. The costs of adverse drug effects are estimated in Section 5.2.3.

5.5.5 Breast cancer medications: Benefits

Avoidance of hospitalisation cost

As discussed in Table 5.2, the average cost per patient day for hospitalisation of neoplastic disorder is $751.13 and the average length of hospital stay is 7.45 days (AIHW 2004). According to the above clinical information, the cost savings of avoidance of hospitalisation of Pioglitazone is calculated to be $5,592.92 ($751.13/day × 7.45 days).

Decrease in visits to general and specialist medical practitioners

Assuming that the conditions of breast cancer are under control, patients attend their general and specialist medical practitioners on a less regular basis. The cost savings from reduced health service consumption are estimated in Section 5.2.3.

Increase in productivity

The average length of hospital stay of the cancer category is 7.45 days. Should hospitalisation be avoided, the loss of work days can be avoided. The increase in productivity of Pioglitazone is calculated to be $1,080.25 (7.45 days × $145.00/day). The increase in productivity due to decrease in visits to medical practitioners is estimated in Section 5.2.3.

Increase in life expectancy

Clinical studies showed that patient receiving Letrozole (Femara®) 2.5mg daily gain an additional 0.714 life-years as compared with patient receiving Tamoxifen 20mg daily (Karnon and Jones 2003). By using the above clinical information and the lower estimates of QALY of $35,395 per year from Table 5.7, the benefit of increased life expectancy for Letrozole is calculated to be $25,272.03 ($35,395/year × 0.714 years).

Complementary medications

When the breast cancer condition is not under control, patients are more likely to resort to complementary medicines (such as vitamins and herbal preparation) or other alternative therapy. With successful medication therapy, patients' cancer conditions go into remission; they are less likely to resort to complementary medicines. The saving for patients and is estimated in Section 5.2.3.

5.6   Respiratory diseases

5.6.1   Asthma and chronic obstructive pulmonary diseases

Asthma and chronic obstructive pulmonary diseases (COPD) are two major respiratory conditions contributing to the disease burden of Australia.

Asthma affects 100 million people worldwide and is one of most common chronic conditions in industrialised countries (Lamb et al. 2000; Markham 2000; Sheth 2002; Lyseng-Williamson 2003). Asthma is a chronic inflammatory disorder of the airways characterised by increased responsiveness of the tracheobronchial tree to multiple stimuli. Asthma is manifested by bronchoconstriction that may be relieved spontaneously or as a result of therapy. It is an episodic disease with reversible symptoms of airflow obstruction. Without proper clinical management, an asthmatic episode can be fatal. Asthmatic patients can experience reduced quality of life and require a range of health services, from general medical practitioner care to emergency department visits or hospital in-patient care.

COPD is characterised by a chronic obstruction to airflow due to chronic bronchitis or emphysema. It is a permanent and progressive disease of the lung. Chronic bronchitis and emphysema are two distinct processes but often coexist. Chronic bronchitis is a condition associated with excessive tracheobronchial mucus production sufficient to cause cough with expectoration for at least three months per year for more than two consecutive years. Emphysema is defined as a distention of the air spaces distal to the terminal bronchiole with destruction of alveolar septa.

5.6.2   Incidence and mortality

According to the National Health Survey 2001, there were approximately 2.2 million (12%) people in Australia suffering from asthma (ABS 2002). Asthma prevalence was the highest among the 5–14-year-olds at 19.2%, followed by 15–24-year-olds at 14.9%. The incidence of asthma increased markedly over the past decade, from 8.5% in the 1989–90 National Health Survey, to 11.5% in 1995 and 12% in 2001.

According to the National Health Survey 2001, there were almost 665,000 (3.5%) people with COPD in Australia (AIHW 2004). The prevalence of the condition based on self-reporting is often underestimated because the disease is only diagnosed at an advanced stage when the disease starts to restrict the lifestyle of the patient.

Asthma was the cause of 397 deaths, 0.3% of all deaths in Australia in 2002 (see Table 5.5). The death rates increased markedly after the age of 50, to 32.2 deaths per 100,000 for patients over 85 years of age. The asthma of older patients is often complicated by the presence of COPD (AIHW 2002). In 2002, COPD was the underlying cause for 5,599 deaths, or 4.2% of all deaths (AIHW 2004).

5.6.3   Health services consumed

In 2001–02, asthma was the principal diagnosis for 40,918 hospital separations, or 0.8% of all hospital separations, with an average length of stay of 2.5 days (AIHW 2004). It was one of the most common reasons for hospitalisation among children aged 0–14. Asthma is often reported as an additional diagnosis in hospital separations, with principal diagnoses of pneumonia, cataract and heart conditions such as angina. A significant proportion of total costs with asthma is due to poor control of the disease, which leads to exacerbations of the condition, thus requiring hospitalisation and emergency visit (Sheth et al. 2002).

COPD is one of the major causes of hospitalisation among the elderly. In 2001–02, COPD was principal diagnosis of 51,621 (0.8%) hospital separations, 39,748 (77%) hospital separations found among patients over 65 years of age. The average length of stay is 7.5 days.

Asthma is one of the most common reasons for visits to emergency departments. In the National Health Survey 1995, an estimated 8,870 asthmatic patients visited a hospital emergency department, and 349 patients had more than one visit. Almost half of the admissions to hospital emergency departments occurred in those aged 0–9 years. Asthma is a major problem managed in the primary health care setting, being the sixth most frequently managed problem by general medical practitioners. A survey of general practice in 2002–03 found that asthma accounted for 2.9% of GP visits. Medications were the most common treatment for asthma prescribed by general medical practitioners. Salbutamol was the most frequent medication prescribed and was the fifth most prescribed medication by general medical practitioners with 4.4 million prescriptions in 2002–03 (AIHW 2004).

COPD was the eighth most frequently managed disease of the respiratory systems, accounting for 3.2% of all problems, and represented 0.5% of all problems managed by general medical practitioners (AIHW 2002). Patients over 45 years of age with COPD required the most care by general medical practitioners.

5.6.4   Burden of asthma and chronic obstructive pulmonary disease

Both asthma and COPD are significantly causes of disability and reduction in quality of life. From the 1998 Survey of Disability, Ageing and Carers, it was estimated that more than 170,902 patients cited asthma and 52,906 patients cited COPD as their main disabling conditions (AIHW 2002).

Cost estimates for asthma indication from developed countries accounts for 2% of the economic cost of all diseases. The cost per asthmatic patient varies between $429 to $1,857 (1991 values) per year in Australia, Canada, Sweden, UK and the US (Markham 2000; Lamb 2000).

Worldwide, COPD is a leading cause of disability, measured by life-years-lost (LYL) and disability-adjusted life-years (DALYs). By 2020, chronic obstructive pulmonary disease is expected to be the fifth leading cause of DALYs, contributing to 4% of the total DALYs. This is compared with 2% in 1990 (Rutten von Molken and Feenstra 2001)

In 1996, asthma accounted for 3% of the disease burden of Australia, 1% of years of life lost due to premature mortality and 5% of 'healthy' life lost due to poor health and disability. COPD was estimated accounted for 4% of the disease burden of Australia, 4% of years of life lost due to premature mortality and 3% of 'healthy' life lost due to poor health and disability (AIHW 2004).

5.6.5 Respiratory medications used in asthma and COPD: Costs

As discussed in Section 3.8, direct costs of respiratory medications used in asthma and COPD include acquisition costs of medications, external program costs such as pharmacy remuneration, as well as internal program costs of the PBS, costs of adverse reactions and other social costs.

The clinical goal of asthma management is to minimise symptoms, exacerbations, use of 'reliever' medications (such as Salbutamol or Terbutaline), and adverse effects of medications, and to maintain optimal peak expiratory flow values and normal activity levels. Treatment of an underlying airway inflammation with corticosteroid aims to prevent the exacerbation of the conditions resulting in excess muscus production, bronchoconstriction, wheezing and shortness of breath.

A long-acting inhaled β_2-agonist plus an inhaled corticosteroid, such as Salmeterol/fluticasone (Seretide®) is recommended for initial maintenance treatments for patients with moderate and severe asthma. Inhaled bronchodilators such as anti-cholinergic agents (such as Tiotropium) and β adrenergic agonists (such as Salbutamol) are the main therapy for patients with Chronic Obstructive Pulmonary Disease). Tiotropium (Spiriva®) is used for long-term maintenance of bronchoplasm and dyspnoea associated with COPD.

Acquisition costs and external program costs of Salmeterol/fluticasone and Tiotropium are listed in Appendix 5.9. Costs of adverse drug effects are estimated in Section 5.2.3. As discussed in previous sections, the internal program cost is insignificant when compared with other costs.

5.6.6 Respiratory medications used in asthma and COPD: Benefits

Improvement in health status

In Australia in 1992, asthma was estimated to cause 523,000 lost work days and 965,000 lost school days accounting for $110 to $120 million per year (Lamb 2000), mainly due to poor asthmatic control. Management guidelines, such as the six-point asthma management plan from the National Asthma Council of Australia, are developed to encourage preventer therapy in order to reduce the cost of asthma-related morbidity. Symptoms of asthma impair the quality of life of a patient. Asthmatic symptoms include shortness of breath, wheezing, chest tightness, and coughing. All these affect the ability of an asthmatic patient to perform daily activities. The Asthma Quality of Life Questionnaire (AQLQ) is a questionnaire consisting of 32 items divided into four domains, namely symptoms, emotional function, activity limitation and environmental stimuli. AQLQ is used to assess the clinical efficacy of inhaled Salmeterol/fluticasone that shows significant improvement when compared with monotherapy. Salmeterol/fluticasone has a dual action as both reliever and preventer for Asthma, and is only administered twice daily; and is a better alternative when compared with separate therapies of preventer and reliever (which can be dosed up to every four hours).

Exacerbations of COPD contribute substantially to the burdens of the disease and significantly reduce the quality of life for patients (Friedmann and Hilleman 2001). Tiotropium helps to provide relief of bronchodilation for patients with COPD. The once daily administration of Tiotropium 18mcg via handihaler is easier when compared with the four times daily administration of inhaled ipratropium and salbutamol via inhaler or nebulisers. The convenience in dosing regimen of Tiotropium helps to increase the medication compliance and the quality of life of COPD patients.

Avoidance of hospitalisation cost

As seen in Table 5.2, the average cost per patient day for hospitalisation of respiratory disorder is $658.73. The average length of hospital stay is 2.5 days for asthma and 7.5 days for COPD. Using the clinical information above, the cost savings of avoidance of hospitalisation for asthma is calculated to be $1,646.83 ($658.73/day × 2.5 days) and that for COPD is calculated to be $4,940.78 ($658.73/day × 7.5 days).

Decrease in visits to general medical practitioners

Assuming that the respiratory conditions of patients are monitored and controlled, there is less need to attend general and specialist medical practitioners. The cost savings from reduced health services consumption are estimated in Section 5.2.3.

Improvement in productivity

As discussed in Section 5.2.3, the average earning for an 8-hour day is $145.00 in 2002. The average length of hospital stay for patients with asthma as principal diagnosis in Australia in 2001–02 is 2.5 days and that for COPD is 7.5 days. Hospitalisation could be avoided with optimal asthmatic control of the patients. The increase in productivity as a result of decreased amount of sick leave due to avoidance of hospitalisation is $362.50 (2.5 days × $145/day) in the case of asthma, and $1,087.50 (7.5 days × $145/day) in the case of COPD. The increase in productivity due to decrease in visits to medical practitioners is estimated in Section 5.2.3.

Increase in life expectancy

Asthma is listed as the underlying cause of 397 deaths accounting for 0.3% of all deaths in 2002. The death rates remain low during early and middle adult life and increases markedly after 50 years of age. COPD is a major cause of mortality in Australia, accounting for 5,599 deaths (4.2%) in 2002, usually among older patients particularly over 70 years of age.

Respiratory diseases are the third major cause of death for patients over 45 years of age. Assuming that the average life expectancy from birth is 80 years of age (82 for females and 76.6 for males), there are potentially 30–35 years of life lost prematurely if there is no health intervention. Respiratory diseases, especially COPD, accounts for 2% of years of equivalent 'healthy' life-years lost through disease, impairment and disability (Rutten von Molken and Feenstra 2001). If the control of asthma and COPD are maintained at an optimal level, the risk of complications (such as infections and pneumonia) is reduced and premature death can be avoided. Using clinical information above and the authors' opinion and judgement, we assumed that 0.7 'healthy' life-years (2% × 35 years) lost is prevented. Using the lower estimates of $35,395/year from Table 5.7, benefit of increased life expectancy for Salmeterol/fluticasone and Tiotropium is estimated to be $24,776.50 ($35,395/year × 0.7 years).

Complementary medications

If the respiratory conditions of patients are controlled, they are less likely to resort to complementary medicines. This represents a substantial saving for the patients and is estimated in Section 5.2.3.

5.7 Conclusion

This chapter has provided the detailed estimates of costs and benefits of the six medications selected, namely Atorvastatin, Clopidogrel, Pioglitazone, Letrozole, Salmeterol/fluticasone and Tiotropium.

The general principles and assumptions in calculating the numerical estimates of costs and benefits of medications are discussed in Section 5.2. In the cost stream, the numerical estimates include acquisition costs of medications, external program costs such as pharmacy remuneration, internal program costs of administering the PBS, costs of adverse reactions as well as the social costs.

In the benefit stream, numerical estimates include cost avoidance of hospitalisation, cost saving from reduced consumption of health services due to improved health status, improvement in economic productivity, cost savings due to reduced consumption of complementary medicines, as well as benefits of improved life expectancy. Clinical information, when available, is used in estimating benefits of the medications. In the absence of published clinical data, authors' expert opinions and social value judgements are use in the benefit estimates of the medications.

The principles are then applied to calculate the numerical estimate of the six medications, namely Atorvastatin, Clopidogrel, Pioglitazone, Letrozole, Salmeterol/fluticasone and Tiotropium. With these estimates of costs and benefits, the cost benefit analysis of these six medications for PBS listing is discussed in the next chapter.

6
New[3] Cost Benefit Analysis of PBS Medications

6.1 Introduction

In this chapter, six medications are selected for hypothetical cost benefit analysis under the type of criteria listed under the Pharmaceutical Benefit Advisory Committee (PBAC) submission guidelines, the standard approach of financial cost benefit analysis and the new[3] cost benefit analysis under the normative social choice approach of new[3] welfare economics.

As discussed in Chapter 5, the six medications are chosen due to the prevalence of medical conditions as well as their burden of disease to the Australian society. Atorvastatin and Clopidogrel are selected for cardiovascular diseases which account for 70% of the total burden of diseases in Australia. Pioglitazone is selected for type 2 diabetes which is a growing epidemic worldwide. Letrozole is selected for breast cancer which is the most common cancer diagnosed among Australian females. Fluticasone/Salmeterol and Tiotropium are selected for respiratory diseases that account for significant mortality and morbidity of the society.

6.2 General framework of cost benefit analysis calculations

The general principles of estimating the costs and benefits of medications for the selected medical conditions are discussed in Chapter 5. These estimates are then applied into the hypothetical

133

cost benefit analysis under the PBAC type of criteria, the financial cost benefit analysis and the new[3] cost benefit analysis.

As discussed in Chapter 5, the analysis is divided into the cost and benefit streams over a period of five years because all the six medical conditions selected are chronic in nature. All costs and benefits of the medication are allocated over the five years and discounted to present values for comparison.

As discussed in Section 2.6, social costs and social benefits (in addition to financial costs and benefits) are evaluated in monetary terms in the cost benefit calculation. A social discount rate of 0% is used to address the issues of intergenerational equity, as health gain in the future is as important as the current health gain. Individual preference is taken into consideration by estimating the willingness-to-pay (WTP) for the medication in the absence of government subsidy.

6.2.1 The cost stream

Under the cost stream, five different costs are identified, namely costs of medications, the external and internal administration costs of the Pharmaceutical Benefits Scheme (PBS), cost of adverse drug effects, as well as the social costs.

As discussed in Chapter 5, the cost of medication is the acquisition cost and is derived from negotiation between the Pharmaceutical Benefits Pricing Authority (PBPA) and pharmaceutical companies. For medications listed on PBS under Section 85 of the *National Health Act*, the acquisition cost of the medication is the 'approved price to pharmacist'. For medications listed on PBS under Section 100 of the *National Health Act*, the acquisition cost of the medication is the 'ex-manufacturer price'. The acquisition cost of medications is listed under the Schedule of Pharmaceutical Benefits published by the Medicare Australia on its website as well as in hardcopy format. Copies of Schedule of Pharmaceutical Benefits are distributed to approved pharmacists and medical practitioners.

The external administration cost of the PBS is the remuneration or government recovery paid to the community or hospital pharmacy for dispensing the prescriptions of the medications. Costs to the government vary according to the entitlement status of the patients. As discussed in Chapters 4 and 5, pharmacy remuneration is specified in the Community Pharmacy Agreement negotiated between the government and the Pharmacy Guild of Australia once every five years.

Assuming that patients fill their prescription monthly, the annual cost of medication is calculated by the multiplying the unit cost of medication by twelve. The external administration cost is calculated by 12 times the maximum government recovery that would be paid for such medications. Although the costs of medications and pharmacy remuneration may change monthly, the fluctuation is usually minimal in the time frame of the calculation. The same annual figures for cost of medication and those for external administration cost are used for the five-year period of the analysis.

The internal administrative cost is the operating cost of the PBS by the Medicare Australia. This is generally insignificant when compared to other costs and is not considered in the cost benefit calculation.

Any medications may have adverse effects, even when patients use their medications correctly. Although the incidence of drug adverse effects, a cost estimate of $29.60 for adverse drug effects is derived from clinical information and is included as the cost stream of the analysis (see Section 5.2.3 for estimates of adverse drug effects).

The social cost is the opportunity cost forgone if the fund (or money) is used to pay for the medications. For the medication conditions discussed, there are a number of different medications available. The social cost of a medication is calculated by the difference between the monthly cost of the medication and that of the cheaper alternatives. That annual social cost is estimated as 12 times that difference in cost.

6.2.2 The benefit stream

As discussed in Chapter 5, benefits are estimated in the form of increase in economic productivity, cost savings as a result of avoidance of hospitalisation, cost savings due to decrease in consumption of health services (visits to medical practitioners), and of complementary medicines due to improved health status, improved life expectancy and WTP of medications in the form of private prescriptions.

Using the clinical information of the average length of stay of the various medical conditions, cost savings from avoidance of hospitalisation is calculated by multiplying the duration of hospitalisation with the average daily cost of that particular category of hospital separation (see Table 5.2). Increase in economic productivity due to avoidance of hospitalisation is estimated as the average length of hospital stay multiplied by daily wage rate of $145.00.

Increase in economic productivity is calculated by multiplying a daily wage rate of $145.00 with the number of days off work due to hospitalisation and medical consultation. The increase in economic productivity due to reduction of visits to general and medical practitioners is a fixed estimate (see Table 5.1). The cost savings from decrease in visits to general and specialist medical practitioners are estimated in Tables 5.3 and 5.4. As discussed in Section 5.2.3, an annual saving of about $400.00 is estimated for reduced consumption of complementary medicines with improvement of health status. The above benefit estimates are from authors' expert opinions and social value judgements.

In estimating the benefits of improved life expectancy, a lower estimate of $35,395 per Quality Adjusted life-year (QALY) under the WTP approach is used in this calculation (see Tables 5.6 and 5.7). The number of QALY gained by using the medication is quoted from scientific information from clinical journals. If such published clinical information is not available, the authors estimated the number of QALY gained (by the medication) by using expert opinions and social value judgement. The benefit of the medication is calculated by multiplying the value of quality adjusted life-year with the number of QALY gained by using the medication.

WTP of a patient is calculated by the amount a patient will pay for that medication in the absence of a government subsidy. According to the recommendation from the Pharmacy Guild of Australia, the price of the medication on private script is calculated by a 10% markup of the cost of medication plus $6.75 dispensing fee.

The general principles of numerical estimates for costs and benefits of individual medications for the selected conditions are discussed in Section 5.2. In the remaining part of this chapter, these principles are applied to the hypothetical cost benefit analysis of the six medications under the PBAC type of submission criteria, the financial cost benefit analysis approach and the new[3] cost benefit analysis. Section 6.3 is the cost benefit analysis for Atorvastatin,

Section 6.4 is for Clopidogrel, Section 6.5 is for Pioglitazone, and Section 6.6 is for Letrozole. Section 6.7 is for Fluticasone/Salmeterol and Section 6.8 for Tiotropium. Section 6.9 is the conclusion.

6.3   Cost benefit analysis of Atorvastatin 40mg

Atorvastatin (Lipitor®) is the most commonly prescribed medication on the PBS in 2003 (see Appendix 5.1). 3-hydroxy-3-methylglutaryl-coenzyme A (HMG-CoA) reductase is the rate-controlling enzyme in the biosynthetic pathway for cholesterol. Atorvastatin is a HMG-CoA reductase inhibitor that blocks hepatic cholesterol synthesis, triggering compensatory reactions that lead to the reduction in plasma low density lipoprotein (LDL).

Atorvastatin is prescribed to control blood lipid profile and to prevent atherosclerosis (hardening and thickening of blood vessel). A daily dose of 40mg Atorvastatin is commonly prescribed to control hyperlipidaemia and to prevent heart attack and control coronary heart disease. The calculation is performed under the hypothetical cost benefit analysis of PBAC type of criteria, of financial cost benefit analysis, and of new³ cost benefit analysis.

6.3.1   Hypothetical cost benefit analysis of Atorvastatin 40mg under PBAC type of criteria

The cost stream

As discussed in Sections 5.3.4 and 6.2.1, costs of medication, external program costs and costs for adverse drug effects are included in the hypothetical cost benefit analysis under the PBAC type of submission criteria. Internal program costs are considered insignificant to be included in the calculation. Social costs and other indirect costs are not considered under the PBAC submission guidelines. The acquisition cost and external program cost of Atorvastatin 40mg and other hypolipidaemic medications are listed in Appendix 5.4. Assuming a patient fills 12 scripts per year, the annual cost of medication for Atorvastatin is $859.32 ($71.61 × 12). As discussed in Section 6.2.1, the drug cost may increase slightly on an annual basis, but this would be offset by a cap on pricing. As the usage volume of Atorvastatin is above the limit, the unit price of the medication will come down. The fluctuation of the unit price of Atorvastatin is thus minimal. For practicality, the same figure of $859.32 is used for the five-year calculation.

The $11.82 per script of external administrative cost is the remuneration paid to approved pharmacies for dispensing prescriptions of Atorvastatin as discussed in Section 6.2.1. If a patient fills 12 scripts per year, the annual dispensing cost (or external program cost) is $141.84 ($11.82 × 12). The same argument applies to the minimal fluctuation of external programs cost over the five-year time frame. For practicality, the same figure of $141.84 is used for the five-year calculation. As discussed in Section 5.2.3, the internal administration cost is insignificant and costs for adverse drug effects are estimated to be $29.60 annually. The social cost is the opportunity cost forgone because the fund is used to pay for Atorvastatin rather than other alternatives, but it is not considered under this approach

The benefit stream

As discussed in Section 5.3.5, the average cost per patient day for cardiovascular type of hospital separation is $999.02. For coronary heart disease, the average length of stay is 4.5 days. By using the above clinical information, the cost of hospital separation for coronary heart disease is calculated to be $4,495.59 ($999.02/day × 4.5 days), assuming that patient's lipid profile is well controlled and monitored and there is no risk for hospitalisation for the next five years. According to authors' value judgement, the avoidance of hospitalisation cost is only counted once at the beginning of the five-year period. The same assumption is used in the financial cost benefit analysis and the new[3] cost benefit analysis.

With patients' health improved, there is a less frequent need for visits to general and specialist medical practitioners. While the PBAC considers the extra costs for additional outcome in the form of incremental ratios, benefit of improved health status is not quantified under the PBAC type of criteria.

Increase of economic production is not considered under the PBAC approach. With improved health status, there is a lesser tendency to consume complementary medical products. As complementary medicines are paid entirely by patients, benefits from such cost-savings are not considered under the PBAC type of criteria.

While it considered the extra dollar cost per extra QALY, the benefit of each QALY is not quantified under the PBAC type of criteria. WTP of the patient to obtain positive changes in health status is also not considered under this approach.

Detailed calculation of the hypothetical cost benefit analysis of Atorvastatin 40mg under the PBAC type of criteria can be referred to in Appendix 6.1. A discount rate of 5% is used. Over the five-year time period, the total discounted cost is $4,685.81 and the total discounted benefit is $4,495.59. The cost benefit ratio is 0.96 and the net present value is –$190.22. Using the decision rules of cost benefit analysis, Atorvastatin should not be listed on the PBS under the PBAC type of submission criteria.

6.3.2 Financial cost benefit analysis of Atorvastatin 40mg

The cost stream

As discussed in the previous section, only costs of medications, external administrative costs and costs for adverse effects are considered. Internal program costs are insignificant and social costs are not included.

The benefit stream

As discussed in Section 5.3.5, increase in economic productivity due to avoidance of hospitalisation is estimated to be $625.50 ($145.00/day × 4.5 days). As discussed in previous section, hospitalisation is assumed to be avoided once in year 0 for the five-year period, the $625.00 of increase in productivity is counted once at year 0.

The estimates for an increase in economic productivity due to a decrease in visits to general and specialist medical practitioners are from author's expert opinion and social value judgement, as discussed Section 5.2.3. The estimate is $725.00 in first two years and is $362.50 in last three years of the five-year period.

Cost savings from avoidance of hospitalisation cost has been discussed in Section 6.3.1. Under the financial cost benefit analysis approach, indirect cost savings from a decrease in visits to general and specialist medical practitioners, as well as those from decreased consumption of complementary medicines (with health improvement) are not considered. Social benefits from improved life expectancy and the WTP of the patient to obtain positive changes in health status are also not considered under the financial cost benefit analysis approach.

Detailed calculation of the financial cost benefit analysis of Atorvastatin 40mg can be found in Appendix 6.2. A discount rate of 5% is used. Over the five-year time period, the total discounted cost is $4,685.81 and the total discounted benefit is $7,476.73. The cost benefit ratio is 1.60 and a net present value is $2,790.92. Using the decision rules of cost benefit analysis, Atorvastatin should be listed on the PBS under the financial cost benefit analysis approach.

6.3.3 New[3] cost benefit analysis of Atorvastatin 40mg

The cost stream

As discussed in Section 6.2.1, five different costs are identified, namely the costs of medications, the internal and external program costs, the costs for adverse drug effects, as well as the social costs. The first four cost items are considered under both cost benefit analysis under the PBAC criteria and financial cost benefit analysis, and are discussed in Sections 6.3.1 and 6.3.2. New[3] cost benefit analysis is the only approach considering social costs.

Social cost is the opportunity cost forgone because the fund is used to pay for Atorvastatin rather than other alternatives. On average, it costs an extra $117.52 per year to use Atorvastatin 40mg daily instead of using Pravastatin 40mg, Fluvastatin 40mg or Simvastatin 80mg daily.

The benefit stream

Benefits from an increase of economic production are calculated in Section 6.3.2. Cost savings from avoidance of hospitalisation are cal-

Table 6.1 Cost comparison between different 'statins'

Medications	Strength & packsize	Govt rec ($)	P'cy markup($)	Cost to govt* ($)
Atorvastatin	40mg × 30 tablets	83.43	11.82	59.73–83.43
Simvastatin	80mg × 30 tablets	111.13	14.34	87.43–111.13
Pravastatin	40mg × 30 tablets	75.65	11.11	51.95–75.65
Fluvastatin	40mg × 30 tablets	34.13	7.34	3.09–34.13

Note: * Cost to government depends on the entitlement status of patients.

culated in Section 6.3.1. As discussed in Section 5.2.3, there is a benefit from reduced health services consumption with the improvement of a patients' health. Cost savings from a decrease in visits to general medical practitioners are estimated to be $458.80 for the first two years and $229.40 for the last three years of the five-year period (see Table 5.3). Cost savings from a decrease in visits to specialist medical practitioners are estimated to be $250.80 for the first two years, and $125.40 for the last three years (see Table 5.4).

As discussed in Section 5.2.3, patients may not resort to complementary medicines if their cardiovascular conditions are controlled. By using authors' expert opinion and value judgement, this annual savings is estimated to be $400 from patients' perspective.

As stated in the PBAC submission guidelines 2002 (p. 74), the main intended outcome of drug therapy is the improvement of health. The ultimate benefit of drug therapy is the improvement in the quality and/or quantity of life. In classical utilitarianism, individual or collective actions are taken to maximise the utility of the whole society. To improve life expectancy is to increase the utility of a society. Page (1977, 1982) commented that 'utility was entirely non-observable' and 'interpersonal comparisons of utility are impossible'. In order to estimate the benefit as a result of an increase in life expectancy, the value of a statistical life is calculated. The value of a statistical life (VSL) is an inference made by evaluating individuals' preferences for risk avoidance or improvement in their situations, and expressing such preferences in monetary terms (Green et al. 2000; Abelson 2003; MEDTAP 2003). As discussed in Section 5.3.5, the benefit of improved life expectancy of Atorvastatin is estimated to be 0.54 QALYs by using authors' expert opinion and value judgements. By using the lower figure of QALY at $35,935 per year, this benefit is estimated to be $19,113.30.

In neoclassical utilitarianism, individuals take actions to maximise their own utility rather than the utility of the whole society. In a hypothetical situation, Atorvastatin is not listed on the PBS. If a patient is concerned with his or her serum lipid profile, he or she is willing to pay for medications through private prescription if there is no government subsidy available for the medication. WTP of a patient for Atorvastatin can then be estimated as the price of the private script. The current pricing practice of private prescription is the cost of medication plus 10% and $6.75 dispensing fee.

Atorvastatin 40mg on a private script will cost patients about $85.50 (cost of $71.61 plus 10% markup plus $6.75 dispensing fee for private script) per month and $1,026.25 per year. Detailed calculation of the new[3] cost benefit analysis of Atorvastatin 40mg can be referred to in Appendix 6.3. A social discount rate of 0% is used. Over the five-year time period, the total discounted cost is $5,741.45 and the total discounted benefit is $36,386.74. The cost benefit ratio is 6.34 and a net present value is $30,645.29. Using the decision rules of cost benefit analysis, Atorvastatin should be listed on the PBS under the new[3] cost benefit analysis approach.

6.4 Cost benefit analysis of Clopidogrel

Clopidogrel (Plavix® or Iscover®) inhibits platelet aggregation within blood vessels. It is commonly prescribed to control acute coronary acute syndrome in order to prevent stroke or recurrence of stroke.

6.4.1 Hypothetical cost benefit analysis of Clopidogrel 75mg under PBAC type of criteria

The cost stream

As discussed in Sections 5.3.4 and 6.2.1, costs of medications, external program costs, as well as costs for adverse drug effects are considered in the hypothetical cost benefit analysis calculation under the PBAC type of submission criteria. Internal program costs are considered insignificant. Social costs and other indirect costs are not included under this approach. The acquisition cost and external program costs of Clopidogrel 75mg are listed in Appendix 5.4. A monthly supply of Clopidogrel 75mg costs $72.16. Assuming that patients fill 12 scripts per year, the annual cost of medication of Clopidogrel is $865.92 ($72.16 × 12). The fluctuation of the drug cost is minimal and the same figure of $865.92 is used for calculation over the five-year period. The $11.88 per script of the external program cost is the remuneration paid to community and hospital pharmacies for dispensing prescriptions of Clopidogrel as discussed in Section 6.2.1. Assuming a patient fills 12 scripts per year, this gives an annual dispensing cost (or external program costs) of $142.56. As discussed in Section 6.2.1, the variation of the dispensing cost per prescription is minimal over the five-year time frame.

For practical calculations, the same figure of \$142.56 is used for each of the five years. The internal administrative cost is insignificant and the estimate for costs of adverse drug effects is \$29.60 annually as discussed in Section 5.2.3. The social cost is not considered under this approach as discussed in Section 6.3.1.

The benefit stream

As discussed in Section 5.3.5, the average cost per patient day for cardiovascular type of hospital separation is \$999.02. The average length of stay for stroke is 9.7 days. By using the clinical information, the cost of hospital separation is \$9,690.50 (\$999.02/day × 9.7 days). As discussed in previous sections, the avoidance of hospitalisation cost is only counted as benefit once at the beginning of the five-year period since it is anticipated that the circulatory profile of patient is well monitored and there is no risk for further hospitalisation for stroke in the next five years.

As discussed in Section 6.3.1, benefits from an increase in economic productivity are not considered under the PBAC approach. Cost savings from a decrease in general and specialist medical practitioner consultation, and decreased consumption of complementary medicines are also not considered under the PBAC approach. Benefits arising from improved life expectancy and WTP of a patient to obtain positive changes in health status are also not considered under this approach. Detailed calculation of the hypothetical cost benefit analysis of Clopidogrel 75mg under the PBAC type of criteria can be referred to in Appendix 6.4. A discount rate of 5% is used. Over the 5-year time period, the total discounted cost is \$4,719.08 and the total discounted benefit is \$9,690.50. The cost benefit ratio is 2.05 and the net present value is \$4,971.42. Using the decision rules of cost benefit analysis, Clopidogrel should be listed on the PBS under the PBAC type of submission criteria.

6.4.2 Financial cost benefit analysis of Clopidogrel 75mg

The cost stream

As discussed in the previous sections, only the costs of medications, external administrative costs and costs for adverse effects are considered. Internal program costs are insignificant and social costs are not included.

The benefit stream

As discussed in Section 5.3.5, the increase in economic productivity due to avoidance of hospitalisation is $1,406.50 (9.7 days × $145.00 per day). Assuming that hospitalisation is avoided once in Year 0 for the five-year period, the benefit of $1,406.50 is counted once at Year 0. With improvement in health status, patients attend general and specialist medical practitioners on a less frequent basis. As discussed in Section 5.2.3, the corresponding increase in economics productivity is estimated to be $725.00 in Year 0 and 1, and $362.50 in Year 2, 3 and 4 (see Table 5.1). Cost savings from avoidance of hospitalisation is estimated to be $9,690.50 as discussed in Section 6.4.1. Indirect cost savings from decrease in consultations with medical practitioners, and decreased consumption of complementary medicines are not considered under the financial cost benefit analysis approach. Social benefits from improved life expectancy and the WTP of a patient to obtain positive changes in health status are also not considered under this approach. Detailed calculation of the financial cost benefit analysis of Clopidogrel 75mg can be referred to in Appendix 6.5. A discount rate of 5% is used. Over the five-year time period, the total discounted cost is $4,719.08 and the total discounted benefit is $13,452.64. The cost benefit ratio is 2.85 and the net present value is $8,733.55. Using the decision rules of cost benefit analysis, Clopidogrel should be listed on the PBS under the financial cost benefit analysis approach.

6.4.3   New[3] cost benefit analysis of Clopidogrel 75mg

The cost stream

As discussed in Section 6.3.3, new[3] cost benefit analysis is the only approach considering social costs. Social cost is the opportunity cost forgone when the fund is used for Clopidogrel rather than other alternatives. On average, it costs an extra $64.77 per month to use Clopidogrel daily instead of using Asasantin® 200–25mg, or Aspirin 100mg. By using authors' expert opinions and value judgements, the social cost of Clopidogrel is estimated to be $772.24 ($64.77 × 12) annually.

The benefit stream

Benefits from an increase in economic productivity are as discussed in Section 6.4.2. Benefits from avoidance of hospitalisation are as

Table 6.2 Cost comparison between Clopidogrel, Asasantin and Aspirin

Medications	Strength & packsize	Govt rec ($)	P'cy markup($)	Cost to govt* ($)
Clopidogrel	75mg × 28 tablets	84.04	11.88	60.34–84.04
Asasantin	200–25mg × 60 tablets	32.42	7.18	8.72–32.42
Aspirin	100mg × 112 tablets	6.13	4.79	0–6.13

Note: *cost to government depends on entitlement status of patients.

discussed in Section 6.4.1. Benefits from a decrease in general and specialist medical practitioner consultation are as discussed in Section 5.2.3 (see Table 5.1). Cost savings from decrease consumption of complementary medicines due to improved health status are estimated to be $400.00 annually (see Section 5.2.3). As discussed in Section 5.3.5, the benefit of improved life expectancy of Clopidogrel 75mg is estimated to be 0.5 QALYs by using clinical information and authors' value judgement. Given QALY at $35,935 per year, the benefit is estimated to be $17,697.50.

Assuming that Clopidogrel 75mg is not listed on the PBS, and that a patient concerned with his circulatory profile is willing to pay for medications through private means without government subsidy, then the WTP of the patient for Clopidogrel 75mg can be estimated as the price of the private script. By using common industry practice, Clopidogrel 75mg on private script is estimated to cost patients about $86.13 (cost of $72.16 plus 10% markup plus $6.75 dispensing fee for a private script) per month and $1,033.51 per year.

Detailed calculation of the new[3] cost benefit analysis of Clopidogrel 75mg can be referred to in Appendix 6.6. A social discount rate of 0% is used. Over the five-year time period, the total discounted cost is $9,076.65 and the total discounted benefit is $40,983.15. The cost benefit ratio is 4.52 and the net present value is $31,906.50. Using the decision rules of cost benefit analysis, Clopidogrel should be listed on the PBS under the new[3] cost benefit analysis approach.

6.5 Cost benefit analysis of Pioglitazone 30mg

Insulin binds to the surface receptors of responsive cells and results in phosphorylation of the receptor and various intracellular insulin receptor substrates. This follows by translocation of glucose transporters to the plasma membrane, and activation of other intracellular enzymes involved in glucose metabolism. In type 2 diabetes, metabolic defects in the intracellular responses to receptor activation lead to the development of insulin resistance. Type 2 diabetes is characterised by decreased glucose transport and utilisation at the level of muscle and adipose tissue and increased glucose production by the liver. During the progression to a clinical diagnosis of type 2 diabetes, a chronic insulin resistance results a compensatory increase in circulating insulin levels, further depleting the reserve of secretory capacity of the β cells of pancreas. The β cell dysfunction and the insulin resistance results in type 2 diabetes (Grossman 2002).

Traditional oral hypoglycaemic agents do not address the underlying insulin resistance. Sulphonylureas (e.g. glibenclamide, gliclazide, glimepiride, and glipizide) reduce blood glucose levels by stimulating the β cells of the pancreas to increase insulin secretion. Biguanides (Metformin) reduces the blood glucose level by reducing hepatic glucose production. As the secretory function of the β cells declines, insulin administration becomes the final therapeutic choice.

Thiazolidinediones (TZDs) are shown to reverse some of the metabolic defects in the development of insulin resistance and ultimately type 2 diabetes. TZDs activate peroxisome proliferator activator receptors (PPAR) and increase insulin sensitivity by enhancing the expression of multiple gene-encoding proteins which modulate glucose and lipid metabolism, thus enhancing insulin sensitivity in the liver, muscle and adipose tissue. These include proteins involved in the insulin-signaling cascade, increased expression of glucose transporters, insulin-stimulated lipoprotein lipase activity, and fatty acid transport protein and acyl-CoA synthase.

Pioglitazone (Actos®) is a TZD that is demonstrated to reduce glucose levels in type 2 diabetic patients by improving hepatic and muscle sensitivity to insulin (Miyazaki et al. 2001). Pioglitazone reduces plasma glucose levels by increasing peripheral glucose utilisation and decreasing hepatic glucose production. Clinical studies have demonstrated that absolute reductions in fasting plasma glucose to the range of 1.7 to 4.4 mmol/L, along with an increase of high density lipoprotein (HDL) cholesterol of 8.7 to 12.6%, and a

Table 6.3 Important considerations in evaluating drug therapies for diabetes mellitus

Efficacy				Economic impact	
Surrogate markers	Clinical endpoints	Effectiveness	Safety	Short term	Long term
% reduction in HbA$_{1c}$ (monotherapy)	Macrovascualr MI Stroke	Compliance	Hypo-glycaemia	Cost of drug	Cost savings from prevention of macro-vascular complications
% reduction in HbA$_{1c}$ (combination therapy)	Microvascular Nephropathy Retinopathy Neuropathy	Adverse effects	Idiosyncratic adverse drug reactions	Cost of monitoring	Cost savings from prevention of micro-vascular complications
Serum lipids Effects on TG, LDL, HDL		Impact on use of other antidiabetic medications	Drug interactions	Cost of weight control (incl medications)	Cost differences due to changes in use of other diabetic medications
Weight gain/loss			Monitoring		Cost issues associated with obesity and related complications

Notes:
HbA$_{1c}$ = glycosylated haemogloblin.
HDL = high density lipoprotein.
LDL = low density lipoprotein.
TG = triglycerides.

Source: Veenstra et al. 2002.

decrease in triglycerides to the range of 18.2 to 26.0%, have no significant effects on LDL or total cholesterol (Grossman 2002).

6.5.1   Hypothetical cost benefit analysis of Pioglitazone 30mg under PBAC type of criteria

The cost stream

As discussed in Section 5.4.6, the costs items considered under the PBAC type of criteria include costs of medications, external program costs, as well as costs for adverse drug effects. Internal program costs are insignificant. Social cost and other indirect costs are not considered under this approach. The acquisition costs and external program costs drug cost of Pioglitazone 30mg are listed in Appendix 5.6. A monthly supply of Pioglitazone 30mg is $85.56. Assuming that patients fill 12 scripts per year, the annual cost of medication is $1,026.72 ($85.56 × 12). As discussed in Section 6.2.1, fluctuation in drug cost is minimal over the five-year period and the same figure of $1,026.72 is used for practical calculations.

The $13.22 per script of external administrative cost is the remuneration paid to approved pharmacies for dispensing prescriptions of Pioglitazone as discussed in Section 6.2.1. Assuming an individual patient fills 12 scripts per year, this gives an annual dispensing cost of $158.64. The fluctuation of the dispensing cost per prescription is minimal over the five-year time frame. For practical calculations, the same figure of $158.64 is used for the five years. The internal administrative cost is insignificant in the cost benefit calculation, and costs for adverse drug effects are estimated to be $29.60 as discussed in Section 5.2.3. Social cost is not considered under this approach as discussed in Section 6.3.1.

The benefit stream

The average cost per patient day for endocrine, nutritional and metabolic type of hospital separation is $789.42 (see Table 5.2). By using the clinical information, the benefit of avoidance of hospitalisation stay for type 2 diabetes is $8,683.62 ($789.42/day × 11.0 days) as discussed in Section 5.4.7. Consider the blood glucose level of patient is well controlled and monitored and there is no risk for hospitalisation for the next five years. According to authors' value judgement, the cost avoidance of hospitalisation is only counted as benefit once at the beginning of the five-year period.

Benefits arising from increase in economic productivity are not considered under this approach. With patients' health improved, there is a decrease in visits to general and specialist medical practitioners. While the PBAC considers the extra costs for additional outcome in the form of incremental ratios, benefit of improved health status is not quantified under this approach. Costs of complementary medicines are borne by patients with no government subsidy. WTP is also a criterion from patients' perspective. Both are not considered under PBAC type of criteria.

Detailed calculation of the hypothetical cost benefit analysis of Pioglitazone 30mg under the PBAC type of criteria can be referred to in Appendix 6.7. A discount rate of 5% is used. Over the five-year time period, the total discounted cost is $5,523.17 and the total discounted benefit is $8,683.62. The cost benefit ratio is 1.57 and the net present value is $3,160.45. Using the decision rules of cost benefit analysis, Pioglitazone 30mg should be listed on the PBS under the PBAC type of criteria.

6.5.2   Financial cost benefit analysis of Pioglitazone 30mg

The cost stream

As discussed in Section 5.4.6, the costs considered under financial cost benefit analysis include costs of medications, external program costs, as well as costs for adverse drug effects. Internal program costs are insignificant. Social cost and other indirect costs are not considered under this approach.

The benefit stream

As discussed in Section 5.4.7, an increase in economic productivity due to avoidance of hospitalisation for type 2 diabetes is $1,595.00 (11.0 days × $145.00 per day). Assuming that hospitalisation is avoided once in Year 0 for the five-year period, the benefit of $1,595.00 is counted once at Year 0.

With improvement in health status, patients attend general and specialist medical practitioners on a less frequent basis. This corresponding increase in economic productivity is estimated to be $725.00 in first two years and $362.50 in the last three years of the five-year period (see Table 5.1), as according to authors' value judgement.

Cost savings from avoidance of hospitalisation are discussed in Section 6.5.1. Benefits from decrease in visits to medical practitioner are not considered under the financial cost benefit analysis. Benefits from decreased consumption of complementary medicines, improved life expectancy and WTP of patient to obtain positive changes in health status are also not considered under the financial cost benefit analysis.

Detailed calculation of the financial cost benefit analysis of Pioglitazone 30mg can be referred to in Appendix 6.8. A discount rate of 5% is used. Over the five-year time period, the total discounted cost is $5,523.17 and the total discounted benefit is $12,634.26. The cost benefit ratio is 2.29 and the net present value is $7,111.09. Using the decision rules of cost benefit analysis, Pioglitazone 30mg should be listed on the PBS under the financial cost benefit analysis approach.

6.5.3   New[3] cost benefit analysis of Pioglitazone 30mg

The cost stream

As discussed in Section 6.3.3, new[3] cost benefit analysis is the only approach considering social costs. The social cost is the opportunity cost forgone when the fund is used for Pioglitazone 30mg rather than other alternatives. On average, it costs an extra $83.76 per month to use Pioglitazone 30mg daily instead of using Metformin or Gliclazide. By using authors' expert opinion and value judgement, the social cost is estimated to be $1,005.12 ($83.76 × 12) annually.

The benefit stream

Benefits from an increase of economic productivity are as discussed in Section 6.5.2. Benefits from avoidance of hospitalisation are as discussed in Section 6.5.1. Benefits from decrease in general and specialist medical practitioner consultation are as discussed in Section

Table 6.4   Cost comparison between Pioglitazone and other oral hypoglycaemics

Medications	Strength & packsize	Govt rec ($)	P'cy markup($)	Cost to govt* ($)
Pioglitazone	30mg × 30 tablets	98.78	13.22	75.08–98.78
Metformin	500mg × 100 tablets	14.70	5.40	0–14.70
Gliclazide	80mg × 100 tablets	15.34	5.63	0–15.34

Note: * Cost to government depends on entitlement status of patients.

5.2.3. Cost savings from a decrease consumption of complementary medicines due to improved health status are as discussed in Section 5.2.3. As discussed in Section 5.4.7, the life expectancy is expected to increase by about 0.35 life-years (Coyle et al. 2002). By using the above clinical information and lower estimate of QALY at $35,935 per year, the benefit of improved life expectancy of Pioglitazone 30mg is estimated to be $12,388.25.

Assuming that Pioglitazone 30mg is not listed on the PBS, patients concerned with their blood glucose level are willing to pay for medications in the absence of government subsidy. Their WTP for Pioglitazone 30mg is estimated as the price of the private script. By using common industry practice, Pioglitazone 30mg on private script costs patients about $100.87 (cost of $85.56 plus 10% markup plus $6.75 dispensing fee for private script) per month and $1,210.44 per year.

Detailed calculation of the new³ cost benefit analysis of Pioglitazone 30mg can be referred to in Appendix 6.9. A social discount rate of 0% is used. Over the five-year time period, the total discounted cost is $11,100.45 and the total discounted benefit is $35,739.92. The cost benefit ratio is 3.22 and the net present value is $24,639.47. Using the decision rules of cost benefit analysis, Pioglitazone 30mg should be listed on the PBS under the new³ cost benefit analysis approach.

6.6   Cost benefit analysis of Letrozole 2.5mg

Letrozole is a third generation aromastase inhibitor that blocks oestrogen production in breast tissue. Letrozole (Femara®) 2.5mg daily is prescribed as treatment of hormone-dependent advanced breast cancer in post-menopausal women. The following calculation is performed under three different approaches namely the hypothetical cost benefit analysis under the PBAC type of submission criteria, the financial cost benefit analysis and new³ cost benefit analysis.

6.6.1   Hypothetical cost benefit analysis of Letrozole 2.5mg under PBAC type of criteria

The cost stream

As discussed in Section 5.5.4, costs of medications, external program costs, as well as costs for adverse drug effects are considered by the

PBAC. Internal program costs are insignificant to be considered in the cost benefit calculation. Social cost and other indirect costs are not considered under this approach.

The acquisition costs and external program costs of Letrozole 2.5mg are listed in Appendix 5.8. A monthly supply of Letrozole 2.5mg is $1,924.39. The $22.66 per script of external administrative cost is the remuneration paid to approved pharmacies for dispensing prescriptions of Letrozole 2.5mg as discussed in Section 6.2.1. Assuming that patients fill 12 prescriptions per year, the annual cost of Letrozole is $2,332.68 ($1,924.39 × 12) and the annual dispensing cost of $271.92 ($22.66 × 12). As discussed in Section 6.2.1, there is minimal fluctuation for drug cost and dispensing cost over the five-year period, the same figures of $2,332.68 and $271.92 are used in the calculation. The internal administrative cost is insignificant to be included in the cost benefit calculation. Costs for adverse drug effects are estimated to be $29.60 annually as discussed in Section 5.2.3. The social cost is not considered under this approach.

The benefit stream

The average cost per patient day for the neoplastic disorder category of hospital separation is $751.13 and the average length of stay is 7.45 days (see Table 5.2). By using the above clinical information, the cost savings of avoidance of hospitalisation is estimated to be $5,592.92 ($751.13/day × 7.45 days). Assuming the patient is receiving treatment such as surgery and/or chemotherapy, and is in remission after two admissions to hospital, and there is no risk of hospitalisation for the remaining five-year period. By using authors' expert opinion and value judgements, the avoidance of hospitalisation costs is only counted annually for the first two years.

Benefits arising from an increase in economic productivity are not considered under the PBAC type of criteria. With the improvement in patients' health, there is a decrease in health services consumption in terms of visits to general and specialist medical practitioners. While the PBAC considers the extra costs for an additional outcome in the form of incremental ratios, the benefit of improved health status is not quantified under the PBAC approach. Cost savings from a decrease in consumption of complementary medicines and WTP are not considered under the PBAC type of criteria.

Detailed calculation of the hypothetical cost benefit analysis of Letrozole 2.5mg under the PBAC type of criteria can be referred to in Appendix 6.10. A discount rate of 5% is used. Over the five-year time period, the total discounted cost is $11,973.57 and the total discounted benefit is $10,919.51. The net present value is –$1,054.07 and the cost benefit ratio is 0.91. Using the decision rules of cost benefit analysis, Letrozole 2.5mg should not be listed on the PBS under the PBAC type of submission criteria.

6.6.2   Financial cost benefit analysis of Letrozole 2.5mg

The cost stream

As discussed in Section 5.5.4, costs of medications, external program costs, as well as costs for adverse drug effects are considered under the financial cost benefit analysis. Internal program costs are insignificant. Social cost and other indirect costs are not considered under this approach.

The benefit stream

As discussed in Section 5.5.5, the increase in economic productivity due to avoidance of hospitalisation for breast cancer is $1,080.25 (7.45 days × $145.00 per day). Assuming that hospitalisation is avoided once in both Year 0 and Year 1, the benefit of $1,080.25 is counted twice for the five-year period as discussed in previous section.

With improvement in health status, patients attend general and specialist medical practitioners on a less frequent basis. This corresponding increase in economic productivity is estimated to be $725.00 in the first two years, and $362.50 for the last three years (see Table 5.1). This gives a total increase in productivity of $1,805.25 in Year 1 and Year 0.

Benefits from avoidance of hospitalisation cost are as discussed in Section 6.6.1. Costs savings from a decrease in general and specialist medical practitioner consultation are not considered under the financial cost benefit analysis approach. Benefits from decreased consumption of complementary medicines, improved life expectancy and WTP of patient to obtain positive changes in health status are also not considered under this approach.

Detailed calculation of the financial cost benefit analysis of Pioglitazone 30mg can be referred to in Appendix 6.11. A discount rate of 5% is used. Over the five-year time period, the total discounted cost is $11,973.57 and the total discounted benefit is $15,384.2. The cost benefit ratio is 1.28 and the net present value is $3,410.63. Using the decision rules of cost benefit analysis, Letrozole 2.5mg should be listed on the PBS under the financial cost benefit analysis approach.

6.6.3 New[3] cost benefit analysis of Letrozole 2.5mg

The cost stream

As discussed in Section 6.3.3, the new[3] cost benefit analysis is the only approach considering social costs. Social cost is the opportunity cost forgone when the fund is used for Letrozole 2.5mg rather than other alternatives. On average, it costs an extra $177.64 per month to use Letrozole 2.5mg daily instead of using Tamxoifen 20mg. By using authors' value judgements, the social cost of Letrozole 2.5mg is estimated to be $2,131.68 ($177.64 × 12) annually.

The benefit stream

Increase in economic productivity with improved health is discussed in Section 6.6.2. Cost savings from avoidance of hospitalisation are as discussed in Section 6.6.1. Benefits from a decrease in visits to general and specialist medical practitioner and cost savings from a decreased consumption of complementary medicines due to improved health are as discussed in Section 5.2.3. As discussed in Section 5.5.5, the improved life expectancy is estimated to be 0.714 years (Karnon and Jones 2003). By using the clinical information and the lower figure of at $35,393 per QALY, the benefit of improved life expectancy due to Letrozole therapy is estimated to be $25,272.03.

Table 6.5 Cost comparison between Letrozole and other medications for breast cancer

Medications	Strength & packsize	Govt rec ($)	P'cy markup($)	Cost to govt* ($)
Letrozole	2.5mg × 30 tablets	217.05	22.66	193.35–217.05
Anastrozole	1mg × 30 tablets	217.05	22.66	193.35–217.05
Tamoxifen	20mg × 60 tablets	78.82	14.10	55.12–78.82

Note: * Cost to government depends on the entitlement status of patients.

Assuming that Letrozole 2.5mg is not listed on the PBS. If a patient is in remission, she is willing to pay for medications in the absence of government subsidy. WTP of the patient for Letrozole 2.5mg is estimated as the price of the private script. By using common industry practice, Letrozole on private scripts costs patients about $220.58 (cost of $194.39 plus 10% markup plus $6.75 dispensing fee for private script) per month and $2,646.95 per year.

Detailed calculation of the new³ cost benefit analysis of Letrozole 2.5mg can be referred to in Appendix 6.12. A social discount rate of 0% is used. Over the five-year time period, the total discounted cost is $23,827.45 and the total discounted benefit is $58,874.22. The cost benefit ratio is 2.47 and the net present value is $35,046.27. Using the decision rules of cost benefit analysis, Letrozole 2.5mg should be listed on the PBS under the new³ cost benefit analysis approach.

6.7   Cost benefit analysis of Fluticasone/Salmeterol 500/50

Fluticasone/Salmeterol is commonly prescribed as initial maintenance therapy for moderate and severe asthma. Fluticasone (corticosteroid) and Salmeterol (long-acting β-agonist) are combined in a single inhalation device (Seretide®) in order to improve patient compliance. Fluticasone and Salmeterol target different aspects of the disease process of asthma. Salmeterol controls symptoms of asthma, while fluticasone reduces inflammation and prevents exacerbations of the condition.

Salmeterol is a selective long-acting β_2 adrenoceptor agonist and at dosages of less than 100mcg twice daily has little measurable cardiovascular effect. Salmeterol has a slower onset of action, but a more effective protection against histamine-induced broncho-constriction as well as a longer duration of broncho-dilation (for 12 hours) than recommended doses of conventional short-acting β_2 agonists such as Salbutamol. The anti-inflammatory activity of fluticasone improves symptomatic control of asthma, allows reduction of other medications, such as reliever bronchodilators, and may limit the risk of decline in lung function over time. Clinical evidence shows that the two drugs produce complementary effects in asthmatic patients (Markham and Adkins 2000). A twice-daily dose of Fluticasone/Salmeterol 500/50mcg (Seretide 500/50®) is commonly prescribed as a combination therapy for asthma. The calculation is performed under the hypothetical cost benefit analysis under the PBAC type of submission criteria, the criteria of financial cost benefit analysis and of new[3] cost benefit analysis.

6.7.1 Hypothetical cost benefit analysis of Fluticasone/ Salmeterol 500/50 under PBAC type of criteria

The cost stream

As discussed in Section 5.6.5, the cost items considered under the PBAC type of criteria include costs of medications, external program costs, and costs for adverse drug effects. Internal program costs are insignificant to be included in the calculation. Social cost and other indirect costs are not considered by the PBAC. The acquisition costs and external program costs of Fluticasone/Salmeterol 500/50mcg accuhaler are listed in Appendix 5.9. The monthly drug cost of Fluticasone/Salmeterol 500/50mcg accuhaler is $68.00, and the $11.46 per script of external administrative cost is the remuneration paid to approved pharmacies for dispensing prescriptions of Fluticasone/Salmeterol 500/50mcg accuhaler as discussed in Section 6.2.1. Assuming that patients fill 12 scripts per year, the annual cost of medication is $816.00 ($68.00 × 12) and the annual dispensing cost is $137.52 ($11.46 × 12). As discussed in Section 6.2.1, the fluctuation in drug cost and dispensing is minimal over the five-year period. For practical calculations, the same figures of $816.00 and $137.52 are used for calculation over the five-year period. The internal administrative cost is insignificant to be included in the cost benefit calculation and the cost for adverse drug effects is estimated to be $29.60 annually as discussed in Section 5.2.3. The social cost is not considered under this approach.

The benefit stream

As discussed in Section 5.6.6, the average cost per patient day for the respiratory category of hospital separation is $658.73 (see Table 5.2) and the average length of stay for asthma is 2.5 days. By using the above clinical information, cost savings of avoidance of hospitalisation is calculated to be $1,646.83. According to authors' expert opinion and value judgement, the benefit of cost avoidance of hospitalisation is counted once in Year 0 for the five-year period, the cost saving ($658.73/day × 2.5 days). Assuming the patient's asthma condition is under control and there is no risk of hospitalisation for the remaining of the five-year period.

Benefits arising from an increase in economic productivity are not considered under the PBAC type of criteria. With patients' health improves, there is a decrease in health services consumption in terms of visits to medical practitioners. While the PBAC considers the extra costs for additional outcome in the form of incremental ratios, benefits of improved health status are not quantified under this approach. Cost savings from decreased consumption of complementary medicines and WTP are both not considered under the PBAC type of criteria.

Detailed calculation of the hypothetical cost benefit analysis of Fluticasone/Salmeterol 500/50mcg accuhaler under the PBAC type of criteria can be referred to in Appendix 6.13. A discount rate of 5% is used. Over the five-year time period, the total discounted cost is $4,469.24 and the total discounted benefit is $1,646.83. The cost benefit ratio is 0.37 and the net present value is –$2,822.41. Using the decision rules of cost benefit analysis, Fluticasone/Salmeterol 500/50mcg accuhaler should not be listed on the PBS under the PBAC type of submission criteria.

6.7.2 Financial cost benefit analysis of Fluticasone/Salmeterol 500/50

The cost stream

As discussed in Section 5.6.5, costs of medications, external program costs, as well as costs for adverse drug effects are considered under the financial cost benefit analysis. Internal program costs are insignificant. Social cost and other indirect costs are not considered under this approach.

The benefit stream

As discussed in Section 5.6.6, the increase in economic productivity due to avoidance of hospitalisation for asthma is $362.50 (2.5 days × $145.00 per day). Assuming patient's asthma condition is under control and there is no risk of hospitalisation for the remaining of the five-year period, and the benefit of $362.50 of cost savings of hospitalisation is only counted once at Year 0.

With improved health, patients visit medical practitioners on a less frequent basis and take less time off work for medical appointment.

The increase in economic productivity is estimated to be $725.00 in Year 0 and 1, and $362.50 in years 2, 3 and 4 (see Table 5.1). Benefits from avoidance of hospitalisation cost are as discussed in Section 6.7.1. Costs savings from less visits to general and specialist medical practitioner and from decreased consumption of complementary medicines are discussed in Section 5.2.3. Improved life expectancy and WTP of a patient to obtain positive changes in health status are not considered under financial cost benefit analysis.

Detailed calculation of the financial cost benefit analysis of Fluticasone/Salmeterol 500/50mcg accuhaler can be referred to in Appendix 6.14. A discount rate of 5% is used. Over the five-year time period, the total discounted cost is $4,469.24 and the total discounted benefit is $4,367.42. The cost benefit ratio is 0.98 and the net present value is –$104.27. Using the decision rules of cost benefit analysis, Fluticasone/Salmeterol 500/50mcg accuhaler should not be listed on the PBS under the financial cost benefit analysis approach.

6.7.3   New[3] cost benefit analysis of Fluticasone/Salmeterol 500/50

The cost stream

As discussed in Section 6.3.3, the new[3] cost benefit analysis is the only approach considering social costs. The social cost is the opportunity cost forgone when the fund is used for Fluticasone/Salmeterol 500/50mcg accuhaler rather than other alternatives. On average, it costs an extra $31.79 per month to use Fluticasone/Salmeterol 500/50mcg accuhaler daily instead of using Beclomethasone and/or Salbutamol inhalers. By using authors' value judgement, the social

Table 6.6   Cost comparison between inhalers for asthma

Medications	Strength & packsize	Govt rec ($)	P'cy markup($)	Cost to govt* ($)
Fluticasone/ Salmeterol	500/50 mcg Accuhaler	79.46	11.49	55.76–79.46
Beclomethasone	100mcg inhaler	31.39	7.69	7.69–31.39
Salbutamol	100mcg inhaler	16.28	5.72	0–16.28

Note: * Cost to government depends on entitlement status of patients.

cost of Fluticasone/Salmeterol 500/50mcg accuhaler is estimated to be $381.48 ($31.79 × 12) annually.

The benefit stream

Benefits from increase in economic productivity are as discussed in Section 6.7.2. Cost savings from avoidance of hospitalisation are as discussed in Section 6.7.1. Benefits from decrease in general and specialist medical practitioner consultation are and cost savings from decrease consumption of complementary medicines due to improved health status are as discussed in Section 5.2.3. As discussed in Section 5.6.6, the improved life expectancy due to Fluticasone/Salmeterol 500/50mcg therapy is estimated to be 0.7 years according to authors' expert opinion and value judgement. Using the lower figure $35,395 per QALY, the benefit of improving life expectancy is estimated to be $24,776.50.

Assuming that the Fluticasone/Salmeterol 500/50mcg accuhaler is not listed on the PBS, and patients prefer to pay for Fluticasone/ Salmeterol 500/50mcg accuhaler in the absence of government subsidy so that their asthma can be under control. Their WTP for Fluticasone/Salmeterol 500/50mcg accuhaler can then be estimated as the price of the private script. By using common industry practice, Fluticasone/Salmeterol 500/50mcg accuhaler on private script costs patients about $81.55 (cost of $68.00 plus 10% markup plus $6.75 dispensing fee for private script) per month and $978.60 per year.

Detailed calculation of the new[3] cost benefit analysis of Fluticasone/Salmeterol 500/50mcg accuhaler can be referred to in Appendix 6.15. A social discount rate of 0% is used. Over the five-year time period, the total discounted cost is $6,823.05 and the total discounted benefit is $38,744.93. The cost benefit ratio is 5.68 and the net present value is $31,921.88. Using the decision rules of cost benefit analysis, Fluticasone/Salmeterol 500/50mcg accuhaler should be listed on the PBS under the new[3] cost benefit analysis approach.

6.8   Cost benefit analysis of Tiotropium

Tiotropium is prescribed as long-term maintenance therapy of bronchospasm and dyspnoea associated with Chronic Obstructive

Pulmonary Disease (COPD). Tiotropium (Spiriva®) is an inhaled anti-cholinergic agent prescribed as maintenance therapy for bronchospasm and dyspnoea in Chronic Obstructive Pulmonary Disease. Tiotropium is a long-acting, specific antimuscarinic (anticholinergic) agent. Randomised double-blind clinical studies of Tiotropium assessed lung function of patients in terms of forced expiratory volume in one second (FEV_1), forced vital capacity (FVC) and peak expiratory flow rate (PEFR). Health outcome measures including dyspnoea, exacerbations, hospitalisation and health-related quality of life (as measured by the St George's Respiratory Questionnaire, SGRQ) were also assessed. Tiotropium significantly reduced the number of both COPD exacerbations and hospitalisations associated with COPD exacerbations. In addition, the time to the first COPD exacerbation and to the first hospitalisation associated with a COPD exacerbation was significantly prolonged. The following calculation is performed under the hypothetical scenario under the PBAC type of submission criteria, the criteria of financial cost benefit analysis and the new[3] cost benefit analysis.

6.8.1   Hypothetical cost benefit analysis of Tiotropium under PBAC type of criteria

The cost stream

As discussed in Section 5.6.5, PBAC considers only costs of medications, external program costs, as well as costs for adverse drug effects. Internal program costs are insignificant to be included in the cost benefit calculation. Social cost and other indirect costs are not considered under this approach.

The acquisition costs and external program costs of Tiotropium 18mcg are listed in Appendix 5.9. A monthly supply of Tiotropium 18mcg is $66.20. The $11.28 per script of external administrative cost is the remuneration paid to approved pharmacies for dispensing prescriptions of Tiotropium 18mcg as discussed in section 5.2.3. Assuming that patients fill 12 scripts per year, the annual cost of medication is $794.40 ($66.20 × 12) and the annual dispensing cost is $135.36 ($11.28 × 12). As discussed in Section 6.2.1, the fluctuation in drug cost and dispensing cost is minimal over the five-year period. For practical calculations, the same figures of $794.40 and $135.36 are used for the five years.

The internal administrative cost is considered insignificant and the cost for adverse drug effects is estimated to be $29.60 annually as discussed in Section 6.2.1. The social cost is not considered under the PBAC approach.

The benefit stream

As discussed in Section 5.6.6, the average cost per patient day for respiratory category of hospital separation is $658.73 (see Table 5.2) and the average length of stay for COPD is 7.5 days. By using the above clinical information, cost savings of avoidance of hospitalisation is calculated to be $4,940.78. According to authors' expert opinion and value judgement, cost savings from avoidance of hospitalisation is counted once in Year 0 for the five-year period. Assuming the patient's asthma condition is under control and there is no risk for hospitalisation for the remaining of the five-year period.

Benefits arising from an increase in economic productivity are not considered under the PBAC type of criteria. With health improvement, patients have a lesser need to visit general and specialist medical practitioners. While the PBAC considers the extra costs for additional outcome in the form of incremental ratios, the benefit of improved health status is not quantified under the PBAC approach. Cost savings from a decrease in consumption of complementary medicines and WTP are both not considered under the PBAC type of criteria.

Detailed calculation of the hypothetical cost benefit analysis of Tiotropium 18mcg under the PBAC type of criteria can be referred to in Appendix 6.16. A discount rate of 5% is used. Over the five-year time period, the total discounted cost is $4,361.23 and the total discounted benefit is $4,940.78. The cost benefit ratio is 1.13 and the net present value is $579.55. Using the decision rules of cost benefit analysis, Tiotropium 18mcg should be listed on PBS under this approach.

6.8.2 Financial cost benefit analysis of Tiotropium

The cost stream

As discussed in Section 5.6.5, costs of medications, external program costs, as well as costs for adverse drug effects are considered under the financial cost benefit analysis. Internal program costs are insignificant. Social costs and other indirect costs are not considered under this approach.

The benefit stream

As discussed in Section 5.6.6, the increase in economic productivity due to avoidance of hospitalisation for COPD is $1,087.50 (7.5 days × $145.00/day). Assuming a patient's respiratory condition is under control, and there is no risk for hospitalisation for the remaining of the five-year period, the benefit of $362.50 of cost savings of hospitalisation is only counted once at Year 0.

With improvement in health status, patients attend general and specialist medical practitioners on a less frequent basis. This corresponding increase in economics productivity is estimated to be $725.00 in Year 0 and 1, and $362.50 in Year 2, 3 and 4 (see Table 5.1).

Benefits from avoidance of hospitalisation cost are as discussed in Section 6.8.1. Costs savings from a decrease in visits to general and specialist medical practitioners and from decreased consumption of complementary medicines are discussed in Section 5.2.3. Improved life expectancy and WTP of a patient to obtain positive changes in health status are not considered under the financial cost benefit analysis.

Detailed calculation of the financial cost benefit analysis of Tiotropium 18mcg can be referred to in Appendix 6.17. A discount rate of 5% is used. Over the five-year time period, the total discounted cost is $4,361.23 and the total discounted benefit is $8,383.92. The cost benefit ratio is 1.92 and the net present value is $4,022.69. Using the decision rules of cost benefit analysis, Tiotropium 18mcg should be listed on the PBS under the financial cost benefit analysis approach.

6.8.3   New[3] cost benefit analysis of Tiotropium

The cost stream

As discussed in Section 6.3.3, the new[3] cost benefit analysis is the only approach considering social costs. Social cost is the opportunity cost forgone when the fund is used for Tiotropium 18mcg rather than other alternatives. On average, it costs an extra $21.70 per month by using Tiotropium 18mcg daily instead of using

Table 6.7   Cost comparison between Tiotropium, Ipratropium and Salbutamol

Medications	Strength & packsize	Govt rec ($)	P'cy markup($)	Cost to govt* ($)
Tiotropium	18mcg × 30 capsules	77.48	11.28	53.78–77.48
Ipratropium	20mcg inhaler	39.50	7.83	15.80–39.50
Salbutamol	100mcg inhaler	16.28	5.72	0–16.28

Note: * Cost to government depends on entitlement of patients.

Ipratropium and/or Salbutamol inhalers. By using authors' value judgement, the social cost of Tiotropium 18mcg is estimated to be $260.40 ($21.70 × 12) annually.

The benefit stream

Benefits from increase in economic productivity are as discussed in Section 6.8.2. Cost savings from avoidance of hospitalisation are as discussed in Section 6.8.1. Benefits from a decrease in general and specialist medical practitioner consultation are and cost savings from a decrease in consumption of complementary medicines due to improved health status are as discussed in Section 5.2.3. As discussed in Section 5.6.6, the improved life expectancy due to Tiotropium 18mcg therapy is estimated to be 0.7 years according to authors' expert opinion and value judgement. Using the lower figure $35,395 per QALY, the benefit of improving life expectancy is estimated to be $24,776.50.

Assuming that Tiotropium 18mcg is not listed on the PBS, patients may be willing to pay for medications in the absence of government subsidy if they prefer to have their COPD under control with Tiotropium 18mcg. WTP of a patient for Tiotropium 18mcg is estimated as the price of the private script. By using common industry practice, Tiotropium 18mcg on private script costs patients about $79.57 (cost of $66.20, plus 10% markup, plus $6.75 dispensing fee) per month and $954.84 per year.

Detailed calculation of the new[3] cost benefit analysis of Tiotropium 18mcg can be referred to in Appendix 6.18. A social discount rate of 0% is used. Over the five-year time period, the total discounted cost is $6,098.85 and the total discounted benefit is $42,600.08. The cost benefit ratio is 6.98 and the net present value is \$36,501.23. Using the decision rules of cost benefit analysis, Tiotropium 18mcg should be listed on the PBS under the new[3] cost benefit analysis approach.

6.9   Sensitivity analysis

In order to deal with uncertainty in the new[3] cost benefit analysis of the six medications, a higher discount rate of 5% and 10% (instead of 0%) is used. The net present values and cost benefit ratios are calculated in Appendices 6.19 to 6.30. Net present values of Atorvastatin, Clopidogrel, Pioglitazone, Fluticasone/Salmeterol, and Tiotropium decrease with an increase in the discount rate from 0% to 5%. However, the net present values of all six medications remain positive even with a higher discount rate. The decision rule does not change with an increase in discount rate.

In addition to discount rate, there can also be uncertainty with the flow of net benefits. The cost benefit calculation is repeated by excluding the different items of net benefit. For sensitivity analysis, the alternatives that we have considered in undertaking cost benefit analysis as follows:

1.   excluding WTP of medication as benefits (results reported in Appendix 7.6);
2.   excluding decrease in consumption of complementary medicines as benefits (results reported in Appendix 7.7);
3.   excluding decrease in consultation with general and specialist medical practitioners as benefits (results reported in Appendix 7.8);
4.   excluding cost avoidance of hospitalisation as benefits (results reported in Appendix 7.9);
5.   excluding increase in economic productivity as benefits (results reported in Appendix 7.10);
6.   excluding increase in life expectancy as benefits (results reported in Appendix 7.11); and
7.   including only 50% increase in life expectancy as benefits (results reported in Appendix 7.12).

The change in cost benefit ratio for the six medications only becomes significant with the exclusion of QALYs gained. However, the net present values of all six medications remain positive and the decision rule does not change.

6.10   Conclusion

Six medications are selected for cost benefit analysis, namely Atorvastatin 40mg, Clopidogrel 75mg, Pioglitazone 30mg, Letrozole 2.5mg, Fluticasone/Salmeterol 500/50mcg and Tiotropium 18mcg. The cost and benefit estimates of the six medications are discussed in Chapter 5.

This chapter has provided the analysis of the costs and benefits of these six medications under three different approaches, namely the PBAC submission criteria, the financial cost benefit analysis and the new³ cost benefit analysis.

Under the new³ cost benefit analysis, all six medications return with positive net present values and with their cost-benefit ratios being greater than 1. Using the decision rules of cost benefit analysis, the results support that all six medications should be listed on the PBS, as they are presently.

Under the PBAC type of criteria, only Clopidogrel, Pioglitazone and Tiotropium return with positive net present values and with cost-benefit ratios greater than 1. Using the decision rules of cost benefit analysis, Atorvastatin, Letrozole and Fluticasone/Salmeterol should not be listed on the PBS.

Under the financial cost benefit analysis, five medications return positive net present values and cost-benefit ratios greater than 1. Using the decision rules of cost benefit analysis, all medications with the exception of Flucticasone/Salmeterol, should be listed on the PBS. For Flucticasone/Salmeterol, the net present value is –$104.27 and the cost-benefit ratio is 0.98 and it should be rejected from PBS listing.

Apart from PBS listing decisions, the net present values and cost-benefit ratios calculated for the six medications can be used in an optimisation program for health sector planning. This will be done in the next chapter.

7
PBS Planning: Modelling and Implications

7.1 Introduction

In the previous chapter, a cost benefit analysis of six medications was performed. That exercise was useful in providing information in decision-making about listing individual medication on the Pharmaceutical Benefit Scheme (PBS) in Australia. However, a realistic exercise of health programs evaluation should also be in the form of proactive health sector planning. In health sector planning, a set of health programs is chosen from alternatives to be financed by the available budget. In this chapter, we develop a PBS sub-sector planning. We apply the new[3] cost benefit analysis developed in Chapter 3 to sub-sector planning of PBS (we call it PBS planning), and discuss the implications of PBS sub-sector planning in selecting a set of medications for PBS listing that can maximise health and social welfare of the society.

This chapter is structured in two parts. In Part A, a PBS sub-sector planning and modelling exercise of PBS decision-making is undertaken. Section 7.2 discusses sector planning in general and Section 7.3 is about the issues and model of PBS sub-sector planning. Section 7.4 discusses the implications of results of the PBS sub-sector planning. Section 7.5 is the sensitivity analysis for project planning under risk and uncertainty. Section 7.6 discusses the principles, issues and modelling in health project planning for sustainable development of the health (and PBS) sector.

In Part B, the implications of this sub-sector planning model along with the implications of the cost benefit analysis in Chapter 6 for drug listing and the PBS related issues are discussed. Part B provides an integrated analysis of the implications of the application of the new[3] cost benefit analysis to the PBS in Australia. Section 7.7 discusses the implications for decision-making in the PBS setting. Section 7.8 discusses the general consideration of the PBS planning model. Section 7.9 discusses the implications of cost benefit analysis in decision-making. Section 7.10 discusses the implications for health sector planning and Section 7.11 discusses the welfare economics implications. Section 7.12 discusses other issues such as generic pricing policy and technological development. Section 7.13 compares the Australian case with other international scenario. Section 7.14 discusses the plausibility of the approach and the result. Section 7.15 presents the conclusion.

Part A   Modelling

7.2   Sector planning via project planning

As discussed in Section 1.2, the objective of this study is to apply social cost benefit analysis in a holistic manner to the PBS setting to go beyond a single program consideration and towards health sector planning. So far we have considered the economic evaluation of individual medications for PBS listing, but the real challenge is the decision-making on a set of medications to be included in a systematic manner. In this situation, economic evaluation needs to be applied to each medication. In order to decide on a set of medications among other alternatives to be included in the PBS, i.e. to prepare a PBS sub-sector planning, we need to apply the principles and methodologies of project planning which are discussed below.

Project planning in the health sector involves identification of a set of health programs to be approved and implemented by the Government. Health sector planning is a sectoral exercise: a sum of money (the sectoral budget) is allocated to the health sector; and certain programs are selected and financed by such a budget on the basis of the principles and methodologies of project planning. In selecting programs to be undertaken in a sector, the relative cost benefit ratios or net present values (NPVs) are used. Formulation of a total sectoral plan for the health sector on the basis of cost benefit analysis by applying some health sector wide mathematical models is not yet a popular practice. Such an exercise will be undertaken in Section 7.3.

7.3 PBS sub-sector planning: Issues and models

7.3.1 The issues in PBS planning

In the area of healthcare, project planning is the decision-making process of selecting a health program among its alternatives. In the context of the PBS in Australia, project planning is about the selection of a set of medication from their alternatives for government subsidy which can be funded by available budget in a particular year or time period. With the aid of economic analysis, a set of medications should be selected on the basis that it achieves the desired health outcomes at the minimum possible cost of resources. When conducting the economic analysis, one should consider the macroeconomic and sector implications, economic efficiency, equity and distributional justice, ethics and moral philosophy, as well as sustainability and issues of intergenerational equity of the project (Hurley 2000; Carter 2001; Asian Development Bank 2002).

Through provision of medications to the public, the PBS aims to preserve or maintain, to restore and hopefully to improve the health status of the Australian population. Fiscal responsibility was identified as one of important measures in the Intergenerational Report 2002 (Costello 2002) for preserving intergenerational equity over a 35-year time span. With the ageing population in Australia, investment in health is important to maintain optimal health status of the population, to preserve and/prolong the productivity of the labour market, and hence the tax revenue of the government.

Early intervention is crucial in the area of health. Without early intervention, most conditions such as cardiovascular diseases and type 2 diabetes will progress to critical stages, resulting in hospitalisation, or even impaired functional status or disability of patients. In the latter case, institutional care such as hostels or nursing homes may become the only viable, and perhaps the most expensive alternative.

At the initial planning stage of the project, one should assess the demands or needs of the project. In the context of the PBS, the demand of a medication can be estimated by epidemiological studies, statistical data on the prevalence of the diseases, and the burden of the diseases to Australia. These data help to establish the economic rationale for public sector involvement. However, a more efficient system, regardless of public or private sector involvement, should be established. As stated in Chapter 4, the PBS in Australia is implemented under a public system, and is administered by the Medicare Australia (formerly Health Insurance Commission). Therefore, economic efficiency of individual medications in the PBS system as well as their social considerations stated above need to be considered in the PBS decision-making.

Another issue in the Australian health sector is the sustainability of the health condition of the population. Sustainability is a concept from environmental economics. Sustainable development refers to the notion that economic development should proceed at a pace and in a manner which conserves the environment and depletable natural resources (see Bannock et al. 1998). In the context of health, sustainability should be considered in implementing health programs aiming at preserving the optimal health status of the Australian population. This is further discussed in Section 7.6.

New[3] cost benefit analysis provides an appropriate framework for addressing the above issues of PBS sub-sector planning. By applying the new[3] cost benefit analysis in PBS planning, the economic and social costs and benefits of medications are valued in monetary terms and compared. A set of medications is selected among other alternatives by using the criteria discussed in Section 3.15, an exercise which addresses the PBS issues discussed above. Health policy on pharmaceutical subsidy formulated under such criteria offers a much broader perspective and caters for the needs of the whole population.

7.3.2 Capital budgeting and operations research techniques

As discussed in Section 2.3.1, a social cost benefit analysis is developed on the basis of the capital budgeting technique and can be considered as capital rationing. Capital budgeting is an operations research technique designed to select a portfolio of projects from a set of alternative proposals in order to achieve maximisation of social welfare or health outcome.

As discussed in Section 1.6, operations research methods have been applied to the healthcare sector since the 1960s. With cost containment being the common theme in public healthcare systems around the world, interest in operations research methods in healthcare delivery is growing. When applying an economic evaluation of a health program such as the PBS, studies of operations research methods in the area of allocation, forecasting demand, as well as quality and efficiency are most relevant (Gass and Harris 2001).

With scarcity of resources, allocation is an important measure to ensure optimal health outcomes. Forecasting helps to establish future demand in healthcare services and resources in order to allow a meaningful proactive project planning exercise. Mathematical programming such as goal programming and integer programming are commonly used in this area of operations research. Mathematical programming is a study of optimising the use and allocation of scarce resources. Linear programming solves the problem by finding the maximum (or minimum) of an objective function $f(x)$ subject to a set of constraints in the form of $g_i(x) \leq b_i$. Stochastic programming deals with optimisation models when available data are subject to significant uncertainty. Stochastic programming is closely related to other paradigms for decision-making under uncertainty. Decision analysis is usually restricted to problems in which discrete choices are evaluated in the view of sequential observations of discrete random variables. The analytic approach allows decision makers to use general preference functions in comparing alternative courses of actions. Theoretically, both single and multiple objectives can be incorporated in the decision-making framework. However, it is not practical to enumerate all choices (decisions) as well as outcomes (of random variables) in the context of decision-making. This approach is usually used when a few strategic alternatives are considered (Gass and Harris 2001)

Optimisation models developed under mathematical programming can then be interpreted under the normative social choice and the new[3] welfare economics framework. By incorporating the social welfare criteria and the static and dynamic constraints of the economy based on new[3] welfare economics, a set of optimal decisions for resource allocation that specifies optimal social welfare and health outcome in the health sector can be formulated (Islam 2001a). These optimisation can also be specified by embedding cost benefit analysis (in the present study new[3] cost benefit analysis) concepts, issues and decision-making problems (Clarke and Islam 2004; Craven and Islam 2005).

7.3.3 Public policy objectives

As discussed in Sections 3.12 and 7.3.1, a social cost benefit analysis should incorporate the underlying government social and economic policies including extra-welfaristic outcomes such as equity, justice, ethics and moral philosophy. When considering the sector planning of PBS, one should take into account macroeconomic and sector implications in addition to benefits and costs of the health program alone. The main objective of a health program is health maximisation, improving the quantity and quality of life of the individuals of a society. Other macroeconomic issues such as employment in the healthcare sector, sustainability of the pharmaceutical industries, viability of a timely and efficient distribution network of PBS medications (through medical practitioners, pharmacies, full-line pharmaceutical wholesalers, for example) should also be considered.

7.3.4 Sector planning models and new[3] cost benefit analysis

It was stated in Chapter 3 that the elements of the new[3] social choice approach to cost benefit analysis (Islam 2001a) are the following:

a. it considers *economics* and *ethics* in estimating costs and benefits in economic evaluation;
b. it assumes *measurability* of social welfare, non-economic costs and benefits on the basis of *social value judgement, preferences* and public policy objectives; and
c. it aims to estimate costs and benefits of the health program by using scientific information, expert opinion and social preferences.

The inclusion of the elements of the new approach in health sector planning model developed in this research will be done by the following methods:

a. including social costs and benefits in estimating the parameters of the values;
b. applying a combination of scientific information, expert opinions and social value judgement in identifying and estimating

parameters and coefficient, equations and objective functions of this model; and

c. including social value judgement and ethical issues in the model through the objective function and constraints and discount rates of the models.

By incorporating social objectives, the objective function represents social value judgement. By adjusting the discount factor, intergenerational equity is considered and emphasis is put on future generations.

In the context of PBS sector planning, new[3] cost benefit analysis is used as an evaluation tool for PBS decision-making by incorporating the elements of new[3] cost benefit analysis discussed above. Firstly, the Therapeutic Goods Administration assesses a medication for its safety and efficacy by using scientific information, in order to determine whether the medication should be approved for the Australian market. Secondly, medical treatment guidelines of the medication are established to determine the clinical indications that are subsidised or funded by the PBS budget. Under the new[3] cost benefit analysis, both social costs and benefits are included in the evaluation. Details of calculation of the costs and benefits estimates are discussed in Chapters 5 and 6. In defining the costs and benefits of medications, social value judgements and ethical considerations are incorporated in the analysis, in addition to the definition of benefits under the Pharmaceutical Benefit Advisory (PBAC) type of criteria where social costs and benefits are excluded (as discussed in previous Chapters 2, 3, 5 and 6).

Thirdly, the percentage of government subsidy on PBS medications depends on the entitlement status of patients. As discussed in Section 4.8, the population is divided into general patients and concessional patients according to their entitlement. The entitlement status of patients is linked to income and is determined by the Treasury as discussed in Section 4.8. In addition to the distributional weights incorporated when calculating costs and benefits, it is important that the government address the distributional issues through taxation system rather than to rely on the process of project selection and design to redistribute income. It is usually outside the terns of references of project analysts to influence government tax and transfer policies (Jack 1999, p. 227).

The cost benefits ratios and NPVs of the six medications, namely Atorvastatin, Clopidogrel, Pioglitazone, Letrozole, Fluticasone/Salmeterol and Tiotropium are calculated in Chapter 6. As discussed in Section 2.4.3, medications should be selected for listing on the PBS if their cost benefit ratios are greater than one, and/or their NPVs are positive. Under the PBAC type of criteria, the NPV of Clopidogrel is $4,971.42 and its cost benefit ratio is 2.05. The NPV of Pioglitazone 30mg is $3,160.45 and its cost benefit ratio is 1.57. The NPV of Tiotropium is $579.55 and its cost benefit ratio is 1.13. All three medications should be accepted on the PBS under the PBAC type of criteria. For the other three, Atorvastatin, Letrozole and Fluticasone/Salmeterol, their NPVs are negative and cost benefit ratios are less than one. The NPV and cost benefit ratio of Atorvastatin is –$190.22 and 0.96. The NPV and cost benefit ratio of Letrozole is –$1,054.07 and 0.91. The NPV and cost benefit ratio of Fluticasone/Salmeterol is –$2,822.41 and 0.37. Using the decision rules of cost benefit analysis, all three medications should be rejected under the PBAC type of criteria (see Appendix 7.1).

Under the financial cost benefit analysis approach, the NPV of Atorvastatin, Clopidogrel, Pioglitazone, Letrozole, and Tiotropium are $2,790.92, $8,733.55, $7,111.09, $3,410.63, and $4,022.69 respectively. The cost benefit ratios of Atorvastatin, Clopidogrel, Pioglitazone, Letrozole, and Tiotropium are 1.60, 2.85, 2.29, 1.28 and 1.92 respectively. The cost benefit ratio of Fluticasone/Salmeterol is 0.98 and its NPV is –$104.27. Based on NPVs and cost benefit ratios, all medications should be selected with the exception of Fluticasone/Salmeterol (see Appendix 7.2).

Under the new[3] cost benefit analysis approach, the NPVs of Atorvastatin, Clopidogrel, Pioglitazone, Letrozole, Fluticasone/Salmeterol and Tiotropium are $30,645.29, $31,906.50, $24,639.47, $35,046.27, $31,921.88 and $36,501.23 respectively. Their cost benefit ratios are 6.34, 4.52, 3.22, 2.47, 5.68 and 6.98 respectively. Based on NPVs and cost benefit ratios, all medications should be selected (see Appendix 7.3).

As discussed in Chapter 5 and Chapter 6, the cost data are obtained from the Schedule of Pharmaceutical Benefits (published by the Medicare Australia) and computer dispensing programs used by community pharmacies. The benefits are calculated from statistical data of health services consumption from the Australian Bureau of Statistics and the AIHW, the Medicare Benefit Scheme, published data of the statistical values of life, and professional opinions of researchers.

7.3.5 PBS planning model

As an exercise for health sub-sector planning, let us assume that selection of medications for listing on the PBS is subject to the constraints of an allocated budget. In addition to the positive NPVs and cost benefit ratios being greater than 1, the net cash flow of that year must be within the allocated budget so that the chosen program is socially and financially viable within that year. The net cash flow of the program is calculated as the net benefits (benefits less costs) of these medications considered for PBS selection.

A PBS planning model

$$\text{Max} \quad \Sigma_i \Sigma_j A_{tj} X_j (1-\xi_j)^t \tag{7.1}$$

$$\text{subject to:} \quad \Sigma_i \Sigma_j R_{tj} X_j \le R_t$$

$$X_j = \{0,1\} \quad j = 1.. \text{ N (drugs)} \quad t = 1.. \text{ T (time)}$$

where:

A_{tj} = net benefit stream of drug j at time t = $(B_{tj} - C_{tj})$;

X_j = 1 if drug j is active, 0 otherwise;

R_{tj} = allocation of resource to drug j at time t;

R_t = total resource to allocate at time t;

ξ_j = the social discount rate of drug j;

B_{tj} = benefit for a drug j at time t; and

C_{tj} = cost for a drug j at time t.

This is a dynamic integer-programming problem for choosing a set of medications in PBS for a planning period. The objective function represents economic efficiency (net benefits) and public policy objectives. The constraints represent the economic and social costs of the medications, and the RHS figures show available PBS budgets. The model results can provide information regarding which medications should be chosen for the PBS in the given period. Public policy objectives derived from extra-welfaristic considerations can be represented by the discount rate, the cost and benefit estimates and the availability of funds. *This objective function explicitly can incorporate both equity and efficiency and other extra-welfaristic elements of social welfare objectives simultaneously,* allowing the choice over the amount of government subsidy and its distribution to be made concurrently, not sequentially (Jack 1999, p. 221).

An Australian PBS Planning Model (PBSPLAN)

Let the decision variables of the Australian PBS model be:

X_1 = Atorvastatin 40mg
X_2 = Clopidogrel 75mg
X_3 = Pioglitazone 30mg
X_4 = Letrozole 2.5mg
X_5 = Fluticasone/Salmeterol 500/50
X_6 = Tiotropium 18mcg

The objective functions

The objective function is derived by maximising the NPVs of the six medications under budget constraints. The government cost of PBS prescription for the year ending 30 June 2004 is 5 billion. Cardiovascular diseases, type 2 diabetes, breast cancer, asthma and chronic obstructive pulmonary diseases together account for about 30% of the disease burden in Australian society. The budget constraint for the six medications is assumed to be 1.5 billion (30% of $5 billion). The government cost of PBS prescriptions increased at 8.5% annually for the last five years (1999–2004). Assuming budget constraints increase by 8.5% annually for the five-year period, objective functions and constraints are derived as follow.

Model 1   PBAC type criteria

Objective function

$$- 190.22X_1 + 4971.42X_2 + 3160.45X_3 - 1054.07X_4$$
$$- 2822.41X_5 + 579.55X_6 \tag{7.3}$$

Subject to budget constraints

Year 0: $3464.82X_1 + 8652.41X_2 + 7468.65X_3 + 2959.01X_4 + 633.7X_5 + 3981.41X_6 \le 1500000000$

Year 1: $- 1030.77X_1 - 1038.09X_2 - 1214.97X_3 + 2959.01X_4 - 983.13X_5 - 959.37X_6 \le 1627500000$

Year 2: $- 1030.77X_1 - 1038.09X_2 - 1214.97X_3 - 2633.91X_4 - 983.13X_5 - 959.37X_6 \le 1773975000$

Year 3: $-1030.77X_1 - 1038.09X_2 - 1214.97X_3 - 2633.91X_4 - 983.13X_5 - 959.37X_6 \leq 1933632750$

Year 4: $-1030.77X_1 - 1038.09X_2 - 1214.97X_3 - 2633.91X_4 - 983.13X_5 - 959.37X_6 \leq 2107659698$

$X_j = \{0,1\}$ $j = 1,2,3,4,5,6$

Model 2 Financial cost benefit analysis

Objective function

$$2790.92X_1 + 8733.55X_2 + 7111.09X_3 + 3410.63X_4 - 104.27X_5 + 4022.69X_6 \tag{7.4}$$

Subject to budget constraints

Year 0: $4815.32X_1 + 10783.91X_2 + 9788.65X_3 + 4764.26X_4 + 1751.20X_5 + 5793.91X_6 \leq 1500000000$

Year 1: $-305.77X_1 - 313.09X_2 - 489.97X_3 + 4764.26X_4 - 258.13X_5 - 234.37X_6 \leq 1627500000$

Year 2: $-668.27X_1 - 675.59X_2 - 852.47X_3 - 2271.41X_4 - 620.63X_5 - 596.87X_6 \leq 1773975000$

Year 3: $-668.27X_1 - 675.59X_2 - 852.47X_3 - 2271.41X_4 - 620.63X_5 - 596.87X_6 \leq 1933632750$

Year 4: $-668.27X_1 - 675.59X_2 - 852.47X_3C2271.41X_4 - 620.63X_5 - 596.87X_6 \leq 2107659698$

$X_j = \{0,1\}$ $j = 1,2,3,4,5,6$

Model 3 New[3] cost benefit analysis

Objective function

$$30645.29X_1 + 31906.50X_2 + 24639.47X_3 + 35046.27X_4 + 31921.88X_5 + 36501.23X_6 \tag{7.5}$$

Subject to budget constraints

Year 0: $25946.95X_1 + 29847.28X_2 + 23491.77X_3 + 31661.16X_4 + 28243.42X_5 + 32374.45X_6 \leq 1500000000$

Year 1: $1712.56X_1 + 1052.78X_2 + 824.90X_3 + 6389.13X_4 + 1839.07X_5 + 1457.59X_6 \leq 1627500000$

Year 2: $995.26X_1 + 335.48X_2 + 107.60X_3 - 1001.34X_4 + 1121.77X_5 + 740.29X_6 \leq 1773975000$

Year 3: $995.26X_1 + 335.48X_2 + 107.60X_3 - 1001.34X_4 +$
$1121.77X_5 + 740.29X_6 \leq 1933632750$
Year 4: $995.26X_1 + 335.48X_2 + 107.60X_3 - 1001.34X_4 +$
$1121.77X_5 + 740.29X_6 \leq 2107659698$
$X_j = \{0,1\}$ $j = 1,2,3,4,5,6$

Results

A dynamic optimisation integer-programming model is used to solve the problem. Under budget constraints of the data above and the parameters, the PBSPLAN model was solved with the GAMS program (Levary et al. 1990; Brooke et al. 1992). The net benefits, NPVs and cost benefit ratios under the PBAC criteria are listed in Appendix 7.1; those under the financial cost benefit approach are listed in Appendix 7.2, and those under the new[3] cost benefit analysis are listed in Appendix 7.3. The GAMS program and output for PBSPLAN is given in Appendix 7.13.

For Model 1, the objective value of the social welfare function is 8711.3522 and the integer solution is $X_2 = X_3 = X_6 = 1$. Within the constraints of the allocated budget constraints, only three medications are selected with ranking in the order of Clopidogrel, Pioglitazone and Tiotropium. Atorvastatin, Letrozole and Fluticasone/Salmeterol are rejected from PBS listing.

For Model 2, the objective value of the social welfare function is 26068.7841 and the integer solution is $X_1 = X_2 = X_3 = X_4 = X_6 = 1$. Within the constraints of the allocated budget constraints, only five medications are selected with ranking in the order of Clopidogrel, Pioglitazone, Tiotropium, Letrozole, and Atorvastatin. Fluticasone/Salmeterol is rejected from PBS listing

For Model 3, the objective value of the social welfare function is 190660.6400 and the integer solution is $X_1 = X_2 = X_3 = X_4 = X_5 = X_6 = 1$. Within the constraints of the allocated budget constraints, all six medications are selected with ranking in the order of Tiotropium, Letrozole, Fluticasone/Salmeterol, Clopidogrel, Atorvastatin and Pioglitazone.

The results from the GAMS modelling support the decision-making from using the NPVs and cost benefit ratios criteria. Under the PBAC criteria, only Clopidogrel, Pioglitazone and Tiotropium are selected. Under the financial cost benefit analysis, Clopidogrel, Pioglitazone, Tiotropium, Letrozole, and Atorvastatin are selected.

Table 7.1 Results of PBSPLAN under different criteria

Cost benefit analysis model	Discount rate	Budget Constraints	Objective function value	Ranking of medications	Medications rejected
1. PBAC criteria	5%	As in Section 7.3.5	8711.3522	X_2, X_3, X_6	X_5, X_4, X_1
2. Financial CBA	5%	As in Section 7.3.5	26068.7841	X_2, X_3, X_6, X_4, X_1	X_5
3. New^3 CBA	0%	As in Section 7.3.5	190660.6400	$X_6, X_4, X_5, X_2, X_1, X_3$	None
4. New^3 CBA	0%	Half of the budget as calculated in Section 7.3.5	190660.6400	$X_6, X_4, X_5, X_2, X_1, X_3$	None
5. New^3 CBA (less benefits of QALY)	0%	As in Section 7.3.5	66636.5600	$X_2, X_3, X_6, X_1, X_4, X_5$	None
6. New^3 CBA	5%	As in Section 7.3.5	189216.3610	$X_6, X_4, X_2, X_5, X_1, X_3$	None
7. New^3 CBA	5%	Increase in the first year budget	189216.3610	$X_6, X_4, X_2, X_5, X_1, X_3$	None
8. New^3 CBA	5%	Increase in the fifth year budget	189216.3610	$X_6, X_4, X_2, X_5, X_1, X_3$	None
9. New^3 CBA	10%	As in Section 7.3.5	187977.8427	$X_6, X_4, X_2, X_5, X_1, X_3$	None
10. New^3 CBA	–5%	As in Section 7.3.5	0	None	All

Notes:

CBA = cost benefit analysis

X_1 = listing Atorvastatin 40mg on PBS.

X_2 = listing Clopidogrel 75mg on PBS.

X_3 = listing Pioglitazone 30mg on PBS.

X_4 = listing Letrozole 2.5mg on PBS.

X_5 = listing Fluticasone/Salmeterol 500/50 on PBS.

X_6 = listing Tiotropium 18mcg on PBS.

Under the new[3] cost benefit analysis, all six medications are selected.

Apart from the criteria under the three models, different parameters are put into the PBSPLAN model in order to test the validity of the model and the effects of discount rate, budget constraints and net benefit estimates on the results and the ranking of the medications selected. Model 1 is the cost benefit analysis under PBAC type of criteria with discount rate of 5%. Model 2 is the financial cost benefit analysis with discount rate of 5%. Model 3 is the new[3] cost benefit analysis with discount rate of 0%. Model 4 is the new[3] cost benefit analysis with discount rate of 0% and half of the allocated budget. Model 5 is the new[3] cost benefit analysis with discount rate of 0% and the exclusion of Quality Adjusted Life-years (QALYs) as benefit measures. Model 6 is the new[3] cost benefit analysis with discount rate of 5%. Model 7 is the new[3] cost benefit analysis with discount rate of 5% and increase in first year budget. Model 8 is the new[3] cost benefit analysis with discount rate of 5% and increase in last year budget. Model 9 is the new[3] cost benefit analysis with discount rate of 10%. Model 10 is the new[3] cost benefit analysis with discount rate of −5%. The value of the objective function, the ranking of the medications selected and the medication rejected changes with different criteria of the model specified. The results are listed in the Table 7.1.

7.4 Project appraisal and planning under risk and uncertainty: Sensitivity analysis

The outcome of many health programs is uncertain. This uncertainty needs to be incorporated into the planning and evaluation of the health program. Sensitivity analysis is used to test the results with changes in estimates of the analysis, such as the discount rate, and efficacy rate of the program. Decision trees or simulation techniques are used to aid decision-making. A decision tree maps out the sequence of events in a decision-making process, allowing for all alternatives at each decision point and chance event. Simulation techniques are used to generate the frequency distributions of possible outcomes for all alternative decisions, as well as to provide inputs for expected utility, certainty equivalent, or risk-adjusted discount rate analysis (Pappas and Hirschey 1985; Campbell and Brown 2003).

There is also uncertainty in the distribution of costs and benefits of health programs. Individuals affected by the program may value the uncertain costs and benefits differently. Results of a social cost benefit analysis may depend on the aggregation of such costs and benefits. To deal with uncertainty in the economic evaluation of health program, the following rules may be incorporated (Pearce and Nash 1981; Campbell and Brown 2003):

1) expected NPV;
2) sensitivity analysis;
3) adjustment for cost with risks-bearing in the decision rules;
4) a risky discount rate based on possibly state-preference theory; and
5) index of pessimism criterion, maximax criterion, maximin criterion, minimax regret criterion and payoff matrix.

Sensitivity analysis is the most common form of method in dealing with risk and uncertainty in cost benefit analysis. Following this tradition, while the sensitivity analyses of evaluation of individual medications were given in Section 6.9, the sensitivity analyses of the PBS sub-sector planning model are undertaken here. In order to deal with uncertainty in the new[3] cost benefit analysis of the six medications, a higher discount rate of 5% and 10% (instead of 0%) is used. The NPVs are calculated and listed in Appendices 7.3 and 7.4. NPVs of Atorvastatin, Clopidogrel, Pioglitazone, Fluticasone/ Salmeterol, and Tiotropium decrease with an increase in the discount rate from 0% to 5%. However, the NPVs of all six medications remain positive even with a higher discount rate. The decision rule does not change with an increase in discount rate.

In addition to discount rate, there can also be uncertainty with the flow of net benefits. The cost benefit calculation is repeated by excluding the different items of net benefit. The change in cost benefit ratio for the six medications only becomes significant with the exclusion of QALYs gained. However, the NPVs of all six medications remain positive and the decision rule does not change. A stochastic integer-programming model can be developed to compute uncertainty in outcomes of a health sector plan. The model is possible, but not attempted in this study.

7.5   Implications of results

After undertaking a cost benefit analysis under the three different approaches in Chapter 6, a set of net benefits, NPVs and cost benefit ratios are calculated. Under the new[3] cost benefit analysis, social value judgement and ethical issues as well as scientific information is incorporated in the definition and estimates of costs and benefits of the medications.

As discussed in Section 7.3.5, the annual PBS budget is used as the constraints of the PBSPLAN model to address the issues of project viability and sustainability. Issues such as burden of diseases and prevalence of the medical condition are factored into the budget constraints in order to address the ethical issues of equity and allocation according to need. Distributional equity is addressed by the entitlement status of patients that determined percentage of government subsidy, as well as the prevalence of diseases in the Australian population. Discount rate is set at 0% in order to address intergenerational equity. Under these criteria, a set of medications is selected under Model 3 new[3] cost benefit analysis leading to optimal, social, health outcome for the Australian public.

From Table 7.1, the value of the objective function is influenced by the discount rate. Comparing Models 3, 6 and 9, the criteria of calculating net benefit estimates and the budget constraints are the same for the three models, the objective function increases in value with the decrease in discount rate. The ranking of medications selected also differs. In Model 3, Fluticasone/Salmeterol is selected ahead of Clopidogrel. The selection order is reversed in Models 6 and 9.

The value of the objective function is also sensitive to the criteria of calculating net benefit estimates of the medications. Comparing Models 3 and 5, the value of objective function decreases substantially with the exclusion of QALY as benefits. The ranking of medications selected also changes with Tiotropium drops from first and third position, Clopidogrel moves from fourth to first position.

When comparing Models 3 and 4, as well as 5, 6 and 7, changes in budget constraints does not affect the value of objective function and ranking of medication selected. All medications seem to be selected under the new[3] cost benefit analysis model regardless of the changes in discount rate, budget constraints and criteria of calculating net benefit estimates. Only six medications are tested for PBS listing using PBSPLAN in this study. In real life setting, there are many more medications considered for PBS listing than the six medications in this study. Some medications among others would be rejected from PBS listing.

However, the new[3] cost benefit analysis approach aids decision-making in PBS to be sustainable and ethically justified, leading to better budget management and more efficient resource allocation. The new[3] cost benefit analysis can provide policy plan that gives high level of social welfare for the Australian community. Therefore, the model produced in this chapter can maximise social welfare for Australia.

7.6 Health project planning for sustainable development

7.6.1 Definition of sustainability

Anand and Sen (2000) have argued that it is essential to achieve sustainable development of a society or economy. Anand and Sen (2000) further argues that redistribution to the poor in the form of improving health and nutrition is important in enhancing their capabilities to lead more fulfilling lives; and considers human development vital in achieving sustainability. Health sector project planning should be developed so that the program will produce sustainable human development. In this section below, we discuss how a sustainable health sector development can be formulated.

The core idea of sustainability is that current policies or decisions should address issues of intergenerational equity and preserve the economic opportunities of the next generation to maintain their living standards (Repetto 1985; Solow 1991). Talbot (1977) argued that preserving opportunities for future generations is a common sense minimal notion of intergenerational justice (Kneese and Schulze 1985). The framework is based on the utilitarian approach of maximising total welfare of different generations, allowing the welfare to be traded off across different generations. Health programs should be based on such criteria and principles of sustainable development.

Sustainability is concerned with giving equal weights to present and future generations in health policy-making. The health of future generations should be treated as equally positive and important as that of the present generation. Future benefits should not be discounted. Translating these principles into the setting of the PBS, the policy objectives of PBAC should encompass the following (Anand and Sen 2000):

a. meeting basic pharmaceutical needs of the Australian general community;
b. protecting the vulnerable, especially for those with chronic and/or multiple medical conditions and those who cannot afford costs of medications;
c. improving the health status of the general public for higher productivity;
d. ensuring intergenerational equity and justice;
e. incorporating altruism, ethics and moral philosophy; and
f. providing intertemporal efficiency with the above objectives.

7.6.2   Sustainability criterion in NPV analysis

All drugs with a positive NPV should be included in the PBS provided that the net impact is non-negative. Medications selected for PBS listing should not have a net negative effect. The use of NPV analysis, by itself, does not address the issues of intergenerational equity nor does it address the issues of irreversibility and therefore cannot, by itself, prescribe a set of sustainable development programs.

The policy objectives discussed in Section 7.6.1 can be incorporated in the PBSPLAN model. Sustainability criterion can be introduced into a cost benefit analysis by including constraints on the depletion of resources, by increasing the budget at the initial period to meet the PBS expenditure in order to improve the health of the general population (see Model 7 in Table 7.1). Sustainability can also be addressed by considering the prevalence of the medical conditions among the population, ensuring that funding is directed towards medications which maximise the health of the population and generate positive impact on the welfare of the society. This criterion is incorporated in setting budget constraints according to the burden of different diseases and medical conditions. Sustainability can also be considered by using zero discount rate so that future health benefits of the society is held equally important as the current health benefits (see Models 3, 4, 5 in Table 7.1).

7.6.3 Proposed methodology

The methodology proposed by Islam and Gigas (1996), for program evaluation method on a sustainable development basis, can be used to formulate a health sector plan for sustainable social development. Using the cost benefit analysis technique as discussed above, non-confounding factors in the program can be valuated. Social benefits of listing a drug on the PBS can be valuated by the methods discussed in chapters 5 and 6. The social benefits of a particular drug can then be incorporated into the new[3] cost benefit analysis.

The proposed discount rate used under this method varies slightly from previous uses of the social discount rate in the project evaluation phase. It may have a premium received for the sustainable growth of the health sector. The cost benefit ratio is calculated to reflect the desirability of listing of the drug on the PBS. The cost benefit ratio is then used as a multiplier on the social discount rate to give the health social discount rate (ξ_j) for each drug j. The issue of intergenerational equity is addressed by altering the expected flow of the benefits and costs of the PBS and balances the needs of current and future generations.

7.6.4 Model for sustainable health programs

$$\text{Max} \quad \Sigma_{\forall t} \, \Sigma_{\forall j} \, A_{tj} \, X_j \, (1 - \xi_j)^t$$

subject to:
$$\Sigma_{\forall t} \, \Sigma_{\forall j} \, (Eb_{tj} - Ec_{tj}) \, X_j \geq 0$$
$$\Sigma_{\forall t} \, \Sigma_{\forall j} \, R_{tj} \, X_j \leq R_t$$
$$X_j = \{0,1\} \qquad j = 1.. \, N \text{ (drugs)} \qquad t = 1.. \, T \text{ (time)}$$

where:

A_{tj} = net benefit stream of drug j at time t;

X_j = 1 if drug j is active, 0 otherwise;

Eb_{tj} = health benefits of drug j at time t;

Ec_{tj} = health costs of drug j at time t;

R_{tj} = allocation of resource to drug j at time t;

R_t = total resource to allocate at time t; and

ξ_j = sustainable SDR of drug j (as in Section 6.6.5).

7.6.5 Sustainability modelling in this study

As discussed in Section 7.6.2, sustainability is incorporated in the present PBSPLAN model by increasing the initial budget of the PBS program (year 0 of the five-year period), by directing PBS funding towards medications for medical conditions that are most prevalent among the Australian population (such as cardiovascular diseases and type 2 diabetes) and by using zero discount rate in the cost benefit calculation of the medications.

The PBSPLAN is also tested with different budget constraints. All the six medications are still selected when the allocated budget is halved, when there is higher allocated budget in the first year, and when there is higher allocated budget in the fifth year (see Table 7.1). When setting the budget constraints, funding is allocated to the model according to the burden of diseases related to the medications considered.

The PBSPLAN is tested with different social discount rate. The social discount rate is set at zero under the sustainability criteria, all six medications are selected under the new[3] cost benefit analysis approach. The model is repeated with discount rates at 5% and 10% respectively, all six medications are still selected, but with different values of social welfare function.

Part B   Implications

7.7   Implications for decision-making

7.7.1   For the six medications analysed

Atorvastatin

Under the new[3] cost benefit analysis, Atorvastatin has a NPV of $30,645.29 and a cost benefit ratio of 6.34 and should be included on the PBS. Under the financial cost benefit analysis, Atorvastatin has a NPV of $2,790.92 and a cost benefit ratio of 1.60 and should be included on the PBS. But under the PBAC type of criteria, Atorvastatin should be rejected for its NPV of –$190.22 and a cost benefit ratio of 0.96.

Despite its negative results under the PBAC type of criteria, Atorvastatin is not only listed on the PBS; it is the highest selling medication by volume on the PBS list in 2004. Atorvastatin is one of the most commonly prescribed medications to control blood cholesterol level. Atorvastatin blocks the hepatic synthesis of cholesterol and triggers a compensatory reaction to lower plasma level of low-density lipoprotein (LDL). By controlling the blood cholesterol level, Atorvastatin helps to prevent atherosclerosis and further end organ damage such as stroke and heart attack. As discussed in Section 5.3.1, coronary heart disease is the largest single cause of death in Australia. Many of those suffering from coronary events (mainly heart attack) are aged 35–69 and are a vital part of the economic productivity of our society. If the listing decision was made strictly on the basis of the NPVs and cost benefit ratios calculated under the PBAC criteria, Atorvastatin would not be listed on the PBS.

Clopidogrel

Under the new[3] cost benefit analysis, Clopidogrel has a NPV of $31,906.50 and a cost benefit ratio of 4.52 and should be included on the PBS. Under the financial cost benefit analysis, Clopidogrel has a NPV of $8,733.55 and a cost benefit ratio of 2.85 and should be included on the PBS. Lastly under the PBAC type of criteria, Clopidogrel has a NPV of $4,971.42 and a cost benefit ratio of 2.05 and should be included on the PBS. For Clopidogrel, the listing decision is the same under all three criteria.

Under the PBS criteria, Clopidogrel is prescribed to prevent recurrence of ischaemic stroke or transient cerebral ischaemic events. As discussed in Section 5.3.1, stroke is the second largest cause of death in Australia. Clopidogrel inhibits platelet aggregation within blood vessel and helps to prevent the cerebral ischaemic episodes.

Pioglitazone

Under the new[3] cost benefit analysis, Pioglitazone has a NPV of $24,639.47 and a cost benefit ratio of 3.22 and should be included on the PBS. Under the financial cost benefit analysis, Pioglitazone has a NPV of $7,111.09 and a cost benefit ratio of 2.29 and should be included on the PBS. Under the PBAC type of criteria, Pioglitazone should be selected for its NPV of $3,160.45 and a cost benefit ratio of 0.89. For Pioglitazone, the listing decision is the same under all three criteria. Under the PBS type of criteria, Pioglitazone is prescribed as dual therapy with either oral hypoglycaemic agents or insulin when the blood glucose control of type 2 diabetes is inadequate despite maximum doses of oral hypoglycaemic or insulin.

As discussed in Section 5.4.1, the incidence of type 2 diabetes has increased dramatically in recent years with obesity being a significant contributing factor. Diabetes itself is a risk factor predisposing patients to cardiovascular diseases. By addressing the underlying insulin resistance, Pioglitazone helps to provide better blood glucose control for patients. It also helps to slow the progression of treatment from oral hypoglycaemic to insulin, improving the quality of life of patients. Type 2 diabetes is predominantly found among middle-aged and elderly people, with the middle-aged group of patients forming a vital part of the workforce of our society.

Letrozole

Under the new[3] cost benefit analysis, Letrozole has a NPV of $35,046.27 and a cost benefit ratio of 2.47 and should be included on the PBS. Under the financial cost benefit analysis, Letrozole has a NPV of $3,410.63 and a cost benefit ratio of 1.28 and should be included on the PBS. But under the PBAC type of criteria, Letrozole should be rejected for its NPV of –$1,054.07 and a cost benefit ratio of 0.91.

Despite its negative results under the PBAC type of criteria, Letrozole is listed on the PBS. Under the PBS type of criteria, Letrozole is prescribed as treatment of hormone-dependent advanced breast cancer in post-menopausal women. Breast cancer is the most common cause of death from cancers among female patients. Patients receiving Letrozole gain an additional 0.714 life-years as compared with those receiving Tamoxifen. If the listing decision is made strictly on the basis of the NPVs and cost benefit ratios calculated under the PBAC type of criteria, Letrozole would not be listed on the PBS.

Fluticasone/Salmeterol

Under the new[3] cost benefit analysis, Fluticasone/Salmeterol has a NPV of $31,921.88 and a cost benefit ratio of 5.68 and should be included in the PBS. Under the financial cost benefit analysis, Fluticasone/Salmeterol should be rejected from PBS listing because its NPV is –$104.27 and its cost benefit ratio is 0.98. Under the PBAC type of criteria, Fluticasone/Salmeterol should be rejected for a cost benefit ratio of 0.37 and its NPV of –$2,822.41. Despite its negative results under the PBAC type of criteria, Fluticasone/Salmeterol is listed on the PBS. Under the PBS type of criteria, Fluticasone/Salmeterol is prescribed for patients with frequent episodes of asthma. Fluticasone/Salmeterol is one of the most commonly prescribed maintenance therapy medications for asthmatic patients. Asthma prevalence is the highest among the group aged 5–24 years and is a common cause of hospitalisation or emergency department visits for the 5–14 year age group. Fluticasone/Salmeterol helps to prevent the onset of an asthmatic attack and improves the quality of life of patients. If the listing decision were made strictly on the basis of the NPVs and cost benefit ratios calculated under the PBAC type of criteria, Fluticasone/ Salmeterol would not be listed on the PBS.

Tiotropium

Under the new[3] cost benefit analysis, Tiotropium has a NPV of $36,501.23 and a cost benefit ratio of 6.98 and should be included on the PBS. Under the financial cost benefit analysis, Tiotropium has a NPV of $4,022.69 and a cost benefit ratio of 1.92 and should be included on the PBS. Under the PBAC type of criteria, Tiotropium has a NPV of $579.55 and a cost benefit ratio of 1.13 and should be included on the PBS. For Tiotropium, the listing decision is the same under all three criteria.

Under the PBS type of criteria, Tiotropium is prescribed for the long-term maintenance of bronchospasm and dyspnoea associated with chronic obstructive pulmonary disease. Chronic obstructive pulmonary disease is the major cause of hospitalisation among elderly patients. Tiotropium helps to control the respiratory symptoms and improve the quality of life of sufferers.

7.7.2 PBS sub-sector planning strategies and policies

As discussed in Section 7.3.4, all six medications are selected under the social choice approach. The results are compared with other approaches. Under the PBAC type of criteria, only Clopidogrel and Tiotropium should be selected. Under the financial cost benefit analysis, all medications except Fluticasone/Salmeterol should be selected. Under the new[3] cost benefit analysis with budget constraints, all six medications should be selected. The results from PBSPLAN supports those from using NPV and cost benefit ratio criteria in decision-making.

7.7.3 Sustainability

Under the sustainability criteria, the social discount rate is set to zero and all six medications are selected under the new[3] cost benefit analysis approach. The PBSPLAN is also tested with half of the original budget allocated, all the six medications are still selected under such budget constraints.

7.7.4   Sensitivity analysis

By changing the discount rate from 0% to 5% and 10%, all the six medications still return with a positive NPVs and a cost benefit ratio greater than one. Under the decision rules of NPVs and cost benefit ratios, are six medications should still be selected. The results of net benefits, NPVs and cost benefit ratios of the six medications under new[3] cost benefit analysis are listed in Appendix 7.4 (discount rate = 5%) and Appendix 7.5 (discount rate = 10%). The results are also tested with exclusion of different items of net benefits, all six medications still return positive NPVs, but with lower cost benefit ratios. The results are listed in Appendices 7.6 to 7.12. Details of calculations can be found in Appendices 7.14 to 7.65.

7.8   General consideration

As discussed in Section 6.8, many medications are included on the PBS list despite their negative NPVs and cost benefit ratio being less than one calculated under the PBAC criteria. If the PBAC adopts the societal perspective in deciding the listing of medications on the PBS, then the resulting negative NPVs of the medications suggest the omission of certain benefits from the analysis. On the other hand, all six medications return a positive NPV under the new[3] cost benefit analysis approach, supporting their listing decisions. Thus, the new[3] cost benefit analysis under the social choice approach represents a better method of estimating the costs and benefits of the medications that support the original listing decision.

By introducing a budget constraint as an additional selection criterion, the result of the analysis remains the same. If a tighter budget constraint is applied, with only half of the budget allocated above is available for the six medications, the result is the same and all six medications are selected.

Impact on the health system

The new social choice approach makes it easier and more operational to estimate the social costs and benefits of different programs (in this case different medications across various therapeutic classes), the analysts can make decision on a more balanced framework based on scientific knowledge, social value judgement, social and individual benefits and costs. The PBSPLAN model allows comparison of social costs and benefits among medications across different therapeutic classes. Medications are selected on the basis on their net social benefits for the general community. It is exactly the comparison among different health programs make health sector planning possible.

7.9 Implications of CBA in decision-making

The predominance of cost effectiveness analysis over cost benefit analysis in the economic evaluation of health programs comes as analysts' concern with the validity of valuation method (Birch et al. 2002). Under the new[3] cost benefit analysis, social benefits of health programs are valuated in monetary terms by combining the human capital approach, the preference approach, scientific information, expert opinions as well as social value judgement. Consequently, we can compare benefits in the same unit, even with medications come from different therapeutic classes. Based on the burden of different diseases to the Australian society, a priority list can be set in selecting medications for PBS listing to maximise the social welfare of the society.

7.10 Implications for health sector planning

By introducing health sector planning perspectives into the decision-making process of the PBS, we attempt to incorporate issues such as macroeconomic and sector implications, equity, efficiency, ethics and moral philosophy. In addition to quantifying the clinical, financial and social benefits of a medication, we also try to address how much of these benefits are needed and can be afforded by the Australian society. Although the new[3] cost-benefit model results suggest the acceptance of all the six medications on the PBS, the actual selection of the medications for a particular planning period depends on the available budget and is determined by the priority suggested by the value of the objective functions of the models.

7.11   Welfare economics implication

By incorporating the social cost into the cost stream calculation, we have also considered the opportunity cost of the forgone capital or fund, in addition to the financial cost of the medications and the program. By incorporating the social benefit into the benefit calculation, we tried to capture benefits beyond the mere cost savings measure of the government. By estimating the improvement in quality of life (health status) and the quantity of life (life expectancy) in addition to saving in health costs and increase in economic productivity, we attempt to measure the improvement in the social welfare/utility rather than just the financial benefit to society.

7.12   Other issues

Generic medications and pricing policy

As discussed in Section 4.10, there is a lack of central policy for generics medication to enter into the market. Firstly, there is no limit on number of generic alternatives of the same medications. Secondly, a generic brand of medication may only be available in one particular strength or formulation of the medications, but not the others. This contributes to patients' confusion when their dosages are adjusted upwardly or downwardly as the same brand of medications may not be available in different strength required. Thirdly, some of the generic brands and 'house brand' from pharmacy banner groups are not available directly from full-line pharmacy wholesaler. The manufacturers of generic medications do not need to guarantee ready, easy and equal access of their products to the whole PBS product available. In other words, not every pharmacy can supply all the different generic brands of medications for their patients. From an economic viewpoint, efficiency is an issue when there are ten to twelve different brands of the same medication available (eg. amoxycillin 500mg capsules as discussed earlier). From a therapeutic viewpoint, continuity of care is an issue when ready, easy and equal access to all different brands of medications is not guaranteed. Increase in number of brands available for substitution contributes to further confusion in patients, decrease in medication compliance, duplication or omission in medications by patients, and possibly other clinical errors.

Generic medication pricing is promoted to the Australian public as a policy to lower prices of medications. However, the savings rest with the Government rather than the general public. This is especially the case with the flow-on effect of 12.5% pricing reduction for generic medications, as well as medications within the same reference pricing groups. Some medications in the same reference pricing group do not produce similar health outcome. These medications are not therapeutically interchangeable, but classified as generic medications in economic and pricing definition by the Government. In August 2005, the four medications listed on the PBS come under the above situation are Topiramate (Topamax®), Levetiracetam (Keppra®), Escitalopram (Lexapro®) and Pemetrexed (Alimta®). Patients are required to pay the additional charges of special patient contribution unless their medical practitioners succeed to obtain authority for exemption on clinical ground.

Technological development

Technological innovations such as PBS online and computer prescribing can be introduced to avoid doctor shopping and pharmacy shopping. Information is available online about the timing of the last dispensing of a medication for a particular patient. This can help to determine whether patients are collecting medications within an approved time interval, and help to discourage patients from stockpiling their medications. These innovations can help to combat the issues of moral hazard. New technologies (such as Smart-card) enable medical and pharmacy professionals to retrieve medical and medication histories, thus helping to prevent duplication in prescribing or dispensing, potential lethal drug interactions, and so on.

7.13 International comparison

Compared with other countries, Australia is one of the few jurisdictions demanding economic data in deciding government subsidy of a medication. Unlike Canada and the UK, cost benefit analysis is not encouraged under the submission guidelines of the PBAC. However, it is not clear how these evaluations are used in practice and the transparency in decision-making process of PBAC is always debatable. The outcome of economic evaluation certainly influences the reimbursement decision and the price of the medication, but it seems to be used as just another factor in the negotiations. There is no clear relationship between the outcome of the economic evaluation and the price (Pinto Prades and Badia Llach 2005).

7.14   Plausibility of the approach and result

7.14.1   Validation of model and result

Model validation is a process of substantiating that the model behaves with a satisfactory level of accuracy and consistency within its domain of applicability. During the validation process, the model is run under the same input conditions that drive the system. The model behaviour is then compared with the system behaviour to check whether the 'right' model has been built (Gass and Harris 2001).

There are three levels of validation tests, namely descriptive, analytical and experimental. There are also three types of validation criteria applied to the three levels of validation tests. For the descriptive level, the validation criteria include the attainment of the objectives of the model, the appropriateness of the model structure and the plausibility of the results. The objective of the PBSPLAN is to select medications among other alternatives to be listed on the PBS in order to maximise the health and social welfare of the Australian community subject to the budget constraints of that time period. For the analytical level, the validation criteria include the characteristics of model solutions and the robustness of the results. The results of the PBSPLAN model support the decision deriving from other criteria such as NPVs, cost benefit ratios, etc. For the experimental level, the validation criteria include the methodological tests related to model documentation, costs and efficiency in model transfer and extension, tests related to model execution such as accuracy and efficiency of the execution, and cost and efficiency in the software transfer and extension.

The model PBSPLAN is a GAMS program used for capital budgeting. The objective of this model is health sector planning with budget constraints. From the experience of this study such as model convergence, results, the plausibility of the results (to be discussed in the next section) and other model validation criteria, it is found to be an appropriate model for health sector planning.

7.14.2 Plausibility of results

The accuracy of the results can be verified by checking the relevance of the optimal solution provided by the model to the expected results, the reported actual values or the historical data set. Several methods are used to check the plausibility of the results, namely intuitive judgement, comparison of results, statistical tests and self-auditing or third party auditing.

Intuitive judgement is used to check whether the results are consistent with the theory in this area and acceptable to the professions. In the PBSPLAN, the results are consistent with the theory, where all the six medications return positive NPVs and a cost benefit ratio greater than one. They are selected in PBSPLAN with the ranking of the six medications being consistent with the order of their NPVs of the six medications and the burden of diseases to the Australian society. The capital budgeting approach to health sector planning is new to the profession.

Results can also be compared with historical data, results from similar studies, and the ability to predict the future performance of the system. It is difficult to compare the results of PBSPLAN with historical data and results from similar studies as the model has not been used previously in health sector planning.

Justification of theoretical foundation

By including the social costs and benefits component, we capture the change in social welfare better than the PBAC and financial approach of cost benefit analysis. The social welfare function of the PBSPLAN incorporates both equity and efficiency issues simultaneously, allowing the decision of the amount of resource allocated and its distribution to be made concurrently rather than sequentially (Jack 1999, p. 221).

7.14.3 Generalisation

The sectoral planning approach developed in this chapter on the basis of new[3] cost benefit analysis is a general approach. The methodology can be applied to other disciples in economics and social sciences other than the PBS and health programs. Apart from performing health sector planning from the pharmaceutical subsidy perspective, the same principles can be applied to all other types of health programs including hospitalisation and other health services consumption.

7.15   Conclusion

In this chapter, we have undertaken a cost benefit analysis for these six medications along with a sector planning exercise. Our exercise implied that the new[3] cost benefit analysis is a suitable methodology in selecting health programs that maximise the social welfare or benefit of the society. Under this approach, social value judgement, ethical issues and scientific information are incorporated in the definition and estimation of costs and benefits of the health program.

In addition, sustainability and intergenerational equity are built-in criteria of the model. As a result, the model under the new[3] cost benefit analysis leads to selection of health programs that maximise the social welfare and health outcome of the general community.

8
Summary and Conclusion

8.1 Introduction

This chapter provides the summary, limitations and conclusion of this study including the justification for the development of a new approach to cost benefit analysis, the application of this new approach to the Pharmaceutical Benefit Scheme (PBS) in Australia, and the implications of the findings for economic evaluation and normative economics with a special emphasis on the implications for health economics.

This chapter is structured as follows. Section 8.2 presents the new approach, its justification, and application. Section 8.3 provides a summary of findings and their plausibility. Sections 8.4 and 8.5 report the limitations and conclusions of this study.

8.2 A new approach: Summary and overview

8.2.1 Justification and theoretical foundation

As discussed in Section 2.7, there are several limitations with the existing practices of cost benefit analysis. There are theoretical difficulties. The mainstream framework of welfare economics of cost benefit analysis assumes utility maximisation, consumer sovereignty, consequentialism and welfarism (Hurley 2000). Under the framework of *new welfare economics*, utility functions are assumed to be ordinal and interpersonal comparison of utility is considered impossible. It is then also impossible to maximise the sum of utilities aggregated across individuals and the concept of consumer sovereignty is also questionable as a result of information asymmetry, lack of adequate professional and/or technical knowledge. In new welfare economics, a democratic social choice is impossible. Cost benefit analysis is fraught with various difficulties in being a useful technique for social choice. Further developments have occurred in welfare economics such as new[2] welfare economics and normative social choice theory. Further extensions to these developments are necessary, as was argued in Preface and Chapters 1, 2 and 3.

In addition, issues of distributional equity as well as incorporation of ethics and moral philosophy do not form part of current practices of cost benefit analysis of health programs. Another issue needs to be addressed is the choice of an appropriate discount rate for ensuring intergenerational equity in the benefits and costs of the health program when conducting a cost benefit analysis. There are other problems in the existing methods for conceptualising and measuring benefits of projects and programs. This has led practitioners to resort to cost effectiveness analysis and other methods, instead of cost benefit analysis.

The objective of this research was to develop a new approach called new[3] cost benefit analysis, based on the elements of new[3] welfare economics, in order to overcome some of the above limitations of current practices of cost benefit analysis and to make it an operational technique for social choice. The new[3] cost benefit analysis can evaluate the full social costs and benefits of health programs, using the PBS as a partially illustrative example.

Under the new[3] cost benefit analysis, a combination of the preference-based and human capital approach method was used to measure social benefits of health programs, in terms of financial benefits (as cost savings in health service consumption and increase in economic productivity), willingness-to-pay (WTP) of patients for a positive health outcome, as well as other measures of social benefits (external, indirect, intangible benefits) based on expert opinions, scientific information and social value judgements.

The new[3] cost benefit analysis aims for the operationalisation of social choice theory, the integration of moral philosophy and ethics into health economics, the provision of appropriate quantitative information for decision-making, and a balanced decision-making or a social choice framework based on scientific knowledge, expert opinions, social value judgements and preferences. This approach is based on a possibility perspective of social choice theory; it integrates individual preferences with social preferences in making social choices. Some other elements of the theoretical foundations of this approach are: measurability and comparability of utility and welfare, the relevance of extra-welfaristic elements in social decision-making, the role of the social welfare function in the specification of social optima, the possibility for explicating social preferences from constitutional and policy documents.

8.2.2 Evaluation in practice: The PBS in Australia

In most OECD countries, the healthcare system is financed either through direct government funding or through tax expenditures. The PBS in Australia is an example of direct government funding where the commonwealth government provides subsidised medications to the general public. The PBS was first implemented in 1950 to provide 139 life-saving and disease-preventing medications free to the whole community. Under the PBS, benefits are only available from an approved pharmacy via a PBS prescription written by an approved medical practitioner. The commonwealth government supplies the PBS stationery and/or computer-prescribing software to the medical practitioners. Patients get medications dispensed at a subsidised price under the PBS.

In order to attract government subsidy, medications must be listed on the PBS. The Pharmaceutical Benefits Advisory Committee (PBAC) makes recommendations to the Minister of Health and Ageing regarding the PBS listing of medications. In 1993, Australia became the first jurisdiction in the world to make economic evaluation mandatory in the submission to the PBAC for applying for a government subsidy of medications. The PBAC issues submission guidelines for the pharmaceutical industries. Although some existing methods adopt a societal perspective in evaluating health projects, cost effectiveness analysis is the dominating methodology and cost benefit analysis is not widely adopted. In this research, we have demonstrated that the new[3] cost benefit analysis is an improved methodology in addressing the societal perspective and assessing the impact on social welfare of listing decisions.

8.2.3 New[3] cost benefit analysis

Medications should be listed on the PBS on the basis of maximising social net benefits in addition to financial net benefits. The new[3] cost benefit analysis reduces all social benefits and costs of the PBS to a single measurement unit (the dollar) in order to allow a meaningful comparison between different medications for making social choices in the health sector. A few major areas are of special significance in the new[3] cost benefit analysis based on the possibility perspective in normative social choice theory and social value judgements and preferences (Chapters 3, 5, 6 and 7):

1) identification and inclusion of indirect, external and intangible costs and benefits on the basis of scientific information, expert opinions and social value judgements;
2) social valuation of benefits and costs;
3) shadow pricing of benefits and costs;
4) the use of altruistic social discount rate;
5) incorporation of public policy objectives, social preferences and value judgements in ranking and decision-making regarding PBS listing;
6) incorporation of ethics and extra-welfaristic elements in cost benefit estimates and models (via the discount rate, terminal conditions, time horizon and modelling structure and equations); and
7) incorporation of issues such as sustainability and fiscal soundness.

Using Bentham's concept of utilitarianism, '*social benefit or welfare*' is defined as an aggregation of individual utility or health gain (Bannock et al. 1972) adjusted, however, by social preferences. Benefits and costs borne by individuals are aggregated into 'social benefits' and 'social costs' by simple addition which are adjusted by expert opinions and social preferences. A medication should be listed on the PBS from an economic perspective if its net social benefit or welfare is positive (Chapters 2, 3 and 6).

The elements of new[3] welfare economics and new[3] cost benefit analysis of medications which are relevant in the Australian PBS setting have been adopted in this study. Following the discussion of the present application of the new[3] cost benefit analysis in Section 3.6.2, economics and ethics have been considered in estimating costs and benefits of listing medications on the PBS in Australia. The present application assumes the measurability of social welfare and other extra-welfaristic components of costs and benefits of listing a medication on the PBS on the basis of social value judgement and public policy objectives. In this PBS application, social welfare is represented by the social benefits of a medication which consists of improvement in productivity, avoidance of hospitalisation and other costs, and improvement in the quality and expectancy of life. In the present application in this study, costs and benefits have been estimated by using scientific information, expert opinions and social preferences. As consideration for equity are addressed in the PBS setting by other health and social support schemes, equity consideration have not been incorporated in the present new[3] cost benefit analysis.

Under the new[3] cost benefit methodology, we captured the social costs and benefits in addition to the financial costs and benefits. In the cost stream, we included the financial costs (in the form of drug costs, internal and external program costs) and the social costs. The social cost was estimated as the social opportunity cost of paying for the six medications instead of their lower cost alternatives. The social cost is thus the differential between the medication cost and its lower cost alternatives.

The ultimate goal of health programs is to improve the health outcome of individual patients. Medications are prescribed to alleviate symptoms, control medical conditions of patients and prevent progression of disease and deterioration of the medical condition, ultimately aiming at improvement in the quantity and quality of the patients' lives.

In the benefit stream, we estimated the monetary value of health gain in terms of improved quality and quantity of life. These estimates were based on expert opinions and the social value judgement of the analyst/researcher. With improved health, a patient will have a less frequent need for visits to general and/or specialist medical practitioners. Patients are less likely to consume complementary medicines if their health is maintained under optimal condition. The benefit of improved life expectancy was estimated by the expected increase in number of health years and the statistical value of life. The WTP of medications was estimated by a patient's preference to get the medication in the absence of government subsidy.

The increase in productivity was calculated as the number of days of potential sick leave multiplied by the average daily wage rate of $145.00 (ABS 2005 Cat. No. 6305.0, 6306.0). There are two components of potential sick leave, hospitalisation and outpatient visit.

Data on hospitalisation come from average length of stay of the medical conditions corresponding to the six medications, as published by the Australian Institute of Health and Welfare. Data of decreased outpatient visits are based on the assumption of the researcher/analyst. The increase in productivity for the six medications is calculated in Chapters 5 and 6.

In many mainstream practices in this area, the inclusion of increase in economic productivity is discouraged. We disagreed with this view and argued that an increase in productivity due to taking a medication should necessarily be included in a cost benefit analysis. Ultimately, the cost of lost productivity is captured by the society. This is why we include the increase in economic productivity as a benefit under the social choice approach.

Avoidance of hospitalisation costs was calculated as the average length of stay multiplied by the average cost per patient day for that medical condition. Both figures are clinical information published by the Australian Institute of Health and Welfare as discussed in Chapters 5 and 6.

The cost savings of decrease in outpatient visits was calculated as the number of visits avoided multiplied by the unit consultation fee. The decrease in the number of visits was based on assumptions of the researcher/analyst. The unit consultation fee to medical practitioners is published in the Medicare Benefits Schedule (Department of Health and Ageing 2004a). The results are reported and discussed in Chapters 5 and 6.

A statistical value of life was used to measure the benefit of improved life expectancy as a result of the medication. The benefit was calculated as the number of healthy life-years lost due to an untreated medical condition multiplied by the average value of quality adjusted life-years. The results are reported in Chapters 5 and 6.

The benefit of improved health status was also measured as the decrease in complementary medicine consumption. An annual savings of $400 is proposed by the researcher/analyst. The WTP of the medication was calculated as the amount a patient pays for the medication supplied on a private prescription in the absence of government subsidy. The results are calculated in Chapters 5 and 6.

Using the estimates of costs and benefits, we then calculated the net present values and cost benefit ratio for each of the six medications. Under the new[3] cost benefit methodology, the results supported the listing decision as all six medications return positive net present values and cost benefit ratio greater than one. This was in line with the real life scenario as all six medications are listed on the PBS.

8.2.4 Sector planning

The new[3] cost benefit methodology allows the comparison of costs and benefits of different medications in a single unit of monetary terms of all projects. These figures were then put into an optimisation model for sector planning for the Australian PBS decision-making using the GAMS computer program in order to test the viability of the listing decisions in the presence of budget constraints (Chapter 7).

As we can now compare the results of medications from different therapeutic classes, we can then proactively determine which medication should be listed, taking into consideration issues such as budget constraints, the burden of different diseases to society, social and individual preferences, and so on. Issues such as sustainability and intergenerational equity are also considered by addressing the social discount rate and the inclusion of social benefits and social value judgements in the decision-making process.

8.3 Summary of findings: Implications, validation and plausibility

Under the new[3] cost benefit methodology, both social costs and benefit components were included in the analysis. Changes in social welfare as a result of listing six medications were better captured in the new[3] cost benefit analysis than the PBAC type of approach and a financial approach of cost benefit analysis.

The new[3] cost benefit methodology was applied to six medications listed on the PBS in chapters 5 and 6. As discussed in Chapter 7, the listing decision of the six medications was supported by the results of the analysis under the new[3] cost benefit methodology. By adjusting the social discount rate from 0% to 5% and 10%, the result of the analysis under the new[3] cost benefit methodology still supports the listing of the six medications.

By enabling comparisons of costs and benefits of medications from different therapeutic classes, a health sector planning exercise was carried out in the PBS setting. The model PBSPLAN is a GAMS program used for capital budgeting. In the health sector planning exercise, we tested the viability of the listing decisions of six medications in the presence of budget constraints. PBSPLAN is an appropriate model and all six medications were selected. The value of the social welfare function of each medication calculated in PBSPLAN guided the priority of medication selection. Ranking of the six medications was consistent with the order of the net present values of the six medications and the burden of diseases to Australian society. This type of capital budgeting approach to health sector planning is new in the literature. It is difficult to compare the results of PBSPLAN with historical data and results from similar studies as the model has not been used previously in health sector planning in the existing literature.

Intuitive judgement was used to check whether the results were consistent with the theory in this area and acceptable to the profession. Under the new[3] cost benefit analysis, all six medications returned positive net present values, with the cost benefit ratio being greater than one. Under the decision rules of cost benefit analysis, the results supported the listing decisions of all six medications.

We found from this research that applications of social choice theory and new[3] welfare economics resulted in new[3] cost benefit analysis provide a more operational and appropriate framework in assessing and analysing costs and benefits of health programs. When compared to the traditional cost benefit analysis method, the new method of new[3] cost benefit analysis is more operational and flexible to incorporate ethics, extra-welfaristic elements and social preferences

8.4   Limitation and areas for further research

In this study, new[3] cost benefit analysis is only performed on six medications as an illustrative example. Further exercise of new[3] cost benefit analysis should be performed on a much wider range of medications. In other medical conditions such as dementia, and Parkinson's disease, and so on, the social costs and benefits of the carers should also be taken into consideration. Further research is necessary to guarantee improved estimates and analysis of the costs and benefits of medications, especially the social costs and benefits for PBS listing.

In this study, only six medications are input into the PBSPLAN model. All six medications are selected. In reality, increase of the number of medications input into the PBSPLAN model or changes in budget constraints will lead to acceptance of some medications for PBS listing and rejection of the others.

Expenditure on pharmaceuticals is only one of the components of healthcare spending. Pharmaceuticals accounted for 16.4% of the total burden of disease to Australian society in 2000–01 (see Appendix 5.1). Expenditure on hospital accounts for 44.8% of total healthcare spending that on aged care homes accounts for 7.9% and that on non-hospital medical services accounts for 17.2%. With the ageing of the Australian population, service consumption on aged care residential facilities and programs will only increase. If an increase in medication usage helps to better control the medical condition and decrease the consumption of other health services such as hospital stays, outpatient visits, residential aged care or mental health facilities, these indirect benefits should be considered.

In terms of health sector planning, we considered the net changes of benefits or welfare of the whole health sector rather than the narrow program-based budget consideration. The new[3] cost benefit analysis is the appropriate methodology to address these important issues, and ensure that medications selected under this approach will deliver the maximum level of benefit and welfare to the society.

8.5   Conclusion

This book has developed a new[3] cost benefit analysis applied to the PBS in Australia under the form of an appropriate normative economic framework based on the integration of economics and ethics, the possibility for normative social choice, measurement of social welfare and interpersonal comparison of utility, in for the inclusion of medications on the PBS in Australia.

The new[3] cost benefit analysis is a preferred approach because it captures social welfare changes better than the existing practice. The results of this new[3] cost benefit analysis supported the listing decision of the six medications. The results further enabled a health sector planning exercise based on plausible policy implications. The new[3] cost benefit analysis turns health sector planning into a proactive decision-making exercise for normative social choice.

The new[3] cost benefit methodology is consistent with the social choice theory of welfare economics and professional judgement in academic research. In addition to the setting of the Australian PBS, practitioners can use this approach in other areas of health economics and the social sciences.

Appendices

Appendix 2.1   Financial Formulae

A general formula of **present value (*PV*)** is as follows:

$$PV = \frac{FV_1}{(1+r)^0} + \frac{FV_2}{(1+r)^1} + \ldots\ldots + \frac{FV_n}{(1+r)^n}$$

where FV_s = the future values
r = discount rate/rate of interest
n = number of years.

The discounted **net present value (*NPV*)** of a program is calculated as:

$$NPV = \frac{B_0 - C_0}{(1+r)^0} + \frac{B_1 - C_1}{(1+r)^1} + \ldots\ldots + \frac{B_n - C_n}{(1+r)^n}$$
$$= \sum_{t=0}^{n} \frac{B^t - C^t}{(1+r)^t}$$

The **cost-benefit (C–B) ratio** reveals the dollars gained on each dollar of cost. The cost-benefit ratio is calculated as follows:

$$\text{C–B ratio} = \frac{\displaystyle\sum_{t=0}^{N} \frac{B_t}{(1+r)^t}}{\displaystyle\sum_{t=0}^{n} \frac{C_t}{(1+r)^t}}$$

Interpretation of the cost-benefit ratio (C–B):
1. If C–B ratio is greater than 1, the program is of value.
2. If C–B ratio is equal to 1, the benefit equals the cost.
3. If C–B ratio is less than 1, the program is not beneficial.

Appendix 2.2   Financial Cost Benefit Analysis of Drug A, discount rate = 5%

Year	0	1	2	3	4
Costs					
Cost of medication	50	50	50	50	50
Dispensing cost	20	20	20	20	20
Administrative cost	10	10	10	10	10
Total costs	80	80	80	80	80
Benefits					
Increased economic production for patients	0	120	120	120	120
Health gain as improved quantity/quality of life	0	20	20	20	20
Total benefit	0	140	140	140	140
Net financial benefit	−80	60	60	60	60
Cost stream	80	80	80	80	80
Discounted cost stream	80	76.19	72.56	69.11	65.82
Total discounted cost	363.68				
Benefit stream	0	140	140	140	140
Discounted benefit stream	0	133.33	126.98	120.94	115.18
Total discounted benefit	496.43				
Cost-benefit ratio	1.37				
Net financial benefits	−80	60	60	60	60
Discounted values of benefits	−80	55.56	54.42	51.83	49.36
Net present value	132.76				

Appendix 3.1   Shadow Pricing Formulae

A comprehensive set of shadow prices is required for economic appraisal of health programmes as market prices are not always efficient prices. We define here the shadow prices, social parameters and social discount rate necessary for project appraisal exercise in the health sector (Bruce 1976; Ray 1984, Islam 2001b), especially in developing countries.

1. Social value of private consumption:

$$W = \frac{w(c)}{w(g)}$$

2. Critical consumption level:

$$c_*^* d = v_c^\beta$$

3. Social value of public income:

$$v = \frac{w(g)}{w(c)} = \frac{(1-s)g}{(i-sq)\beta_c}\left[1 - \frac{(1+sg)^{t+1}}{(1+i)}\right]$$

4. Income specific distribution parameters:

$$d_i = \left[c^-\middle/_c\right]^n$$

5. Social discount rate/Social accounting rate of interest:

$$r = sq + (1-s)\frac{q}{v}$$

6. Conversion factor for labour:

$$\beta_1 = \frac{SWR}{W}$$

7. Shadow wage rate (SWR):

$$\beta_0 = m_c + \Delta c\beta_c - \Delta c.\frac{d}{v}$$

8. Consumption rate of interest:
$$i = \eta g + \rho$$

9. Conversion factors for non-traded goods:
   (a) Standard Conversion Factor:

$$\alpha = \frac{\sum \varepsilon X_i + \sum \eta M_i}{\sum \varepsilon X_i(1 + t_x) + \sum \eta M_i(1 + t_m)}$$

   (b) Conversion factor for consumption goods:
       The same formula as in (a), but only consumption goods are included in the estimation of β_C.

The definitions of the parameters and variables:
W = marginal wage rate
m = value of the foregone marginal product of labour
c = average consumption
Δc = incremental consumption

g   = compound rate of growth of consumption
i   = consumption rate of interest
r   = social accounting rate of interest
q   = marginal productivity of capital
SWR = shadow wage rate
m_c = value of the foregone marginal product of labour
t_m = average rate of tariffs on imports
t_x = average rate of taxes on exports
ε   = elasticity of export supply
η   = elasticity of import demand
w   = social price of private consumption
v   = social price of public income
c^* = critical consumption level
d   = weighted average income distribution parameters
d_i = income-specific distribution parameter
ρ   = rate of pure time preference
n   = elasticity of marginal utility with respect consumption time
t   = time
w(c) = welfare value of a unit of private consumption
w(g) = welfare value of a unit of public income
s   = private marginal propensity to save out of public sector investment
(1-s) = private marginal propensity to consume out of public sector
        investment
α   = standard conversion factor
$β_C$ = conversion factor for consumption goods
$β_1$ = conversion factor for labour
M   = value of imports
X   = value of exports

Appendix 3.2 Cost Benefit Analysis of Drug A under PBAC type of criteria, discount rate = 5%

Year	0	1	2	3	4
Costs					
Cost of medication	50	50	50	50	50
Dispensing cost	20	20	20	20	20
Administrative cost	10	10	10	10	10
Total costs	80	80	80	80	80
Benefits					
Cost avoidance of hospitalisation or other treatment	0	20	20	20	20
Total benefit	0	20	20	20	20
Net financial benefit	–80	–60	–60	–60	–60
Cost stream	80	80	80	80	80
Discounted cost stream	80	76.19	72.56	69.11	65.82
Total discounted cost	363.68				
Benefit stream	0	20	20	20	20
Discounted benefit stream	0	19.05	18.14	17.28	16.45
Total discounted benefit	70.92				
Cost-benefit ratio	0.20				
Net benefits	–80	–60	–60	–60	–60
Discounted values of net benefits stream	–80	–57.14	–54.42	–51.83	–49.36
Net present value	–292.76				

Appendix 3.3   Social Cost Benefit Analysis of Drug A, discount rate = 0%

Year	0	1	2	3	4
Costs					
Cost of medications	50	50	50	50	50
Dispensing cost	20	20	20	20	20
Administrative cost	10	10	10	10	10
Social cost (opportunity cost of funds forgone)	10	10	10	10	10
Total costs	90	90	90	90	90
Social welfare/benefits					
Increased economic production for patients	0	120	120	120	120
Cost avoidance of hospitalisation or other treatment	0	20	20	20	20
Health gain as improved quantity/quality of life	0	10	10	10	10
Total benefits	0	150	150	150	150
Net benefits	−90	60	60	60	60
Cost stream	90	90	90	90	90
Discounted cost stream	90	90	90	90	90
Total discounted cost	450				
Benefit stream	0	150	150	150	150
Discounted benefit stream	0	150	150	150	150
Total discounted benefit	600				
Cost-benefit ratio	1.33				
Net benefits	−90	60	60	60	60
Discounted values of net benefits stream	−90	60	60	60	60
Net present value	150				

Appendix 3.4 Social Cost Benefit Analysis of Drug A, discount rate = 0%, incorporating public policy objectives

Year	0	1	2	3	4
Costs					
Cost of medications	50	50	50	50	50
Dispensing cost	20	20	20	20	20
Administrative cost	10	10	10	10	10
Social cost (opportunity cost of funds forgone)	10	10	10	10	10
Total costs	90	90	90	90	90
Social welfare/benefits					
Increased economic production for patients	0	120	120	120	120
Improved employment	0	10	10	10	10
Cost avoidance of hospitalisation or other treatment	0	20	20	20	20
Health gain as improved quantity/quality of life	0	10	10	10	10
Total benefits	0	160	160	160	160
Net benefits	–90	70	70	70	70
Cost stream	90	90	90	90	90
Discounted cost stream	90	90	90	90	90
Total discounted cost	450				
Benefit stream	0	160	160	160	160
Discounted benefit stream	0	160	160	160	160
Total discounted benefit	640				
Cost-benefit ratio	1.42				
Net benefits	–90	70	70	70	70
Discounted values of net benefits stream	–90	70	70	70	70
Net present value	190				

Appendix 3.5   Social Cost Benefit Analysis of Drug A, discount rate = 0%, incorporating distributional weights

Year	0	1	2	3	4
Costs					
Cost of medications	50	50	50	50	50
Dispensing cost	20	20	20	20	20
Administrative cost	10	10	10	10	10
Social cost (opportunity cost of funds forgone)	10	10	10	10	10
Total costs	90	90	90	90	90
Social welfare/benefits					
Increased economic production for patients	0	120	120	120	120
Cost avoidance of hospitalisation or other treatment	0	20	20	20	20
Health gain as improved quantity/quality of life	0	10	10	10	10
Extra health gain, incorporating distributional weights	0	5	5	5	5
Total benefits	0	155	155	155	155
Net benefits	−90	65	65	65	65
Cost stream	90	90	90	90	90
Discounted cost stream	90	90	90	90	90
Total discounted cost	450				
Benefit stream	0	155	155	155	155
Discounted benefit stream	0	155	155	155	155
Total discounted benefit	620				
Cost-benefit ratio	1.38				
Net benefits	−90	65	65	65	65
Discounted values of net benefits stream	−90	65	65	65	65
Net present value	170				

Appendix 4.1 Annual PBS and RPBS Government Cost, July 1997–June 2004

Year ending	June 1998	June 1999	June 2000	June 2001	June 2002	June 2003	June 2004
Category – PBS							
Conc non-safety net	1576058096	1739534530	2000633063	2359644872	2569555585	2747329765	2972331634
Conc safety net	439989321	467079112	547828759	660301391	778411796	907524352	1004522779
General non-safety net	411856192	469041337	521014426	662096086	691204687	750543943	824130608
General safety net	98613376	106618435	107012550	128173669	148498520	169805201	190682979
Drs Bag	14953823	13370491	10754395	10343534	9803682	9510606	9408669
Total	2541470808	2795643906	3187243193	3820559552	4197474271	4584713868	5001076669
Category – RPBS							
Repat non-safety net	140469272	161780364	193937997	228440705	321163595	*	*
Repat safety net	64246360	68089097	78385266	96701658	49828999	*	*
Total	204715632	229869461	272323263	325142363	370992593	425979488	456229564

Notes: Conc = concessional. Repat = repatriation. * Breakdown figures between Repat safety net and Repat non-safety net not available.

Source: PBS Statistics, HIC website.

Appendix 4.2 Annual PBS and RPBS Prescription Volume, July 1997–June 2004

Year ending	June 1998	June 1999	June 2000	June 2001	June 2002	June 2003	June 2004
Category – PBS							
Conc non-safety net	86389807	88475299	94281689	99284880	102010392	101459056	104619866
Conc safety net	20060505	20608073	23078245	25420093	28406601	31177491	32827303
General non-safety net	14087393	15153955	16296571	18526030	19292053	20694131	22443338
General safety net	3945591	4111088	3928739	4340355	4813037	5188492	5544618
Drs Bag	628496	572753	496306	478999	448179	437516	426976
Total	125111792	128921168	138081550	148050357	154970262	158956686	165862101
Category – RPBS							
Repat non-safety net	7074992	7734955	8773952	9387366	12389719	*	*
Repat safety net	2853493	2955956	3271643	3711666	1842814	*	*
Total	9928485	10690911	12045595	13099032	14232533	15362691	15627475

Notes: Conc = concessional. Repat = repatriation. * Breakdown figures between Repat safety net and Repat non-safety net not available.

Source: PBS Statistics, HIC website.

Appendix 4.3 Changes in Level of Patient Contribution of PBS

Date of change	Amount ($) general	% of average cost of 'general' benefit	Amount ($) concessional	% of average cost of 'concessional' benefit
March 1960	0.50	22%		
November 1971	1.00	40%		
September 1975	1.50	51%		
March 1976	2.00	59%		
July 1978	2.50	60%		
September 1979	2.75	60%		
December 1981	3.20	62%		
January 1983	4.00	69%	2.00	34%
July 1985	5.00	73%	2.00	32%
July 1986	5.00	64%	2.00	29%
November 1986	Max $10.00	54%	2.50	27%
July 1988	Max $11.00	51%	2.50	27%
July 1989	Max $11.00	53%	2.50	25%
July 1990	Max $11.00	49%	2.50	23%
November 1990	Max $15.00	55%	2.50	21%
August 1991	Max $15.70	57%	2.50	21%
October 1991	Max $15.70	57%	2.60	22%
August 1992	Max $15.90	45%	2.60	20%
August 1993	Max $16.00	47%	2.60	18%
August 1994	Max $16.20	45%	2.60	16%
August 1995	Max $16.80	45%	2.60	15%
August 1996	Max $17.40	43%	2.70	14%
January 1997	Max $20.00	44%	3.20	16%
January 1999	Max $20.30	40%	3.20	14%
January 2000	Max $20.60	40%	3.30	14%
January 2001	Max $21.90	42%	3.50	14%
January 2002	Max $22.40	42%	3.60	14%
January 2003	Max $23.10	40%	3.70	13%
January 2004	Max $23.70	39%	3.80	12%
January 2005	Max $28.60	–	4.60	–

Source: Pharmacy Guild Digest (2004).

Appendix 4.4 Population to Pharmacy Ratios in Australia

Year (30 June)	Population	Number of pharmacies	Population: pharmacy ratio
1970	12 663 469	5876	2155
1975	13 893 000	5566	2496
1980	14 695 400	5417	2713
1985	15 788 300	5484	2879
1986	16 018 400	5549	2887
1987	16 263 300	5559	2926
1988	16 532 200	5609	2947
1989	16 814 400	5612	2996
1990	17 065 100	5625	3034
1991	17 284 000	5351	3230
1992	17 489 100	5091	3435
1993	17 656 400	5018	3519
1994	17 847 400	4980	3584
1995	18 063 300	4949	3650
1996	18 310 714	4953	3697
1997	18 532 247	4954	3741
1998	18 7303 59	4952	3782
1999	18 871 800	4942	3819
2000	19 080 200	4925	3874
2001	19 334 200	4925	3926
2002	19 657 400	4926	3991
2003	19 757 900	4907	4026
2004	20 009 000	4910	4075

Source: Pharmacy Guild Digest (2004).

Appendix 5.1 Diseases and Injury of Disease Chapter: Health System Cost by Health Sector, 2000–01 ($ million)

Burden of Disease Chapter	Hospital[a]	Aged care home	Non-hospital medical	Dental & others[b]	Total pharmaceuticals[c]	Research	Total	% of total
Cardiovascular	2533	526	782	78	1411	153	5484	11.2
Nervous system	1115	2168	573	410	468	201	4878	9.9
Muscoskeletal	1828	482	879	760	680	55	4684	9.5
Injuries	2830	105	622	284	184	6	4031	8.2
Respiratory	1437	88	840	64	1189	35	3654	7.4
Oral Health	189	0	15	3110	34	27	3374	6.9
Mental disorder	1196	366	499	144	616	109	2929	6.0
Digestive system	1571	34	347	204	637	31	2825	5.7
Neoplasms	1988	37	258	24	183	215	2705	5.5
Genitourinary	1317	14	469	31	233	13	2078	4.2
Endocrine & metabolic	396	14	340	64	714	68	1594	3.2
Skin diseases	562	13	341	103	344	13	1376	2.8
Maternal condition	1178	0	107	10	9	11	1315	2.7
Infectious & parasites	478	8	366	27	209	139	1226	2.5
Diabetes Mellitus	289	38	183	36	234	35	814	1.7
Neonatal	334	0	12	0	1	11	357	0.7
Congenital anomalies	158	6	19	1	2	37	221	0.5
Others	2633	0	1802	174	996	21	5626	11.4
Total	22030	3899	8454	5524	805	1182	49174	100.0
As percent of total	44.8	7.9	17.2	11.2	16.4	2.4		100.0

Notes:

a. Includes public and private acute hospitals, and psychiatric facilities.

b. Includes dental and other paramedical professional services such as physiotherapists, podiatrists, osteopaths, chiropractors, etc.

c. Includes prescriptions medications, over-the-counter medications as well as complementary medications.

Source: Australia's Health (AIHW 2004 p. 254).

Appendix 5.2 Top Generic Medications by Defined Daily Dose and Volume, 2001–02 and 2002–3

Generic name	Action	2000-01 DDD PBS/RPBS	2000-01 DDD Total^a	2000-01 Volume ('000) PBS/RPBS	2000-01 Volume ('000) Total	2002-03 DDD PBS/RPBS	2002-03 DDD Total	2002-03 Volume ('000) PBS/RPBS	2002-03 Volume ('000) Total	% difference 2000-01 to 20002-03 DDD PBS/RPBS	% difference DDD Total	% difference Volume ('000) PBS/RPBS	% difference Volume ('000) Total
Atorvastatin	Hypolipidaemic	44.4	44.4	4747	4752	66.0	66.1	6203	6215	48.8	48.8	30.7	30.8
Simvastatin	Hypolipidaemic	32.4	32.5	4787	4792	43.5	43.5	5461	5466	34.0	34.0	14.1	14.1
Diltiazem hydrochloride	Anti-hypertensive Anti-angina	57.8	57.9	1487	1488	41.1	41.	1529	1531	-29.0	-28.7	2.9	2.8
Salbutamol	Bronchodilator	22.2	30.2	3589	4736	20.4	27.9	3318	4389	-8.0	-7.5	-7.6	-7.3
Ramipril	Anti-hypertensive	12.8	12.9	1561	1593	26.3	26.9	2501	2637	105.6	108.8	60.3	65.5
Omeprazole	Anti-ulcerant	15.3	15.4	2762	2782	22.6	22.7	4665	4675	47.6	46.9	68.9	68.0
Rofecoxib	Anti-inflammatory	4.2	4.0	669	677	20.6	20.8	2929	2948	385.8	385.3	337.7	335.3
Frusemide	Diuretic	20.0	21.6	1367	1482	19.5	20.7	1376	1467	-2.8	-4.3	0.7	-0.9
Irbesartan	Anti-hypertensive	14.6	14.6	2458	2460	18.1	18.2	3074	3114	23.8	24.4	25.1	26.6
Irbesartan with hydrochlorothiazide	Anti-hypertensive	7.8	7.8	1076	1076	17.6	17.7	2381	2386	126.3	126.8	121.3	121.8
Aspirin	Anti-platelet aggregation	12.9	14.0	1257	1378	15.6	16.7	1352	1456	21.5	19.6	7.6	5.6
Amlodipine besylate	Anti-hypertensive	15.1	15.9	2337	2504	15.2	16.2	2327	2568	0.2	2.2	-0.5	2.6
Celecoxib	Anti-inflammatory	29.0	29.4	3852	3966	15.8	15.9	3535	3567	-45.7	-45.9	-8.2	-10.1
Sertraline	Anti-depressant	14.3	14.4	2257	2267	15.7	15.8	2441	2454	10.1	10.2	8.1	8.3
Thyroxine sodium	Thyroid hormone replacement	8.6	13.3	548	827	9.6	14.5	624	922	11.8	9.1	13.8	8.3

Note:
a. Total figure is more than that subsidised under the PBS/RPBS because costs of private scripts or scripts less than patient copayments are paid by patients directly.

Source: Australia's Health (AIHW 2004 pp. 315, 440).

Appendix 5.3 Age-standardised Death Rates,* 1921–2002 (per 100,000 population)

ICD-10 Chapter of disease	1921	1941	1961	1971	1981	1991	2000	2001	2002
Circulatory diseases	856	1404	1554	1559	1129	786	541	517	506
Neoplasms	358	394	388	416	439	444	403	402	399
Respiratory diseases	423	318	187	200	161	139	124	116	122
Endocrine, nutritional	47	73	40	52	40	42	45	45	47
All causes	3589	3305	2658	2632	2090	1714	1405	1359	1364

Note: * Age-standardised the total Australian population at 30 June 2001.

Source: AIHW National Mortality Databases.

Appendix 5.4   Cost of Cardiovascular Medications

Medications	Strength & packsize	Drug cost ($)	Pharmacy markup ($)	Govt rec ($)	Cost to govt*($)
Atorvastatin	10mg × 30 tablets	34.97	8.46	43.13	19.43–43.13
	20mg × 30 tablets	49.95	9.66	59.61	35.91–59.61
	40mg × 30 tablets	71.61	11.82	83.43	59.73–83.43
	80mg × 30 tablets	102.45	14.91	117.36	93.66–117.36
Simvastatin	10mg × 30 tablets	33.05	7.97	41.02	17.32–41.02
	20mg × 30 tablets	47.19	9.38	56.57	32.87–56.57
	40mg × 30 tablets	67.60	11.42	79.02	55.32–79.02
	80mg × 30 tablets	96.79	14.34	111.13	87.43–111.13
Clopidogrel	75mg × 28 tablets	72.16	11.88	84.04	60.34–84.04

Note: cost to government ranges according to the entitlement status of patients.

Source: HIC PBS, May 2004.

Appendix 5.5   Examples of the Costs of Type 2 Diabetes

Direct Costs
Medications and treatment of adverse events
Laboratory costs
Equipment and supplies (including those for home blood glucose
   monitoring and injections)
General Physician visits
Nurse and other health professional visits
Endocrinologist and other specialist physician consultations (including
   eye and podiatry examinations)
Emergency department visits
Hospitalisation
Treatment of complications, including dialysis and surgery
Nursing home or other long-term care
Social services
Preventative strategies
Education of patients
Patient travel
Patient out-of-pocket expenses

Indirect Costs
Loss of productivity due to illness or disability
Loss of productivity due to premature death

Source: Foster and Plosker (2000).

Appendix 5.6 Cost of Type 2 Diabetic Medications

Medications	Strength & packsize	Drug cost ($)	Pharmacy markup ($)	Govt rec ($)	Cost to govt*($)
Pioglitazone	15mg × 30 tablets	55.61	10.22	65.83	42.13–65.83
	30mg × 30 tablets	85.56	13.22	98.78	75.08–98.78
	45mg × 30 tablets	108.59	15.52	124.11	100.41–124.11
Rosiglitazone	4mg × 30 tablets	51.77	9.84	61.61	37.91–61.61
	8mg × 30 tablets	79.63	12.62	92.25	68.55–92.25
Glimepiride	1mg × 30 tablets	3.66	5.03	8.69	0–8.69
	2mg × 30 tablets	7.00	5.36	12.36	0–12.36
	3mg × 30 tablets	9.00	5.56	14.56	0–14.56
	4mg × 30 tablets	11.00	5.76	16.76	0–16.76
Glipizide	5mg × 100 tablets	4.93	5.15	10.08	0–10.08
Gliclazide	80mg × 100 tablets	4.93	5.63	15.34	0–15.34
	30mg × 100 tablets	9.71	9.44	19.45	0–19.45
Metformin	500mg × 100 tablets	10.01	5.40	14.70	0–14.70
	850mg × 60 tablets	9.13	9.37	18.50	0–18.50
	1000mg × 90 tablets	9.13	7.80	23.70	0–23.70

Note: Cost to government ranges according to the entitlement status of patients.

Source: HIC PBS, May (2004).

Appendix 5.7 Five-year Relative Survival Ratios for all Registrable Cancers of Females in Australia

Cancer site	Diagnosis period		
	1982–86	1987–91	1992–94
Thyroid	87.8	91.9	95.6
Melanoma	90.9	93.5	94.6
Hodgkin's lymphoma	73.8	79.9	84.4
Breast	72.3	77.8	84.0
Uterus	76.1	78.5	81.4
Cervix	69.6	72.0	74.6
Bladder	67.2	65.2	64.7
Rectum	52.3	56.0	60.6
Colon	51.3	54.7	58.7
Kidney	49.4	52.7	57.5
Non-Hodgkin's lymphoma	49.9	54.6	55.8
Leukaemia	39.4	44.2	43.2
Ovary	34.4	37.7	42.0
Stomach	21.1	21.8	24.8
Brain	24.1	25.3	23.8
Lung	11.8	11.9	14.0
Unknown primary	10.4	10.9	11.5
Pancreas	4.1	5.4	5.2
All registrable cancers	55.3	59.1	63.4

Source: Australia's Health (AIHW 2002 p. 52).

Appendix 5.8 Cost of Breast Cancer Medications

Medications	Strength & packsize	Drug cost ($)	Pharmacy markup ($)	Govt rec ($)	Cost to govt*($)
Letrozole	2.5mg × 30 tablets	194.39	22.66	217.05	193.35–217.05
Anastrozole	1mg × 30 tablets	194.39	22.66	217.05	193.35–217.05
Tamoxifen	20mg × 60 tablets	64.72	14.10	78.82	55.12–78.82

Note: Cost to government ranges according to the entitlement status of patients.

Source: HIC PBS, May (2004).

Appendix 5.9   Cost of Asthma and COPD Medications

Medications	Strength & packsize	Drug cost ($)	Pharmacy markup ($)	Govt rec ($)	Cost to govt*($)
Fluticasone/ Salmeterol	50/25mcg inhaler	37.49	8.41	45.90	22.20–45.90
	125/25mcg inhaler	49.69	9.63	59.32	35.62–59.32
	250/25mcg inhaler	68.00	11.49	79.46	55.76–79.46
	100/50mcg accuhaler	37.49	8.41	45.90	22.20–45.90
	250/50mcg accuhaler	49.69	9.63	59.32	35.62–59.32
	500/50mcg accuhaler	68.00	11.49	79.46	55.76–79.46
Beclo- methasone	50mcg inhaler	11.57	5.82	17.39	0–17.39
	100mcg inhaler	24.30	7.69	31.39	7.69–31.39
	50mcg autohaler	19.28	6.59	25.87	2.17–25.87
	100mcg autohaler	29.39	7.60	36.99	13.29–36.99
Salbutamol	100mcg inhaler × 2	10.56	5.72	16.28	0–16.28
	100mcg autohaler × 2	28.91	7.55	36.46	12.76–36.46
	2.5mg nebules	17.15	6.37	23.52	0–23.52
	5mg nebules	18.13	6.47	24.60	0.90–24.60
Tiotropium	18mcg capsules 30s	66.20	11.28	77.48	53.78–77.48
Ipratropium	20mcg inhaler × 2	31.67	7.83	39.50	15.80–39.50
	250mcg nebules	42.25	8.89	51.14	27.44–51.14
	500mcg nebules	49.95	9.65	59.60	35.90–59.60

Note: Cost to government ranges according to the entitlement status of patients.

Source: HIC PBS, May (2004).

Appendix 6.1   Hypothetical Cost Benefit Analysis of Atorvastatin 40mg under PBAC type of criteria, discount rate = 5%

Year	0	1	2	3	4
Costs					
Cost of medication	859.32	859.32	859.32	859.32	859.32
External administrative cost	141.84	141.84	141.84	141.84	141.84
Internal administrative cost	Insig.	Insig.	Insig.	Insig.	Insig.
Cost of adverse drug effects	29.61	29.61	29.61	29.61	29.61
Social cost	n.c.	n.c.	n.c.	n.c.	n.c.
Total costs	1030.77	1030.77	1030.77	1030.77	1030.77
Benefits					
Increase in economic productivity of patients	n.c.	n.c.	n.c.	n.c.	n.c.
Cost avoidance of hospitalisation	4495.59	0.00	0.00	0.00	0.00
Decrease consumption of health services – GP consultation	n.c.	n.c.	n.c.	n.c.	n.c.
Decrease consumption of health services – specialist consultation	n.c.	n.c.	n.c.	n.c.	n.c.
Improved health status – decreased consumption of complementary medicines	n.c.	n.c.	n.c.	n.c.	n.c.
Health gain – improvement in life expectancy – QALYs gained	n.c.	n.c.	n.c.	n.c.	n.c.
Willingness-to-pay of patient to obtain positive changes in health status	n.c.	n.c.	n.c.	n.c.	n.c.
Total benefits	4495.59	0.00	0.00	0.00	0.00
Cost stream					
Discounted cost stream	1030.77	981.68	934.93	890.41	848.01
Total discounted cost	4685.81				
Benefit stream					
Discounted benefit stream	4495.59	0.00	0.00	0.00	0.00
Total discounted benefit	4495.59				
Cost-benefit ratio	0.96				
Net financial benefits	3464.82	–1030.77	–1030.77	–1030.77	–1030.77
Discounted values of benefits	3464.82	–981.68	–934.93	–890.41	–848.01
Net present value	–190.22				

Notes:
Insig. = insignificant.
n.c. = not considered under this approach.

Appendix 6.2 Financial Cost Benefit Analysis of Atorvastatin 40mg, discount rate = 5%

Year	0	1	2	3	4
Costs					
Cost of medication	859.32	859.32	859.32	859.32	859.32
External administrative cost	141.84	141.84	141.84	141.84	141.84
Internal administrative cost	Insig.	Insig.	Insig.	Insig.	Insig.
Cost of adverse drug effects	29.61	29.61	29.61	29.61	29.61
Social cost	n.c.	n.c.	n.c.	n.c.	n.c.
Total costs	1030.77	1030.77	1030.77	1030.77	1030.77
Benefits					
Increase in economic productivity of patients	1350.50	725.00	362.50	362.50	362.50
Cost avoidance of hospitalisation	4495.59	0.00	0.00	0.00	0.00
Decrease consumption of health services – GP consultation	n.c.	n.c.	n.c.	n.c.	n.c.
Decrease consumption of health services – specialist consultation	n.c.	n.c.	n.c.	n.c.	n.c.
Improved health status – decreased consumption of complementary medicines	n.c.	n.c.	n.c.	n.c.	n.c.
Health gain – improvement in life expectancy – QALYs gained	n.c.	n.c.	n.c.	n.c.	n.c.
Willingness-to-pay of patient to obtain positive changes in health status	n.c.	n.c.	n.c.	n.c.	n.c.
Total benefits	5846.09	725.00	362.50	362.50	362.50
Cost stream					
Discounted cost stream	1030.77	981.68	934.93	890.41	848.01
Total discounted cost	4685.81				
Benefit stream					
Discounted benefit stream	5846.09	690.48	328.79	313.14	298.23
Total discounted benefit	7476.73				
Cost-benefit ratio	1.60				
Net financial benefits	4815.32	–305.77	–668.27	–668.27	–668.27
Discounted values of benefits	4815.32	–291.21	–606.13	–577.27	–549.79
Net present value	2790.92				

Notes:
Insig. = insignificant.
n.c. = not considered under this approach.

Appendix 6.3   New[3] Cost Benefit Analysis of Atorvastatin 40mg, discount rate = 0%

Year	0	1	2	3	4
Costs					
Cost of medication	859.32	859.32	859.32	859.32	859.32
External administrative cost	141.84	141.84	141.84	141.84	141.84
Internal administrative cost	Insig.	Insig.	Insig.	Insig.	Insig.
Cost of adverse drug effects	29.61	29.61	29.61	29.61	29.61
Social cost	117.52	117.52	117.52	117.52	117.52
Total costs	1148.29	1148.29	1148.29	1148.29	1148.29
Benefits					
Increase in economic productivity of patients	1350.50	725.00	362.50	362.50	362.50
Cost avoidance of hospitalisation	4495.59	0.00	0.00	0.00	0.00
Decrease consumption of health services – GP consultation	458.80	458.80	229.40	229.40	229.40
Decrease consumption of health services – specialist consultation	250.80	250.80	125.40	125.40	125.40
Improved health status – decreased consumption of complementary medicines	400.00	400.00	400.00	400.00	400.00
Health gain – improvement in life expectancy – QALYs gained	19113.30	0.00	0.00	0.00	0.00
Willingness-to-pay of patient to obtain positive changes in health status	1026.25	1026.25	1026.25	1026.25	1026.25
Total benefits/ social welfare	27095.24	2860.85	2143.55	2143.55	2143.55
Cost stream					
Discounted cost stream	1148.29	1148.29	1148.29	1148.29	1148.29
Total discounted cost	5741.45				
Benefit stream					
Discounted benefit stream	27095.24	2860.85	2143.55	2143.55	2143.55
Total discounted benefit	36386.74				
Cost-benefit ratio	6.34				
Net financial benefits	25946.95	1712.56	995.26	995.26	995.26
Discounted values of benefits	25946.95	1712.56	995.26	995.26	995.26
Net present value/ social welfare	30645.29				
Total benefits/ social welfare	27095.24	2860.85	2143.55	2143.55	2143.55

Note: Insig. = insignificant.

Appendix 6.4 Hypothetical Cost Benefit Analysis of Clopidogrel 75mg under PBAC type of criteria, discount rate = 5%

Year	0	1	2	3	4
Costs					
Cost of medication	865.92	865.92	865.92	865.92	865.92
External administrative cost	142.56	142.56	142.56	142.56	142.56
Internal administrative cost	Insig.	Insig.	Insig.	Insig.	Insig.
Cost of adverse drug effects	29.61	29.61	29.61	29.61	29.61
Social cost	n.c.	n.c.	n.c.	n.c.	n.c.
Total costs	1038.09	1038.09	1038.09	1038.09	1038.09
Benefits					
Increase in economic productivity of patients	n.c.	n.c.	n.c.	n.c.	n.c.
Cost avoidance of hospitalisation	9690.50	0.00	0.00	0.00	0.00
Decrease consumption of health services – GP consultation	n.c.	n.c.	n.c.	n.c.	n.c.
Decrease consumption of health services – specialist consultation	n.c.	n.c.	n.c.	n.c.	n.c.
Improved health status – decreased consumption of complementary medicines	n.c.	n.c.	n.c.	n.c.	n.c.
Health gain – improvement in life expectancy – QALYs gained	n.c.	n.c.	n.c.	n.c.	n.c.
Willingness-to-pay of patient to obtain positive changes in health status	n.c.	n.c.	n.c.	n.c.	n.c.
Total benefits	9690.50	0.00	0.00	0.00	0.00
Cost stream					
Discounted cost stream	1038.09	988.66	941.57	896.73	854.04
Total discounted cost	4719.08				
Benefit stream					
Discounted benefit stream	9690.50	0.00	0.00	0.00	0.00
Total discounted benefit	9690.50				
Cost-benefit ratio	2.05				
Net financial benefits	8652.41	–1038.09	–1038.09	–1038.09	–1038.09
Discounted values of benefits	8652.41	–988.66	–941.57	–896.73	–854.04
Net present value	4971.42				

Notes:
Insig. = insignificant.
n.c. = not considered under this approach.

Appendix 6.5   Financial Cost Benefit Analysis of Clopidogrel 75mg, discount rate = 5%

Year	0	1	2	3	4
Costs					
Cost of medication	865.92	865.92	865.92	865.92	865.92
External administrative cost	142.56	142.56	142.56	142.56	142.56
Internal administrative cost	Insig.	Insig.	Insig.	Insig.	Insig.
Cost of adverse drug effects	29.61	29.61	29.61	29.61	29.61
Social cost	n.c.	n.c.	n.c.	n.c.	n.c.
Total costs	1038.09	1038.09	1038.09	1038.09	1038.09
Benefits					
Increase in economic productivity of patients	2131.50	725.00	362.50	362.50	362.50
Cost avoidance of hospitalisation	9690.50	0.00	0.00	0.00	0.00
Decrease consumption of health services – GP consultation	n.c.	n.c.	n.c.	n.c.	n.c.
Decrease consumption of health services – specialist consultation	n.c.	n.c.	n.c.	n.c.	n.c.
Improved health status – decreased consumption of complementary medicines	n.c.	n.c.	n.c.	n.c.	n.c.
Health gain – improvement in life expectancy – QALYs gained	n.c.	n.c.	n.c.	n.c.	n.c.
Willingness-to-pay of patient to obtain positive changes in health status	n.c.	n.c.	n.c.	n.c.	n.c.
Total benefits	11822.00	725.00	362.50	362.50	362.50
Cost stream					
Discounted cost stream	1038.09	988.66	941.57	896.73	854.04
Total discounted cost	4719.08				
Benefit stream					
Discounted benefit stream	11822.00	690.48	328.79	313.14	298.23
Total discounted benefit	13452.64				
Cost-benefit ratio	2.85				
Net financial benefits	10783.91	–313.09	–675.59	–675.59	–675.59
Discounted values of benefits	10783.91	–298.18	–612.77	–583.59	–555.81
Net present value	8733.55				

Notes:
Insig. = insignificant.
n.c. = not considered under this approach.

Appendix 6.6 New[3] Cost Benefit Analysis of Clopidogrel 75mg, discount rate = 0%

Year	0	1	2	3	4
Costs					
Cost of medication	865.92	865.92	865.92	865.92	865.92
External administrative cost	142.56	142.56	142.56	142.56	142.56
Internal administrative cost	Insig.	Insig.	Insig.	Insig.	Insig.
Cost of adverse drug effects	29.61	29.61	29.61	29.61	29.61
Social cost	777.24	777.24	777.24	777.24	777.24
Total costs	1815.33	1815.33	1815.33	1815.33	1815.33
Benefits					
Increase in economic productivity of patients	2131.50	725.00	362.50	362.50	362.50
Cost avoidance of hospitalisation	9690.50	0.00	0.00	0.00	0.00
Decrease consumption of health services – GP consultation	458.80	458.80	229.40	229.40	229.40
Decrease consumption of health services – specialist consultation	250.80	250.80	125.40	125.40	125.40
Improved health status – decreased consumption of complementary medicines	400.00	400.00	400.00	400.00	400.00
Health gain – improvement in life expectancy – QALYs gained	17697.50	0.00	0.00	0.00	0.00
Willingness-to-pay of patient to obtain positive changes in health status	1033.51	1033.51	1033.51	1033.51	1033.51
Total benefits/ social welfare	31662.61	2868.11	2150.81	2150.81	2150.81
Cost stream					
Discounted cost stream	1815.33	1815.33	1815.33	1815.33	1815.33
Total discounted cost	9076.65				
Benefit stream					
Discounted benefit stream	31662.61	2868.11	2150.81	2150.81	2150.81
Total discounted benefit	40983.15				
Cost-benefit ratio	4.52				
Net financial benefits	29847.28	1052.78	335.48	335.48	335.48
Discounted values of benefits	29847.28	1052.78	335.48	335.48	335.48
Net present value/ social welfare	31906.50				

Note: Insig. = insignificant.

Appendix 6.7   Hypothetical Cost Benefit Analysis of Pioglitazone 30mg under PBAC type of criteria, discount rate = 5%

Year	0	1	2	3	4
Costs					
Cost of medication	1026.72	1026.72	1026.72	1026.72	1026.72
External administrative cost	158.64	158.64	158.64	158.64	158.64
Internal administrative cost	Insig.	Insig.	Insig.	Insig.	Insig.
Cost of adverse drug effects	29.61	29.61	29.61	29.61	29.61
Social cost	n.c.	n.c.	n.c.	n.c.	n.c.
Total costs	1214.97	1214.97	1214.97	1214.97	1214.97
Benefits					
Increase in economic productivity of patients	n.c.	n.c.	n.c.	n.c.	n.c.
Cost avoidance of hospitalisation	8683.62	0.00	0.00	0.00	0.00
Decrease consumption of health services – GP consultation	n.c.	n.c.	n.c.	n.c.	n.c.
Decrease consumption of health services – specialist consultation	n.c.	n.c.	n.c.	n.c.	n.c.
Improved health status – decreased consumption of complementary medicines	n.c.	n.c.	n.c.	n.c.	n.c.
Health gain – improvement in life expectancy – QALYs gained	n.c.	n.c.	n.c.	n.c.	n.c.
Willingness-to-pay of patient to obtain positive changes in health status	n.c.	n.c.	n.c.	n.c.	n.c.
Total benefits	8683.62	0.00	0.00	0.00	0.00
Cost stream					
Discounted cost stream	1214.97	1157.11	1102.00	1049.53	999.56
Total discounted cost	5523.17				
Benefit stream					
Discounted benefit stream	8683.62	0.00	0.00	0.00	0.00
Total discounted benefit	8683.62				
Cost-benefit ratio	1.57				
Net financial benefits	7468.65	–1214.97	–1214.97	–1214.97	–1214.97
Discounted values of benefits	7468.65	–1157.11	–1102.00	–1049.53	–999.56
Net present value	3160.45				

Notes:
Insig. = insignificant.
n.c. = not considered under this approach.

Appendix 6.8   Financial Cost Benefit Analysis of Pioglitazone 30mg, discount rate = 5%

Year	0	1	2	3	4
Costs					
Cost of medication	1026.72	1026.72	1026.72	1026.72	1026.72
External administrative cost	158.64	158.64	158.64	158.64	158.64
Internal administrative cost	Insig.	Insig.	Insig.	Insig.	Insig.
Cost of adverse drug effects	29.61	29.61	29.61	29.61	29.61
Social cost	n.c.	n.c.	n.c.	n.c.	n.c.
Total costs	1214.97	1214.97	1214.97	1214.97	1214.97
Benefits					
Increase in economic productivity of patients	2320.00	725.00	362.50	362.50	362.50
Cost avoidance of hospitalisation	8683.62	0.00	0.00	0.00	0.00
Decrease consumption of health services – GP consultation	n.c.	n.c.	n.c.	n.c.	n.c.
Decrease consumption of health services – specialist consultation	n.c.	n.c.	n.c.	n.c.	n.c.
Improved health status – decreased consumption of complementary medicines	n.c.	n.c.	n.c.	n.c.	n.c.
Health gain – improvement in life expectancy – QALYs gained	n.c.	n.c.	n.c.	n.c.	n.c.
Willingness-to-pay of patient to obtain positive changes in health status	n.c.	n.c.	n.c.	n.c.	n.c.
Total benefits	11003.62	725.00	362.50	362.50	362.50
Cost stream					
Discounted cost stream	1214.97	1157.11	1102.00	1049.53	999.56
Total discounted cost	5523.17				
Benefit stream					
Discounted benefit stream	11003.62	690.48	328.79	313.14	298.23
Total discounted benefit	12634.26				
Cost-benefit ratio	2.29				
Net financial benefits	9788.65	−489.97	−852.47	−852.47	−852.47
Discounted values of benefits	9788.65	−466.64	−773.21	−736.39	−701.33
Net present value	7111.09				

Notes:
Insig. = insignificant.
n.c. = not considered under this approach.

Appendix 6.9   New[3] Cost Benefit Analysis of Pioglitazone 30mg, discount rate = 0%

Year	0	1	2	3	4
Costs					
Cost of medication	1026.72	1026.72	1026.72	1026.72	1026.72
External administrative cost	158.64	158.64	158.64	158.64	158.64
Internal administrative cost	Insig.	Insig.	Insig.	Insig.	Insig.
Cost of adverse drug effects	29.61	29.61	29.61	29.61	29.61
Social cost	1005.12	1005.12	1005.12	1005.12	1005.12
Total costs	2220.09	2220.09	2220.09	2220.09	2220.09
Benefits					
Increase in economic productivity of patients	2320.00	725.00	362.50	362.50	362.50
Cost avoidance of hospitalisation	8683.62	0.00	0.00	0.00	0.00
Decrease consumption of health services – GP consultation	458.80	458.80	229.40	229.40	229.40
Decrease consumption of health services – specialist consultation	250.80	250.80	125.40	125.40	125.40
Improved health status – decreased consumption of complementary medicines	400.00	400.00	400.00	400.00	400.00
Health gain – improvement in life expectancy – QALYs gained	12388.25	0.00	0.00	0.00	0.00
Willingness-to-pay of patient to obtain positive changes in health status	1210.39	1210.39	1210.39	1210.39	1210.39
Total benefits/ social welfare	25711.86	3044.99	2327.69	2327.69	2327.69
Cost stream					
Discounted cost stream	2220.09	2220.09	2220.09	2220.09	2220.09
Total discounted cost	11100.45				
Benefit stream					
Discounted benefit stream	25711.86	3044.99	2327.69	2327.69	2327.69
Total discounted benefit	35739.92				
Cost-benefit ratio	3.22				
Net financial benefits	23491.77	824.90	107.60	107.60	107.60
Discounted values of benefits	23491.77	824.90	107.60	107.60	107.60
Net present value/ social welfare	24639.47				

Note: Insig. = insignificant.

Appendix 6.10 Hypothetical Cost Benefit Analysis of Letrozole 2.5mg under PBAC type of criteria, discount rate = 5%

Year	0	1	2	3	4
Costs					
Cost of medication	2332.38	2332.38	2332.38	2332.38	2332.38
External administrative cost	271.92	271.92	271.92	271.92	271.92
Internal administrative cost	Insig.	Insig.	Insig.	Insig.	Insig.
Cost of adverse drug effects	29.61	29.61	29.61	29.61	29.61
Social cost	n.c.	n.c.	n.c.	n.c.	n.c.
Total costs	2633.91	2633.91	2633.91	2633.91	2633.91
Benefits					
Increase in economic productivity of patients	n.c.	n.c.	n.c.	n.c.	n.c.
Cost avoidance of hospitalisation	5592.92	5592.92	0.00	0.00	0.00
Decrease consumption of health services – GP consultation	n.c.	n.c.	n.c.	n.c.	n.c.
Decrease consumption of health services – specialist consultation	n.c.	n.c.	n.c.	n.c.	n.c.
Improved health status – decreased consumption of complementary medicines	n.c.	n.c.	n.c.	n.c.	n.c.
Health gain – improvement in life expectancy – QALYs gained	n.c.	n.c.	n.c.	n.c.	n.c.
Willingness-to-pay of patient to obtain positive changes in health status	n.c.	n.c.	n.c.	n.c.	n.c.
Total benefits	5592.92	5592.92	0.00	0.00	0.00
Cost stream					
Discounted cost stream	2633.91	2508.48	2389.01	2275.25	2166.92
Total discounted cost	11973.57				
Benefit stream					
Discounted benefit stream	5592.92	5326.59	0.00	0.00	0.00
Total discounted benefit	10919.51				
Cost-benefit ratio	0.91				
Net financial benefits	2959.01	2959.01	−2633.91	−2633.91	−2633.91
Discounted values of benefits	2959.01	2818.10	−2389.01	−2275.25	−2166.92
Net present value	−1054.07				

Notes:
Insig. = insignificant.
n.c. = not considered under this approach.

Appendix 6.11   Financial Cost Benefit Analysis of Letrozole 2.5mg, discount rate = 5%

Year	0	1	2	3	4
Costs					
Cost of medication	2332.38	2332.38	2332.38	2332.38	2332.38
External administrative cost	271.92	271.92	271.92	271.92	271.92
Internal administrative cost	Insig.	Insig.	Insig.	Insig.	Insig.
Cost of adverse drug effects	29.61	29.61	29.61	29.61	29.61
Social cost	n.c.	n.c.	n.c.	n.c.	n.c.
Total costs	2633.91	2633.91	2633.91	2633.91	2633.91
Benefits					
Increase in economic productivity of patients	1805.25	1805.25	362.50	362.50	362.50
Cost avoidance of hospitalisation	5592.92	5592.92	0.00	0.00	0.00
Decrease consumption of health services – GP consultation	n.c.	n.c.	n.c.	n.c.	n.c.
Decrease consumption of health services – specialist consultation	n.c.	n.c.	n.c.	n.c.	n.c.
Improved health status – decreased consumption of complementary medicines	n.c.	n.c.	n.c.	n.c.	n.c.
Health gain – improvement in life expectancy – QALYs gained	n.c.	n.c.	n.c.	n.c.	n.c.
Willingness-to-pay of patient to obtain positive changes in health status	n.c.	n.c.	n.c.	n.c.	n.c.
Total benefits	7398.17	7398.17	362.50	362.50	362.50
Cost stream					
Discounted cost stream	2633.91	2508.48	2389.01	2275.25	2166.92
Total discounted cost	11973.57				
Benefit stream					
Discounted benefit stream	7398.17	7045.87	328.79	313.14	298.23
Total discounted benefit	15384.20				
Cost-benefit ratio	1.28				
Net financial benefits	4764.26	4764.26	–2271.41	–2271.41	–2271.41
Discounted values of benefits	4764.26	4537.39	–2060.21	–1962.11	–1868.69
Net present value	3410.63				

Notes:
Insig. = insignificant.
n.c. = not considered under this approach.

Appendix 6.12   New[3] Cost Benefit Analysis of Letrozole 2.5mg, discount rate = 0%

Year	0	1	2	3	4
Costs					
Cost of medication	2332.38	2332.38	2332.38	2332.38	2332.38
External administrative cost	271.92	271.92	271.92	271.92	271.92
Internal administrative cost	Insig.	Insig.	Insig.	Insig.	Insig.
Cost of adverse drug effects	29.61	29.61	29.61	29.61	29.61
Social cost	2131.68	2131.68	2131.68	2131.68	2131.68
Total costs	4765.59	4765.59	4765.59	4765.59	4765.59
Benefits					
Increase economic productivity of patients	1805.25	1805.25	362.50	362.50	362.50
Cost avoidance of hospitalisation	5592.92	5592.92	0.00	0.00	0.00
Decrease consumption of health services – GP consultation	458.80	458.80	229.40	229.40	229.40
Decrease consumption of health services – specialist consultation	250.80	250.80	125.40	125.40	125.40
Improved health status – decreased consumption of complementary medicines	400.00	400.00	400.00	400.00	400.00
Health gain – improvement in life expectancy – QALYs gained	25272.03	0.00	0.00	0.00	0.00
Willingness-to-pay of patient to obtain positive changes in health status	2646.95	2646.95	2646.95	2646.95	2646.95
Total benefits/ social welfare	36426.75	11154.72	3764.25	3764.25	3764.25
Cost stream					
Discounted cost stream	4765.59	4765.59	4765.59	4765.59	4765.59
Total discounted cost	23827.95				
Benefit stream					
Discounted benefit stream	36426.75	11154.72	3764.25	3764.25	3764.25
Total discounted benefit	58874.22				
Cost-benefit ratio	2.47				
Net financial benefits	31661.16	6389.13	–1001.34	–1001.34	–1001.34
Discounted values of benefits	31661.16	6389.13	–1001.34	–1001.34	–1001.34
Net present value/ social welfare	35046.27				

Note: Insig. = insignificant.

Appendix 6.13   Hypothetical Cost Benefit Analysis of Fluticasone/Salmeterol under PBAC type of criteria, discount rate = 5%

Year	0	1	2	3	4
Costs					
Cost of medication	816.00	816.00	816.00	816.00	816.00
External administrative cost	137.52	137.52	137.52	137.52	137.52
Internal administrative cost	Insig.	Insig.	Insig.	Insig.	Insig.
Cost of adverse drug effects	29.61	29.61	29.61	29.61	29.61
Social cost	n.c.	n.c.	n.c.	n.c.	n.c.
Total costs	983.13	983.13	983.13	983.13	983.13
Benefits					
Increase economic productivity of patients	n.c.	n.c.	n.c.	n.c.	n.c.
Cost avoidance of hospitalisation	1646.83	0.00	0.00	0.00	0.00
Decrease consumption of health services – GP consultation	n.c.	n.c.	n.c.	n.c.	n.c.
Decrease consumption of health services – specialist consultation	n.c.	n.c.	n.c.	n.c.	n.c.
Improved health status – decreased consumption of complementary medicines	n.c.	n.c.	n.c.	n.c.	n.c.
Health gain – improvement in life expectancy – QALYs gained	n.c.	n.c.	n.c.	n.c.	n.c.
Willingness-to-pay of patient to obtain positive changes in health status	n.c.	n.c.	n.c.	n.c.	n.c.
Total benefits	1646.83	0.00	0.00	0.00	0.00
Cost stream					
Discounted cost stream	983.13	936.31	891.72	849.26	808.82
Total discounted cost	4469.24				
Benefit stream					
Discounted benefit stream	1646.83	0.00	0.00	0.00	0.00
Total discounted benefit	1646.83				
Cost-benefit ratio	0.37				
Net financial benefits	663.70	–983.13	–983.13	–983.13	–983.13
Discounted values of benefits	663.70	–936.31	–891.72	–849.26	–808.82
Net present value	–2822.41				

Notes:
Insig. = insignificant.
n.c. = not considered under this approach.

Appendix 6.14 Financial Cost Benefit Analysis of Fluticasone/Salmeterol, discount rate = 5%

Year	0	1	2	3	4
Costs					
Cost of medication	816.00	816.00	816.00	816.00	816.00
External administrative cost	137.52	137.52	137.52	137.52	137.52
Internal administrative cost	Insig.	Insig.	Insig.	Insig.	Insig.
Cost of adverse drug effects	29.61	29.61	29.61	29.61	29.61
Social cost	n.c.	n.c.	n.c.	n.c.	n.c.
Total costs	983.13	983.13	983.13	983.13	983.13
Benefits					
Increase economic productivity of patients	1087.50	725.00	362.50	362.50	362.50
Cost avoidance of hospitalisation	1646.83	0.00	0.00	0.00	0.00
Decrease consumption of health services – GP consultation	n.c.	n.c.	n.c.	n.c.	n.c.
Decrease consumption of health services – specialist consultation	n.c.	n.c.	n.c.	n.c.	n.c.
Improved health status – decreased consumption of complementary medicines	n.c.	n.c.	n.c.	n.c.	n.c.
Health gain – improvement in life expectancy – QALYs gained	n.c.	n.c.	n.c.	n.c.	n.c.
Willingness-to-pay of patient to obtain positive changes in health status	n.c.	n.c.	n.c.	n.c.	n.c.
Total benefits	2734.33	725.00	365.20	362.50	362.50
Cost stream					
Discounted cost stream	983.13	936.31	891.72	849.26	808.82
Total discounted cost	4469.24				
Benefit stream					
Discounted benefit stream	2734.33	690.48	331.24	313.14	298.23
Total discounted benefit	4367.42				
Cost-benefit ratio	0.98				
Net financial benefits	1751.20	−258.13	−617.93	−620.63	−620.63
Discounted values of benefits	1751.20	−245.84	−560.47	−536.12	−510.59
Net present value	−104.27				

Notes:
Insig. = insignificant.
n.c. = not considered under this approach.

Appendix 6.15   New[3] Cost Benefit Analysis of Fluticasone/Salmeterol, discount rate = 0%

Year	0	1	2	3	4
Costs					
Cost of medication	816.00	816.00	816.00	816.00	816.00
External administrative cost	137.52	137.52	137.52	137.52	137.52
Internal administrative cost	Insig.	Insig.	Insig.	Insig.	Insig.
Cost of adverse drug effects	29.61	29.61	29.61	29.61	29.61
Social cost	381.48	381.48	381.48	381.48	381.48
Total costs	1364.61	1364.61	1364.61	1364.61	1364.61
Benefits					
Increase in economic productivity of patients	1087.50	725.00	362.50	362.50	362.50
Cost avoidance of hospitalisation	1646.83	0.00	0.00	0.00	0.00
Decrease consumption of health services – GP consultation	458.80	458.80	229.40	229.40	229.40
Decrease consumption of health services – specialist consultation	250.80	250.80	125.40	125.40	125.40
Improved health status – decreased consumption of complementary medicines	400.00	400.00	400.00	400.00	400.00
Health gain – improvement in life expectancy – QALYs gained	24776.50	0.00	0.00	0.00	0.00
Willingness-to-pay of patient to obtain positive changes in health status	987.60	987.60	987.60	987.60	987.60
Total benefits/ social welfare	29608.03	2822.20	2104.90	2104.90	2104.90
Cost stream					
Discounted cost stream	1364.61	1364.61	1364.61	1364.61	1364.61
Total discounted cost	6823.05				
Benefit stream					
Discounted benefit stream	29608.03	2822.20	2104.90	2104.90	2104.90
Total discounted benefit	38744.93				
Cost-benefit ratio	5.68				
Net financial benefits	28243.42	1457.59	740.29	740.29	740.29
Discounted values of benefits	28243.42	1457.59	740.29	740.29	740.29
Net present value/ social welfare	31921.88				

Notes:
Insig. = insignificant.
n.c. = not considered under this approach.

Appendix 6.16 Hypothetical Cost Benefit Analysis of Tiotropium 18mcg under PBAC type of criteria, discount rate = 5%

Year	0	1	2	3	4
Costs					
Cost of medication	794.40	794.40	794.40	794.40	794.40
External administrative cost	135.36	135.36	135.36	135.36	135.36
Internal administrative cost	Insig.	Insig.	Insig.	Insig.	Insig.
Cost of adverse drug effects	29.61	29.61	29.61	29.61	29.61
Social cost	n.c.	n.c.	n.c.	n.c.	n.c.
Total costs	959.37	959.37	959.37	959.37	959.37
Benefits					
Increase in economic productivity of patients	n.c.	n.c.	n.c.	n.c.	n.c.
Cost avoidance of hospitalisation	4940.78	0.00	0.00	0.00	0.00
Decrease consumption of health services – GP consultation	n.c.	n.c.	n.c.	n.c.	n.c.
Decrease consumption of health services – specialist consultation	n.c.	n.c.	n.c.	n.c.	n.c.
Improved health status – decreased consumption of complementary medicines	n.c.	n.c.	n.c.	n.c.	n.c.
Health gain – improvement in life expectancy – QALYs gained	n.c.	n.c.	n.c.	n.c.	n.c.
Willingness-to-pay of patient to obtain positive changes in health status	n.c.	n.c.	n.c.	n.c.	n.c.
Total benefits	4940.78	0.00	0.00	0.00	0.00
Cost stream					
Discounted cost stream	959.37	913.68	870.17	828.73	789.27
Total discounted cost	4361.23				
Benefit stream					
Discounted benefit stream	4940.78	0.00	0.00	0.00	0.00
Total discounted benefit	4940.78				
Cost-benefit ratio	1.13				
Net financial benefits	3981.41	–959.37	–959.37	–959.37	–959.37
Discounted values of benefits	3981.41	–913.68	–870.17	–828.73	–789.27
Net present value	579.55				

Notes:
Insig. = insignificant.
n.c. = not considered under this approach.

Appendix 6.17   Financial Cost Benefit Analysis of Tiotropium 18mcg, discount rate = 5%

Year	0	1	2	3	4
Costs					
Cost of medication	794.40	794.40	794.40	794.40	794.40
External administrative cost	135.36	135.36	135.36	135.36	135.36
Internal administrative cost	Insig.	Insig.	Insig.	Insig.	Insig.
Cost of adverse drug effects	29.61	29.61	29.61	29.61	29.61
Social cost	n.c.	n.c.	n.c.	n.c.	n.c.
Total costs	959.37	959.37	959.37	959.37	959.37
Benefits					
Increase in economic productivity of patients	1812.50	725.00	362.50	362.50	362.50
Cost avoidance of hospitalisation	4940.78	0.00	0.00	0.00	0.00
Decrease consumption of health services – GP consultation	n.c.	n.c.	n.c.	n.c.	n.c.
Decrease consumption of health services – specialist consultation	n.c.	n.c.	n.c.	n.c.	n.c.
Improved health status – decreased consumption of complementary medicines	n.c.	n.c.	n.c.	n.c.	n.c.
Health gain – improvement in life expectancy – QALYs gained	n.c.	n.c.	n.c.	n.c.	n.c.
Willingness-to-pay of patient to obtain positive changes in health status	n.c.	n.c.	n.c.	n.c.	n.c.
Total benefits	6753.28	725.00	362.50	362.50	362.50
Cost stream					
Discounted cost stream	959.37	913.68	870.17	828.73	789.27
Total discounted cost	4361.23				
Benefit stream					
Discounted benefit stream	6753.28	690.48	328.79	313.14	298.23
Total discounted benefit	8383.92				
Cost-benefit ratio	1.92				
Net financial benefits	5793.91	–234.37	–596.87	–596.87	–596.87
Discounted values of benefits	5793.91	–223.21	–541.37	–515.59	–491.04
Net present value	4022.69				

Notes:
Insig. = insignificant.
n.c. = not considered under this approach.

Appendix 6.18 New[3] Cost Benefit Analysis of Tiotropium, discount rate = 0%

Year	0	1	2	3	4
Costs					
Cost of medication	794.40	794.40	794.40	794.40	794.40
External administrative cost	135.36	135.36	135.36	135.36	135.36
Internal administrative cost	Insig.	Insig.	Insig.	Insig.	Insig.
Cost of adverse drug effects	29.61	29.61	29.61	29.61	29.61
Social cost	260.4	260.4	260.4	260.4	260.4
Total costs	1219.77	1219.77	1219.77	1219.77	1219.77
Benefits					
Increase in economic productivity of patients	1812.50	725.00	362.50	362.50	362.50
Cost avoidance of hospitalisation	4940.78	0.00	0.00	0.00	0.00
Decrease consumption of health services – GP consultation	458.80	458.80	229.40	229.40	229.40
Decrease consumption of health services – specialist consultation	250.80	250.80	125.40	125.40	125.40
Improved health status – decreased consumption of complementary medicines	400.00	400.00	400.00	400.00	400.00
Health gain – improvement in life expectancy – QALYs gained	24776.50	0.00	0.00	0.00	0.00
Willingness-to-pay of patient to obtain positive changes in health status	954.84	954.84	954.84	954.84	954.84
Total benefits/ social welfare	33594.22	2789.44	2072.14	2072.14	2072.14
Cost stream					
Discounted cost stream	1219.77	1219.77	1219.77	1219.77	1219.77
Total discounted cost	6098.85				
Benefit stream					
Discounted benefit stream	33594.22	2789.44	2072.14	2072.14	2072.14
Total discounted benefit	42600.08				
Cost-benefit ratio	6.98				
Net financial benefits	32374.45	1569.67	852.37	852.37	852.37
Discounted values of benefits	32374.45	1569.67	852.37	852.37	852.37
Net present value/ social welfare	954.84				

Notes: Insig. = insignificant.

Appendix 6.19   New[3] Cost Benefit Analysis of Atorvastatin 40mg, discount rate = 5%

Year	0	1	2	3	4
Costs					
Cost of medication	859.32	859.32	859.32	859.32	859.32
External administrative cost	141.84	141.84	141.84	141.84	141.84
Internal administrative cost	Insig.	Insig.	Insig.	Insig.	Insig.
Cost of adverse drug effects	29.61	29.61	29.61	29.61	29.61
Social cost	117.52	117.52	117.52	117.52	117.52
Total costs	1148.29	1148.29	1148.29	1148.29	1148.29
Benefits					
Increase in economic productivity of patients	1350.50	725.00	362.50	362.50	362.50
Cost avoidance of hospitalisation	4495.59	0.00	0.00	0.00	0.00
Decrease consumption of health services – GP consultation	458.80	458.80	229.40	229.40	229.40
Decrease consumption of health services – specialist consultation	250.80	250.80	125.40	125.40	125.40
Improved health status – decreased consumption of complementary medicines	400.00	400.00	400.00	400.00	400.00
Health gain – improvement in life expectancy – QALYs gained	19113.30	0.00	0.00	0.00	0.00
Willingness-to-pay of patient to obtain positive changes in health status	1026.25	1026.25	1026.25	1026.25	1026.25
Total benefits/ social welfare	27095.24	2860.85	2143.55	2143.55	2143.55
Cost stream					
Discounted cost stream	1148.29	1093.61	1041.52	991.93	944.70
Total discounted cost	5220.05				
Benefit stream					
Discounted benefit stream	27095.24	2724.62	1944.24	1851.66	1763.50
Total discounted benefit	35379.26				
Cost-benefit ratio	6.78				
Net financial benefits	25946.95	1712.56	995.26	995.26	995.26
Discounted values of benefits	25946.95	1631.01	902.72	859.74	818.80
Net present value/ social welfare	30159.21				

Note: Insig. = insignificant.

Appendix 6.20 New[3] Cost Benefit Analysis of Atorvastatin 40mg, discount rate = 10%

Year	0	1	2	3	4
Costs					
Cost of medication	859.32	859.32	859.32	859.32	859.32
External administrative cost	141.84	141.84	141.84	141.84	141.84
Internal administrative cost	Insig.	Insig.	Insig.	Insig.	Insig.
Cost of adverse drug effects	29.61	29.61	29.61	29.61	29.61
Social cost	117.52	117.52	117.52	117.52	117.52
Total costs	1148.29	1148.29	1148.29	1148.29	1148.29
Benefits					
Increase in economic productivity of patients	1350.50	725.00	362.50	362.50	362.50
Cost avoidance of hospitalisation	4495.59	0.00	0.00	0.00	0.00
Decrease consumption of health services – GP consultation	458.80	458.80	229.40	229.40	229.40
Decrease consumption of health services – specialist consultation	250.80	250.80	125.40	125.40	125.40
Improved health status – decreased consumption of complementary medicines	400.00	400.00	400.00	400.00	400.00
Health gain – improvement in life expectancy – QALYs gained	19113.30	0.00	0.00	0.00	0.00
Willingness-to-pay of patient to obtain positive changes in health status	1026.25	1026.25	1026.25	1026.25	1026.25
Total benefits/ social welfare	27095.24	2860.85	2143.55	2143.55	2143.55
Cost stream					
Discounted cost stream	1148.29	1043.90	949.00	862.72	784.29
Total discounted cost	4788.21				
Benefit stream					
Discounted benefit stream	27095.24	2600.77	1771.54	1610.47	1464.07
Total discounted benefit	34542.08				
Cost-benefit ratio	7.21				
Net financial benefits	25946.95	1712.56	995.26	995.26	995.26
Discounted values of benefits	25946.95	1556.87	822.53	747.75	679.77
Net present value/ social welfare	29753.88				

Note: Insig. = insignificant.

Appendix 6.21   New[3] Cost Benefit Analysis of Clopidogrel 75mg, discount rate = 5%

Year	0	1	2	3	4
Costs					
Cost of medication	865.92	865.92	865.92	865.92	865.92
External administrative cost	142.56	142.56	142.56	142.56	142.56
Internal administrative cost	Insig.	Insig.	Insig.	Insig.	Insig.
Cost of adverse drug effects	29.61	29.61	29.61	29.61	29.61
Social cost	777.24	777.24	777.24	777.24	777.24
Total costs	1815.33	1815.33	1815.33	1815.33	1815.33
Benefits					
Increase in economic productivity of patients	2131.50	725.00	362.50	362.50	362.50
Cost avoidance of hospitalisation	9690.50	0.00	0.00	0.00	0.00
Decrease consumption of health services – GP consultation	458.80	458.80	229.40	229.40	229.40
Decrease consumption of health services – specialist consultation	250.80	250.80	125.40	125.40	125.40
Improved health status – decreased consumption of complementary medicines	400.00	400.00	400.00	400.00	400.00
Health gain – improvement in life expectancy – QALYs gained	17697.50	0.00	0.00	0.00	0.00
Willingness-to-pay of patient to obtain positive changes in health status	1033.51	1033.51	1033.51	1033.51	1033.51
Total benefits/ social welfare	31662.61	2868.11	2150.81	2150.81	2150.81
Cost stream					
Discounted cost stream	1815.33	1728.88	1646.54	1568.14	1493.47
Total discounted cost	8252.36				
Benefit stream					
Discounted benefit stream	31662.61	2731.53	1950.83	1857.93	1769.47
Total discounted benefit	39972.37				
Cost-benefit ratio	4.84				
Net financial benefits	29847.28	1052.78	335.48	335.48	335.48
Discounted values of benefits	29847.28	1002.65	304.29	289.80	276.00
Net present value/ social welfare	31720.01				

Note: Insig. = insignificant.

Appendix 6.22 New[3] Cost Benefit Analysis of Clopidogrel 75mg, discount rate = 10%

Year	0	1	2	3	4
Costs					
Cost of medication	865.92	865.92	865.92	865.92	865.92
External administrative cost	142.56	142.56	142.56	142.56	142.56
Internal administrative cost	Insig.	Insig.	Insig.	Insig.	Insig.
Cost of adverse drug effects	29.61	29.61	29.61	29.61	29.61
Social cost	777.24	777.24	777.24	777.24	777.24
Total costs	1815.33	1815.33	1815.33	1815.33	1815.33
Benefits					
Increase in economic productivity of patients	2131.50	725.00	362.50	362.50	362.50
Cost avoidance of hospitalisation	9690.50	0.00	0.00	0.00	0.00
Decrease consumption of health services – GP consultation	458.80	458.80	229.40	229.40	229.40
Decrease consumption of health services – specialist consultation	250.80	250.80	125.40	125.40	125.40
Improved health status – decreased consumption of complementary medicines	400.00	400.00	400.00	400.00	400.00
Health gain – improvement in life expectancy – QALYs gained	17697.50	0.00	0.00	0.00	0.00
Willingness-to-pay of patient to obtain positive changes in health status	1033.51	1033.51	1033.51	1033.51	1033.51
Total benefits/ social welfare	31662.61	2868.11	2150.81	2150.81	2150.81
Cost stream					
Discounted cost stream	1815.33	1650.30	1500.28	1363.88	1239.89
Total discounted cost	7569.67				
Benefit stream					
Discounted benefit stream	31662.61	2607.37	1777.54	1615.93	1469.02
Total discounted benefit	39132.47				
Cost-benefit ratio	5.17				
Net financial benefits	29847.28	1052.78	335.48	335.48	335.48
Discounted values of benefits	29847.28	957.07	277.26	252.05	229.14
Net present value/ social welfare	31562.79				

Note: Insig. = insignificant.

Appendix 6.23 New[3] Cost Benefit Analysis of Pioglitazone 30mg, discount rate = 5%

Year	0	1	2	3	4
Costs					
Cost of medication	1026.72	1026.72	1026.72	1026.72	1026.72
External administrative cost	158.64	158.64	158.64	158.64	158.64
Internal administrative cost	Insig.	Insig.	Insig.	Insig.	Insig.
Cost of adverse drug effects	29.61	29.61	29.61	29.61	29.61
Social cost	1005.12	1005.12	1005.12	1005.12	1005.12
Total costs	2220.09	2220.09	2220.09	2220.09	2220.09
Benefits					
Increase in economic productivity of patients	2320.00	725.00	362.50	362.50	362.50
Cost avoidance of hospitalisation	8683.62	0.00	0.00	0.00	0.00
Decrease consumption of health services – GP consultation	458.80	458.80	229.40	229.40	229.40
Decrease consumption of health services – specialist consultation	250.80	250.80	125.40	125.40	125.40
Improved health status – decreased consumption of complementary medicines	400.00	400.00	400.00	400.00	400.00
Health gain – improvement in life expectancy – QALYs gained	12388.25	0.00	0.00	0.00	0.00
Willingness-to-pay of patient to obtain positive changes in health status	1210.39	1210.39	1210.39	1210.39	1210.39
Total benefits/ social welfare	25711.86	3044.99	2327.69	2327.69	2327.69
Cost stream					
Discounted cost stream	2220.09	2114.37	2013.67	1917.78	1826.47
Total discounted cost	10092.37				
Benefit stream					
Discounted benefit stream	25711.86	2899.99	2111.26	2010.73	1914.99
Total discounted benefit	34648.83				
Cost-benefit ratio	3.43				
Net financial benefits	23491.77	824.90	107.60	107.60	107.60
Discounted values of benefits	23491.77	785.62	97.60	92.95	88.52
Net present value/ social welfare	24556.45				

Note: Insig. = insignificant.

Appendix 6.24   New[3] Cost Benefit Analysis of Pioglitazone 30mg, discount rate = 10%

Year	0	1	2	3	4
Costs					
Cost of medication	1026.72	1026.72	1026.72	1026.72	1026.72
External administrative cost	158.64	158.64	158.64	158.64	158.64
Internal administrative cost	Insig.	Insig.	Insig.	Insig.	Insig.
Cost of adverse drug effects	29.61	29.61	29.61	29.61	29.61
Social cost	1005.12	1005.12	1005.12	1005.12	1005.12
Total costs	2220.09	2220.09	2220.09	2220.09	2220.09
Benefits					
Increase in economic productivity of patients	2320.00	725.00	362.50	362.50	362.50
Cost avoidance of hospitalisation	8683.62	0.00	0.00	0.00	0.00
Decrease consumption of health services – GP consultation	458.80	458.80	229.40	229.40	229.40
Decrease consumption of health services – specialist consultation	250.80	250.80	125.40	125.40	125.40
Improved health status – decreased consumption of complementary medicines	400.00	400.00	400.00	400.00	400.00
Health gain – improvement in life expectancy – QALYs gained	12388.25	0.00	0.00	0.00	0.00
Willingness-to-pay of patient to obtain positive changes in health status	1210.39	1210.39	1210.39	1210.39	1210.39
Total benefits/ social welfare	25711.86	3044.99	2327.69	2327.69	2327.69
Cost stream					
Discounted cost stream	2220.09	2018.26	1834.79	1667.98	1516.34
Total discounted cost	9257.46				
Benefit stream					
Discounted benefit stream	25711.86	2768.17	1923.72	1748.82	1589.84
Total discounted benefit	33742.40				
Cost-benefit ratio	3.64				
Net financial benefits	23491.77	824.90	107.60	107.60	107.60
Discounted values of benefits	23491.77	749.91	88.93	80.84	73.49
Net present value/ social welfare	24484.94				

Note: Insig. = insignificant.

Appendix 6.25 New[3] Cost Benefit Analysis of Letrozole 2.5mg, discount rate = 5%

Year	0	1	2	3	4
Costs					
Cost of medication	2332.38	2332.38	2332.38	2332.38	2332.38
External administrative cost	271.92	271.92	271.92	271.92	271.92
Internal administrative cost	Insig.	Insig.	Insig.	Insig.	Insig.
Cost of adverse drug effects	29.61	29.61	29.61	29.61	29.61
Social cost	2131.68	2131.68	2131.68	2131.68	2131.68
Total costs	4765.59	4765.59	4765.59	4765.59	4765.59
Benefits					
Increase economic productivity of patients	1805.25	1805.25	362.50	362.50	362.50
Cost avoidance of hospitalisation	5592.92	5592.92	0.00	0.00	0.00
Decrease consumption of health services – GP consultation	458.80	458.80	229.40	229.40	229.40
Decrease consumption of health services – specialist consultation	250.80	250.80	125.40	125.40	125.40
Improved health status – decreased consumption of complementary medicines	400.00	400.00	400.00	400.00	400.00
Health gain – improvement in life expectancy – QALYs gained	25272.03	0.00	0.00	0.00	0.00
Willingness-to-pay of patient to obtain positive changes in health status	2646.95	2646.95	2646.95	2646.95	2646.95
Total benefits/ social welfare	36426.75	11154.72	3764.25	3764.25	3764.25
Cost stream					
Discounted cost stream	4765.59	4538.65	4322.49	4116.66	3920.65
Total discounted cost	21664.04				
Benefit stream					
Discounted benefit stream	36426.75	10623.53	3414.25	3251.67	3096.85
Total discounted benefit	56813.05				
Cost-benefit ratio	2.62				
Net financial benefits	31661.16	6389.13	–1001.34	–1001.34	–1001.34
Discounted values of benefits	31661.16	6084.88	–908.24	–864.99	–823.80
Net present value/ social welfare	35149.01				

Note: Insig. = insignificant.

Appendix 6.26   New[3] Cost Benefit Analysis of Letrozole 2.5mg, discount rate = 10%

Year	0	1	2	3	4
Costs					
Cost of medication	2332.38	2332.38	2332.38	2332.38	2332.38
External administrative cost	271.92	271.92	271.92	271.92	271.92
Internal administrative cost	Insig.	Insig.	Insig.	Insig.	Insig.
Cost of adverse drug effects	29.61	29.61	29.61	29.61	29.61
Social cost	2131.68	2131.68	2131.68	2131.68	2131.68
Total costs	4765.59	4765.59	4765.59	4765.59	4765.59
Benefits					
Increase economic productivity of patients	1805.25	1805.25	362.50	362.50	362.50
Cost avoidance of hospitalisation	5592.92	5592.92	0.00	0.00	0.00
Decrease consumption of health services – GP consultation	458.80	458.80	229.40	229.40	229.40
Decrease consumption of health services – specialist consultation	250.80	250.80	125.40	125.40	125.40
Improved health status – decreased consumption of complementary medicines	400.00	400.00	400.00	400.00	400.00
Health gain – improvement in life expectancy – QALYs gained	25272.03	0.00	0.00	0.00	0.00
Willingness-to-pay of patient to obtain positive changes in health status	2646.95	2646.95	2646.95	2646.95	2646.95
Total benefits/ social welfare	36426.75	11154.72	3764.25	3764.25	3764.25
Cost stream					
Discounted cost stream	4765.59	4332.35	3938.52	3580.44	3254.95
Total discounted cost	19871.84				
Benefit stream					
Discounted benefit stream	36426.75	10140.64	311.10	2828.12	2571.02
Total discounted benefit	52277.63				
Cost-benefit ratio	2.63				
Net financial benefits	31661.16	6389.13	−1001.34	−1001.34	−1001.34
Discounted values of benefits	31661.16	5808.29	−3627.43	−752.32	−683.93
Net present value/ social welfare	32405.79				

Note: Insig. = insignificant.

Appendix 6.27   New[3] Cost Benefit Analysis of Fluticasone/Salmeterol, discount rate = 5%

Year	0	1	2	3	4
Costs					
Cost of medication	816.00	816.00	816.00	816.00	816.00
External administrative cost	137.52	137.52	137.52	137.52	137.52
Internal administrative cost	Insig.	Insig.	Insig.	Insig.	Insig.
Cost of adverse drug effects	29.61	29.61	29.61	29.61	29.61
Social cost	381.48	381.48	381.48	381.48	381.48
Total costs	1364.61	1364.61	1364.61	1364.61	1364.61
Benefits					
Increase in economic productivity of patients	1087.50	725.00	362.50	362.50	362.50
Cost avoidance of hospitalisation	1646.83	0.00	0.00	0.00	0.00
Decrease consumption of health services – GP consultation	458.80	458.80	229.40	229.40	229.40
Decrease consumption of health services – specialist consultation	250.80	250.80	125.40	125.40	125.40
Improved health status – decreased consumption of complementary medicines	400.00	400.00	400.00	400.00	400.00
Health gain – improvement in life expectancy – QALYs gained	24776.50	0.00	0.00	0.00	0.00
Willingness-to-pay of patient to obtain positive changes in health status	987.60	987.60	987.60	987.60	987.60
Total benefits/ social welfare	29608.03	2822.20	2104.90	2104.90	2104.90
Cost stream					
Discounted cost stream	1364.61	1299.63	1237.73	1178.79	1122.66
Total discounted cost	6203.42				
Benefit stream					
Discounted benefit stream	29608.03	2687.81	1909.19	1818.28	1731.70
Total discounted benefit	37755.00				
Cost-benefit ratio	6.09				
Net financial benefits	28243.42	1457.59	740.29	740.29	740.29
Discounted values of benefits	28243.42	1388.18	671.46	639.48	609.04
Net present value/ social welfare	31551.58				

Notes: Insig. = insignificant.

Appendix 6.28 New[3] Cost Benefit Analysis of Fluticasone/Salmeterol, discount rate = 10%

Year	0	1	2	3	4
Costs					
Cost of medication	816.00	816.00	816.00	816.00	816.00
External administrative cost	137.52	137.52	137.52	137.52	137.52
Internal administrative cost	Insig.	Insig.	Insig.	Insig.	Insig.
Cost of adverse drug effects	29.61	29.61	29.61	29.61	29.61
Social cost	381.48	381.48	381.48	381.48	381.48
Total costs	1364.61	1364.61	1364.61	1364.61	1364.61
Benefits					
Increase in economic productivity of patients	1087.50	725.00	362.50	362.50	362.50
Cost avoidance of hospitalisation	1646.83	0.00	0.00	0.00	0.00
Decrease consumption of health services – GP consultation	458.80	458.80	229.40	229.40	229.40
Decrease consumption of health services – specialist consultation	250.80	250.80	125.40	125.40	125.40
Improved health status – decreased consumption of complementary medicines	400.00	400.00	400.00	400.00	400.00
Health gain – improvement in life expectancy – QALYs gained	24776.50	0.00	0.00	0.00	0.00
Willingness-to-pay of patient to obtain positive changes in health status	987.60	987.60	987.60	987.60	987.60
Total benefits/ social welfare	29608.03	2822.20	2104.90	2104.90	2104.90
Cost stream					
Discounted cost stream	1364.61	1240.55	1127.78	1025.25	932.04
Total discounted cost	5690.23				
Benefit stream					
Discounted benefit stream	29608.03	2565.63	1739.59	1581.43	1437.67
Total discounted benefit	36932.36				
Cost-benefit ratio	6.49				
Net financial benefits	28243.42	1457.59	740.29	740.29	740.29
Discounted values of benefits	28243.42	1325.08	611.81	556.19	505.63
Net present value/ social welfare	31242.13				

Notes: Insig. = insignificant.

Appendix 6.29   New[3] Cost Benefit Analysis of Tiotropium, discount rate = 5%

Year	0	1	2	3	4
Costs					
Cost of medication	794.40	794.40	794.40	794.40	794.40
External administrative cost	135.36	135.36	135.36	135.36	135.36
Internal administrative cost	Insig.	Insig.	Insig.	Insig.	Insig.
Cost of adverse drug effects	29.61	29.61	29.61	29.61	29.61
Social cost	260.4	260.4	260.4	260.4	260.4
Total costs	1219.77	1219.77	1219.77	1219.77	1219.77
Benefits					
Increase in economic productivity of patients	1812.50	725.00	362.50	362.50	362.50
Cost avoidance of hospitalisation	4940.78	0.00	0.00	0.00	0.00
Decrease consumption of health services – GP consultation	458.80	458.80	229.40	229.40	229.40
Decrease consumption of health services – specialist consultation	250.80	250.80	125.40	125.40	125.40
Improved health status – decreased consumption of complementary medicines	400.00	400.00	400.00	400.00	400.00
Health gain – improvement in life expectancy – QALYs gained	24776.50	0.00	0.00	0.00	0.00
Willingness-to-pay of patient to obtain positive changes in health status	954.84	954.84	954.84	954.84	954.84
Total benefits/ social welfare	33594.22	2789.44	2072.14	2072.14	2072.14
Cost stream					
Discounted cost stream	1219.77	1161.68	1106.36	1053.67	1003.50
Total discounted cost	5544.99				
Benefit stream					
Discounted benefit stream	33594.22	2656.61	1879.47	1789.98	1704.75
Total discounted benefit	41625.03				
Cost-benefit ratio	7.51				
Net financial benefits	32374.45	1569.67	852.37	852.37	852.37
Discounted values of benefits	32374.45	1494.92	773.12	736.30	701.24
Net present value/ social welfare	36080.04				

Notes: Insig. = insignificant.

Appendix 6.30 New[3] Cost Benefit Analysis of Tiotropium, discount rate = 10%

Year	0	1	2	3	4
Costs					
Cost of medication	794.40	794.40	794.40	794.40	794.40
External administrative cost	135.36	135.36	135.36	135.36	135.36
Internal administrative cost	Insig.	Insig.	Insig.	Insig.	Insig.
Cost of adverse drug effects	29.61	29.61	29.61	29.61	29.61
Social cost	260.4	260.4	260.4	260.4	260.4
Total costs	1219.77	1219.77	1219.77	1219.77	1219.77
Benefits					
Increase in economic productivity of patients	1812.50	725.00	362.50	362.50	362.50
Cost avoidance of hospitalisation	4940.78	0.00	0.00	0.00	0.00
Decrease consumption of health services – GP consultation	458.80	458.80	229.40	229.40	229.40
Decrease consumption of health services – specialist consultation	250.80	250.80	125.40	125.40	125.40
Improved health status – decreased consumption of complementary medicines	400.00	400.00	400.00	400.00	400.00
Health gain – improvement in life expectancy – QALYs gained	24776.50	0.00	0.00	0.00	0.00
Willingness-to-pay of patient to obtain positive changes in health status	954.84	954.84	954.84	954.84	954.84
Total benefits/ social welfare	33594.22	2789.44	2072.14	2072.14	2072.14
Cost stream					
Discounted cost stream	1219.77	1108.88	1008.08	916.43	833.12
Total discounted cost	5086.27				
Benefit stream					
Discounted benefit stream	33594.22	2535.85	1712.52	1556.82	1415.29
Total discounted benefit	40814.70				
Cost-benefit ratio	8.02				
Net financial benefits	32374.45	1569.67	852.37	852.37	852.37
Discounted values of benefits	32374.45	1426.97	704.44	640.39	582.18
Net present value/ social welfare	35728.43				

Notes: Insig. = insignificant.

Appendix 7.1 Net Benefits and Net Present Values of the Six Medications under PBAC Type of Criteria, discount rate = 5%

Medications		Atorvastatin	Clopidogrel	Pioglitazone	Letrozole	Fluticasone/ Salmeterol	Tiotropium
Year	PVF	Net benefits	Net benefits	Net benefits	Net benefits	Net benefits	Net benefits
0	1	3464.82	8652.41	7468.65	2959.01	663.70	3981.41
1	0.95238	−1030.77	−1038.09	−1214.97	2959.01	−983.13	−959.37
2	0.90702	−1030.77	−1038.09	−1214.97	−2633.91	−983.13	−959.37
3	0.86383	−1030.77	−1038.09	−1214.97	−2633.91	−983.13	−959.37
4	0.82270	−1030.77	−1038.09	−1214.97	−2633.91	−983.13	−959.37
Net present value		−190.22	4971.42	3160.45	−1054.07	−2822.41	579.55
C-B ratio		0.96	2.05	1.57	0.91	0.37	1.13

Notes: PVF = present value factor. C-B ratio = cost-benefit ratio.

Appendix 7.2 Net Benefits and Net Present Values of the Six Medications under Financial Cost Benefit Analysis, discount rate = 5%

Medications		Atorvastatin	Clopidogrel	Pioglitazone	Letrozole	Fluticasone/ Salmeterol	Tiotropium
Year	PVF	Net benefits	Net benefits	Net benefits	Net benefits	Net benefits	Net benefits
0	1	4815.32	10783.91	9788.65	4764.26	1751.20	5793.91
1	0.95238	−305.77	−313.09	−489.97	4764.26	−258.13	−234.37
2	0.90702	−668.27	−675.59	−852.47	−2271.41	−620.93	−596.87
3	0.86383	−668.27	−675.59	−852.47	−2271.41	−620.93	−596.87
4	0.82270	−668.27	−675.59	−852.47	−2271.41	−620.93	−596.87
Net present value		2790.92	8733.55	7111.09	3410.63	−104.27	4022.69
C-B ratio		1.60	2.85	2.29	1.28	0.98	1.92

Notes: PVF = present value factor. C-B ratio = cost-benefit ratio.

Appendix 7.3 Net Benefits and Net Present Values of the Six Medications under New[3] Cost Benefit Analysis, discount rate = 0%

Medications		Atorvastatin	Clopidogrel	Pioglitazone	Letrozole	Fluticasone/ Salmeterol	Tiotropium
Year	PVF	Net benefits	Net benefits	Net benefits	Net benefits	Net benefits	Net benefits
0	1	25946.95	29847.28	23491.77	31661.16	28243.42	32374.45
1	1	1712.56	1052.78	824.90	6389.13	1457.59	1569.67
2	1	995.26	335.48	107.60	-1001.34	740.29	852.37
3	1	995.26	335.48	107.60	-1001.34	740.29	852.37
4	1	995.26	335.48	107.60	-1001.34	740.29	852.37
Net present value		30645.29	31906.50	24639.47	35046.27	31921.88	36501.23
C-B ratio		6.34	4.52	3.22	2.47	5.68	6.98

Notes: PVF = present value factor. C-B ratio = cost-benefit ratio.

Appendix 7.4 Net Benefits and Net Present Values of the Six Medications under New[3] Cost Benefit Analysis, discount rate = 5%

Medications		Atorvastatin	Clopidogrel	Pioglitazone	Letrozole	Fluticasone/ Salmeterol	Tiotropium
Year	PVF	Net benefits	Net benefits	Net benefits	Net benefits	Net benefits	Net benefits
0	1	25946.95	29847.28	23491.77	31661.16	28243.42	32374.45
1	0.95238	1712.56	1052.78	824.90	6389.13	1457.59	1569.67
2	0.90702	995.26	335.48	107.60	−1001.34	740.29	852.37
3	0.86383	995.26	335.48	107.60	−1001.34	740.29	852.37
4	0.82270	995.26	335.48	107.60	−1001.34	740.29	852.37
Net present value		30159.21	31720.01	24556.45	35149.01	31551.58	36080.04
C-B ratio		6.78	4.84	3.43	2.62	6.09	7.51

Notes: PVF = present value factor. C-B ratio = cost-benefit ratio.

Appendix 7.5 Net Benefits and Net Present Values of the Six Medications under New[3] Cost Benefit Analysis, discount rate = 10%

Medications		Atorvastatin	Clopidogrel	Pioglitazone	Letrozole	Fluticasone/Salmeterol	Tiotropium
Year	PVF	Net benefits	Net benefits	Net benefits	Net benefits	Net benefits	Net benefits
0	1	25946.95	29847.28	23491.77	31661.16	28243.42	32374.45
1	0.95238	1712.56	1052.78	824.90	6389.13	1457.59	1569.67
2	0.90702	995.26	335.48	107.60	-1001.34	740.29	852.37
3	0.86383	995.26	335.48	107.60	-1001.34	740.29	852.37
4	0.82270	995.26	335.48	107.60	-1001.34	740.29	852.37
Net present value		30159.21	31720.01	24556.45	35149.01	31551.58	36080.04
C-B ratio		6.78	4.84	3.43	2.62	6.09	7.51

Notes: PVF = present value factor. C-B ratio = cost-benefit ratio.

Appendix 7.6 Net Benefits and Net Present Values of the Six Medications under New[3] Cost Benefit Analysis (excluding Willingness-to-pay as Benefit), discount rate = 0%

Medications		Atorvastatin	Clopidogrel	Pioglitazone	Letrozole	Fluticasone/ Salmeterol	Tiotropium
Year	PVF	Net benefits	Net benefits	Net benefits	Net benefits	Net benefits	Net benefits
0	1	24920.70	28813.77	22281.38	29014.21	27255.82	31419.61
1	0.90909	686.31	19.27	−385.49	3742.18	469.99	614.83
2	0.82645	−30.99	−698.03	−1102.79	−3648.29	−247.31	−102.47
3	0.75131	−30.99	−698.03	−1102.79	−3648.29	−247.31	−102.47
4	0.68301	−30.99	−698.03	−1102.79	−3648.29	−247.31	−102.47
Net present value		25514.04	26738.95	18587.52	21811.52	26983.88	31727.03
C-B ratio		5.44	3.95	2.67	1.92	4.95	6.20

Notes: PVF = present value factor. C-B ratio = cost-benefit ratio.

Appendix 7.7 Net Benefits and Net Present Values of the Six Medications under New[3] Cost Benefit Analysis (excluding savings from decreased consumption of complementary medicines as benefit), discount rate = 0%

Medications		Atorvastatin	Clopidogrel	Pioglitazone	Letrozole	Fluticasone/Salmeterol	Tiotropium
Year	PVF	Net benefits	Net benefits	Net benefits	Net benefits	Net benefits	Net benefits
0	1	25546.95	29447.28	23091.77	31261.16	27873.42	31974.45
1	0.90909	1312.56	652.78	424.90	5989.13	1057.59	1169.67
2	0.82645	595.26	−64.52	−292.40	−1401.34	340.29	452.37
3	0.75131	595.26	−64.52	−292.40	−1401.34	340.29	452.37
4	0.68301	595.26	−64.52	−292.40	−1401.34	340.29	452.37
Net present value		28645.29	29906.50	22639.47	33046.27	29921.88	34501.23
C-B ratio		5.99	4.29	3.04	2.39	5.39	6.66

Notes: PVF = present value factor. C-B ratio = cost-benefit ratio.

Appendix 7.8   Net Benefits and Net Present Values of the Six Medications under New[3] Cost Benefit Analysis (excluding savings from decreased GP and specialist consultation as benefit), discount rate = 0%

Medications		Atorvastatin	Clopidogrel	Pioglitazone	Letrozole	Fluticasone/ Salmeterol	Tiotropium
Year	PVF	Net benefits	Net benefits	Net benefits	Net benefits	Net benefits	Net benefits
0	1	25237.35	29137.68	22782.17	30951.56	27533.82	31644.85
1	0.90909	1002.96	343.18	115.30	5679.53	749.99	860.07
2	0.82645	640.46	–19.32	–247.20	–1356.14	385.49	497.57
3	0.75131	640.46	–19.32	–247.20	–1356.14	385.49	497.57
4	0.68301	640.46	–19.32	–247.20	–1356.14	385.49	497.57
Net present value		28161.69	29422.90	22639.47	22155.87	29438.28	34017.63
C-B ratio		5.90	4.24	3.04	3.00	5.31	6.58

Notes: PVF = present value factor. C-B ratio = cost-benefit ratio.

Appendix 7.9 Net Benefits and Net Present Values of the Six Medications under New[3] Cost Benefit Analysis (excluding savings from cost avoidance of hospitalisation as benefit), discount rate = 0%

Medications	PVF	Atorvastatin	Clopidogrel	Pioglitazone	Letrozole	Fluticasone/ Salmeterol	Tiotropium
Year		Net benefits	Net benefits	Net benefits	Net benefits	Net benefits	Net benefits
0	1	21451.36	20156.78	14808.15	26068.24	26596.59	27433.67
1	0.90909	1712.56	1052.78	824.90	796.21	1457.59	1569.67
2	0.82645	995.26	335.48	107.60	-1001.34	740.29	852.37
3	0.75131	995.26	335.48	107.60	-1001.34	740.29	852.37
4	0.68301	995.26	335.48	107.60	-1001.34	740.29	852.37
Net present value		26149.70	22216.00	15955.85	23860.43	30275.05	31560.45
C-B ratio		5.55	3.65	2.44	2.00	5.44	6.17

Notes: PVF = present value factor. C-B ratio = cost-benefit ratio.

Appendix 7.10 Net Benefits and Net Present Values of the Six Medications under New[3] Cost Benefit Analysis (excluding increase in economic productivity as benefit), discount rate = 0%

Medications		Atorvastatin	Clopidogrel	Pioglitazone	Letrozole	Fluticasone/ Salmeterol	Tiotropium
Year	PVF	Net benefits	Net benefits	Net benefits	Net benefits	Net benefits	Net benefits
0	1	24596.45	27715.78	21171.77	29855.91	27155.92	30561.95
1	0.90909	987.56	327.78	99.90	4583.88	732.59	844.67
2	0.82645	632.76	−27.02	−254.90	−1363.84	377.79	489.87
3	0.75131	632.76	−27.02	−254.90	−1363.84	377.79	489.87
4	0.68301	632.76	−27.02	−254.90	−1363.84	377.79	489.87
Net present value		27482.29	27962.50	20506.97	30348.27	29021.88	32876.23
C-B ratio		5.79	4.08	2.85	2.27	5.25	6.39

Notes: PVF present value factor. C-B ratio = cost-benefit ratio.

Appendix 7.11 Net Benefits and Net Present Values of the Six Medications under New[3] Cost Benefit Analysis (excluding increase in life expectancy as benefit), discount rate = 0%

Medications		Atorvastatin	Clopidogrel	Pioglitazone	Letrozole	Fluticasone/Salmeterol	Tiotropium
Year	PVF	Net benefits	Net benefits	Net benefits	Net benefits	Net benefits	Net benefits
0	1	6833.65	12149.78	11103.52	6389.13	3466.92	7597.95
1	0.90909	1712.56	1052.78	824.90	6389.13	1457.59	1569.67
2	0.82645	995.26	335.48	107.60	-1001.34	740.29	852.37
3	0.75131	995.26	335.48	107.60	-1001.34	740.29	852.37
4	0.68301	995.26	335.48	107.60	-1001.34	740.29	852.37
Net present value		11531.99	14209.00	12251.22	9774.24	7145.38	11724.73
C-B ratio		3.01	2.57	2.10	1.41	2.05	2.92

Notes: PVF = present value factor. C-B ratio = cost-benefit ratio.

Appendix 7.12 Net Benefits and Net Present Values of the Six Medications under New[3] Cost Benefit Analysis (including 50% increase in life expectancy as benefit), discount rate = 0%

Medications		Atorvastatin	Clopidogrel	Pioglitazone	Letrozole	Fluticasone/ Salmeterol	Tiotropium
Year	PVF	Net benefits	Net benefits	Net benefits	Net benefits	Net benefits	Net benefits
0	1	16930.30	20998.53	17297.65	19025.15	15855.17	19986.20
1	0.90909	1712.56	1052.78	824.90	6389.13	1457.59	1569.67
2	0.82645	995.26	335.48	107.60	-1001.34	740.29	852.37
3	0.75131	995.26	335.48	107.60	-1001.34	740.29	852.37
4	0.68301	995.26	335.48	107.60	-1001.34	740.29	852.37
Net present value		24112.98	21088.64	23057.75	18445.35	22410.26	19533.63
C-B ratio		4.67	3.54	2.66	1.94	3.86	4.95

Notes: PVF = present value factor. C-B ratio = cost-benefit ratio.

Appendix 7.13   PBSPLAN GAMS program, discount rate = 0%

GAMS 2.25.085   386/486 DOS   01/04/80 05:04:27   PAGE 1
G e n e r a l   A l g e b r a i c   M o d e l i n g   S y s t e m
C o m p i l a t i o n

This is the GAMS program named PBSPLAN used to solve the model health sectoral plan for 6 drugs, 5 time periods. It computes a mixed integer programming problem for listing drugs in the PBS. This program is developed on the basis of the GAMS methods presented in Thompson and Thore (1992) and Brook et al. (1997).

```
 9
10    SETS
11    J   Time / 1*5/
12    I   drugs / x1, x2, x3, x4, x5, x6/
13
14
15    *Cash flows:
16    TABLE
17    A(J,I)        cash flows in period J from drugs I
18          x1          x2          x3          x4          x5          x6
19      1   25946.95    29847.28    23491.77    31661.16    28243.42    32374.45
20      2   1712.56     1052.78     824.90      6389.13     1457.59     1569.67
21      3   995.26      335.48      107.60      -1001.34    740.29      852.37
22      4   995.26      335.48      107.60      -1001.34    740.29      852.37
23      5   995.26      335.48      107.60      -1001.34    740.29      852.37;
24
25
26    *Budget constraint:
27    PARAMETER
28        RHS(J)   Govt. health budget constraints in period J
29               /1    1500000000
30                2    1627500000
31                3    1773975000
32                4    1933632750
33                5    2107659698 /
34
35
36    NPSB(I)      net present social benefit of drug I;
37        NPSB(I) = SUM(J, A(J,I) /(1.00**(ORD(J)-1))) ;
38    *       NPSB(I) = SUM(J, A(J,I) /(1.00**(ORD(J)-1))) ;
39
40    VARIABLES
41        SOCVALUE    total net present value of social benefit
42
```

Appendix 7.13   PBSPLAN GAMS program, discount rate = 0% – *continued*

```
43   BINARY VARIABLES
44     x(I)    drugs;
45
46   EQUATIONS
47     OBJECTIVE        total NPSB of all listed drugs
48     CONSTRAINT(J)    budget constraint in time period J;
49
50   OBJECTIVE..      SOCVALUE =E= SUM(I, NPSB(I)*x(I));
51   CONSTRAINT(J)..  SUM(I, -A(J, I)*x(I)) =L= RHS(J);
52
53   model PBSPLAN /all/;
54   solve PBSPLAN maximizing SOCVALUE using mip;
55
56
```

GAMS 2.25.085   386/486 DOS   01/04/80 05:04:27   PAGE   2
G e n e r a l   A l g e b r a i c   M o d e l i n g   S y s t e m
C o m p i l a t i o n

COMPILATION TIME   =   0.050 SECONDS   VERID MW2-25-085

GAMS 2.25.085   386/486 DOS   01/04/80 05:04:27   PAGE   3
G e n e r a l   A l g e b r a i c   M o d e l i n g   S y s t e m
Equation Listing   SOLVE PBSPLAN USING MIP FROM LINE 54

—— OBJECTIVE   =E=   total NPSB of all listed drugs

OBJECTIVE..   SOCVALUE – 30645.29*X(X1) – 31906.5*X(X2) –
24639.47*X(X3) – 35046.27*X(X4) – 31921.88*X(X5) – 36501.23*X(X6) =E=
0 ; (LHS = 0)

—— CONSTRAINT   =L=   budget constraint in time period J

CONSTRAINT(1)..   – 25946.95*X(X1) – 29847.28*X(X2) – 23491.77*X(X3) –
31661.16*X(X4) – 28243.42*X(X5) – 32374.45*X(X6) =L= 1.5000000E+9 ;
(LHS = 0)

CONSTRAINT(2)..   – 1712.56*X(X1) – 1052.78*X(X2) – 824.9*X(X3) –
6389.13*X(X4) – 1457.59*X(X5) – 1569.67*X(X6) =L= 1.6275000E+9 ;
(LHS = 0)

CONSTRAINT(3)..   – 995.26*X(X1) – 335.48*X(X2) – 107.6*X(X3) +
1001.34*X(X4) – 740.29*X(X5) – 852.37*X(X6) =L= 1.7739750E+9 ;
(LHS = 0)

REMAINING 2 ENTRIES SKIPPED

Appendix 7.13   PBSPLAN GAMS program, discount rate = 0% – *continued*

GAMS 2.25.085   386/486 DOS   01/04/80 05:04:27 PAGE   4
G e n e r a l   A l g e b r a i c   M o d e l i n g   S y s t e m
Column Listing   SOLVE PBSPLAN USING MIP FROM LINE 54

—— SOCVALUE   total net present value of social benefit

SOCVALUE
(.LO, .L, .UP = -INF, 0, +INF)
1   OBJECTIVE

—— X drugs
X(X1)
	(.LO, .L, .UP = 0, 0, 1)
–30645.29	OBJECTIVE
–25946.95	CONSTRAINT(1)
–1712.56	CONSTRAINT(2)
–995.26	CONSTRAINT(3)
–995.26	CONSTRAINT(4)
–995.26	CONSTRAINT(5)

X(X2)
	(.LO, .L, .UP = 0, 0, 1)
–31906.5	OBJECTIVE
–29847.28	CONSTRAINT(1)
–1052.78	CONSTRAINT(2)
–335.48	CONSTRAINT(3)
–335.48	CONSTRAINT(4)
–335.48	CONSTRAINT(5)

X(X3)
	(.LO, .L, .UP = 0, 0, 1)
–24639.47	OBJECTIVE
–23491.77	CONSTRAINT(1)
–824.9	CONSTRAINT(2)
–107.6	CONSTRAINT(3)
–107.6	CONSTRAINT(4)
–107.6	CONSTRAINT(5)

REMAINING 3 ENTRIES SKIPPED

GAMS 2.25.085   386/486 DOS   01/04/80 05:04:27   PAGE   5
G e n e r a l   A l g e b r a i c   M o d e l i n g   S y s t e m
Model Statistics   SOLVE PBSPLAN USING MIP FROM LINE 54

MODEL STATISTICS

BLOCKS OF EQUATIONS	2	SINGLE EQUATIONS	6
BLOCKS OF VARIABLES	2	SINGLE VARIABLES	7
NON ZERO ELEMENTS	37	DISCRETE VARIABLES	6

Appendix 7.13 PBSPLAN GAMS program, discount rate = 0% – *continued*

GENERATION TIME = 0.660 SECONDS

EXECUTION TIME = 0.720 SECONDS VERID MW2-25-085

GAMS 2.25.085 386/486 DOS 01/04/80 05:04:27 PAGE 6
G e n e r a l A l g e b r a i c M o d e l i n g S y s t e m
Solution Report SOLVE PBSPLAN USING MIP FROM LINE 54

S O L V E S U M M A R Y

MODEL	PBSPLAN	OBJECTIVE	SOCVALUE
TYPE	MIP	DIRECTION	MAXIMIZE
SOLVER	ZOOM	FROM LINE	54

**** SOLVER STATUS 1 NORMAL COMPLETION
**** MODEL STATUS 1 OPTIMAL
**** OBJECTIVE VALUE 190660.6400

RESOURCE USAGE, LIMIT 0.170 1000.000
ITERATION COUNT, LIMIT 7 1000
You do not have a full license for this solver, Continue to run in demonstration mode.
The following size restrictions apply:
Total nonzero elements: 1000
Discrete variables: 20

Work space allocated – 0.01 Mb

	Iterations	Time
Initial LP	7	0.00
Heuristic	0	0.00
Branch and bound	0	0.00
Final LP	0	0.00

	LOWER	LEVEL	UPPER	MARGINAL
—— EQU OBJECTIVE	.	.	.	1.000

OBJECTIVE total NPSB of all listed drugs

—— EQU CONSTRAINT budget constraint in time period J

	LOWER	LEVEL	UPPER	MARGINAL
1	–INF	–1.716E+5	1.5000E+9	.
2	–INF	–1.301E+4	1.6275E+9	.
3	–INF	–2029.660	1.7740E+9	.
4	–INF	–2029.660	1.9336E+9	.
5	–INF	–2029.660	2.1077E+9	.

	LOWER	LEVEL	UPPER	MARGINAL
—— VAR SOCVALUE	–INF	1.9066E+5	+INF	.

SOCVALUE total net present value of social benefit

Appendix 7.13 PBSPLAN GAMS program, discount rate = 0% – *continued*

GAMS 2.25.085   386/486 DOS   01/04/80 05:04:27   PAGE   7
G e n e r a l   A l g e b r a i c   M o d e l i n g   S y s t e m
Solution Report   SOLVE PBSPLAN USING MIP FROM LINE 54

—— VAR X   drugs

	LOWER	LEVEL	UPPER	MARGINAL
X1	.	1.000	1.000	30645.290
X2	.	1.000	1.000	31906.500
X3	.	1.000	1.000	24639.470
X4	.	1.000	1.000	35046.270
X5	.	1.000	1.000	31921.880
X6	.	1.000	1.000	36501.230

**** REPORT SUMMARY :   0 NONOPT
                                    0 INFEASIBLE
                                    0 UNBOUNDED

EXECUTION TIME   =   0.170 SECONDS   VERID MW2-25-085

USER: Dr. S.M.N. Islam   G950901:1341AR-MW2
        Centre for Strategic Economics Studies, Victoria University

**** FILE SUMMARY

INPUT   C:\GAMS386\HEALTH51.GMS
OUTPUT   C:\GAMS386\HEALTH51.LST

Appendix 7.14 New[3] Cost Benefit Analysis of Atorvastatin 40mg (excluding willingness-to-pay as benefit), discount rate = 0%

Year	0	1	2	3	4
Costs					
Cost of medication	859.32	859.32	859.32	859.32	859.32
External administrative cost	141.84	141.84	141.84	141.84	141.84
Internal administrative cost	Insig.	Insig.	Insig.	Insig.	Insig.
Cost of adverse drug effects	29.61	29.61	29.61	29.61	29.61
Social cost	117.52	117.52	117.52	117.52	117.52
Total costs	1148.29	1148.29	1148.29	1148.29	1148.29
Benefits					
Increase in economic productivity of patients	1350.50	725.00	362.50	362.50	362.50
Cost avoidance of hospitalisation	4495.59	0.00	0.00	0.00	0.00
Decrease consumption of health services – GP consultation	458.80	458.80	229.40	229.40	229.40
Decrease consumption of health services – specialist consultation	250.80	250.80	125.40	125.40	125.40
Improved health status – decreased consumption of complementary medicines	400.00	400.00	400.00	400.00	400.00
Health gain – improvement in life expectancy – QALYs gained	19113.30	0.00	0.00	0.00	0.00
Willingness-to-pay of patient to obtain positive changes in health status	0.00	0.00	0.00	0.00	0.00
Total benefits/ social welfare	26068.99	1834.60	1117.30	1117.30	1117.30
Cost stream					
Discounted cost stream	1148.29	1148.29	1148.29	1148.29	1148.29
Total discounted cost	5741.45				
Benefit stream					
Discounted benefit stream	26068.99	1834.60	1117.30	1117.30	1117.30
Total discounted benefit	31255.49				
Cost-benefit ratio	5.44				
Net financial benefits	24920.70	686.31	–30.99	–30.99	–30.99
Discounted values of benefits	24920.70	686.31	–30.99	–30.99	–30.99
Net present value/ social welfare	25514.04				

Note: Insig. = insignificant.

Appendix 7.15   New[3] Cost Benefit Analysis of Atorvastatin 40mg (excluding savings from decreased consumption of complementary medicines as benefit), discount rate = 0%

Year	0	1	2	3	4
Costs					
Cost of medication	859.32	859.32	859.32	859.32	859.32
External administrative cost	141.84	141.84	141.84	141.84	141.84
Internal administrative cost	Insig.	Insig.	Insig.	Insig.	Insig.
Cost of adverse drug effects	29.61	29.61	29.61	29.61	29.61
Social cost	117.52	117.52	117.52	117.52	117.52
Total costs	1148.29	1148.29	1148.29	1148.29	1148.29
Benefits					
Increase in economic productivity of patients	1350.50	725.00	362.50	362.50	362.50
Cost avoidance of hospitalisation	4495.59	0.00	0.00	0.00	0.00
Decrease consumption of health services – GP consultation	458.80	458.80	229.40	229.40	229.40
Decrease consumption of health services – specialist consultation	250.80	250.80	125.40	125.40	125.40
Improved health status – decreased consumption of complementary medicines	0.00	0.00	0.00	0.00	0.00
Health gain – improvement in life expectancy – QALYs gained	19113.30	0.00	0.00	0.00	0.00
Willingness-to-pay of patient to obtain positive changes in health status	1026.25	1026.25	1026.25	1026.25	1026.25
Total benefits/ social welfare	26695.24	2460.85	1743.55	1743.55	1743.55
Cost stream					
Discounted cost stream	1148.29	1148.29	1148.29	1148.29	1148.29
Total discounted cost	5741.45				
Benefit stream					
Discounted benefit stream	26695.24	2460.85	1743.55	1743.55	1743.55
Total discounted benefit	34386.74				
Cost-benefit ratio	5.99				
Net financial benefits	25546.95	1312.56	595.26	595.26	595.26
Discounted values of benefits	25546.95	1312.56	595.26	595.26	595.26
Net present value/ social welfare	28645.29				

Note: Insig. = insignificant.

Appendix 7.16 New[3] Cost Benefit Analysis of Atorvastatin 40mg (excluding savings from decreased GP and specialist consultation as benefit), discount rate = 0%

Year	0	1	2	3	4
Costs					
Cost of medication	865.92	865.92	865.92	865.92	865.92
External administrative cost	142.56	142.56	142.56	142.56	142.56
Internal administrative cost	Insig.	Insig.	Insig.	Insig.	Insig.
Cost of adverse drug effects	29.61	29.61	29.61	29.61	29.61
Social cost	777.24	777.24	777.24	777.24	777.24
Total costs	1815.33	1815.33	1815.33	1815.33	1815.33
Benefits					
Increase in economic productivity of patients	1350.50	725.00	362.50	362.50	362.50
Cost avoidance of hospitalisation	4495.59	0.00	0.00	0.00	0.00
Decrease consumption of health services – GP consultation	0.00	0.00	0.00	0.00	0.00
Decrease consumption of health services – specialist consultation	0.00	0.00	0.00	0.00	0.00
Improved health status – decreased consumption of complementary medicines	400.00	400.00	400.00	400.00	400.00
Health gain – improvement in life expectancy – QALYs gained	19113.30	0.00	0.00	0.00	0.00
Willingness-to-pay of patient to obtain positive changes in health status	1026.25	1026.25	1026.25	1026.25	1026.25
Total benefits/ social welfare	26385.64	2151.25	1788.75	1788.75	1788.75
Cost stream					
Discounted cost stream	1148.29	1148.29	1148.29	1148.29	1148.29
Total discounted cost	5741.45				
Benefit stream					
Discounted benefit stream	26385.64	2151.25	1788.75	1788.75	1788.75
Total discounted benefit	33903.14				
Cost-benefit ratio	5.90				
Net financial benefits	25237.35	1002.96	640.46	640.46	640.46
Discounted values of benefits	25237.35	1002.96	640.46	640.46	640.46
Net present value/ social welfare	28161.69				

Note: Insig. = insignificant.

Appendix 7.17   New[3] Cost Benefit Analysis of Atorvastatin 40mg (excluding savings from cost avoidance from hospitalisation as benefit), discount rate = 0%

Year	0	1	2	3	4
Costs					
Cost of medication	865.92	865.92	865.92	865.92	865.92
External administrative cost	142.56	142.56	142.56	142.56	142.56
Internal administrative cost	Insig.	Insig.	Insig.	Insig.	Insig.
Cost of adverse drug effects	29.61	29.61	29.61	29.61	29.61
Social cost	777.24	777.24	777.24	777.24	777.24
Total costs	1815.33	1815.33	1815.33	1815.33	1815.33
Benefits					
Increase in economic productivity of patients	1350.50	725.00	362.50	362.50	362.50
Cost avoidance of hospitalisation	0.00	0.00	0.00	0.00	0.00
Decrease consumption of health services – GP consultation	458.80	458.80	229.40	229.40	229.40
Decrease consumption of health services – specialist consultation	250.80	250.80	125.40	125.40	125.40
Improved health status – decreased consumption of complementary medicines	400.00	400.00	400.00	400.00	400.00
Health gain – improvement in life expectancy – QALYs gained	19113.30	0.00	0.00	0.00	0.00
Willingness-to-pay of patient to obtain positive changes in health status	1026.25	1026.25	1026.25	1026.25	1026.25
Total benefits/ social welfare	22599.65	2860.85	2143.55	2143.55	2143.55
Cost stream					
Discounted cost stream	1148.29	1148.29	1148.29	1148.29	1148.29
Total discounted cost	5741.45				
Benefit stream					
Discounted benefit stream	22599.65	2860.85	2143.55	2143.55	2143.55
Total discounted benefit	31891.15				
Cost-benefit ratio	5.55				
Net financial benefits	21451.36	1712.56	995.26	995.26	995.26
Discounted values of benefits	21451.36	1712.56	995.26	995.26	995.26
Net present value/ social welfare	26149.70				

Note: Insig. = insignificant.

Appendix 7.18   New[3] Cost Benefit Analysis of Atorvastatin 40mg (excluding increase in productivity as benefit), discount rate = 0%

Year	0	1	2	3	4
Costs					
Cost of medication	1026.72	1026.72	1026.72	1026.72	1026.72
External administrative cost	158.64	158.64	158.64	158.64	158.64
Internal administrative cost	Insig.	Insig.	Insig.	Insig.	Insig.
Cost of adverse drug effects	29.61	29.61	29.61	29.61	29.61
Social cost	1005.12	1005.12	1005.12	1005.12	1005.12
Total costs	2220.09	2220.09	2220.09	2220.09	2220.09
Benefits					
Increase in economic productivity of patients	0.00	0.00	0.00	0.00	0.00
Cost avoidance of hospitalisation	4495.59	0.00	0.00	0.00	0.00
Decrease consumption of health services – GP consultation	458.80	458.80	229.40	229.40	229.40
Decrease consumption of health services – specialist consultation	250.80	250.80	125.40	125.40	125.40
Improved health status – decreased consumption of complementary medicines	400.00	400.00	400.00	400.00	400.00
Health gain – improvement in life expectancy – QALYs gained	19113.30	0.00	0.00	0.00	0.00
Willingness-to-pay of patient to obtain positive changes in health status	1026.25	1026.25	1026.25	1026.25	1026.25
Total benefits/ social welfare	25744.74	2135.85	1781.05	1781.05	1781.05
Cost stream					
Discounted cost stream	1148.29	1148.29	1148.29	1148.29	1148.29
Total discounted cost	5741.45				
Benefit stream					
Discounted benefit stream	25744.74	2135.85	1781.05	1781.05	1781.05
Total discounted benefit	33223.74				
Cost-benefit ratio	5.79				
Net financial benefits	24596.45	987.56	632.76	632.76	632.76
Discounted values of benefits	24596.45	987.56	632.76	632.76	632.76
Net present value/ social welfare	27482.29				

Note: Insig. = insignificant.

Appendix 7.19   New[3] Cost Benefit Analysis of Atorvastatin 40mg (excluding increase in life expectancy as benefit), discount rate = 0%

Year	0	1	2	3	4
Costs					
Cost of medication	1026.72	1026.72	1026.72	1026.72	1026.72
External administrative cost	158.64	158.64	158.64	158.64	158.64
Internal administrative cost	Insig.	Insig.	Insig.	Insig.	Insig.
Cost of adverse drug effects	29.61	29.61	29.61	29.61	29.61
Social cost	1005.12	1005.12	1005.12	1005.12	1005.12
Total costs	2220.09	2220.09	2220.09	2220.09	2220.09
Benefits					
Increase in economic productivity of patients	1350.50	725.00	362.50	362.50	362.50
Cost avoidance of hospitalisation	4495.59	0.00	0.00	0.00	0.00
Decrease consumption of health services – GP consultation	458.80	458.80	229.40	229.40	229.40
Decrease consumption of health services – specialist consultation	250.80	250.80	125.40	125.40	125.40
Improved health status – decreased consumption of complementary medicines	400.00	400.00	400.00	400.00	400.00
Health gain – improvement in life expectancy – QALYs gained	0.00	0.00	0.00	0.00	0.00
Willingness-to-pay of patient to obtain positive changes in health status	1026.25	1026.25	1026.25	1026.25	1026.25
Total benefits/ social welfare	7981.94	2860.85	2143.55	2143.55	2143.55
Cost stream					
Discounted cost stream	1148.29	1148.29	1148.29	1148.29	1148.29
Total discounted cost	5741.45				
Benefit stream					
Discounted benefit stream	7981.94	2860.85	2143.55	2143.55	2143.55
Total discounted benefit	17273.44				
Cost-benefit ratio	3.01				
Net financial benefits	6833.65	1712.56	995.26	995.26	995.26
Discounted values of benefits	6833.65	1712.56	995.26	995.26	995.26
Net present value/ social welfare	11531.99				

Note: Insig. = insignificant.

Appendix 7.20　New[3] Cost Benefit Analysis of Atorvastatin 40mg (including 50% of benefit of increase in life expectancy), discount rate = 0%

Year	0	1	2	3	4
Costs					
Cost of medication	2332.38	2332.38	2332.38	2332.38	2332.38
External administrative cost	271.92	271.92	271.92	271.92	271.92
Internal administrative cost	Insig.	Insig.	Insig.	Insig.	Insig.
Cost of adverse drug effects	29.61	29.61	29.61	29.61	29.61
Social cost	2131.68	2131.68	2131.68	2131.68	2131.68
Total costs	4765.59	4765.59	4765.59	4765.59	4765.59
Benefits					
Increase economic productivity of patients	1350.50	725.00	362.50	362.50	362.50
Cost avoidance of hospitalisation	4495.59	0.00	0.00	0.00	0.00
Decrease consumption of health services – GP consultation	458.80	458.80	229.40	229.40	229.40
Decrease consumption of health services – specialist consultation	250.80	250.80	125.40	125.40	125.40
Improved health status – decreased consumption of complementary medicines	400.00	400.00	400.00	400.00	400.00
Health gain – improvement in life expectancy – QALYs gained	9556.65	0.00	0.00	0.00	0.00
Willingness-to-pay of patient to obtain positive changes in health status	1026.25	1026.25	1026.25	1026.25	1026.25
Total benefits/ social welfare	17538.59	2860.85	2143.55	2143.55	2143.55
Cost stream					
Discounted cost stream	1148.29	1148.29	1148.29	1148.29	1148.29
Total discounted cost	5741.45				
Benefit stream					
Discounted benefit stream	17538.59	2860.85	2143.55	2143.55	2143.55
Total discounted benefit	26830.09				
Cost-benefit ratio	4.67				
Net financial benefits	16390.30	1712.56	995.26	995.26	995.26
Discounted values of benefits	16390.30	1712.56	995.26	995.26	995.26
Net present value/ social welfare	21088.64				

Note: Insig. = insignificant.

Appendix 7.21   New[3] Cost Benefit Analysis of Clopidogrel 75mg (excluding willingness-to-pay as benefit), discount rate = 0%

Year	0	1	2	3	4
Costs					
Cost of medication	859.32	859.32	859.32	859.32	859.32
External administrative cost	141.84	141.84	141.84	141.84	141.84
Internal administrative cost	Insig.	Insig.	Insig.	Insig.	Insig.
Cost of adverse drug effects	29.61	29.61	29.61	29.61	29.61
Social cost	117.52	117.52	117.52	117.52	117.52
Total costs	1148.29	1148.29	1148.29	1148.29	1148.29
Benefits					
Increase in economic productivity of patients	2131.50	725.00	362.50	362.50	362.50
Cost avoidance of hospitalisation	9690.50	0.00	0.00	0.00	0.00
Decrease consumption of health services – GP consultation	458.80	458.80	229.40	229.40	229.40
Decrease consumption of health services – specialist consultation	250.80	250.80	125.40	125.40	125.40
Improved health status – decreased consumption of complementary medicines	400.00	400.00	400.00	400.00	400.00
Health gain – improvement in life expectancy – QALYs gained	17697.50	0.00	0.00	0.00	0.00
Willingness-to-pay of patient to obtain positive changes in health status	0.00	0.00	0.00	0.00	0.00
Total benefits/ social welfare	30629.10	1834.60	1117.30	1117.30	1117.30
Cost stream					
Discounted cost stream	1815.33	1815.33	1815.33	1815.33	1815.33
Total discounted cost	9076.65				
Benefit stream					
Discounted benefit stream	30629.10	1834.60	1117.30	1117.30	1117.30
Total discounted benefit	35815.60				
Cost-benefit ratio	3.95				
Net financial benefits	28813.77	19.27	–698.03	–698.03	–698.03
Discounted values of benefits	28813.77	19.27	–698.03	–698.03	–698.03
Net present value/ social welfare	26738.95				

Note: Insig. = insignificant.

Appendix 7.22 New[3] Cost Benefit Analysis of Clopidogrel 75mg (excluding savings from decreased consumption of complementary medicines as benefit), discount rate = 0%

Year	0	1	2	3	4
Costs					
Cost of medication	859.32	859.32	859.32	859.32	859.32
External administrative cost	141.84	141.84	141.84	141.84	141.84
Internal administrative cost	Insig.	Insig.	Insig.	Insig.	Insig.
Cost of adverse drug effects	29.61	29.61	29.61	29.61	29.61
Social cost	117.52	117.52	117.52	117.52	117.52
Total costs	1148.29	1148.29	1148.29	1148.29	1148.29
Benefits					
Increase in economic productivity of patients	2131.50	725.00	362.50	362.50	362.50
Cost avoidance of hospitalisation	9690.50	0.00	0.00	0.00	0.00
Decrease consumption of health services – GP consultation	458.80	458.80	229.40	229.40	229.40
Decrease consumption of health services – specialist consultation	250.80	250.80	125.40	125.40	125.40
Improved health status – decreased consumption of complementary medicines	0.00	0.00	0.00	0.00	0.00
Health gain – improvement in life expectancy – QALYs gained	17697.50	0.00	0.00	0.00	0.00
Willingness-to-pay of patient to obtain positive changes in health status	1033.51	1033.51	1033.51	1033.51	1033.51
Total benefits/ social welfare	31262.61	2468.11	1750.81	1750.81	1750.81
Cost stream					
Discounted cost stream	1815.33	1815.33	1815.33	1815.33	1815.33
Total discounted cost	9076.65				
Benefit stream					
Discounted benefit stream	31262.61	2468.11	1750.81	1750.81	1750.81
Total discounted benefit	38983.15				
Cost-benefit ratio	4.29				
Net financial benefits	29447.28	652.78	–64.52	–64.52	–64.52
Discounted values of benefits	29447.28	652.78	–64.52	–64.52	–64.52
Net present value/ social welfare	29906.50				

Note: Insig. = insignificant.

Appendix 7.23   New[3] Cost Benefit Analysis of Clopidogrel 75mg (excluding savings from decreased GP and specialist consultation as benefit), discount rate = 0%

Year	0	1	2	3	4
Costs					
Cost of medication	865.92	865.92	865.92	865.92	865.92
External administrative cost	142.56	142.56	142.56	142.56	142.56
Internal administrative cost	Insig.	Insig.	Insig.	Insig.	Insig.
Cost of adverse drug effects	29.61	29.61	29.61	29.61	29.61
Social cost	777.24	777.24	777.24	777.24	777.24
Total costs	1815.33	1815.33	1815.33	1815.33	1815.33
Benefits					
Increase in economic productivity of patients	2131.50	725.00	362.50	362.50	362.50
Cost avoidance of hospitalisation	9690.50	0.00	0.00	0.00	0.00
Decrease consumption of health services – GP consultation	0.00	0.00	0.00	0.00	0.00
Decrease consumption of health services – specialist consultation	0.00	0.00	0.00	0.00	0.00
Improved health status – decreased consumption of complementary medicines	400.00	400.00	400.00	400.00	400.00
Health gain – improvement in life expectancy – QALYs gained	17697.50	0.00	0.00	0.00	0.00
Willingness-to-pay of patient to obtain positive changes in health status	1033.51	1033.51	1033.51	1033.51	1033.51
Total benefits/ social welfare	30953.01	2158.51	1796.01	1796.01	1796.01
Cost stream					
Discounted cost stream	1815.33	1815.33	1815.33	1815.33	1815.33
Total discounted cost	9076.65				
Benefit stream					
Discounted benefit stream	30953.01	2158.51	1796.01	1796.01	1796.01
Total discounted benefit	38499.55				
Cost-benefit ratio	4.24				
Net financial benefits	29137.68	343.18	–19.32	–19.32	–19.32
Discounted values of benefits	29137.68	343.18	–19.32	–19.32	–19.32
Net present value/ social welfare	29422.90				

Note: Insig. = insignificant.

Appendix 7.24 New[3] Cost Benefit Analysis of Clopidogrel 75mg (excluding savings from cost avoidance from hospitalisation as benefit), discount rate = 0%

Year	0	1	2	3	4
Costs					
Cost of medication	865.92	865.92	865.92	865.92	865.92
External administrative cost	142.56	142.56	142.56	142.56	142.56
Internal administrative cost	Insig.	Insig.	Insig.	Insig.	Insig.
Cost of adverse drug effects	29.61	29.61	29.61	29.61	29.61
Social cost	777.24	777.24	777.24	777.24	777.24
Total costs	1815.33	1815.33	1815.33	1815.33	1815.33
Benefits					
Increase in economic productivity of patients	2131.50	725.00	362.50	362.50	362.50
Cost avoidance of hospitalisation	0.00	0.00	0.00	0.00	0.00
Decrease consumption of health services – GP consultation	458.80	458.80	229.40	229.40	229.40
Decrease consumption of health services – specialist consultation	250.80	250.80	125.40	125.40	125.40
Improved health status – decreased consumption of complementary medicines	400.00	400.00	400.00	400.00	400.00
Health gain – improvement in life expectancy – QALYs gained	17697.50	0.00	0.00	0.00	0.00
Willingness-to-pay of patient to obtain positive changes in health status	1033.51	1033.51	1033.51	1033.51	1033.51
Total benefits/ social welfare	21972.11	2868.11	2150.81	2150.81	2150.81
Cost stream					
Discounted cost stream	1815.33	1815.33	1815.33	1815.33	1815.33
Total discounted cost	9076.65				
Benefit stream					
Discounted benefit stream	21972.11	2868.11	2150.81	2150.81	2150.81
Total discounted benefit	31292.65				
Cost-benefit ratio	3.45				
Net financial benefits	20156.78	1052.78	335.48	335.48	335.48
Discounted values of benefits	20156.78	1052.78	335.48	335.48	335.48
Net present value/ social welfare	22216.00				

Note: Insig. = insignificant.

Appendix 7.25   New[3] Cost Benefit Analysis of Clopidogrel 75mg (excluding increase in productivity as benefit), discount rate = 0%

Year	0	1	2	3	4
Costs					
Cost of medication	1026.72	1026.72	1026.72	1026.72	1026.72
External administrative cost	158.64	158.64	158.64	158.64	158.64
Internal administrative cost	Insig.	Insig.	Insig.	Insig.	Insig.
Cost of adverse drug effects	29.61	29.61	29.61	29.61	29.61
Social cost	1005.12	1005.12	1005.12	1005.12	1005.12
Total costs	2220.09	2220.09	2220.09	2220.09	2220.09
Benefits					
Increase in economic productivity of patients	0.00	0.00	0.00	0.00	0.00
Cost avoidance of hospitalisation	9690.50	0.00	0.00	0.00	0.00
Decrease consumption of health services – GP consultation	458.80	458.80	229.40	229.40	229.40
Decrease consumption of health services – specialist consultation	250.80	250.80	125.40	125.40	125.40
Improved health status – decreased consumption of complementary medicines	400.00	400.00	400.00	400.00	400.00
Health gain – improvement in life expectancy – QALYs gained	17697.50	0.00	0.00	0.00	0.00
Willingness-to-pay of patient to obtain positive changes in health status	1033.51	1033.51	1033.51	1033.51	1033.51
Total benefits/ social welfare	29531.11	2143.11	1788.31	1788.31	1788.31
Cost stream					
Discounted cost stream	1815.33	1815.33	1815.33	1815.33	1815.33
Total discounted cost	9076.65				
Benefit stream					
Discounted benefit stream	29531.11	2143.11	1788.31	1788.31	1788.31
Total discounted benefit	37039.15				
Cost-benefit ratio	4.08				
Net financial benefits	27715.78	327.78	–27.02	–27.02	–27.02
Discounted values of benefits	27715.78	327.78	–27.02	–27.02	–27.02
Net present value/ social welfare	27962.50				

Note: Insig. = insignificant.

Appendix 7.26 New[3] Cost Benefit Analysis of Clopidogrel 75mg (excluding increase in life expectancy as benefit), discount rate = 0%

Year	0	1	2	3	4
Costs					
Cost of medication	1026.72	1026.72	1026.72	1026.72	1026.72
External administrative cost	158.64	158.64	158.64	158.64	158.64
Internal administrative cost	Insig.	Insig.	Insig.	Insig.	Insig.
Cost of adverse drug effects	29.61	29.61	29.61	29.61	29.61
Social cost	1005.12	1005.12	1005.12	1005.12	1005.12
Total costs	2220.09	2220.09	2220.09	2220.09	2220.09
Benefits					
Increase in economic productivity of patients	2131.50	725.00	362.50	362.50	362.50
Cost avoidance of hospitalisation	9690.50	0.00	0.00	0.00	0.00
Decrease consumption of health services – GP consultation	458.80	458.80	229.40	229.40	229.40
Decrease consumption of health services – specialist consultation	250.80	250.80	125.40	125.40	125.40
Improved health status – decreased consumption of complementary medicines	400.00	400.00	400.00	400.00	400.00
Health gain – improvement in life expectancy – QALYs gained	0.00	0.00	0.00	0.00	0.00
Willingness-to-pay of patient to obtain positive changes in health status	1033.51	1033.51	1033.51	1033.51	1033.51
Total benefits/ social welfare	13965.11	2868.11	2150.81	2150.81	2150.81
Cost stream					
Discounted cost stream	1815.33	1815.33	1815.33	1815.33	1815.33
Total discounted cost	9076.65				
Benefit stream					
Discounted benefit stream	13965.11	2868.11	2150.81	2150.81	2150.81
Total discounted benefit	23285.65				
Cost-benefit ratio	2.57				
Net financial benefits	12149.78	1052.78	335.48	335.48	335.48
Discounted values of benefits	12149.78	1052.78	335.48	335.48	335.48
Net present value/ social welfare	14209.00				

Note: Insig. = insignificant.

Appendix 7.27   New[3] Cost Benefit Analysis of Clopidogrel 75mg (including 50% of benefit of increase in life expectancy), discount rate = 0%

Year	0	1	2	3	4
Costs					
Cost of medication	2332.38	2332.38	2332.38	2332.38	2332.38
External administrative cost	271.92	271.92	271.92	271.92	271.92
Internal administrative cost	Insig.	Insig.	Insig.	Insig.	Insig.
Cost of adverse drug effects	29.61	29.61	29.61	29.61	29.61
Social cost	2131.68	2131.68	2131.68	2131.68	2131.68
Total costs	4765.59	4765.59	4765.59	4765.59	4765.59
Benefits					
Increase economic productivity of patients	2131.50	725.00	362.50	362.50	362.50
Cost avoidance of hospitalisation	9690.50	0.00	0.00	0.00	0.00
Decrease consumption of health services – GP consultation	458.80	458.80	229.40	229.40	229.40
Decrease consumption of health services – specialist consultation	250.80	250.80	125.40	125.40	125.40
Improved health status – decreased consumption of complementary medicines	400.00	400.00	400.00	400.00	400.00
Health gain – improvement in life expectancy – QALYs gained	8848.75	0.00	0.00	0.00	0.00
Willingness-to-pay of patient to obtain positive changes in health status	1033.51	1033.51	1033.51	1033.51	1033.51
Total benefits/ social welfare	22813.86	2868.11	2150.81	2150.81	2150.81
Cost stream					
Discounted cost stream	1815.33	1815.33	1815.33	1815.33	1815.33
Total discounted cost	9076.65				
Benefit stream					
Discounted benefit stream	22813.86	2868.11	2150.81	2150.81	2150.81
Total discounted benefit	32134.40				
Cost-benefit ratio	3.54				
Net financial benefits	20998.53	1052.78	335.48	335.48	335.48
Discounted values of benefits	20998.53	1052.78	335.48	335.48	335.48
Net present value/ social welfare	23057.75				

Note: Insig. = insignificant.

Appendix 7.28 New[3] Cost Benefit Analysis of Pioglitazone 30mg (excluding willingness-to-pay as benefit), discount rate = 0%

Year	0	1	2	3	4
Costs					
Cost of medication	859.32	859.32	859.32	859.32	859.32
External administrative cost	141.84	141.84	141.84	141.84	141.84
Internal administrative cost	Insig.	Insig.	Insig.	Insig.	Insig.
Cost of adverse drug effects	29.61	29.61	29.61	29.61	29.61
Social cost	117.52	117.52	117.52	117.52	117.52
Total costs	1148.29	1148.29	1148.29	1148.29	1148.29
Benefits					
Increase in economic productivity of patients	2320.00	725.00	362.50	362.50	362.50
Cost avoidance of hospitalisation	8683.62	0.00	0.00	0.00	0.00
Decrease consumption of health services – GP consultation	458.80	458.80	229.40	229.40	229.40
Decrease consumption of health services – specialist consultation	250.80	250.80	125.40	125.40	125.40
Improved health status – decreased consumption of complementary medicines	400.00	400.00	400.00	400.00	400.00
Health gain – improvement in life expectancy – QALYs gained	12388.25	0.00	0.00	0.00	0.00
Willingness-to-pay of patient to obtain positive changes in health status	0.00	0.00	0.00	0.00	0.00
Total benefits/ social welfare	24501.47	1834.60	1117.30	1117.30	1117.30
Cost stream					
Discounted cost stream	2220.09	2220.09	2220.09	2220.09	2220.09
Total discounted cost	11100.45				
Benefit stream					
Discounted benefit stream	24501.47	1834.60	1117.30	1117.30	1117.30
Total discounted benefit	29687.97				
Cost-benefit ratio	2.67				
Net financial benefits	22281.38	–385.49	–1102.79	–1102.79	–1102.79
Discounted values of benefits	22281.38	–385.49	–1102.79	–1102.79	–1102.79
Net present value/ social welfare	18587.52				

Note: Insig. = insignificant.

Appendix 7.29 New[3] Cost Benefit Analysis of Pioglitazone 30mg (excluding savings from decreased consumption of complementary medicines as benefit), discount rate = 0%

Year	0	1	2	3	4
Costs					
Cost of medication	859.32	859.32	859.32	859.32	859.32
External administrative cost	141.84	141.84	141.84	141.84	141.84
Internal administrative cost	Insig.	Insig.	Insig.	Insig.	Insig.
Cost of adverse drug effects	29.61	29.61	29.61	29.61	29.61
Social cost	117.52	117.52	117.52	117.52	117.52
Total costs	1148.29	1148.29	1148.29	1148.29	1148.29
Benefits					
Increase in economic productivity of patients	2320.00	725.00	362.50	362.50	362.50
Cost avoidance of hospitalisation	8683.62	0.00	0.00	0.00	0.00
Decrease consumption of health services – GP consultation	458.80	458.80	229.40	229.40	229.40
Decrease consumption of health services – specialist consultation	250.80	250.80	125.40	125.40	125.40
Improved health status – decreased consumption of complementary medicines	0.00	0.00	0.00	0.00	0.00
Health gain – improvement in life expectancy – QALYs gained	12388.25	0.00	0.00	0.00	0.00
Willingness-to-pay of patient to obtain positive changes in health status	1210.39	1210.39	1210.39	1210.39	1210.39
Total benefits/ social welfare	25311.86	2644.99	1927.69	1927.69	1927.69
Cost stream					
Discounted cost stream	2220.09	2220.09	2220.09	2220.09	2220.09
Total discounted cost	11100.45				
Benefit stream					
Discounted benefit stream	25311.86	2644.99	1927.69	1927.69	1927.69
Total discounted benefit	33739.92				
Cost-benefit ratio	3.04				
Net financial benefits	23091.77	424.90	–292.40	–292.40	–292.40
Discounted values of benefits	23091.77	424.90	–292.40	–292.40	–292.40
Net present value/ social welfare	22639.47				

Note: Insig. = insignificant.

Appendix 7.30   New[3] Cost Benefit Analysis of Pioglitazone 30mg (excluding savings from decreased GP and specialist consultation as benefit), discount rate = 0%

Year	0	1	2	3	4
Costs					
Cost of medication	865.92	865.92	865.92	865.92	865.92
External administrative cost	142.56	142.56	142.56	142.56	142.56
Internal administrative cost	Insig.	Insig.	Insig.	Insig.	Insig.
Cost of adverse drug effects	29.61	29.61	29.61	29.61	29.61
Social cost	777.24	777.24	777.24	777.24	777.24
Total costs	1815.33	1815.33	1815.33	1815.33	1815.33
	2320.00	725.00	362.50	362.50	362.50
	8683.62	0.00	0.00	0.00	0.00
	0.00	0.00	0.00	0.00	0.00
	0.00	0.00	0.00	0.00	0.00
improved health status – decreased consumption of complementary medicines	400.00	400.00	400.00	400.00	400.00
Health gain – improvement in life expectancy – QALYs gained	12388.25	0.00	0.00	0.00	0.00
Willingness-to-pay of patient to obtain positive changes in health status	1210.39	1210.39	1210.39	1210.39	1210.39
Total benefits/ social welfare	25002.26	2335.39	1972.89	1972.89	1972.89
Cost stream					
Discounted cost stream	2220.09	2220.09	2220.09	2220.09	2220.09
Total discounted cost	11100.45				
Benefit stream					
Discounted benefit stream	25002.26	2335.39	1972.89	1972.89	1972.89
Total discounted benefit	33256.32				
Cost-benefit ratio	3.00				
Net financial benefits	22782.17	115.30	–247.20	–247.20	–247.20
Discounted values of benefits	22782.17	115.30	–247.20	–247.20	–247.20
Net present value/ social welfare	22155.87				

Note: Insig. = insignificant.

Appendix 7.31 New[3] Cost Benefit Analysis of Pioglitazone 30mg (excluding savings from cost avoidance from hospitalisation as benefit), discount rate = 0%

Year	0	1	2	3	4
Costs					
Cost of medication	865.92	865.92	865.92	865.92	865.92
External administrative cost	142.56	142.56	142.56	142.56	142.56
Internal administrative cost	Insig.	Insig.	Insig.	Insig.	Insig.
Cost of adverse drug effects	29.61	29.61	29.61	29.61	29.61
Social cost	777.24	777.24	777.24	777.24	777.24
Total costs	1815.33	1815.33	1815.33	1815.33	1815.33
Benefits					
Increase in economic productivity of patients	2320.00	725.00	362.50	362.50	362.50
Cost avoidance of hospitalisation	0.00	0.00	0.00	0.00	0.00
Decrease consumption of health services – GP consultation	458.80	458.80	229.40	229.40	229.40
Decrease consumption of health services – specialist consultation	250.80	250.80	125.40	125.40	125.40
Improved health status – decreased consumption of complementary medicines	400.00	400.00	400.00	400.00	400.00
Health gain – improvement in life expectancy – QALYs gained	12388.25	0.00	0.00	0.00	0.00
Willingness-to-pay of patient to obtain positive changes in health status	1210.39	1210.39	1210.39	1210.39	1210.39
Total benefits/ social welfare	17028.24	3044.99	2327.69	2327.69	2327.69
Cost stream					
Discounted cost stream	2220.09	2220.09	2220.09	2220.09	2220.09
Total discounted cost	11100.45				
Benefit stream					
Discounted benefit stream	17028.24	3044.99	2327.69	2327.69	2327.69
Total discounted benefit	27056.30				
Cost-benefit ratio	2.44				
Net financial benefits	14808.15	824.90	107.60	107.60	107.60
Discounted values of benefits	14808.15	824.90	107.60	107.60	107.60
Net present value/ social welfare	15955.85				

Note: Insig. = insignificant.

Appendix 7.32 New[3] Cost Benefit Analysis of Pioglitazone 30mg (excluding increase in productivity as benefit), discount rate = 0%

Year	0	1	2	3	4
Costs					
Cost of medication	1026.72	1026.72	1026.72	1026.72	1026.72
External administrative cost	158.64	158.64	158.64	158.64	158.64
Internal administrative cost	Insig.	Insig.	Insig.	Insig.	Insig.
Cost of adverse drug effects	29.61	29.61	29.61	29.61	29.61
Social cost	1005.12	1005.12	1005.12	1005.12	1005.12
Total costs	2220.09	2220.09	2220.09	2220.09	2220.09
Benefits					
Increase in economic productivity of patients	0.00	0.00	0.00	0.00	0.00
Cost avoidance of hospitalisation	8683.62	0.00	0.00	0.00	0.00
Decrease consumption of health services – GP consultation	458.80	458.80	229.40	229.40	229.40
Decrease consumption of health services – specialist consultation	250.80	250.80	125.40	125.40	125.40
Improved health status – decreased consumption of complementary medicines	400.00	400.00	400.00	400.00	400.00
Health gain – improvement in life expectancy – QALYs gained	12388.25	0.00	0.00	0.00	0.00
Willingness-to-pay of patient to obtain positive changes in health status	1210.39	1210.39	1210.39	1210.39	1210.39
Total benefits/ social welfare	23391.86	2319.99	1965.19	1965.19	1965.19
Cost stream					
Discounted cost stream	2220.09	2220.09	2220.09	2220.09	2220.09
Total discounted cost	11100.45				
Benefit stream					
Discounted benefit stream	23391.86	2319.99	1965.19	1965.19	1965.19
Total discounted benefit	31607.42				
Cost-benefit ratio	2.85				
Net financial benefits	21171.77	99.90	−254.90	−254.90	−254.90
Discounted values of benefits	21171.77	99.90	−254.90	−254.90	−254.90
Net present value/ social welfare	20506.97				

Note: Insig. = insignificant.

Appendix 7.33   New[3] Cost Benefit Analysis of Pioglitazone 30mg (excluding increase in life expectancy as benefit), discount rate = 0%

Year	0	1	2	3	4
Costs					
Cost of medication	1026.72	1026.72	1026.72	1026.72	1026.72
External administrative cost	158.64	158.64	158.64	158.64	158.64
Internal administrative cost	Insig.	Insig.	Insig.	Insig.	Insig.
Cost of adverse drug effects	29.61	29.61	29.61	29.61	29.61
Social cost	1005.12	1005.12	1005.12	1005.12	1005.12
Total costs	2220.09	2220.09	2220.09	2220.09	2220.09
Benefits					
Increase in economic productivity of patients	2320.00	725.00	362.50	362.50	362.50
Cost avoidance of hospitalisation	8683.62	0.00	0.00	0.00	0.00
Decrease consumption of health services – GP consultation	458.80	458.80	229.40	229.40	229.40
Decrease consumption of health services – specialist consultation	250.80	250.80	125.40	125.40	125.40
Improved health status – decreased consumption of complementary medicines	400.00	400.00	400.00	400.00	400.00
Health gain – improvement in life expectancy – QALYs gained	0.00	0.00	0.00	0.00	0.00
Willingness-to-pay of patient to obtain positive changes in health status	1210.39	1210.39	1210.39	1210.39	1210.39
Total benefits/ social welfare	13323.61	3044.99	2327.69	2327.69	2327.69
Cost stream					
Discounted cost stream	2220.09	2220.09	2220.09	2220.09	2220.09
Total discounted cost	11100.45				
Benefit stream					
Discounted benefit stream	13323.61	3044.99	2327.69	2327.69	2327.69
Total discounted benefit	23351.67				
Cost-benefit ratio	2.10				
Net financial benefits	11103.52	824.90	107.60	107.60	107.60
Discounted values of benefits	11103.52	824.90	107.60	107.60	107.60
Net present value/ social welfare	12251.22				

Note: Insig. = insignificant.

Appendix 7.34 New[3] Cost Benefit Analysis of Pioglitazone 30mg (including 50% of benefit of increase in life expectancy), discount rate = 0%

Year	0	1	2	3	4
Costs					
Cost of medication	2332.38	2332.38	2332.38	2332.38	2332.38
External administrative cost	271.92	271.92	271.92	271.92	271.92
Internal administrative cost	Insig.	Insig.	Insig.	Insig.	Insig.
Cost of adverse drug effects	29.61	29.61	29.61	29.61	29.61
Social cost	2131.68	2131.68	2131.68	2131.68	2131.68
Total costs	4765.59	4765.59	4765.59	4765.59	4765.59
Benefits					
Increase economic productivity of patients	2320.00	725.00	362.50	362.50	362.50
Cost avoidance of hospitalisation	8683.62	0.00	0.00	0.00	0.00
Decrease consumption of health services – GP consultation	458.80	458.80	229.40	229.40	229.40
Decrease consumption of health services – specialist consultation	250.80	250.80	125.40	125.40	125.40
Improved health status – decreased consumption of complementary medicines	400.00	400.00	400.00	400.00	400.00
Health gain – improvement in life expectancy – QALYs gained	6194.13	0.00	0.00	0.00	0.00
Willingness-to-pay of patient to obtain positive changes in health status	1210.39	1210.39	1210.39	1210.39	1210.39
Total benefits/ social welfare	19517.74	3044.99	2327.69	2327.69	2327.69
Cost stream					
Discounted cost stream	2220.09	2220.09	2220.09	2220.09	2220.09
Total discounted cost	11100.45				
Benefit stream					
Discounted benefit stream	19517.74	3044.99	2327.69	2327.69	2327.69
Total discounted benefit	29545.80				
Cost-benefit ratio	2.66				
Net financial benefits	17297.65	824.90	107.60	107.60	107.60
Discounted values of benefits	17297.65	824.90	107.60	107.60	107.60
Net present value/ social welfare	18445.35				

Note: Insig. = insignificant.

Appendix 7.35   New[3] Cost Benefit Analysis of Letrozole 2.5mg (excluding willingness-to-pay as benefit), discount rate = 0%

Year	0	1	2	3	4
Costs					
Cost of medication	859.32	859.32	859.32	859.32	859.32
External administrative cost	141.84	141.84	141.84	141.84	141.84
Internal administrative cost	Insig.	Insig.	Insig.	Insig.	Insig.
Cost of adverse drug effects	29.61	29.61	29.61	29.61	29.61
Social cost	117.52	117.52	117.52	117.52	117.52
Total costs	1148.29	1148.29	1148.29	1148.29	1148.29
Benefits					
Increase in economic productivity of patients	1805.25	1805.25	362.50	362.50	362.50
Cost avoidance of hospitalisation	5592.92	5592.92	0.00	0.00	0.00
Decrease consumption of health services – GP consultation	458.80	458.80	229.40	229.40	229.40
Decrease consumption of health services – specialist consultation	250.80	250.80	125.40	125.40	125.40
Improved health status – decreased consumption of complementary medicines	400.00	400.00	400.00	400.00	400.00
Health gain – improvement in life expectancy – QALYs gained	25272.03	0.00	0.00	0.00	0.00
Willingness-to-pay of patient to obtain positive changes in health status	0.00	0.00	0.00	0.00	0.00
Total benefits/ social welfare	33779.80	8507.77	1117.30	1117.30	1117.30
Cost stream					
Discounted cost stream	4765.59	4765.59	4765.59	4765.59	4765.59
Total discounted cost	23827.95				
Benefit stream					
Discounted benefit stream	33779.80	8507.77	1117.30	1117.30	1117.30
Total discounted benefit	45639.47				
Cost-benefit ratio	1.92				
Net financial benefits	29014.21	3742.18	–3648.29	–3648.29	–3648.29
Discounted values of benefits	29014.21	3742.18	–3648.29	–3648.29	–3648.29
Net present value/ social welfare	21811.52				

Note: Insig. = insignificant.

Appendix 7.36   New[3] Cost Benefit Analysis of Letrozole 2.5mg (excluding savings from decreased consumption of complementary medicines as benefit), discount rate = 0%

Year	0	1	2	3	4
Costs					
Cost of medication	859.32	859.32	859.32	859.32	859.32
External administrative cost	141.84	141.84	141.84	141.84	141.84
Internal administrative cost	Insig.	Insig.	Insig.	Insig.	Insig.
Cost of adverse drug effects	29.61	29.61	29.61	29.61	29.61
Social cost	117.52	117.52	117.52	117.52	117.52
Total costs	1148.29	1148.29	1148.29	1148.29	1148.29
Benefits					
Increase in economic productivity of patients	1805.25	1805.25	362.50	362.50	362.50
Cost avoidance of hospitalisation	5592.92	5592.92	0.00	0.00	0.00
Decrease consumption of health services – GP consultation	458.80	458.80	229.40	229.40	229.40
Decrease consumption of health services – specialist consultation	250.80	250.80	125.40	125.40	125.40
Improved health status – decreased consumption of complementary medicines	0.00	0.00	0.00	0.00	0.00
Health gain – improvement in life expectancy – QALYs gained	25272.03	0.00	0.00	0.00	0.00
Willingness-to-pay of patient to obtain positive changes in health status	2646.95	2646.95	2646.95	2646.95	2646.95
Total benefits/ social welfare	36026.75	10754.72	3364.25	3364.25	3364.25
Cost stream					
Discounted cost stream	4765.59	4765.59	4765.59	4765.59	4765.59
Total discounted cost	23827.95				
Benefit stream					
Discounted benefit stream	36026.75	10754.72	3364.25	3364.25	3364.25
Total discounted benefit	56874.22				
Cost-benefit ratio	2.39				
Net financial benefits	31261.16	5989.13	–1401.34	–1401.34	–1401.34
Discounted values of benefits	31261.16	5989.13	–1401.34	–1401.34	–1401.34
Net present value/ social welfare	33046.27				

Note: Insig. = insignificant.

Appendix 7.37   New[3] Cost Benefit Analysis of Letrozole 2.5mg (excluding savings from decreased GP and specialist consultation as benefit), discount rate = 0%

Year	0	1	2	3	4
Costs					
Cost of medication	865.92	865.92	865.92	865.92	865.92
External administrative cost	142.56	142.56	142.56	142.56	142.56
Internal administrative cost	Insig.	Insig.	Insig.	Insig.	Insig.
Cost of adverse drug effects	29.61	29.61	29.61	29.61	29.61
Social cost	777.24	777.24	777.24	777.24	777.24
Total costs	1815.33	1815.33	1815.33	1815.33	1815.33
Benefits					
Increase in economic productivity of patients	1805.25	1805.25	362.50	362.50	362.50
Cost avoidance of hospitalisation	5592.92	5592.92	0.00	0.00	0.00
Decrease consumption of health services – GP consultation	0.00	0.00	0.00	0.00	0.00
Decrease consumption of health services – specialist consultation	0.00	0.00	0.00	0.00	0.00
Improved health status – decreased consumption of complementary medicines	400.00	400.00	400.00	400.00	400.00
Health gain – improvement in life expectancy – QALYs gained	25272.03	0.00	0.00	0.00	0.00
Willingness-to-pay of patient to obtain positive changes in health status	2646.95	2646.95	2646.95	2646.95	2646.95
Total benefits/ social welfare	35717.15	10445.12	3409.45	3409.45	3409.45
Cost stream					
Discounted cost stream	4765.59	4765.59	4765.59	4765.59	4765.59
Total discounted cost	23827.95				
Benefit stream					
Discounted benefit stream	35717.15	10445.12	3409.45	3409.45	3409.45
Total discounted benefit	56390.62				
Cost-benefit ratio	2.37				
Net financial benefits	30951.56	5679.53	–1356.14	–1356.14	–1356.14
Discounted values of benefits	30951.56	5679.53	–1356.14	–1356.14	–1356.14
Net present value/ social welfare	32562.67				

Note: Insig. = insignificant.

Appendix 7.38 New[3] Cost Benefit Analysis of Letrozole 2.5mg (excluding savings from cost avoidance from hospitalisation as benefit), discount rate = 0%

Year	0	1	2	3	4
Costs					
Cost of medication	865.92	865.92	865.92	865.92	865.92
External administrative cost	142.56	142.56	142.56	142.56	142.56
Internal administrative cost	Insig.	Insig.	Insig.	Insig.	Insig.
Cost of adverse drug effects	29.61	29.61	29.61	29.61	29.61
Social cost	777.24	777.24	777.24	777.24	777.24
Total costs	1815.33	1815.33	1815.33	1815.33	1815.33
Benefits					
Increase in economic productivity of patients	1805.25	1805.25	362.50	362.50	362.50
Cost avoidance of hospitalisation	0.00	0.00	0.00	0.00	0.00
Decrease consumption of health services – GP consultation	458.80	458.80	229.40	229.40	229.40
Decrease consumption of health services – specialist consultation	250.80	250.80	125.40	125.40	125.40
Improved health status – decreased consumption of complementary medicines	400.00	400.00	400.00	400.00	400.00
Health gain – improvement in life expectancy – QALYs gained	25272.03	0.00	0.00	0.00	0.00
Willingness-to-pay of patient to obtain positive changes in health status	2646.95	2646.95	2646.95	2646.95	2646.95
Total benefits/ social welfare	30833.83	5561.80	3764.25	3764.25	3764.25
Cost stream					
Discounted cost stream	4765.59	4765.59	4765.59	4765.59	4765.59
Total discounted cost	23827.95				
Benefit stream					
Discounted benefit stream	30833.83	5561.80	3764.25	3764.25	3764.25
Total discounted benefit	47688.38				
Cost-benefit ratio	2.00				
Net financial benefits	26068.24	796.21	–1001.34	–1001.34	–1001.34
Discounted values of benefits	26068.24	796.21	–1001.34	–1001.34	–1001.34
Net present value/ social welfare	23860.43				

Note: Insig. = insignificant.

Appendix 7.39   New[3] Cost Benefit Analysis of Letrozole 2.5mg (excluding increase in productivity as benefit), discount rate = 0%

Year	0	1	2	3	4
Costs					
Cost of medication	1026.72	1026.72	1026.72	1026.72	1026.72
External administrative cost	158.64	158.64	158.64	158.64	158.64
Internal administrative cost	Insig.	Insig.	Insig.	Insig.	Insig.
Cost of adverse drug effects	29.61	29.61	29.61	29.61	29.61
Social cost	1005.12	1005.12	1005.12	1005.12	1005.12
Total costs	2220.09	2220.09	2220.09	2220.09	2220.09
Benefits					
Increase in economic productivity of patients	0.00	0.00	0.00	0.00	0.00
Cost avoidance of hospitalisation	5592.92	5592.92	0.00	0.00	0.00
Decrease consumption of health services – GP consultation	458.80	458.80	229.40	229.40	229.40
Decrease consumption of health services – specialist consultation	250.80	250.80	125.40	125.40	125.40
Improved health status – decreased consumption of complementary medicines	400.00	400.00	400.00	400.00	400.00
Health gain – improvement in life expectancy – QALYs gained	25272.03	0.00	0.00	0.00	0.00
Willingness-to-pay of patient to obtain positive changes in health status	2646.95	2646.95	2646.95	2646.95	2646.95
Total benefits/ social welfare	34621.50	9349.47	3401.75	3401.75	3401.75
Cost stream					
Discounted cost stream	4765.59	4765.59	4765.59	4765.59	4765.59
Total discounted cost	23827.95				
Benefit stream					
Discounted benefit stream	34621.50	9349.47	3401.75	3401.75	3401.75
Total discounted benefit	54176.22				
Cost-benefit ratio	2.27				
Net financial benefits	29855.91	4583.88	–1363.84	–1363.84	–1363.84
Discounted values of benefits	29855.91	4583.88	–1363.84	–1363.84	–1363.84
Net present value/ social welfare	30348.27				

Note: Insig. = insignificant.

Appendix 7.40 New[3] Cost Benefit Analysis of Letrozole 2.5mg (excluding increase in life expectancy as benefit), discount rate = 0%

Year	0	1	2	3	4
Costs					
Cost of medication	1026.72	1026.72	1026.72	1026.72	1026.72
External administrative cost	158.64	158.64	158.64	158.64	158.64
Internal administrative cost	Insig.	Insig.	Insig.	Insig.	Insig.
Cost of adverse drug effects	29.61	29.61	29.61	29.61	29.61
Social cost	1005.12	1005.12	1005.12	1005.12	1005.12
Total costs	2220.09	2220.09	2220.09	2220.09	2220.09
Benefits					
Increase in economic productivity of patients	1805.25	1805.25	362.50	362.50	362.50
Cost avoidance of hospitalisation	5592.92	5592.92	0.00	0.00	0.00
Decrease consumption of health services – GP consultation	458.80	458.80	229.40	229.40	229.40
Decrease consumption of health services – specialist consultation	250.80	250.80	125.40	125.40	125.40
Improved health status – decreased consumption of complementary medicines	400.00	400.00	400.00	400.00	400.00
Health gain – improvement in life expectancy – QALYs gained	0.00	0.00	0.00	0.00	0.00
Willingness-to-pay of patient to obtain positive changes in health status	2646.95	2646.95	2646.95	2646.95	2646.95
Total benefits/ social welfare	11154.72	11154.72	3764.25	3764.25	3764.25
Cost stream					
Discounted cost stream	4765.59	4765.59	4765.59	4765.59	4765.59
Total discounted cost	23827.95				
Benefit stream					
Discounted benefit stream	11154.72	11154.72	3764.25	3764.25	3764.25
Total discounted benefit	33602.19				
Cost-benefit ratio	1.41				
Net financial benefits	6389.13	6389.13	–1001.34	–1001.34	–1001.34
Discounted values of benefits	6389.13	6389.13	–1001.34	–1001.34	–1001.34
Net present value/ social welfare	9774.24				

Note: Insig. = insignificant.

Appendix 7.41 New[3] Cost Benefit Analysis of Letrozole 2.5mg (including 50% of benefit of increase in life expectancy), discount rate = 0%

Year	0	1	2	3	4
Costs					
Cost of medication	2332.38	2332.38	2332.38	2332.38	2332.38
External administrative cost	271.92	271.92	271.92	271.92	271.92
Internal administrative cost	Insig.	Insig.	Insig.	Insig.	Insig.
Cost of adverse drug effects	29.61	29.61	29.61	29.61	29.61
Social cost	2131.68	2131.68	2131.68	2131.68	2131.68
Total costs	4765.59	4765.59	4765.59	4765.59	4765.59
Benefits					
Increase economic productivity of patients	1805.25	1805.25	362.50	362.50	362.50
Cost avoidance of hospitalisation	5592.92	5592.92	0.00	0.00	0.00
Decrease consumption of health services – GP consultation	458.80	458.80	229.40	229.40	229.40
Decrease consumption of health services – specialist consultation	250.80	250.80	125.40	125.40	125.40
Improved health status – decreased consumption of complementary medicines	400.00	400.00	400.00	400.00	400.00
Health gain – improvement in life expectancy – QALYs gained	12636.02	0.00	0.00	0.00	0.00
Willingness-to-pay of patient to obtain positive changes in health status	2646.95	2646.95	2646.95	2646.95	2646.95
Total benefits/ social welfare	23790.74	11154.72	3764.25	3764.25	3764.25
Cost stream					
Discounted cost stream	4765.59	4765.59	4765.59	4765.59	4765.59
Total discounted cost	23827.95				
Benefit stream					
Discounted benefit stream	23790.74	11154.72	3764.25	3764.25	3764.25
Total discounted benefit	46238.21				
Cost-benefit ratio	1.94				
Net financial benefits	19025.15	6389.13	–1001.34	–1001.34	–1001.34
Discounted values of benefits	19025.15	6389.13	–1001.34	–1001.34	–1001.34
Net present value/ social welfare	22410.26				

Note: Insig. = insignificant.

Appendix 7.42 New[3] Cost Benefit Analysis of Fluticasone/Salmeterol 500/50 (excluding willingness-to-pay as benefit), discount rate = 0%

Year	0	1	2	3	4
Costs					
Cost of medication	859.32	859.32	859.32	859.32	859.32
External administrative cost	141.84	141.84	141.84	141.84	141.84
Internal administrative cost	Insig.	Insig.	Insig.	Insig.	Insig.
Cost of adverse drug effects	29.61	29.61	29.61	29.61	29.61
Social cost	117.52	117.52	117.52	117.52	117.52
Total costs	1148.29	1148.29	1148.29	1148.29	1148.29
Benefits					
Increase in economic productivity of patients	1087.50	725.00	362.50	362.50	362.50
Cost avoidance of hospitalisation	1646.83	0.00	0.00	0.00	0.00
Decrease consumption of health services – GP consultation	458.80	458.80	229.40	229.40	229.40
Decrease consumption of health services – specialist consultation	250.80	250.80	125.40	125.40	125.40
Improved health status – decreased consumption of complementary medicines	400.00	400.00	400.00	400.00	400.00
Health gain – improvement in life expectancy – QALYs gained	24776.50	0.00	0.00	0.00	0.00
Willingness-to-pay of patient to obtain positive changes in health status	0.00	0.00	0.00	0.00	0.00
Total benefits/ social welfare	28620.43	1834.60	1117.30	1117.30	1117.30
Cost stream					
Discounted cost stream	1364.61	1364.61	1364.61	1364.61	1364.61
Total discounted cost	6823.05				
Benefit stream					
Discounted benefit stream	28620.43	1834.60	1117.30	1117.30	1117.30
Total discounted benefit	33806.93				
Cost-benefit ratio	4.95				
Net financial benefits	27255.82	469.99	–247.31	–247.31	–247.31
Discounted values of benefits	27255.82	469.99	–247.31	–247.31	–247.31
Net present value/ social welfare	26983.88				

Note: Insig. = insignificant.

Appendix 7.43   New[3] Cost Benefit Analysis of Fluticasone/Salmeterol 500/50 (excluding savings from decreased consumption of complementary medicines as benefit), discount rate = 0%

Year	0	1	2	3	4
Costs					
Cost of medication	859.32	859.32	859.32	859.32	859.32
External administrative cost	141.84	141.84	141.84	141.84	141.84
Internal administrative cost	Insig.	Insig.	Insig.	Insig.	Insig.
Cost of adverse drug effects	29.61	29.61	29.61	29.61	29.61
Social cost	117.52	117.52	117.52	117.52	117.52
Total costs	1148.29	1148.29	1148.29	1148.29	1148.29
Benefits					
Increase in economic productivity of patients	1087.50	725.00	362.50	362.50	362.50
Cost avoidance of hospitalisation	1646.83	0.00	0.00	0.00	0.00
Decrease consumption of health services – GP consultation	458.80	458.80	229.40	229.40	229.40
Decrease consumption of health services – specialist consultation	250.80	250.80	125.40	125.40	125.40
Improved health status – decreased consumption of complementary medicines	0.00	0.00	0.00	0.00	0.00
Health gain – improvement in life expectancy – QALYs gained	24776.50	0.00	0.00	0.00	0.00
Willingness-to-pay of patient to obtain positive changes in health status	987.60	987.60	987.60	987.60	987.60
Total benefits/ social welfare	29208.03	2422.20	1704.90	1704.90	1704.90
Cost stream					
Discounted cost stream	1364.61	1364.61	1364.61	1364.61	1364.61
Total discounted cost	6823.05				
Benefit stream					
Discounted benefit stream	29208.03	2422.20	1704.90	1704.90	1704.90
Total discounted benefit	36744.93				
Cost-benefit ratio	5.39				
Net financial benefits	27843.42	1057.59	340.29	340.29	340.29
Discounted values of benefits	27843.42	1057.59	340.29	340.29	340.29
Net present value/ social welfare	29921.88				

Note: Insig. = insignificant.

Appendix 7.44　New[3] Cost Benefit Analysis of Fluticasone/Salmeterol 500/50 (excluding savings from decreased GP and specialist consultation as benefit), discount rate = 0%

Year	0	1	2	3	4
Costs					
Cost of medication	865.92	865.92	865.92	865.92	865.92
External administrative cost	142.56	142.56	142.56	142.56	142.56
Internal administrative cost	Insig.	Insig.	Insig.	Insig.	Insig.
Cost of adverse drug effects	29.61	29.61	29.61	29.61	29.61
Social cost	777.24	777.24	777.24	777.24	777.24
Total costs	1815.33	1815.33	1815.33	1815.33	1815.33
Benefits					
Increase in economic productivity of patients	1087.50	725.00	362.50	362.50	362.50
Cost avoidance of hospitalisation	1646.83	0.00	0.00	0.00	0.00
Decrease consumption of health services – GP consultation	0.00	0.00	0.00	0.00	0.00
Decrease consumption of health services – specialist consultation	0.00	0.00	0.00	0.00	0.00
Improved health status – decreased consumption of complementary medicines	400.00	400.00	400.00	400.00	400.00
Health gain – improvement in life expectancy – QALYs gained	24776.50	0.00	0.00	0.00	0.00
Willingness-to-pay of patient to obtain positive changes in health status	987.60	987.60	987.60	987.60	987.60
Total benefits/ social welfare	28898.43	2112.60	1750.10	1750.10	1750.10
Cost stream					
Discounted cost stream	1364.61	1364.61	1364.61	1364.61	1364.61
Total discounted cost	6823.05				
Benefit stream					
Discounted benefit stream	28898.43	2112.60	1750.10	1750.10	1750.10
Total discounted benefit	36261.33				
Cost-benefit ratio	5.31				
Net financial benefits	27533.82	747.99	385.49	385.49	385.49
Discounted values of benefits	27533.82	747.99	385.49	385.49	385.49
Net present value/ social welfare	29438.28				

Note: Insig. = insignificant.

Appendix 7.45   New[3] Cost Benefit Analysis of Fluticasone/Salmeterol 500/50 (excluding savings from cost avoidance from hospitalisation as benefit), discount rate = 0%

Year	0	1	2	3	4
Costs					
Cost of medication	865.92	865.92	865.92	865.92	865.92
External administrative cost	142.56	142.56	142.56	142.56	142.56
Internal administrative cost	Insig.	Insig.	Insig.	Insig.	Insig.
Cost of adverse drug effects	29.61	29.61	29.61	29.61	29.61
Social cost	777.24	777.24	777.24	777.24	777.24
Total costs	1815.33	1815.33	1815.33	1815.33	1815.33
Benefits					
Increase in economic productivity of patients	1087.50	725.00	362.50	362.50	362.50
Cost avoidance of hospitalisation	0.00	0.00	0.00	0.00	0.00
Decrease consumption of health services – GP consultation	458.80	458.80	229.40	229.40	229.40
Decrease consumption of health services – specialist consultation	250.80	250.80	125.40	125.40	125.40
Improved health status – decreased consumption of complementary medicines	400.00	400.00	400.00	400.00	400.00
Health gain – improvement in life expectancy – QALYs gained	24776.50	0.00	0.00	0.00	0.00
Willingness-to-pay of patient to obtain positive changes in health status	987.60	987.60	987.60	987.60	987.60
Total benefits/ social welfare	27961.20	2822.20	2104.90	2104.90	2104.90
Cost stream					
Discounted cost stream	1364.61	1364.61	1364.61	1364.61	1364.61
Total discounted cost	6823.05				
Benefit stream					
Discounted benefit stream	27961.20	2822.20	2104.90	2104.90	2104.90
Total discounted benefit	37098.10				
Cost-benefit ratio	5.44				
Net financial benefits	26596.59	1457.59	740.29	740.29	740.29
Discounted values of benefits	26596.59	1457.59	740.29	740.29	740.29
Net present value social welfare	30275.05/				

Note: Insig. = insignificant.

Appendix 7.46   New[3] Cost Benefit Analysis of Fluticasone/Salmeterol 500/50 (excluding increase in productivity as benefit), discount rate = 0%

Year	0	1	2	3	4
Costs					
Cost of medication	1026.72	1026.72	1026.72	1026.72	1026.72
External administrative cost	158.64	158.64	158.64	158.64	158.64
Internal administrative cost	Insig.	Insig.	Insig.	Insig.	Insig.
Cost of adverse drug effects	29.61	29.61	29.61	29.61	29.61
Social cost	1005.12	1005.12	1005.12	1005.12	1005.12
Total costs	2220.09	2220.09	2220.09	2220.09	2220.09
Benefits					
Increase in economic productivity of patients	0.00	0.00	0.00	0.00	0.00
Cost avoidance of hospitalisation	1646.83	0.00	0.00	0.00	0.00
Decrease consumption of health services – GP consultation	458.80	458.80	229.40	229.40	229.40
Decrease consumption of health services – specialist consultation	250.80	250.80	125.40	125.40	125.40
Improved health status – decreased consumption of complementary medicines	400.00	400.00	400.00	400.00	400.00
Health gain – improvement in life expectancy – QALYs gained	24776.50	0.00	0.00	0.00	0.00
Willingness-to-pay of patient to obtain positive changes in health status	987.60	987.60	987.60	987.60	987.60
Total benefits/ social welfare	28520.53	2097.20	1742.40	1742.40	1742.40
Cost stream					
Discounted cost stream	1364.61	1364.61	1364.61	1364.61	1364.61
Total discounted cost	6823.05				
Benefit stream					
Discounted benefit stream	28520.53	2097.20	1742.40	1742.40	1742.40
Total discounted benefit	35844.93				
Cost-benefit ratio	5.25				
Net financial benefits	27155.92	732.59	377.79	377.79	377.79
Discounted values of benefits	27155.92	732.59	377.79	377.79	377.79
Net present value/ social welfare	29021.88				

Note: Insig. = insignificant.

Appendix 7.47   New[3] Cost Benefit Analysis of Fluticasone/Salmeterol 500/50 (excluding increase in life expectancy as benefit), discount rate = 0%

Year	0	1	2	3	4
Costs					
Cost of medication	1026.72	1026.72	1026.72	1026.72	1026.72
External administrative cost	158.64	158.64	158.64	158.64	158.64
Internal administrative cost	Insig.	Insig.	Insig.	Insig.	Insig.
Cost of adverse drug effects	29.61	29.61	29.61	29.61	29.61
Social cost	1005.12	1005.12	1005.12	1005.12	1005.12
Total costs	2220.09	2220.09	2220.09	2220.09	2220.09
Benefits					
Increase in economic productivity of patients	1087.50	725.00	362.50	362.50	362.50
Cost avoidance of hospitalisation	1646.83	0.00	0.00	0.00	0.00
Decrease consumption of health services – GP consultation	458.80	458.80	229.40	229.40	229.40
Decrease consumption of health services – specialist consultation	250.80	250.80	125.40	125.40	125.40
Improved health status – decreased consumption of complementary medicines	400.00	400.00	400.00	400.00	400.00
Health gain – improvement in life expectancy – QALYs gained	0.00	0.00	0.00	0.00	0.00
Willingness-to-pay of patient to obtain positive changes in health status	987.60	987.60	987.60	987.60	987.60
Total benefits/ social welfare	4831.53	2822.20	2104.90	2104.90	2104.90
Cost stream					
Discounted cost stream	1364.61	1364.61	1364.61	1364.61	1364.61
Total discounted cost	6823.05				
Benefit stream					
Discounted benefit stream	4831.53	2822.20	2104.90	2104.90	2104.90
Total discounted benefit	13968.43				
Cost-benefit ratio	2.05				
Net financial benefits	3466.92	1457.59	740.29	740.29	740.29
Discounted values of benefits	3466.92	1457.59	740.29	740.29	740.29
Net present value/ social welfare	7145.38				

Note: Insig. = insignificant.

Appendix 7.48   New[3] Cost Benefit Analysis of Fluticasone/Salmeterol 500/50 (including 50% of benefit of increase in life expectancy), discount rate = 0%

Year	0	1	2	3	4
Costs					
Cost of medication	2332.38	2332.38	2332.38	2332.38	2332.38
External administrative cost	271.92	271.92	271.92	271.92	271.92
Internal administrative cost	Insig.	Insig.	Insig.	Insig.	Insig.
Cost of adverse drug effects	29.61	29.61	29.61	29.61	29.61
Social cost	2131.68	2131.68	2131.68	2131.68	2131.68
Total costs	4765.59	4765.59	4765.59	4765.59	4765.59
Benefits					
Increase economic productivity of patients	1087.50	725.00	362.50	362.50	362.50
Cost avoidance of hospitalisation	1646.83	0.00	0.00	0.00	0.00
Decrease consumption of health services – GP consultation	458.80	458.80	229.40	229.40	229.40
Decrease consumption of health services – specialist consultation	250.80	250.80	125.40	125.40	125.40
Improved health status – decreased consumption of complementary medicines	400.00	400.00	400.00	400.00	400.00
Health gain – improvement in life expectancy – QALYs gained	12388.25	0.00	0.00	0.00	0.00
Willingness-to-pay of patient to obtain positive changes in health status	987.60	987.60	987.60	987.60	987.60
Total benefits/ social welfare	17219.78	2822.20	2104.90	2104.90	2104.90
Cost stream					
Discounted cost stream	1364.61	1364.61	1364.61	1364.61	1364.61
Total discounted cost	6823.05				
Benefit stream					
Discounted benefit stream	17219.78	2822.20	2104.90	2104.90	2104.90
Total discounted benefit	26356.68				
Cost-benefit ratio	3.86				
Net financial benefits	15855.17	1457.59	740.29	740.29	740.29
Discounted values of benefits	15855.17	1457.59	740.29	740.29	740.29
Net present value/ social welfare	19533.63				

Note: Insig. = insignificant.

Appendix 7.49   New[3] Cost Benefit Analysis of Tiotropium 18mcg (excluding willingness-to-pay as benefit), discount rate = 0%

Year	0	1	2	3	4
Costs					
Cost of medication	859.32	859.32	859.32	859.32	859.32
External administrative cost	141.84	141.84	141.84	141.84	141.84
Internal administrative cost	Insig.	Insig.	Insig.	Insig.	Insig.
Cost of adverse drug effects	29.61	29.61	29.61	29.61	29.61
Social cost	117.52	117.52	117.52	117.52	117.52
Total costs	1148.29	1148.29	1148.29	1148.29	1148.29
Benefits					
Increase in economic productivity of patients	1812.50	725.00	362.50	362.50	362.50
Cost avoidance of hospitalisation	4940.78	0.00	0.00	0.00	0.00
Decrease consumption of health services – GP consultation	458.80	458.80	229.40	229.40	229.40
Decrease consumption of health services – specialist consultation	250.80	250.80	125.40	125.40	125.40
Improved health status – decreased consumption of complementary medicines	400.00	400.00	400.00	400.00	400.00
Health gain – improvement in life expectancy – QALYs gained	24776.50	0.00	0.00	0.00	0.00
Willingness-to-pay of patient to obtain positive changes in health status	0	0	0	0	0
Total benefits/ social welfare	32639.38	1834.60	1117.30	1117.30	1117.30
Cost stream					
Discounted cost stream	1219.77	1219.77	1219.77	1219.77	1219.77
Total discounted cost	6098.85				
Benefit stream					
Discounted benefit stream	32639.38	1834.60	1117.30	1117.30	1117.30
Total discounted benefit	37825.88				
Cost-benefit ratio	6.20				
Net financial benefits	31419.61	614.83	−102.47	−102.47	−102.47
Discounted values of benefits	31419.61	614.83	−102.47	−102.47	−102.47
Net present value/ social welfare	31727.03				

Note: Insig. = insignificant.

Appendix 7.50 New[3] Cost Benefit Analysis of Tiotropium 18mcg (excluding savings from decreased consumption of complementary medicines as benefit), discount rate = 0%

Year	0	1	2	3	4
Costs					
Cost of medication	859.32	859.32	859.32	859.32	859.32
External administrative cost	141.84	141.84	141.84	141.84	141.84
Internal administrative cost	Insig.	Insig.	Insig.	Insig.	Insig.
Cost of adverse drug effects	29.61	29.61	29.61	29.61	29.61
Social cost	117.52	117.52	117.52	117.52	117.52
Total costs	1148.29	1148.29	1148.29	1148.29	1148.29
Benefits					
Increase in economic productivity of patients	1812.50	725.00	362.50	362.50	362.50
Cost avoidance of hospitalisation	4940.78	0.00	0.00	0.00	0.00
Decrease consumption of health services – GP consultation	458.80	458.80	229.40	229.40	229.40
Decrease consumption of health services – specialist consultation	250.80	250.80	125.40	125.40	125.40
Improved health status – decreased consumption of complementary medicines	0.00	0.00	0.00	0.00	0.00
Health gain – improvement in life expectancy – QALYs gained	24776.50	0.00	0.00	0.00	0.00
Willingness-to-pay of patient to obtain positive changes in health status	954.84	954.84	954.84	954.84	954.84
Total benefits/ social welfare	33194.22	2389.44	1672.14	1672.14	1672.14
Cost stream					
Discounted cost stream	1219.77	1219.77	1219.77	1219.77	1219.77
Total discounted cost	6098.85				
Benefit stream					
Discounted benefit stream	33194.22	2389.44	1672.14	1672.14	1672.14
Total discounted benefit	40600.08				
Cost-benefit ratio	6.66				
Net financial benefits	31974.45	1169.67	452.37	452.37	452.37
Discounted values of benefits	31974.45	1169.67	452.37	452.37	452.37
Net present value/ social welfare	34501.23				

Note: Insig. = insignificant.

Appendix 7.51   New[3] Cost Benefit Analysis of Tiotropium 18mcg (excluding savings from decreased GP and specialist consultation as benefit), discount rate = 0%

Year	0	1	2	3	4
Costs					
Cost of medication	865.92	865.92	865.92	865.92	865.92
External administrative cost	142.56	142.56	142.56	142.56	142.56
Internal administrative cost	Insig.	Insig.	Insig.	Insig.	Insig.
Cost of adverse drug effects	29.61	29.61	29.61	29.61	29.61
Social cost	777.24	777.24	777.24	777.24	777.24
Total costs	1815.33	1815.33	1815.33	1815.33	1815.33
Benefits					
Increase in economic productivity of patients	1812.50	725.00	362.50	362.50	362.50
Cost avoidance of hospitalisation	4940.78	0.00	0.00	0.00	0.00
Decrease consumption of health services – GP consultation	0.00	0.00	0.00	0.00	0.00
Decrease consumption of health services – specialist consultation	0.00	0.00	0.00	0.00	0.00
Improved health status – decreased consumption of complementary medicines	400.00	400.00	400.00	400.00	400.00
Health gain – improvement in life expectancy – QALYs gained	24776.50	0.00	0.00	0.00	0.00
Willingness-to-pay of patient to obtain positive changes in health status	954.84	954.84	954.84	954.84	954.84
Total benefits/ social welfare	32884.62	2079.84	1717.34	1717.34	1717.34
Cost stream					
Discounted cost stream	1219.77	1219.77	1219.77	1219.77	1219.77
Total discounted cost	6098.85				
Benefit stream					
Discounted benefit stream	32884.62	2079.84	1717.34	1717.34	1717.34
Total discounted benefit	40116.48				
Cost-benefit ratio	6.58				
Net financial benefits	31664.85	860.07	497.57	497.57	497.57
Discounted values of benefits	31664.85	860.07	497.57	497.57	497.57
Net present value/ social welfare	34017.63				

Note: Insig. = insignificant.

Appendix 7.52 New[3] Cost Benefit Analysis of Tiotropium 18mcg (excluding savings from cost avoidance from hospitalisation as benefit), discount rate = 0%

Year	0	1	2	3	4
Costs					
Cost of medication	865.92	865.92	865.92	865.92	865.92
External administrative cost	142.56	142.56	142.56	142.56	142.56
Internal administrative cost	Insig.	Insig.	Insig.	Insig.	Insig.
Cost of adverse drug effects	29.61	29.61	29.61	29.61	29.61
Social cost	777.24	777.24	777.24	777.24	777.24
Total costs	1815.33	1815.33	1815.33	1815.33	1815.33
Benefits					
Increase in economic productivity of patients	1812.50	725.00	362.50	362.50	362.50
Cost avoidance of hospitalisation	0.00	0.00	0.00	0.00	0.00
Decrease consumption of health services – GP consultation	458.80	458.80	229.40	229.40	229.40
Decrease consumption of health services – specialist consultation	250.80	250.80	125.40	125.40	125.40
Improved health status – decreased consumption of complementary medicines	400.00	400.00	400.00	400.00	400.00
Health gain – improvement in life expectancy – QALYs gained	24776.50	0.00	0.00	0.00	0.00
Willingness-to-pay of patient to obtain positive changes in health status	954.84	954.84	954.84	954.84	954.84
Total benefits/ social welfare	28653.44	2789.44	2072.14	2072.14	2072.14
Cost stream					
Discounted cost stream	1219.77	1219.77	1219.77	1219.77	1219.77
Total discounted cost	6098.85				
Benefit stream					
Discounted benefit stream	28653.44	2789.44	2072.14	2072.14	2072.14
Total discounted benefit	37659.30				
Cost-benefit ratio	6.17				
Net financial benefits	27433.67	1569.67	852.37	852.37	852.37
Discounted values of benefits	27433.67	1569.67	852.37	852.37	852.37
Net present value/ social welfare	31560.45				

Note: Insig. = insignificant.

Appendix 7.53 New[3] Cost Benefit Analysis of Tiotropium 18mcg (excluding increase in productivity as benefit), discount rate = 0%

Year	0	1	2	3	4
Costs					
Cost of medication	1026.72	1026.72	1026.72	1026.72	1026.72
External administrative cost	158.64	158.64	158.64	158.64	158.64
Internal administrative cost	Insig.	Insig.	Insig.	Insig.	Insig.
Cost of adverse drug effects	29.61	29.61	29.61	29.61	29.61
Social cost	1005.12	1005.12	1005.12	1005.12	1005.12
Total costs	2220.09	2220.09	2220.09	2220.09	2220.09
Benefits					
Increase in economic productivity of patients	0.00	0.00	0.00	0.00	0.00
Cost avoidance of hospitalisation	4940.78	0.00	0.00	0.00	0.00
Decrease consumption of health services – GP consultation	458.80	458.80	229.40	229.40	229.40
Decrease consumption of health services – specialist consultation	250.80	250.80	125.40	125.40	125.40
Improved health status – decreased consumption of complementary medicines	400.00	400.00	400.00	400.00	400.00
Health gain – improvement in life expectancy – QALYs gained	24776.50	0.00	0.00	0.00	0.00
Willingness-to-pay of patient to obtain positive changes in health status	954.84	954.84	954.84	954.84	954.84
Total benefits/ social welfare	31781.72	2064.44	1709.64	1709.64	1709.64
Cost stream					
Discounted cost stream	1219.77	1219.77	1219.77	1219.77	1219.77
Total discounted cost	6098.85				
Benefit stream					
Discounted benefit stream	31781.72	2064.44	1709.64	1709.64	1709.64
Total discounted benefit	38975.08				
Cost-benefit ratio	6.39				
Net financial benefits	30561.95	844.67	489.87	489.87	489.87
Discounted values of benefits	30561.95	844.67	489.87	489.87	489.87
Net present value/ social welfare	32876.23				

Note: Insig. = insignificant.

Appendix 7.54   New[3] Cost Benefit Analysis of Tiotropium 18mcg (excluding increase in life expectancy as benefit), discount rate = 0%

Year	0	1	2	3	4
Costs					
Cost of medication	1026.72	1026.72	1026.72	1026.72	1026.72
External administrative cost	158.64	158.64	158.64	158.64	158.64
Internal administrative cost	Insig.	Insig.	Insig.	Insig.	Insig.
Cost of adverse drug effects	29.61	29.61	29.61	29.61	29.61
Social cost	1005.12	1005.12	1005.12	1005.12	1005.12
Total costs	2220.09	2220.09	2220.09	2220.09	2220.09
Benefits					
Increase in economic productivity of patients	1812.50	725.00	362.50	362.50	362.50
Cost avoidance of hospitalisation	4940.78	0.00	0.00	0.00	0.00
Decrease consumption of health services – GP consultation	458.80	458.80	229.40	229.40	229.40
Decrease consumption of health services – specialist consultation	250.80	250.80	125.40	125.40	125.40
Improved health status – decreased consumption of complementary medicines	400.00	400.00	400.00	400.00	400.00
Health gain – improvement in life expectancy – QALYs gained	0.00	0.00	0.00	0.00	0.00
Willingness-to-pay of patient to obtain positive changes in health status	954.84	954.84	954.84	954.84	954.84
Total benefits/ social welfare	8817.72	2789.44	2072.14	2072.14	2072.14
Cost stream					
Discounted cost stream	1219.77	1219.77	1219.77	1219.77	1219.77
Total discounted cost	6098.85				
Benefit stream					
Discounted benefit stream	8817.72	2789.44	2072.14	2072.14	2072.14
Total discounted benefit	17823.58				
Cost-benefit ratio	2.92				
Net financial benefits	7597.95	1569.67	852.37	852.37	852.37
Discounted values of benefits	7597.95	1569.67	852.37	852.37	852.37
Net present value/ social welfare	11724.73				

Note: Insig. = insignificant.

Appendix 7.55   New[3] Cost Benefit Analysis of Tiotropium 18mcg (including 50% of benefit of increase in life expectancy), discount rate = 0%

Year	0	1	2	3	4
Costs					
Cost of medication	2332.38	2332.38	2332.38	2332.38	2332.38
External administrative cost	271.92	271.92	271.92	271.92	271.92
Internal administrative cost	Insig.	Insig.	Insig.	Insig.	Insig.
Cost of adverse drug effects	29.61	29.61	29.61	29.61	29.61
Social cost	2131.68	2131.68	2131.68	2131.68	2131.68
Total costs	4765.59	4765.59	4765.59	4765.59	4765.59
Benefits					
Increase economic productivity of patients	1812.50	725.00	362.50	362.50	362.50
Cost avoidance of hospitalisation	4940.78	0.00	0.00	0.00	0.00
Decrease consumption of health services – GP consultation	458.80	458.80	229.40	229.40	229.40
Decrease consumption of health services – specialist consultation	250.80	250.80	125.40	125.40	125.40
Improved health status – decreased consumption of complementary medicines	400.00	400.00	400.00	400.00	400.00
Health gain – improvement in life expectancy – QALYs gained	12388.25	0.00	0.00	0.00	0.00
Willingness-to-pay of patient to obtain positive changes in health status	954.84	954.84	954.84	954.84	954.84
Total benefits/ social welfare	21205.97	2789.44	2072.14	2072.14	2072.14
Cost stream					
Discounted cost stream	1219.77	1219.77	1219.77	1219.77	1219.77
Total discounted cost	6098.85				
Benefit stream					
Discounted benefit stream	21205.97	2789.44	2072.14	2072.14	2072.14
Total discounted benefit	30211.83				
Cost-benefit ratio	4.95				
Net financial benefits	19986.20	1569.67	852.37	852.37	852.37
Discounted values of benefits	19986.20	1569.67	852.37	852.37	852.37
Net present value/ social welfare	24112.98				

Note: Insig. = insignificant.

Bibliography

Abbott, T.A. III 1995, 'Price regulation in the pharmaceutical industry: Prescription or placebo?', *Journal of Health Economics*, 14: 551–65.

Abbott, T. 2004, 'AUSFTA – Implementation of the obligations to improve transparency of the PBS through an independent review mechanism, hearings before the PBAC and transparency of decision making', a public consultation document, 25 July, AUSFTA, Canberra.

Abel-Smith, B. 1967, 'An international study of health expenditure and its relevance for health planning', Public Health Papers no. 32, World Health Organisation, Geneva.

Abel-Smith, B. 1985, 'Global perspectives on health service financing', *Social Science and Medicine*, 21(9): 95–163.

Abelson, P. 2003, 'The value of life and health for public policy', *The Economic Record*, 79: s2–s13.

Ackerman, F. 1997, 'Applied welfare economics: Externalities, valuation and cost-benefit analysis' in F. Ackerman, D. Kiron, N. Goodwin, J. Harris and K. Gallagher (eds), *Human Well-Being and Economic Goals*, Island Press, Washington D.C.

Acton, J.P. 1973, *Evaluating Public Programs to Save Lives: The Case of Heart Attacks*, RAND report, RAND Corporation.

Allen, F. and Gale, D. (eds) 2001, *Comparing Financial Systems*, MIT Press, Cambridge, Ma.

Altman, M. 1996, *Human Agency and Material Welfare: Revisions in Microeconomics and their Implications for Public Policy*, Kluwer Academic Publisher, Dordrecht.

Anand, S. and Sen, A.K. 2000, *Sustainable Human Development: Concepts and Priorities*, United Nations Development Program, New York.

Aristides, M. and Mitchell, A. 1994, 'Applying the Australian guidelines for the reimbursement of pharmaceuticals ', *PharmacoEconomics*, 6: 196–201.

Aronsson, T., Johansson, P. and Lofgren, K. 1997, *Welfare Measurement, Sustainability and Green National Accounting: A Growth Theoretical Approach*, New Horizons in Environmental Economic Series, Edward Elgar, Cheltenham.

Arrow, K. and Hurwicz L. 1960, 'Decentralization and Computation in Resource Allocation', in R. Pfout (ed.), *Essays in Economic and Econometrics in Honour of Harold Hotelling*, University of North Carolina Press, Chapel Hill.

Arrow, K. 1950, 'A Difficulty in the Concept of Social Welfare', *Journal of Political Economy*, 58: 328–346.

Arrow, K. 1951, *Social Choice and Individual Values*, Wiley, New York.

Arrow, K. 1963, 'Uncertainty and the economics of medical care', *American Economic Review*, 53: 941–973.

Arrow, K. and Scitovsky, T. eds 1969, Reading in Welfare, Allan and Unwin, London.

Arrow, K. 1982, 'The Rate of Discount on Public Investments with Imperfect Capital Markets', in Lind 1982.

Arrow, K., Sen, A. and Suzumura, K. 2003, *Handbook of Social Choice and Welfare Economics*, North Holland Publishing Co., Amsterdam.

Asian Development Bank 2000, *Handbook for the Economic Analysis of Health Sector Projects*, Manila, Philippines.

Australian Bureau of Statistics 2005, Cat. No. 6301.0, 6302.0, 6305.0, 6306.0, on www.abs.gov.au

Australian Bureau of Statistics 2002, *2001 National Health Survey: Summary of results*, ABS Cat. No. 4364.0, Canberra ABS.

Australian Institute of Health and Welfare 2004, *Australia's Health 2004: The Ninth Biennial Health Report of the Australian Institute of Health and Welfare*, AIHW, Canberra.

Australian Institute of Health and Welfare 2003, *Australia's Welfare 2003: The Sixth Biennial Welfare Report of the Australian Institute of Health and Welfare*, AIHW, Canberra.

Australian Institute of Health and Welfare 2002, *Australia's Health 2002: The Eighth Biennial Health Report of the Australian Institute of Health and Welfare*, AIHW, Canberra.

Avineri, S. and de Shalit, A. 1992, *Communitarianism and Individualism*, Oxford University Press, Oxford.

Aylward, B. and Porras, I. 1998, 'An analysis of private and social discount rates in Costa Rica', Collaborative Research in the Economics of Environment and Development (CREED) Working Paper No. 20.

Bakhai, A. 2004, 'The burden of coronary, cerebrovascular and peripheral arterial disease', *PharmacoEconomics*, 22(suppl 4): 11–18.

Bala, M.V., Mauskopf, J.A. and Wood, L.L. 1999, 'Willingness to pay as a measure of health benefits', *PharmacoEconomics*, 15: 9–18.

Bannock, G., Baxter, R.E. and Davis, E. 1998, *Dictionary of Economics*, Penguin, London.

Barry, M., Tilson, L. and Ryan, M. 2004, 'Pricing and reimbursement of drugs in Ireland', *The European Journal of Health Economics*, 5(2): 190–194.

Basu, K. 1980, *Revealed Preference of Government*, Cambridge University Press, Cambridge.

Bateman, E.D. 2001, 'Using clinical measures of disease control to reduce the burden of asthma', *PharmacoEconomics*, 19 suppl(2): 7–12.

Becker, G.S. 1964, *Human Capital*, University of Chicago Press, Chicago, Illinois.

Benninga, S. 2000, *Financial Modelling*, MIT Press, Cambridge, Ma.

Bentham, J. 1789, *An introduction to the Principles of Morals and Legislation*, Payne, London (republished in 1907, Clarendon Press, Oxford).

Bergson, A. 1938, 'A reformulation of certain aspects of welfare economics', *Quarterly Journal of Economics*, 52: 310–334.

Berndt, E.R. 2002, 'Pharmaceuticals in U.S. health care: Determinants of quantity and price', *Journal of Economic Perspectives*, 16(4): 45–66.

Birch, S. and Gafni, A. 2003, 'Economics and the evaluation of health care programs: Generalisability of methods and the implications for generalisability of results', *Health Policy*, 64: 207–219.

Birch, S. and Gafni, A. 2002, ' On being NICE in the UK: Guidelines for technology appraisal for the NHS in England and Wales', *Health Economics*, 11:185–191.

Birch, S. and Gafni, A. 1992, 'Cost effectiveness/utility: Do current decision rules lead us to where we want to be?', *Journal of Health Economics*, 11: 279–296.

Birch, S. and Donaldson, C. 1987, 'Applications of cost-benefit analysis to health care: Departures from welfare economics theory', *Journal of Health Economics*, 6: 211–225.

Birkett, D.J. 1999, 'Economic analysis: A response', *Australian Prescriber*, 22: 51–52.

Birkett, D.J., Mitchell, A.S. and McManus, P. 2001, 'A cost-effectiveness approach to drug subsidy and pricing in Australia', *Health Affairs*, 20(3): 104–114.

Black, S. and Moersch, M. (eds) 1998, *Competition and Convergence in Financial Markets: The German and Anglo-American Models*, North-Holland Elsevier, Amsterdam.

Bleichrodt, H. and Quiggin, J. 1999, 'Life-cycle preferences over consumption and health: When is cost-effectiveness analysis equivalent to cost-benefit analysis?', *Journal of Health Economics*, 18: 681–708.

Bleichrodt, H. and Johannesson, M. 1997, 'Standard Gamble, time trade-off and rating scale: Experimental results on the ranking properties of QALYS', *Journal of Health Economics*, 16: 155–175.

Blomquist, G.C. 2001, 'Economics of value of life', in *International Encyclopedia of the Social and Behavioural Sciences*, Elsevier Science.

Bloor, K. and Freemantle, N. 1996a, 'Lessons from international experience in controlling pharmaceutical expenditure I: Influencing patients', *British Medical Journal*, 312(7044): 1469–1471.

Bloor, K. and Freemantle, N. 1996b, 'Lessons from international experience in controlling pharmaceutical expenditure II: Influencing doctors', *British Medical Journal*, 312(7045): 1525–1528.

Bloor, K., Maynard, A. and Freemantle, N. 1996, 'Lessons from international experience in controlling pharmaceutical expenditure III: Regulating industry', *British Medical Journal*, 313(7048): 33–38.

Blumstein, J.F. 1997, 'The Oregon experiment: The role of cost-benefit analysis in the allocation of medicaid fund', *Social Science and Medicine*, 45(4): 545–554.

Boadway, R. and Bruce, N. 1984, *Welfare Economics*, Basil Blackwell, Oxford.

Bonner, J. 1986, *The Introduction to the Theory of Social Choice*, the John Hopkins University Press, Baltimore.

Bootman, J., Townsend, R. and McGhan, W. 1996, *Principles of Pharmacoeconomics*, Harvey Whiteney, Cincinnati.

Borda, J.C. 1781, 'Mémoire sur les Élections au Scrutin' *Histoire de l'Académe Royale des Sciences (Paris)*, translated by Alfred de Grazia, 'Mathematical Derivation of an Election', *Isis*, June 1953, 44: 42–51.

Bosanquet, N. and Zammit-Lucia, J. 1995, 'The effect of competition on drug prices', *PharmacoEconomics*, 8(6): 473–478.

Braae, R., McNee, W. and Moore, D. 1999, 'Managing pharmaceutical expenditure while increasing access the pharmaceutical management agency (PHARMAC) experience', *PharmacoEconomics*, 16(6): 649–660.

Brandimarte, P. 2002, *Numerical Methods in Finance: A MATLA-Based Introduction*, Wiley, New York.

Braunwald, E., Isselbacher, K.J., Petersdorf, R.G., Wilson, J.D., Martin, J.B. and Fauci, A.S. 1987, *Harrison's Principles of Internal Medicine*, 11th edn, McGraw, New York.

Brent, R.J. 1990, *Project Appraisal for Developing Countries*, Harvester Wheatsheaf, New York.

Brent, R.J. 1998, *Cost-Benefit Analysis for Developing Countries*, Edward Elgar, Cheltenham.

Brent, R.J. 2003, *Cost-Benefit Analysis and Health Care Evaluations*, Edward Elgar, Massachusetts.

Briggs, A. and Sculpher, M. 1998, 'An introduction to Markov modeling for economic evaluation', *PharmacoEconomics*, 13: 397–409.

Britt, H., Miller, G.C. and Knox, S. 2003, *General Practice Activity in Australia 2002–03*, AIHW General Practice Series No. 14, Canberra.

Brooke, A., Kendrick, D. and Meeraus, A. 1992, *GAMS: A User's Guide*, Boyd and Fraser, Cambridge, Ma.

Broome, J. 1999, *Ethics Out of Economics*, Cambridge University Press, Cambridge.

Brown, J. and Sculpher, M. 1999, 'Benefit valuation in economic evaluation of cancer therapies: A systemic review of the published literature', *PharmacoEconomics*, 16: 17–31.

Brown, S. 1983, 'A note on environmental risk and the rate of discount', *Journal of Environmental Economics and Management*, 10: 282–286.

Bruce, C. 1976, *Social Cost-Benefit Analysis*, Staff Working Paper No. 39, World Bank, Washington DC.

Buller, N., Gillen, D., Casciano, R., Doyle, J. and Wilson, K. 2003, 'A pharmacoeconomic evaluation of the myocardial ischaemia reduction with aggressive cholesterol lowering (MIRACL) study in the United Kingdom', *PharmacoEconomics*, 21(Suppl 1): 25–32.

Cabello Ballesteros, L., Fernandez San Martin, M. I., Sanz Cuesta, T., Escortell Mayor, E., Lopez Bilbao, C. and the VICAF Group 2001, 'The cost of inadequate prescriptions of hypolipidaemic drugs'", *PharmacoEconomics*, 19(5): 513–522.

Campell, H. and Brown, R. 2003, *Benefit-Cost Analysis: Financial and Economic Appraisal Using Spreadsheets*, Cambridge University Press, Cambridge.

Candler, W. and Norton, R. 1997, *Multi-Level Programming and Development Policy*, World Bank Working Paper No. 258, World Bank, Washington.

Cannon, C.P. 2004, 'Cost-Effectiveness of Clopidogrel', *PharmacoEconomics*, 22(suppl 4): 1–3.

Carmine, B. 1996, 'Update and evaluation of Australian guidelines: Industry perspective', *Med Care*, 34(12 supp): DS226–232.

Carter, R. and Harris, A. 1999, 'Evaluation of Health Services', in G. Mooney and R. Scotton (eds), *Economics and Australian Health Policy*, Allen and Unwin, St Leonard.

Carter, R. 2001, *The Macro Economic Evaluation Model (MEEM): An Approach to Priority Setting in Health Sector*, PhD Thesis, Monash University, Melbourne.

Cartwright, T. 1993, *Modelling the World in a Spreadsheet*, John Hopkins University Press, Baltimore.

Clarke, M. and Islam, S. 2004, *Economic Growth and Social Welfare: Operationalising Normative Social Choice Theory*, Elsevier, North Holland.

Clayton, A. and Radcliffe, N. 1996, *Sustainability: A Systems Approach*, Earthscan Publications, London.

Cleanthous, P. 2002, Patient welfare implications of innovation in the U.S. antidepressant market, Department of Economics, Yale University.

Cockburn, I.M. and Anis, A.H. 1998, 'Hedonic analysis of arthritic drugs', NBER Working Paper 6574, May, NBER, Cambridge, Ma.

Colagiuri, S., Walker, A. and McLennan, M. 1999, 'Cost-benefit model of diabetes prevention and care', paper presented at the International Conference on Health Outcomes, Canberra, July.

Comanor, W.S. 1986, 'The political economy of the pharmaceutical industry', *Journal of Economic Literature*, 24: 1178–1217.

Condorcet, Marquis de. 1785, *Essai sur l'application de l'analyse à la probabilite des decisions rendues a la pluralité des voix*. Paris: l'Imprimerie Royale.

Conyers, D. and Hills, P. 1984, *An Introduction to Development Planning in the Third World*, John Wiley and Sons, New York.

Costello, P. 2002, '*Intergenerational Report 2002*', 2002–03 Budget Paper No. 5, Canberra.

Coyle, D., Lee, K.M. and O'Brien, B.J. 2002, 'The role of models within economic analysis', *PharmacoEconomics*, 20(Suppl 1): 11–19.

Coyle, D., Palmer, A.J. and Tam, R. 2002, 'Economic evaluation of Pioglitazone hydrochloride in the management of Type 2 diabetes mellitus in Canada', *PharmacoEconomics*, 20(Suppl 1): 31–42.

Craven, B. and Islam, S.M.N. 2005, *Optimisation in Economics and Finance: Some Advances in Non-Linear, Dynamic, Multi-Criteria, and Stochastic Models*, Series: Dynamic Optimisation and Econometrics in Economics and Finance, Vol. 7, Springer, Heidelberg.

Craven, B. and Islam, S.M.N. 2006, *Operations Research Methods: Some Selected Production, Distribution and Inventory Management Applications*, ICFAI University Press, Hyderabad.

Crum, R. and Derkinderen, F.G. 1981, *Capital Budgeting Under Conditions of Uncertainty*, Nijeurode Studies in Business, Vol. 5, Martinus Nijhoff Publishing, Boston.

Culyer, A.J. 1989, 'The normative economics of health care finance and provision', *Oxford Review of Economic Policy*, 5(1): 34–58.

Culyer, A.J. 1990, 'Commodities, characteristics of commodities, characteristics of people, utilities, and quality of life', in S. Baldwin, C. Godfrey and C. Propper (eds), *Quality of Life: Perspective and Policies*, Routledge, London, 9–27.

Culyer, A.J. 1991, 'The normative economics of health care finance and provision' in A. McGuire, P. Fenn and K. Mayhew *Providing health care: The economics of alternative systems of finance and delivery*, Oxford University Press, Oxford, 65–98.

Culyer, A.J. and Maynard, A. (eds) 1997, *Being Reasonable about the Economics of Health: Selected Essays by Alan Williams*, Edward Elgar, Cheltenham.

Culyer, A.J. 2000, *The Economics of Health*, vols 1 and 2, Edward Elgar, London.

Cummings, R.G., Brookshire, D.S. and Schulze, W.D. 1986, *Valuing Environmental Goods: A State of the Art Assessment of the Contingent Valuation Method*, Rowan and Allenheld, Ottawa.

Dantzig, G.B. and Wolfe, P. 1961, 'The decomposition algorithm for linear programs', *Econometrics*, 29: 767–768.

Danzon, P.M. 1997, *Pharmaceutical Price Regulation National Policies versus Global Interests*, The AEI Press, Washington.

Danzon, P.M. and Furukawa, F. 2003, 'Prices and availability of pharmaceuticals: Evidence from nine countries', *Health Affairs*, Web Exclusive, 29 October, W3: 521–536.

Danzon, P.M. and Kim, J.D. 1998, 'International price comparisons for pharmaceuticals, measurement and policy issues', *PharmacoEconomics*, Suppl 1: 115–128.

Danzon, P.M. and Kim, J.D. 2002, *The Life cycle of pharmaceuticals: A cross-national perspective*, Office of Health Economics, April.

Dao, T.D. 1985, 'Cost-benefit and cost-effectiveness analysis of drug therapy', *American Journal of Hospital Pharmacy*, 42: 791–802.

Darba, J. 2003, 'Pharmaceutical expenditure in Spain', *The European Journal of Health Economics*, 4: 151–157.

Davie, A.P. 2000, 'ACE inhibitors after myocardial infarction: Clinical and economic considerations', *PharmacoEconomics*, 17(3): 237–243.

Detsky, A. 1993, 'Guidelines for economic analysis of pharmaceutical products: A draft document for Ontario and Canada', *PharmacoEconomics*, 3: 354–361.

Department of Health and Ageing 2004a, *Medicare Benefits Schedule Effective from 1 May 2004*, Commonwealth of Australia, Canberra.

Department of Health and Ageing 2004b, *Schedule of Pharmaceutical Benefits: For approved Pharmacists and Medical Practitioners effective from 1 May 2004*, Commonwealth of Australia, Canberra.

Department of Health and Ageing 2002, 'Guidelines for the pharmaceutical industry on preparation of submissions to the Pharmaceutical Benefits Advisory Committee', September 2002, www.health.gov.au

Department of Health and Aged Care 2000, 'PBS expenditure and prescriptions, cited 21 January 2003, www.health.gov.au

Diener, A., O'Brien, B. and Gafni, A. 1998, 'Health care contingent valuation studies: A review and classification of the literature', *Health Economics*, 7: 313–326.

Dinwiddy, C. and Teal, F. 1996, *Principles of Cost-Benefit Analysis for Developing Countries*, Cambridge University Press, Cambridge.

Dixon, J.A. and Hufschmidt, M.M. 1986, *Economic Valuation Techniques for the Environment*, John Hopkins University Press, Baltimore.

Dolan, P., Gudex, C., Kind, P. and Williams, A. 1996, 'Valuing health states: A comparison of methods', *Journal of Health Economics*, 15: 209–231.

Donaldson, C., Birch, S. and Gafni, A. 2002, 'The distribution problem in economic evaluation: income and the valuation of costs and consequences of health care programs', *Health Economics*, 11: 55–70.

Drahos, P., Faunce, T., Goddard, M. and Henry, D. 2004, *The FTA and the PBS*, submission to the Senate Select Committee on the US-Australia Free Trade Agreement, Canberra.

Drummond, M., Cooke, J. and Walley, T. 1997, 'Economic evaluation under managed competition: evidence from the U.K.', *Social Science and Medicine*, 45(4): 583–595.

Drummond, M., O'Brien, B., Stoddart G. and Torrance, G. 1997, *Methods for Economic Evaluation of Health Care Programs*, Oxford University Press, Oxford.

Drummond, M. 1994, 'Value-for-money assessments in Australia and beyond', *Decision Resources*, 55: 1–7.

Drummond, M., Maynard, A. and Wells, N. (eds) 1993, *Purchasing and Providing Cost-Effective Health Care*, Churchill Livingstone, London.

Drummond, M., Bloom, B., Freund, D., Evans, D., Henry, D. and Dittus, R. 1992, 'Peer review: Prescription policy in Australia', *Health Affairs*, 11: 191–206.

Drummond, M. 1992, 'Cost-effectiveness guidelines for re-imbursement of pharmaceuticals: Is economic analysis ready for its enhanced status?' *Health Economics*, 1: 85–92.

Drummond, M. 1992, 'Australian guidelines for cost-effectiveness studies of pharmaceuticals: The thin end of the boomerang?', *PharmacoEconomics* (Supp1): 69–69.

Duffield, J.W. and Patterson, D.A. 1991, 'Field testing existing values: an instream flow trust fund for Montana rivers', paper presented at the annual meeting of the American Economic Association, New Orleans.

Dunstan et al. 2002, *Diabetes: Australian Facts*, Australian Institute of Health and Welfare, Canberra.

Dupuit J. 1844, 'De la mesure de l'utilité des travaux public', *Annalis des Ponts et Chausséds*, s. II, 2nd series, 332–375; English translation 'On the measurement of the Utility of Public Works', by R.H. Barback, International Economics Paper (1952), n. 2, pp. 83–110.

Durand-Zaleski, I. and Bertrand, M. 2004, 'The value of Clopidogrel versus Aspirin in reducing atherothrombotic events: The CAPRIE study', *PharmacoEconomics*, 22(Suppl 4): 19–27.

Edgeworth, F.T. 1881, *Mathematical psychics: An essay on the application of mathematics to the moral sciences*, Kegan Paul, London.

Ehrlich, P. et al. 1999, 'Knowledge and the Environment', *Ecological Economics*, 30: 267–284.

Elsinga, E. and Rutten, F.H. 1997, 'Economic evaluation in support of national health policy: The case of the Netherlands', *Social Science and Medicine*, 45(4): 605–620.

Ess, S.M, Schneeweiss, S. and Szucs, T.D. 2003, 'European healthcare policies for controlling drug expenditure', *PharmacoEconomics* 21(2): 89–103.

Essink-Bot, M., Bonsel, G.J. and Van der Maas, P.J. 1990, 'Valuation of health states by the general public: The feasibility of a standardized measurement procedure', *Social Science and Medicine*, 31: 1201–1206.

Ettaro, L., Songer, Thomas J., Zhang, P. and Engelgau, M. 2004, 'Cost-of-illness studies in diabetes mellitus', *PharmacoEconomics* 22(3): 149–164.

Fisher, I. 1906, *The Nature of Capital and Income*, Augustus M. Kelly, New York (reprinted 1965).

Foster, R.H. and Plosker, G.L. 2002, 'Glipizide: A review of the pharmaco-economic implications of the extended-release formulation in Type 2 diabetes mellitus', *PharmacoEconomics* 18(3): 289–306.

Fox, K., Sengupta, J. and Thorbecke, E. 1973, *Theory of Quantitative Economic Policy*, North Holland, Amsterdam.

Freemantle, N. 1999, 'Does the UK National Health Service need a fourth hurdle for pharmaceutical reimbursement to encourage the more efficient prescribing of pharmaceuticals?' *Health Policy*, 46: 255–265

Freund, D., Mitchell, a. and Carmine, B. 1996, 'Speaking from experience: Australia', *Medical Care*, 34(12 Supp): DS211–235.

Friedman, M. and Hilleman, D.E. 2001, 'Economic burden of chronic obstructive pulmonary disease: Impact of new treatment options', *PharmacoEconomics*, 19(3): 245–254.

Froberg, D.G. and Kane, R.L. 1989a, 'Methodology for measuring health state preferences I: Measurement strategies', *Journal of Clinical Epidemiology*, 42: 345–354.

Froberg, D.G. and Kane, R.L. 1989b, 'Methodology for measuring health state preferences II: Scaling methods', *Journal of Clinical Epidemiology*, 42: 459–471.

Froberg, D.G. and Kane, R.L. 1989c, 'Methodology for measuring health state preferences III: Population and context effects', *Journal of Clinical Epidemiology*, 42: 585–592.

Froberg, D.G. and Kane, R.L. 1989d, 'Methodology for measuring health state preferences IV: Progress and a research agenda', *Journal of Clinical Epidemiology*, 42: 675–685.

Gabel, M.J. and Siphan, C.R. 2004, 'A social choice approach to expert consensus panel', *Journal of Health Economics,* 23(3): 543–564.

Gafni, A. 1991, 'Using willingness-to-pay as a measure of benefits: What is the relevant questions to ask in the context of public decision making about health care programs', *Medical Care*, 29: 1246–1252.

Gafni, A. and Birch, S. 1991, 'Equity considerations in utility-based measures of health outcomes in economic appraisals: An adjustment algorithm' *Journal of Health Economics*, 10: 329–342.

Gaspert, F. 1997, 'Objective Measures of Well-being and the Co-operative Production Problem', *Social Choice and Welfare*, 15(1): 95–112.

Gass, S.I. and Harris, C.M. 2001, '*Encyclopedia of Operations Research and Management Science*', Kluwer Academic Publishers, Boston.

George, B., Harris, A. and Mitchell, A. 1997, 'Reimbursement decisions and the implied value of life: Cost effectiveness analysis and decisions to reimburse pharmaceuticals in Australia 1993–1996', presented at the Nineteenth Australian Conference of Health Economists, Melbourne, July.

Ginsberg, G., Shani, S. and Lev, B. 1998, 'Cost-Benefit Analysis of Risperidone and Clozapine in the treatment of schizophrenia in Israel', *PharmacoEconomics*, 13: 231–241.

Glasziou, P. and Mitchell, A. 1996, 'Use of pharmacoeconomic data by regulatory authorities' in B. Spilker (eds) *Quality of Life and Pharmacoeconomics in Clinical Trials* 2nd edn, Lippincott-Raven, Philadelphia, 1141–1147.

Gold, M.R., Siegel, J.E., Russell, L.B. and Weinstein, M.C. (eds) 1996, *Cost Effectiveness in Health and Medicines*, Oxford University Press, Oxford.

Goreux, L. and Manne, A.S. (eds) 1973, *Multi-Level Planning: Case Studies in Mexico*, North Holland, Amsterdam.

Gorham, P. 1995, 'Cost-effectiveness guidelines: The experience of Australian Manufacturers', *PharmacoEconomics*, 5: 369–373.

Grabowski, H. and Mullins, C.D. 1997, 'Pharmacy benefit management, cost-effectiveness analysis and drug formulary decision', *Social Science and Medicine*, 45(4): 535–544.

Green, C., Brazier, J. and Deverill, M. 2000, 'Valuing health-related quality of life', *PharmacoEconomics*, 17(20): 151–165.

Grobler, M. et al. 1996, 'Industry comment on the 1995 revised Australian Pharmacoeconomic guidelines', *PharmacoEconomics*, 9: 353–356.

Grossman, L. 2002, 'New solutions for Type 2 diabetes mellitus', *Pharmaco-Economics*, 20(S1): 1–9.

Harberger, A. 1984, 'Basic needs versus distributional weights in social cost benefit analysis', *Economic Development and Cultural Change*, 32: 455–474.

Hailey, D. 1997, 'Australian economic evaluation and government decisions on pharmaceuticals, compared to assessment of other health technologies', *Social Science and Medicine*, 45(4): 563–581.

Hall, J., Gafni, A. and Birch, S. 2005, 'Are health economics critique of welfarism "non-Sen's" approach? An exploration of compatibility with Sen's capabilities approach.' paper presented to Australian Health Economics Society Annual Conference, Auckland, September.

Hammer, J. 1997, 'Prices and protocols in public health care', *World Bank Economic Review*, 11(3): 409–432.

Hammer, J. and Berman, P. 1995, 'Ends and means in public health policy in developing countries', in P. Berman (ed.), *Health Sector Reform in Developing Countries: Making Health Development Sustainable*, Harvard School of Public Health, Cambridge, Massachusetts.

Harris, A. 1994, 'Economic appraisal in the regulation of pharmaceuticals in Australia: Its rationale and potential impact', *Australian Economic Review*, 2nd Quarter: 99–104.

Hausman, D. and McPherson, M. 1996, *Economic Analysis and Moral Philosophy*, Cambridge University Press, Cambridge.

Hausman, J. A. 1993, *Contingent valuation: A critical assessment*, North-Holland, Amsterdam.

Heal, G.M. 1973, *The Theory of Economic Planning*, North Holland Publishing Company, Amsterdam.

Henriksson, F. 2002, 'Application of Economic Models in Healthcare: The Introduction of Pioglitazone in Sweden', *PharmacoEconomics*, 20(Suppl 1): 43–53.

Henry, D. and Hill, S. 1999, 'Assessing new health technologies: Lessons to be learnt from drugs', *Medical Journal of Australia*, 171: 554–556.

Henry, D. and Lopert, R. 1999, 'Pharmacoeconomics and policy decisions: The Australian health care system', *Clinical Therapeutics*, 21(5): 909–915.

Henry, D. 1992a, 'Should indirect costs and benefits be included?' *PharmacoEconomics*, 1: 462.

Henry, D. 1992b, 'Economic analysis as an aid to subsidisation decisions: The development of Australian guidelines for pharmaceuticals' *Pharmaco-Economics*, 1: 54–67.

Hicks, J.R. 1941, 'The foundation of welfare economics', *Economic Journal*, 49: 696–712.

Higa, G.M. 2000, 'New generation aromatase inhibitors in breast cancer: Weighing out potential costs and benefits', *PharmacoEconomics*, 17(2): 121–132.

Hill, S., Mitchell, A. and Henry, D. 2000, 'Problems with the interpretation of pharmacoeconomic analyses: A review of submissions to the Australian Pharmaceutical Benefits Scheme', *Journal of American Medical Association*, 283: 2116–2121.

Hill, S., Henry D, Pekarsky, B. and Mitchell, A. 1997, 'Economic evaluation on pharmaceuticals: What are reasonable standards for clinical evidence – the Australian experience', *British Journal of Clinical Pharmacology*, 44: 421–425.

Hillegass, W.B., Newman, A.R. and Raco, D.L. 2001, 'Glycoprotein IIb/IIIa receptor therapy in percutaneous coronary intervention and non-ST segment elevation acute coronary syndromes: estimating the economic implications', *PharmacoEconomics*, 19(1): 41–55.

Hirth, R., Chernew, M., Miller, E., Fendrick, A. and Weissert, W. 2000, 'Willingness-to-pay for a quality-adjusted life year: in search of a standard.' *Med Decis Making*, 20(3): 332–42.

Hornberger, J., Redelmeier, D. and Petersen, J. 1992, 'Variability among methods to assess patients' well-being and consequent effect on a cost-effectiveness analysis', *Journal of Clinical Epidemiology*, 45: 505–512.

Hurley, S., Kaldor, J.M., Gardiner, S., Carlin, J.B., Assuncao, R.M. and Evans, D.B. 1996, 'Life cost of Human Immunodeficiency Virus related health care', *Journal of Acquired Immune Deficiency Syndromes and Human Retrovirology*, 12: 371–378.

Hurley, J. 2000, 'An overview of the normative economics of the health sector' in A.J. Culyer and J.P. Newhouse (eds), *Handbook of Health Economics*, Elsevier, Amsterdam.

Hussey, J. and Hussey, R. 1997, *Business Research: A Practical Guide for Undergraduate and Postgraduate Students*, Macmillan Business, London.

Imboden, N. 1978, *A Management Approach to Project Appraisal and Evaluation*, OECD, Paris.

Islam, S. 2001a, *Applied Welfare Economics*, Centre for Strategic Economic Studies, Victoria University, Melbourne.

Islam, S.N. 2001b, *Optimal Growth Economics: An Investigation of the Contemporary Issues, and Sustainability Implications*, North Holland Publishing, Series – Contributions to Economic Analysis, Amsterdam.

Islam, S. 1998, *Mathematical Economics of Multi-Level Optimization: Theory and Application*, Contributions to Economics Series, Springer-Verlag.

Islam, S., Clarke, M. and Mak, C. 2002, 'Incorporating ethics and moral philosophy in health economics: A new framework', paper presented at the Australian Association for Professional and Applied Ethics Annual Conference, Victoria University, Melbourne, 2–4 October.

Islam, S. and Clarke, M. 2000, 'Social welfare and GDP: Can we still use GDP for welfare measurement?' seminar paper, Centre for Strategic Economic Studies, Victoria University, Melbourne.

Islam, S. and Gigas, J. 1996, 'Economics of project appraisal and sustainable economic development', paper presented at the Pacific Rim Allied Economic Organisations Conference, Hong Kong, 10–15 January.

Islam, S. and Gigas, J. 1995, 'Social time preference, climate change and the future of the Australian economy: Findings from the Australian Dynamic Integrated Climate Economic Model (ADICE)', in *Proceedings of Conference of the Australia New Zealand Society of Ecological Economists*, Coffs Harbour, Sydney.

Islam, S., Mak, C. and McCallum, J. 2005, 'Estimation and analysis of costs and benefits of PBS: A social choice approach', paper accepted for the 27th Australian Conference for Health Economists, Auckland, 29–30 Sept.

Islam, S. and Mak, C. 2002a, 'Social cost benefit analysis of the Pharmaceutical Benefits Scheme' *The Otemon Journal of Australian Studies*, 28: 1–33.

Islam, S. and Mak, C. 2002b, 'A modified social cost benefit analysis and operations research model for evaluating health programs', paper presented at the Australian Health Economics Society Annual Conference, Sydney, 18–19 July.

Islam, S. and Mak, C. 2000, 'Welfare economics of health programs: Social cost benefit analysis of the Pharmaceutical Benefits Scheme' seminar paper, Centre for Strategic Economic Studies, Victoria University, Melbourne.

Islam, S. and Oh, K.B. 2003, *Applied Financial Econometrics in E-Commerce*, North Holland, Amsterdam.

Jack, W. 1999, *Principles of Health Economics for Developing Countries*, World Bank Institute Development Series, Washington D.C.

Jenkins, G.P. and Harberger, A.C. 1991, *Manual Cost-Benefit Analysis of Investment Decisions*, Program on Investment Appraisal and Management, Harvard Institute for International Development, Cambridge, Mass.

328   *Bibliography*

Jensen, M. and Meckling, W. 1976, 'Theory of the firm: Managerial behaviour agency costs and ownership structure', *Journal of Financial Economics*, 39(4): 1021–39.

Jevons, W. 1871, 'The Theory of Political Economy', in R. Black (ed.), *Jevons: The Theory of Political Economy*, Penguin, Middlesex.

Jimenez, F.J., Guallar-Castillon, P., Terres, C.R. and Guallar, E. 1999, 'Cost-benefit analysis of *Haemophilus influenzae* Type b vaccination in children in Spain', *PharmacoEconomics*, 15: 75–83.

Johannesson, M. 2000, *Theory and Methods of Economic Evaluation of Health Care*, Kluwer Academic Publishers, Dordrecht.

Johannesson, M. 1996, 'A note on the relationship between *ex ante* and expected willingness to pay for health', *Social Science and Medicine*, 42(3): 305–311.

Johannesson, M. and Henry, D. 1992, 'The Australian guidelines for subsidization of pharmaceuticals: The road to cost-effective, *PharmacoEconomics*, 2: 355–362, 422–426.

Johannesson, M., Jonsson, B. and Borgquist, L. 1991, 'Willingness to pay for antihypertensive therapy: Results of a Swedish pilot study', *Journal of Health Economics*, 10: 461–474.

Johansson, P.O. 1991, *An Introduction to Modern Welfare Economics*, Cambridge University Press, Cambridge.

Johnson, D. 1996, *Poverty, Inequality and Social Welfare in Australia*, Physica-Verlag, Heidelberg.

Johnston, M.A. 1990, 'Australia's Pharmaceutical Pricing Strategy', unpublished PhD thesis, Harvard University.

Jonsson, B. 1997, 'Economic evaluation of medical technologies in Sweden', *Social Science and Medicine*, 45(4): 597–604.

Jonsson, B. 2004, 'Changing health environment: The challenge to demonstrate cost-effectiveness of new compounds', *PharmacoEconomics*, 22(Suppl 4): 5–10.

Juniper, E.F. 2001, 'Using humanistic health data in asthma', *PharmacoEconomics*, 19 suppl(2): 7–12.

Kaldor, N. 1934, 'Welfare propositions of economics and interpersonal comparison of utility', *Economic Journal*, 49: 549–552.

Kanavos, P. 2001, 'Overview of pharmaceutical pricing and reimbursement regulation in Europe', European Commission, November.

Kane, N.M. 1997, 'Pharmaceutical cost containment and innovation in the United States', *Health Policy* 41(Suppl): s71-s89.

Karnon, J. and Brown, J. 2002, 'Tamoxifen plus chemotherapy versus Tamoxifen alone as adjuvant therapies for node-positive, postmenopausal women with early breast cancer: A stochastic economic evaluation', *PharmacoEconomics*, 20(2): 139–142.

Karnon, J. and Jones, T. 2003, 'A stochastic economic evaluation of Letrozole versus Tamoxifen as a first-line hormonal therapy: for advanced breast cancer in postmenopausal patients', *PharmacoEconomics*, 21(7): 513–525.

Kemp, R. and Wlodarczyk, J. 1994, 'Australian pharmaceutical pricing guidelines: Preliminary practical experience', *PharmacoEconomics*, 5(6): 465–471.

Kenkel, D. 1997, 'On valuing morbidity, cost-effectiveness analysis and being rude', *Journal of Health Economics*, 16: 749–758.

Keong, L.C. (eds) 2002, *Corporate Governance: An Asia-Pacific Critique*, Sweet and Maxwell Asia, Hong Kong.

Kneese, A.V. and Schulze, W.D. 1985, 'Ethics and environmental economics', in A.V. Kneese and J.L. Sweeney(eds), *Handbook of Natural Resource and Energy Economics*, North-Holland, Elsevier, Amsterdam.

Kontozamanis, V., Mantzouneas, E. and Stoforos, C. 2003, 'An overview of the Greek pharmaceutical market', *The European Journal of Health Economics*, 4(4): 327–333.

Kornai, J. and Liptak, T. 1965, 'Two level planning', *Econometrica*, 33: 141–169.

Krutilla, J.V. and Fisher, A.C. 1985, *The Economics of Natural Environments* (revised edition), John Hopkins University Press for Resources for the Future, Baltimore.

Kula, E. 1984, 'Derivation of social time preference rates for the United States and Canada', *Quarterly Journal of Economics*, 99: 873–882.

Kula, E. 1985, 'An empirical investigation on the social time preference rate for the United Kingdom', *Environment and Planning*, 7: 99–22.

Kumar, S. 1991, *Recent Developments in Mathematical Programming*, Gordon and Breach Science Publishers, Melbourne.

Lahiri, K. and Moore, G. 1991, *Leading Economic Indicators*, Cambridge University Press, Melbourne.

Lal, D. 1977, 'Distributional weights, shadow wages, and the accounting rate of interest: estimates for India', *Indian Economic Review*, 2(2).

Lamb, H.M., Culy, C.R. and Faulds, D. 2000, 'Inhale Fluticasone proprionate: A pharmacoeconomic review of its use in the management of asthma', *PharmacoEconomics*, 18(5): 487–510.

Langley, P. 1996, 'The November 1995 revised Australian guidelines for the economic evaluation of pharmaceuticals', *PharmacoEconomics*, 9: 341–352.

Langley, P. 1993, 'The role of pharmacoeconomic guidelines for formulary approval: The Australian experience', *Clinical Therapeutics*, 15(6): 1154–1176.

Lavigne, J.E., Phelps, C.E., Mushlin, A. and Lednar, W.M. 2003, 'Reductions in individual work productivity associated with Type 2 diabetes mellitus', *PharmacoEconomics*, 21(15): 1123–1134.

Lele, S.M. 1991, 'Sustainable Development: A Critical Review', *World Development*, 19(6): 607–21.

Le Pen, C. 1997, 'Pharmaceutical economy and the economic assessment of drugs in France', *Social Science & Medicine*, 45(4): 635–643.

Levary, R. et al. 1990, *Quantitative Methods for Capital Budgeting*, South-Western Pub. Co. Cincinnati.

Lichfield, N. et al. 1975, *Evaluation in the Planning Process*, Pergamon Press, Oxford.

Lichtenberg, F. 1996, 'Do (more and better) drugs keep people out of hospitals?', *Health Economics*, 86(2): 384–388.

Lichtenberg, F. 2001, 'Are the benefits of newer drugs worth their cost? Evidence from the 1996 MEPS', *Health Affairs*, September/October.

Lichtenberg, F. 2002a, 'Benefits and cost of newer drugs: An update', Working Paper 8996, NBER, Cambridge.

Lichtenberg, F. 2002b, 'The economic benefits of new drugs', *Economic Realities in Health Care Policy (Pfizer)*, 2 (2): 14–19.

Lightwood, J.M. and Glantz, S.A. 1997, 'Short-term economic and health benefits of smoking cessation, myocardial infarction and stroke', *Circulation*, 96: 1089–1096.

Liljas, B. 1998, 'How to calculate indirect costs in economic evaluation', *PharmacoEconomics*, 13: 1–7.

Lind, R. 1982, *Discounting for Time and Risk in Energy Policy*, John Hopkins University Press, Baltimore.

Little, I.M.D. and Mirlees, J.A. 1974, *Project Appraisal and Planning for Developing Countries*, Heinemann Educational Books, London.

Lloyd, A., Schmieder, C. and Marchant, N. 2003, 'Financial and health costs of uncontrolled blood pressure in the United Kingdom, *Pharmaco-Economics*, 21(Suppl 1): 33–41.

Lofgren, H. 2001, 'Pharmaceutical benefits in Australia and Sweden: Welfare policy and the cost of prescription drugs', *Australian Journal of Social Issues*, 36(3): 207–220.

Loomes, G. and McKenzie, L. 1989, 'The Use of QALYs in Health Care Decision Making', *Social Science and Medicine*, 28: 299–308.

Lyles, A., Luce, B.R. and Rentz, A.M. 1997, 'Managed care pharmacy, socio-economic assessments and drug adoption decisions', *Social Science and Medicine*, 45(4): 511–521.

Lyseng-Williamson, K.A. and Plosker, G.L. 2003, 'Inhaled Salmeterol/ Fluticasone proprinate combination: A pharmacoeconomic review of its use in the management of astham', *PharmacoEconomics*, 21(13): 951–985.

Maetzel, A., Ruof, J., Covington, M. and Wolf, A. 2003, 'Economic evaluation of Orlistat in overweight and obese patients with type 2 diabetes mellitus', *PharmacoEconomics*, 21(7): 501–512.

Mak, C. and Islam, S. 2004a, 'Moral philosophy and health economics: A new framework', paper presented at the CESifo Conference on Human Biology and Economics, Munich, 2–6 June.

Mak, C. and Islam, S. 2004b, 'Estimation and analysis of costs and benefits of PBS: A social choice approach', paper presented at the 26th Australian Conference of Health Economists, Melbourne, 30 Sept–1 Oct.

Mak, C. and Islam, S. 2004c, 'Quality of life: Its role in cost and benefit analysis of health', paper presented at the 6th Australian Conference on Quality of Life, Melbourne, 25 November.

Mak, C. and Islam, S. 2005, 'Economic Evaluation for including drugs in PBS: A case study of Respiratory Diseases Drugs', paper presented at the conference on 'Beyond Fragmented Government: Governance in the Public Sector', Centre for International Corporate Governance Research, Victoria University, Melbourne, 15–17 August.

Maler, K. 1985, 'Welfare Economics and the Environment' in A. Kneese and J. Sweeney (eds) *Handbook of Natural Resources and Energy Economics*, North-Holland, Amsterdam.

Markham, A. and Adkins, J.C. 2000, 'Inhaled Salmeterol/Fluticasone propri-onate combination: A pharmacoeconomic review of its use in the manage-ment of astham', *PharmacoEconomics*, 18(6): 591–608.

Marshall, A. 1890, *Principles of Economics*, 9th edn (1961), Macmillan, London.

Mashayekhi, A. 1980, *Shadow Prices for Project Appraisal in Turkey*, World Bank Staff Working Paper 392, Washington DC.

Mathers, C., Vos, T. and Stevenson, C. 1999, *The Burden of Disease and Injury in Australia*, AIHW, Canberra.

McDaid, D., Mossialos, E. and Mrazek, M.F. 2002, 'Making use of economic evaluation', *International Journal of Risk and Safety in Medicine*, 15: 67–74.

McIntosh, E., Donaldson, C. and Ryan, M. 1999, 'Recent advances in the methods of cost-benefit analysis in health care: Matching the art to the science', *PharmacoEconomics*, 15: 357–367.

McPake, B., Kumaranayake, L. and Normand, C. 2002, *Health Economics: An International Perspective*, Routledge, London.

MEDTAP International 2003, 'The value of investment in health care: Better care, better lives', at www.MEDTAP.com

Menendez, R., Stanford, H.R., Edwards, L., Kalberg, C. and Rickard, K. 2001, 'Cost-efficacy analysis of Fluticasone Proprionate versus Zafirlukast in patients with persistent asthma', *PharmacoEconomics*, 19(8): 865–874.

Miller Jr, R. D. and Frech III, H. E. 2002, 'The productivity of health care and pharmaceuticals: Quality of life, cause of death and the role of obesity', Economics Department, University of California, Santa Barbara, July.

Mills, J. 1863, *Utilitarianism*, Macmillan, London.

Mishan, E. 1976, *Elements of Cost-Benefit Analysis,* George Allen and Unwin, London.

Mitchell, R.C. and Carson, R.T. 1989, *Using Surveys of Public Goods: The Contingent Valuation Method*, Resources for the Future, Washington DC.

Mitchell, A. 1997, 'Use of health outcomes measurements for the Pharmaceutical Benefits Scheme', in *Integrating Health Outcomes Measurement in Routine Health Care Conference 1996 Proceedings*, AIHW 134–138.

Mitchell, A. 1996, 'Current experience in Australia', *Drug Information Journal*, 30: 495–502.

Mithcell, A. 1995, 'Pharmaceutical Guidelines: Current position and possible changes', in S. Smith and M. Drummond (eds), *Economic Evaluation in Australian Health Care*, AGPS, Canberra, 118–124.

Mithcell, A. 1993, 'The Australian perspective on the development of pharmacoeconomic guidelines, in S. Smith and M. Drummond (eds), *Proceedings of the Canadian Collaborative Workshop on Pharmacoeconomics*, Princeton Excerpta Medica, 3–7.

Mitchell, A. and Henry, D. 1992, 'Is the drug cost-effective?', *Australian Prescriber*, 15: 74–75.

Montagne, O., Chaix, C., Harf, A., Castaigne, A. and Durand-Zaleski, I. 2000, 'Costs for acute myocardial infarction in a tertiary care centre and nation-wide in France', *PharmacoEconomics*, 17(6): 603–609.

Mooney, G. 1993, *Economics, Medicines and Healthcare,* 2nd edn, Harvester Wheatsheaf, Hampstead, UK.

Mooney, G. 1996, 'And now for vertical equity? A health economist's perspective', *Journal of Medical Ethics,* 15(3): 148–152.

Mooney, G. 1998, '"Communitarian claims" as an ethical basis for allocating health care resources', *Social Science and Medicine,* 47(9): 1171–80.

Mooney, G. 2001, 'Communitarianism and Health Economics' in J. B. Davis (ed), *The social economics of health care,* London and New York, Routledge, 40–60.

Mooney, G. and Scotton, R. 1999, *Economics and Australian Health Policy,* Allen and Unwin, St Leonard.

Mullins, C. D. 1995, 'Toward an understanding of pharmaceutical pricing strategies through the use of simple game theoretic models', *Journal of Research in Pharmaceutical Economics,* 6(3): 1–14.

Murphy, K. and Topel, R. 1999, *The Economic Value of Medical Research,* University of Chicago Press, Chicago.

Musgrave, T. 1959, *The Theory of Public Finance,* MacGraw-Hills, New York.

Ng, Y. 1979, Welfare Economics, Macmillian Press, London.

Nord, E., Pinto, J.L., Richardson, J., Menzal, P. and Ubel, P. 1999, 'Incorporating societal concerns for fairness in numerical valuations of health programmes', *Health Economics,* 8(1): 25–39.

Nord, E. 1992, 'An alternative to QALYs: The saved young life equivalent (SAVE)', *British Medical Journal,* 305: 875–877.

Nordhaus, W. 2002, 'The health of nations: The contribution of improved health to living standards', NBER Working Paper 8818, National Bureau of Economic Research, Cambridge, MA.

Nuijten, M.J.C. 1998, 'The selection of data sources for use in modeling studies', *PharmacoEconomics,* 13: 305–316.

Nuijten, M.J.C., Szende, A., Koza, J., Mogyorosy, Z., Kramberger, B., Nemecek, K., Tomek, D., Oreskovic, S. and Laskowska, M. 2003, 'Health care reform in six Central European countries', *The European Journal of Health Economics,* 4(4): 286–291.

OECD 1998, *OECD Health Ddata 98: Comparative Analysis of 28 Countries,* OECD, Paris.

Olsen, J.A. 1993, 'Some methodological issues in economic evaluation in health care', PhD Thesis, Department of Economics, University of Tromso.

Olsen, J.A. and Donaldson, C. 1998, 'Helicopters, hearts and hips: Using willingness to pay to set priorities for public sector health programs', *Social Science and Medicine,* 46: 1–12.

Olsen, J.A. and Richardson, J. et al. 2003, 'The moral relevance of personal characteristics in setting health care priorities', *Social Science and Medicine,* 57(7): 1163–1172.

O'Neill, J. 2001, 'Sustainability: Ethics, Politics and the Environment', in J. O'Neill, R. Turner and I Bateman, eds, *Environmental Ethics and Philosophy,* Edward Edgar, Cheltenham.

Ontario Ministry of Health 1994, Ontario *Guidelines for Economic Analysis of Pharmaceutical Products,* Toronto.

Osberg, L. and Sharpe, A. 1998, An Index of Economic Well-being for Canada', paper presented at CLCS Conference on the State of Living Standards and Quality of Life, Ottawa, October 30–31.

Oser, J. and Brue, S. 1988, *The Evolution of Economic Thought*, Harcourt Bruce Jovanovich, New York.

Overseas Development Administration 1977, *Guide to the Economic Appraisal of Projects in Developing Countries*, HMSO, London.

Paavola, J. and Bromley, D. 2002, 'Contested Choices' in D. Bromley and J. Paavola (eds) *Economics, Ethics and Environmental Policy*, Blackwell Publishing, Oxford.

Paladino, J.A. 1994, 'Cost-effectiveness comparison of cefepime and ceftazidime using decision analysis', *PharmacoEconomics*, 5(6): 505–512.

Page, T. 1977, *Conservation and Economics Efficiency*, John Hopkins Press for Resources for the Future, Inc., Baltimore.

Page, T. and Talbot, P. 1982, 'Intergenerational justice as opportunity', in D. MacLean and P. Brown (eds), *Energy and the Future*, Rowman and Littlefield, Totowa.

Pappas, J.L. and Hirschey, M. 1985, *Fundamentals of Managerial Economics*, Dryden Press, New York.

Pareto, V. 1906, Manual of Political Economy, translated by A. Schwier, Macmillan, London(reprinted 1972).

Paul, D. 1995, *Child Labour in Context*, World Vision Australia, Melbourne.

Pauly, M. 1995, 'Valuing health care benefits in money terms', in F. Sloan (ed.) *Valuing Health Care: Costs, Benefits and Effectiveness of Pharmaceuticals and Other Medical Technologies,*, Cambridge University Press, Cambridge.

Pearce, D., Barbier, E. and Markandya, A. 1994, *Sustainable Development: Economics and Environment in the Third World*, Earthscan Publications, London.

Pearce, D. and Nash, C. 1981, *The Social Appraisal of Projects: A Text in Cost-Benefit Analysis*, Macmillan Press, London.

Pedersen, K.M. 2003, 'Pricing and reimbursement of drugs in Denmark', *The European Journal of Health Economics*, 4(1): 60–65.

Peirson, G., Bird, R., Brown, R. and Howard, P. 1995, *Business Finance*, McGraw-Hill Book Company, New York.

Perkins, F. 1994, *Practical Cost Benefit Analysis: Basic Concepts and Applications*, Macmillan Education Australia, Melbourne.

Pezzey, J. 2001, 'Sustainability Policy and Environmental Policy', mimeo, Centre for Resource and Environmental Studies, Australian National University, Canberra.

Pezzey, J. 2002, 'Concern for Sustainable Development in a Sexual World', mimeo, Centre for Resource and Environmental Studies, Australian National University, Canberra.

Pharma in Focus 20 Dec 2004–16 Jan 2005, Lush Media, printed 13 January 2005.

Pharmacy Guild of Australia 2005, *Pharmacy Guild Digest 2004*, Canberra.

Pigou, A.C. 1912, *Wealth and Welfare*, Macmillan, London.

Pigou, A.C. 1920, *The Economics of Welfare*, Macmillan, London.

Pigou, A.C. 1947, *Socialism Versus Capitalism*, Macmillan, London.

Pinto Prades, J.L. and Badia Llach, X. 2005, 'Economic evaluation and pharmaceutical policy', in J. Puig-Junoy (ed) *The Public Financing of Pharmaceuticals: An Economic Approach*, Edward Elgar, Cheltenham, U.K.

Poretz, D.M., Woolard, D., Eron, L.J., Goldenberg, R.I., Rising, J. and Sparks, S. 1984, 'Outpatient use of ceftriaxone: A cost-benefit analysis', *American Journal of Medicine*, 77: 77–83.

Price, C. 1993, *Time, Discounting and Value*, Blackwell, Oxford.

Price, M.J. and Briggs, A. H. 2002, 'Development of an economic model to assess the cost effectiveness of asthma management strategies', *Pharmaco-Economics*, 20(3): 183–194.

Prince, R. 1985, 'A note on environmental risk and the rate of discount: Comment', *Journal of Environmental Economics and Management*, 12: 179–80.

Productivity Commission 2001, *International Pharmaceutical Price Differences*, Research Report, Productivity Commission, July.

Productivity Commission 2003, *Evaluation of the Pharmaceutical Industry Investment Program*, Research Report, January.

Puig-Junoy, J. 2003, *Incentives and Pharmaceutical Reimbursement Reforms in Spain*, Research Centre for Health and Economics, Pompeu Fabra University, Barcelona, Spain, April.

Quiggin, J. 1996, *Great Expectations: Microeconomic Reform and Australia*, Allen and Unwin, Sydney.

Quirk, J. and Saposnik, R. 1968, *Introduction to General Equilibrium Theory and Welfare Economics*, McGraw-Hill, New York.

Radice, D. and Radealli, A. 2003, 'Breast cancer management: Quality of life and cost considerations', *PharmacoEconomics*, 21(6): 383–396.

Ragsdale, C. 2001, *Spreadsheet Modeling and Decision Analysis*, Thomson Learning, Melbourne.

Ravallion, M. 1994, *Poverty Comparisons*, Harwood Economic Publishers, Chur, Switzerland.

Rawls, J. 1974, 'Concepts of distributional equity: Some reasons for the maximin criterion', American Economic Review, *Papers and Proceedings*, 64:141–46.

Ray, A. 1984, *Cost-Benefit Analysis*, John Hopkins University Press, Baltimore.

Reinhardt, U. 1992 'Reflections on the meaning of efficiency: Can efficiency be separated from equity?" *Yale Law and Policy Review*, 10(2): 302–15.

Reinhardt, U. 1997, 'Making economic evaluations respectable', *Social Science and Medicine*, 45(4): 555–562.

Reiter, S. 1986, 'Information incentive and performance in the (new)[2] welfare economics', in S. Reiter (ed.), *Studies in Mathematical Economics*, 25(MAA studies in Mathematics), Mathematical Association of America.

Repetto, R. (eds) 1985, *The Global Possible. Resources, Development and the New Century*. New Haven: Yale University Press.

Rice, D. 1967, ' Estimating the cost of illness', *American Journal of Public Health*, 57: 424–440.

Richardson, J. 1991, 'Economic assessment of health care: Theory and practice', *The Australian Economic Review*, 1st Quarter: 1–21.

Richardson, J. 2002, 'The poverty of ethical analyses in economics and the unwarranted disregard of evidence' in C. Murray, J. Salomon, C. Mathers and A. Lopez, World Health Organisation, Geneva, 627–640.

Richardson, J. and McKie, J. 2005, 'Empiricism, ethics and orthodox economic theory: what is the appropriate basis for decision-making in the health sector?', *Social Science and Medicine*, 60(2): 265–275.

Richter, A. 2004, 'Duct tape for decision makers: The use of OR models in pharmacoeconomics', in *Operations Research and Health Care: A Handbook of Methods and Applications*, Kluwer, Amsterdam.

Ringel, J.S., Hosek, S.D., Vollaard, B.A. and Mahnowski, S. 2002, *The Elasticity of Demand for Health Care*, RAND.

Roberts, K. 1984, 'The theoretical limits of redistribution', *Review of Economic Studies*, 51(2): 177–195.

Robinson, R. 1993, 'Cost-benefit analysis', *British Medical Journal*, 307: 924–926.

Ruchlin, H.S. and Dasbach, E.J. 2001, 'An economic overview of chronic obstructive pulmonary disease', *PharmacoEconomics*, 19(6): 623–642.

Rutten von-Molken, M. and Feenstra, T.L. 2001, 'The burden of asthma and chronic obstructive pulmonary disease data from the Netherlands', *PharmacoEconomics*, 19 suppl(2): 1–6.

Salkeld, G., Mitchell, A. and Hill, S. 1999, 'Pharmaceuticals', in G. Mooney and R. Scotton (eds), *Economics and Australian Health Policy*, Allen and Unwin, St Leonard.

Salvaris, M. 1998, 'Citizenship and Progress', in R. Eckersley (ed.) *Measuring Progress*, CSIRO publishing, Melbourne.

Samuelson, P.A. 1947, *Foundations of Economic Analysis*, Harvard University Press, Cambridge MA.

Schelling, T. 1968, 'The life you save may be your own', in Samuel B. Chase, Jr., ed., *Problems in Public Expenditure Analysis*, The Brookings Institution, Washington D.C., 127–162.

Sculpter, M. 2001, 'Using economic evaluations to reduce the burden of asthma and chronic obstructive pulmonary disease', *PharmacoEconomics*, 19 suppl(2): 21–25.

Schleinitz, M., Weiss, J. and Owens, D. 2004, 'Clopidogrel versus aspirin for secondary prophylaxis of vascular events: A cost-effectiveness analysis', *American Journal of Medicine*, 116: 797–806.

Schweitzer, S.O. 1997, *Pharmaceutical Economics and Policy*, Oxford University Press, London.

Seitz, N.E. et al. 1995, *Capital Budgeting and Long Term Financial Decisions*, Dryden Press.

Sekeran, U. 1992, *Research Methods for Business: A Skill-building Approach*, John Wiley and Sons, New York.

Sen, A. 1967, 'Isolation, assurance, and the social rate of discount', *Quarterly Journal of Economics*, 81(1).

Sen, A. 1970a, *Collective Choices and Social Welfare*, Holden-Day, San Francisco, CA

Sen, A. 1970b, 'Interpersonal Aggregation and Partial Comparability' *Econometrica*, 38(3): 393–409.

Sen, A. 1977, 'Rational Fools: A Critique of the Behavioural Foundations of Economic Theory', *Philosophy and Public Affairs*, 6: 317–344.

Sen, A. 1979a, 'Personal Utilities and Public Judgments: Or What's Wrong with Welfare Economics', *Economic Journal*, 89: 537–558.

Sen, A. 1979b, 'The Welfare Basis of Real Income Comparisons: A Survey', Journal of Economic Literature, 17: 1–45.

Sen, A. 1982, *Choices, Welfare and Measurement*, Basil Blackwell, Oxford.

Sen, A. 1984, *Resources, Values and Development*, Basil Blackwell, Oxford.

Sen, A. 1985a, *Commodities and Capabilities*, North Holland, Amsterdam.

Sen, A. 1985b, 'Well-being Agency and Freedom', *The Journal of Philosophy*, 82: 169–221.

Sen, A. 1992, Inequality reexamined, Harvard University Press, Cambridge, MA.

Sen, A. 1995, 'Rationality and social choice', *American Economic Review*, 85: 1–24.

Sen, A. 1999a, *Beyond the Crisis: Development Strategies in Asia,* Institute of Southeast Asian Studies, Singapore.

Sen, A. 1999b, 'The Possibility of Social Choice', *American Economic Review*, 89(3): 349–378.

Sen, A. 2002, 'Why Health Equity?', *Health Economics*, 11: 659–666.

Sendi, P., Gafni, A. and Birch, S. 2002, 'Opportunity costs and uncertainty in the economic evaluation of health care interventions', *Health Economics*, 11:23–31.

Sever, P.S., Dahlof, B., Poulter, N.R. et al. 2003, 'Prevention of coronary and stroke events with Atorvastatin in hypertensive patients who have average or lower-than-average cholesterol concentrations, in the Anglo-Scandinavian Cardiac Outc – Lipid Lowering Arm (ASCOT-LLA): A multi-centre randomised controlled trial', *Lancet*, 361: 1149–1158.

Shaw, J.W., Horrace, W.C. and Vogel, R.J. 2002, *The Productivity of Pharmaceuticals in Improving Health: An Analysis of the OECD Health Data*, University of Arizona, Tucson.

Sheenan, P. 1999, *The Challenge of Pharmaceutical Policy in Australia: Multiple Objectives and Global Change*, Report to the Department of Industry Science and Resources, Centre for Strategic Economic Studies, Victoria University, Melbourne.

Sheehan, P. and Sweeny, K. 2002, *Competition and Drug Pricing in the PBS: An Economic Interpretation*, Pharmaceutical Industry Project Working Paper No 12, Centre for Strategic Economic Studies, Victoria University, Melbourne.

Sheth, K., Borker, R., Emmett, A., Rickard, K. and Dorinsky, P. 2002, 'Cost-effectiveness comparison of Salmeterol/Fluticasone propionate versus Montelukast in the treatment of adults with persistent asthma', *Pharmaco-Economics*, 20(13): 909–918.

Slesnick, D. 1998, 'Empirical Approaches to the Measurement of Welfare', *Journal of Economic Literature*, 36: 2108–2165.

Sloan, C., 1995, *A History of the Pharmaceutical Benefits Scheme 1947–1993*, Commonwealth Department of Human Services and Health, Canberra.

Sloan, F., Whetten-Goldstein, K. and Wilson, A. 1997, 'Hospital pharmacy decisions, cost containment and the use of cost-effectiveness analysis', *Social Science and Medicine*, 45(4): 523–533.

Sloan, F. (ed.) 1995, *Valuing Health Care: Costs, Benefits and Effectiveness of Pharmaceuticals and Other Medical Technologies*, Cambridge University Press, Cambridge.

Smith, A. 1776, An Inquiry into the Nature and Cause of the Wealth of Nation, London: W. Strahan and T. Cadell (republished London: Home University, 1910).

Smith, D.G. and McBurney, C.R. 2003, 'An economic analysis of the Atorvastatin comparative cholesterol efficacy and safety study (ACCESS)', *PharmacoEconomics*, 21(Suppl)1: 13–23.

Solow, R.M. 1991, 'Sustainability: An Economist's Perspective', The Eighteenth J Seward Johnson Lecture to the Marine Policy Centre, Woods Hole Oceanographic Institution in Dorfman, Robert and Dorfman, Nancy S. (eds) *Economics of the Environment: Selected Readings*. New York: Norton, 179–187.

Squires, L. and van der Tak, H.G. 1975, *Economic Analysis of Projects*, John Hopkins University Press, Baltimore.

Squire, L., van der Tak, H.G. and Durdag, M. 1979, *An Application of Shadow Pricing to Country Economic Analysis with an Illustration from Pakistan*, World Bank Working Paper No. 330, World Bank, Washington DC.

Stiglitz, J. 1988, *Economics of the Public Sector*, W.W. Norton, New York.

Stiglitz, J. 2000, 'Development Thinking of the Millenium' in *proceedings from the Annual Bank Conference on Development Economics 2000*, World Bank, Washington D.C.

Stoleru, L. 1975, *Economic Equilibrium and Growth*, North-Holland, Amsterdam.

Stratton, I.M., Adler, A.I., Neil, H.A.W. et al. 2000, 'Association of glycaemia with macrovascular and microvascular complications of type 2 diabetes (UKPDS 35): Prospective observational study', *British Medical Journal*, 321: 405–12.

Streeting, M. 1990, *A Survey of the Hedonic Price Technique*, Resource Assessment Commission, Canberra.

Sugden, R. and Williams, A. 1981, *The Principles of Practical Cost-Benefit Analysis*, Oxford University Press, Oxford.

Sussex, J. and Marchant, N. (eds.) 1996, *Risk and Return in the Pharmaceutical Industry*, Office of Health Economics, London.

Sweeny, K. 2002a, *Trends in the Use and Cost of Pharmaceuticals Under the Pharmaceutical Benefits Scheme*, Pharmaceutical Industry Project Working Paper No 5, Centre for Strategic Economic Studies, Victoria University, Melbourne.

Sweeny, K. 2002b, *Demand and Price Dynamics in Pharmaceutical Markets: Some International Comparisons*, Pharmaceutical Industry Project Working Paper No 11, Centre for Strategic Economic Studies, Victoria University, Melbourne.

Szuba, T.J. 1986, 'International comparison of drug consumption: Impact of prices', *Social Sciences and Medicine*, 22(10): 1019–1025.

Talbot, P. 1977, *Conservation and Economics Efficiency*, John Hopkins Press for Resources for the Future Inc., Baltimore.

Thompson, G. and Thore, S. 1992, *Computational Economics*, Scientific Press, San Francisco.

Tolley, G.S., Kenkel, D. and Fabian R. 1994, *Valuing Health for Policy: An Economic Approach*, University Press, Oxford.

Torrance, G.W. 1986, 'Measurement of health state utilities for economic appraisal', *Journal of Health Economics*, 5: 1–30.

Turner, R.K, Pearce, D.W. and Bateman, I. 1993, *Environmental Economics: An Elementary Introduction*, John Hopkins University Press, Baltimore.

Van der Pol, M. and Cairns, J. 2000, 'Negative and zero time preference for health' *Health Economics*, 9: 171–175.

Veenstra, D.L., Ramsey, S.D. and Sullivan S.D. 2002, 'A Guide for the use of pharmacoeconomic models of diabetes treatment in US managed-care environment', *PharmacoEconomics*, 20(Suppl 1): 21–30.

Vernon, J.A. 2003, 'The relationship between price regulation and pharmaceutical profit margins', *Applied Economic Letters*, 10: 467–470.

Viscusi, W.K., Magat W.A. and Huber, J. 1987, 'An investigation of the rationality of consumer valuations of multiple health risks', *Rand Journal of Economics*, 18: 465–479.

Viscusi, W.K., Magat, W.A. and Huber, J. 1991, 'Pricing environmental health risks: Survey assessments of risk-risk, and risk-dollar trade-offs for chronic bronchitis', *Journal of Environmental Economics and Management*, 21: 32–51.

Viscusi, W.K 2003, 'The value of a statistical life: a critical review of market estimates throughout the world', Working Paper 9487, NBER, Cambridge.

Vogel, R.J. 2002, 'Pharmaceutical patents and price controls', *Clinical Therapeutics*, 24(7): 1204–1222.

Von der Schulenburg, J.M.G. 1997, 'Economic evaluation of medical technologies from theory to practice: The German perspective', *Social Science and Medicine*, 45(4): 621–633.

Wagner, H.M. 1975, *Principles of Operations Research*, Prentice-Hall, New Jersey.

Wagstaff, A. and van Doorslaer, E. 2000, 'Equity in health care finance and delivery' in A.J. Culyer and J.P. Newhouse (eds), *Handbook of Health Economics*, Elsevier. Amsterdam.

Watsham, T. and Parramore, T. 1997, *Quantitative Methods in Finance*, International Thomson Business Press, Melbourne.

Weinstein, M.C. and Stason, W.B. 1977, 'Foundations of cost-effectiveness analysis for health and medical practices', *New England Journal of Medicine*, 296: 716–21.

Weintraub, W., Jonsson, B. and Bertrand, M. 2004, 'The value of Clopidogrel in addition to standard therapy in reducing atherothrombotic events: The CAPRIE study', *PharmacoEconomics*, 22(Suppl 4): 29–41.

Weisbrod, B.A. 1961, *Economics of Public Health*, University of Pennsylvania Press, Philadelphia.

Weisbrod, B.A. 1971, 'Cost and benefits of medical research', *Journal of Political Economy*, 79: 527–544.

Wilkes, L.C. 1990, *A Survey of the Contingent Valuation Method*, Research Paper No 2, Resource Assessment Commission, Canberra.

Williams, A.H. 1997, 'Intergenerational equity: An exploration of the "fair innings" argument', *Health Economics*, 6: 117–132.

Williams, A.H. 1993, 'Equity in health care: The role of ideology', in E. van Doorslaer, A. Wagstaff and F. Rutten (eds), *Equity in the Finance and Delivery of Health Care*, Oxford University Press, Oxford.

Williams, A.H. 1983, 'The economic role of health-indicators', in G. Teeling Smith (ed.), *Measuring the Social Benefits of Medicines*, Office of Health Economics, London.

Wilson, K., Marriott, J., Fuller, S., Lacey, L. and Gillen, L. 2003, 'A model to assess the cost effectiveness of Statins in achieving the UK national health service framework target cholesterol levels', *PharmacoEconomics*, 21(Suppl 1): 1–11.

World Commission on Environment and Development (WCED) 1987, *Our Common Future*, Oxford University Press, Oxford.

Youman, P., Wilson, K., Harraf, F. and Kalra, L. 2003, 'The economic burden of stroke in the United Kingdom', *PharmacoEconomics*, 21(Suppl 1): 43–50.

Zarnke, K.B., Levine, M.A.H. and O'Brien, B.J. 1997, 'Cost-benefit analysis in the health care literature: Don't judge a study by its label', *Journal of Clinical Epidemiology*, 50: 813–822.

Zikmund, W. G. 1994, *Business Research Methods*, Dryden Press, Philadelphia.

Zillich, A., Blumenschein, K., Johannesson, M. and Freeman, P. 2002, 'Assessment of the relationship between measures of disease severity, quality of life, and willingness to pay in asthma', *PharmacoEconomics*, 20(4): 257–265.

Index